D1592748

~~WITHDRAWN~~

Please remember that this is a library book,
and that it belongs only temporarily to each
person who uses it. Be considerate. Do
not write in this, or any, library book.

AAQ-1777
Griffin

black madonnas

BLACK

feminism, religion,

Lucia Chiavola Birnbaum

MADONNAS

and politics in Italy

Northeastern University Press ▪ BOSTON

Northeastern University Press

Copyright 1993 by Lucia Chiavola Birnbaum

All rights reserved. Except for the quotation of short passages for
the purposes of criticism and review, no part of this book may be
reproduced in any form or by any means, electronic or
mechanical, including photocopying, recording, or any
information storage and retrieval system now known or to be
invented, without written permission of the publisher.

The madonna on the title page is La Sipontina, fifth century C.E.,
now in the duomo at Manfredonia. Photograph by Wallace
Birnbaum.

Library of Congress Cataloging-in-Publication Data

Birnbaum, Lucia Chiavola, 1924–
    Black madonnas : feminism, religion, and politics in Italy /
    Lucia Chiavola Birnbaum.
        p.   cm.
        Includes bibliographical references and index.
        ISBN 1-55553-156-3
        1. Black Virgins—Italy.   2. Italy—Religious life and
    customs.   3. Feminist theory.   4. Feminism—Italy.
    5. Feminist theology.   6. Italy—Politics and government—
    1976–   .   I. Title.
    BT670.B55B57   1993
    232.91—dc20   92-47384

Designed by Ann Twombly

Composed in Perpetua by Coghill Composition Co., Richmond,
Virginia. Printed and bound by Thomson-Shore, Inc., Dexter,
Michigan. The paper is Glatfelter Offset, an acid-free sheet.

MANUFACTURED IN THE UNITED STATES OF AMERICA

97   96   95   94   93   5   4   3   2   1

*alla memoria di mia madre, Kate Cipolla Chiavola,
e di mio padre, Turiddu Chiavola*

TO WALLY

The goddess-centered religion existed for a very long time, much longer than the Indo-European and the Christian . . . leaving an indelible imprint on the Western psyche.

—Marija Gimbutas, *The Language of the Goddess*

■   ■   ■

Yes, I am black! and radiant—
O city women watching me—
As black as Kedar's goathair tents
Or Solomon's fine tapestries.

—The Song of Songs

■   ■   ■

In Italy, where traces persist of the ancient Mediterranean earth mother who nurtured diverse peoples and a multiplicity of beliefs, where pluralism mixes beliefs of an unedited gospel with an unedited marxism, and feminists laugh as well as rage, the vision [of a libertarian and genuinely egalitarian socialism] is as real as the dark wheat and red poppies of Sicily.

—Lucia Chiavola Birnbaum, *Liberazione della donna—*
Feminism in Italy

■   ■   ■

The struggle is inner: Chicano, indio, American Indian, Mojado, Mexicano, immigrant Latino, Anglo in power, working class Anglo, Black, Asian—our psyches resemble the bordertowns and are populated by the same people. The struggle has always been inner, and is played in the outer terrains. Awareness of our situation must come before inner changes, which in turn come before changes in society. Nothing happens in the "real" world unless it first happens in the images of our heads.

—Gloria Anzaldúa, *Borderlands: La Frontera*

■　　■　　■

[In fables] every voice has a right, every subject can put her/himself at the periphery or at the center, every knowledge has its possibilities.

    —Convegno, "Il femminile nella fiaba"

■　　■　　■

The earth is a loan to humans to cultivate and enjoy its fruits, like the air, the water, and sunlight, things that nobody can catch and possess.

    —*La Gana* (story of a witch trial)

■　　■　　■

We have found water in the depths of the earth and a forest has been born that can be seen from afar. And you will see that it will grow, that it will grow.

    —Students of *Novanta* of Italy

contents

illustrations

xi

1. Oropa	9. Spoleto	17. Crotone
2. Padua	10. Rome	18. Palmi
3. Venice	11. Naples	19. Seminara
4. Bologna	12. Pomigliano d'Arco	20. Messina
5. Florence	13. Lucera	21. Tindari
6. Montenero	14. Montevergine	22. Milicia
(Leghorn)	15. Foggia	23. Trapani
7. Loreto	16. Siponto	24. Chiaramonte Gulfi
8. Siena	(Manfredonia)	25. Cagliari

Significant sanctuaries of black madonnas in Italy.

xiii

acknowledgments

THE WISDOM of my grandmothers, Giuseppina Lombardo Cipolla and Lucia Poidomani Chiavola, inspired this book. My mother's passion against injustice and my father's dreams are implicit in the dedication. My sister, Joie Chiavola Mellenbruch, embodies the nurturance of the goddess; my brother, Louis Chiavola, helps me understand why brothers were central to ancient sacred civilizations.

Among the many (not always agreeing) who assisted or encouraged this work are Margaret Alafi, Georgina and Kim Atchison, Helene Aylon, Jennifer Birnbaum, Dorothy Bryant, Sydney Carson, Kati Chavaria, Pat Cody, Toby Cole, Barbara Davidson, Diane Di Prima, Jan Doninelli, Pamela Eakins, Marcia Falk, Clare B. Fischer, Elinor Gadon, China Galland, Nancy B. Greenspan, Dellareese Grigsby, Jean Rosenthal Harris, Estelle Jelinek, Rachel Kahn-Hut, Phyllis Koestenbaum, Marge Lasky, Joan Levinson, Alison Lingo, Bogna Lorenz-Kot, Lorraine Macchello, the late and courageous Florence MacDonald, Ann Machung, Celeste MacLeod, Rita Maran, Phylis Martinelli, Glenna Matthews, Jean Terrace May, Katie Jo Mellenbruch, Maresi Nerad, Karen Offen, Jill Polansky, Maria Polansky, Ruth Rosen, the late Cecilia Ross (who taught me Italian), Rose Scherini, Charlene Spretnak, Eula Thomas, Beverly Voloshin, Eileen Ward, Emily W. White, Jean Wilkinson, the staff and scholars of the American Academy in Rome and of the Istituto Italiano di Cultura of San Francisco, the students in my seminar at the California College of Arts and Crafts, the Women's Network of the American Italian Historical Association, the Women and Work group and the Organization of American Women, both of Berkeley, the Moon Club of Moss Beach, and the Institute for Research on Women and Gender of Stanford University. The late Rena Vassar is my beacon of integrity and high standards of scholarship.

Sicilian aunts, now gone, helped me understand Italian vernacular cultures: Concettina Chiavola, Carmela Giurato, Serafina Panettiere, and Giorgia Monteleone. Sicilian American aunts, Mary Pollaro, Anne Connole, the late Jennie Cipolla, Rose Davis, Pearl Burk, and Lottie Hermida, have helped me understand what happened to these beliefs transplanted to the United States.

Italian women pivotal to this study include Dacia Maraini, who pointed out the significance of the prehistoric woman divinity when I was ready to listen, Lidia Menapace, who encouraged me to turn my research on black madonnas into a journey of discovery, and Maria Occhipinti, who introduced me to the cultural and political radicalism of my father's ancestral Ragusa. Sara Poli's intuition and knowledge have been critical. Simona Mafai, feminist communist stateswoman, reminds me that cultural and political transformation are inseparable.

Many Italians have helped me learn what is meant by *le culture sommerse.* They include Claudio and Enrica De Pra and Anna Papone of Genoa, Carla and Pietro Lasagna of Ameglia, Franca Bimbi and Leopoldina Fortunati of Padua, Maria Luisa and Alberto L'Abate of Florence, Vincenzo Coniglio of Catania, San Francisco, and Rome, Graziella Lanzallotto Fontanini of Calabria and Rome, *Le Papesse* of Catania, Gigliola Lo Cascio and Eugenia Bono of Palermo, Grazia Borrini of Pisa and Berkeley, Biancamaria Colavecchio, Mario Cavaceppi and Nino Cagnetta of Putignano, Gabriella Gondoli Diotallevi and Anna Maria Belardinelli of Perugia, and the late Professor Matteo Sansone of Mattinata.

Scholars of Italian culture in Australia offered many insights: Antonio Comin and Margaret Baker of Flinders University of South Australia, Dino Bressan of the University of Melbourne, Roslyn Pesman of the University of Sydney, Mirna Cicione of La Trobe University, Giuliana Vuocolo of Melbourne, and Josie Ciavola Black of Victoria.

Italians now living in the United States who have helped include Maria Elisa Ciavarelli of the Marche and Glassboro, Lilia Dannenberg of the Friuli and San Francisco, Ivana D'Avanzo of Rome and Sausalito, Pina Piccolo of Seminara and Berkeley, Carmela Riotto and Giovanni Piccolo of Seminara and Concord, Paola Sensi Isolani of Florence, England, and Berkeley,

Filomena Lo Curcio Stefanelli of Stromboli and New Jersey, Laura Stortoni of Sicily, Milan, and Berkeley, and Marilena Tamburello of Palermo and Berkeley. U.S. scholars of Italian studies who have offered insights include Gian Banchero, Lawrence DiStasi, Fred Gardaphe, Renate Holub, Rose Romano, Itala T. C. Rutter, Anthony Tamburri, and Justin Vitiello.

Dr. Norman Birnbaum listens to his patients and sent information about the black madonna of Milicia. Will Canby's historical insight was invaluable. British friends Pat and Tony Jarrett brought wit and perception to our visit to a *festa dei serpari* at Cocullo. The late American anthropologist Leonard Moss first awakened my interest in black madonnas; the Italian anthropologist Tullio Tentori helped me understand them, as well as left catholicism.

I thank William Frohlich for his early encouragement, and Northeastern University Press members Kristen Hatch, Ann Twombly, Frank Austin, Susan M. Kuc, and Jill Bahcall for helping to bring the book to fruition.

Our children, Linda and Stefan, Nancy and Marc, and Barbara and Naury, leaven my research and my life. Our grandchildren, Stefanie, Jake, and Courtney, Nicolas and Matthew, and Jessica, Sabrina, and Joshua, ask questions and embody why the study of the past is important for the future.

Dr. Wallace Birnbaum accompanies me on research trips to Italy and did the photography for this book. In the firestorm in the Oakland hills of October 20, 1991, he rescued the computer containing what follows, and knows why the book is dedicated to him. Tim Ward, architect, translated my poem about black madonnas ("bamboo and acanthus spring from the rubble . . . green") into the design of our new home on the site of the old.

■   ■   ■

ALL TRANSLATIONS, unless otherwise noted, and all mistakes are mine. I have adopted the style of contemporary Italians, used in my *Liberazione della donna—Feminism in Italy,* in removing capitals from as many words as possible, particularly from words connoting hegemony. In direct quotation, I have left people to their own judgments about capitals.

foreword

How, I have been asked, *did you come to write a book about black madonnas?*

All madonnas were white in the Italian-American community of Kansas City, Missouri, where I grew up. No madonnas existed in my U.S. education, capped by a doctoral dissertation on the protestant origins of behaviorist psychology. My uppermost concerns, particularly since the 1960s, have been political; I helped to found the Peace and Freedom party and, as an assistant professor of history at San Francisco State University, encouraged the student strike opposing the war in Vietnam and challenging education designed to uphold the hegemony of some cultural groups.

In search of my roots I went to Italy in 1969, where I found five million workers in the streets and a feminist movement whose banners declared *Non c'è rivoluzione senza liberazione della donna; non c'è liberazione della donna senza rivoluzione* (There is no revolution without women's liberation; there is no women's liberation without revolution). An independent scholar after 1969, I commenced a new life pattern of regular research stays in Italy.

After *Liberazione della donna—Feminism in Italy* was published in 1986, the question persisted: *Why were Italian feminists so grounded, spiritually and politically?* The question became a hundred questions when I discovered that the Sicilian birthplaces of my grandmothers, my grandfathers, and my father were located near archaeological sites of the primordial goddess and sanctuaries of black madonnas, and that these were places of intense beliefs and politics. In the late nineteenth century, these were socialist; in the late twentieth century, beliefs and politics whose themes are justice and responsibility for life, and opposition to hierarchy, violence, and destruction of the earth.

black madonnas

CHAPTER 1

metaphor of black madonnas •

argument and underlying assumptions

BLACK MADONNAS may be considered a metaphor for a
memory of the time when the earth was believed to
be the body of a woman and all creatures were equal, a memory transmitted
in vernacular traditions of earth-bonded cultures, historically expressed in
cultural and political resistance, and glimpsed today in movements aiming
for transformation.

Differing from white madonnas, who may be said to embody church
doctrine of obedience and patience, and differing in shades of dark, what all
black madonnas have in common is location on or near archaeological
evidence of the prechristian woman divinity, and the popular perception
that they are black. Elusive, they are frequently removed from religious and
political implication by art historians, who call them "Byzantine," and by
the church hierarchy, which has "retouched" several of them white. Black is
the color of the earth and the ancient color of regeneration, a matter of
perception, imagination, and beliefs often not conscious, a phenomenon
suggested in people's continuing to call a madonna black even after the
image has been whitened by the church, as at Lucera, Montenero, Avellino,
Chiaramonte Gulfi, and other places.

Differing from liberation theologies centering on the son, the contemporary Italian amalgam of heretical and radical beliefs appears to be stirred by

3

women's insistence on their difference and suggested in the moral and political difference of black madonnas from the subordinated and passive white madonna of the church.[1]

This book explores the hypothesis that veneration of the indigenous goddess of Old Europe merged with African, Middle Eastern, and Asian dark goddesses and persisted in the christian era in vernacular beliefs and rituals associated with black madonnas. The term "vernacular" connotes submerged beliefs visible in the everyday activities of people Antonio Gramsci described as "subaltern classes." Women, historically subordinated culturally, as well as economically and politically, by hegemonies of church, society, and state, may be said to pertain, along with other colonized peoples, to the subaltern classes.

Vernacular ways of knowing and believing, bypassing established knowledge and belief, are implied in the metaphor of black madonnas.[2] In this sense, this study participates in what Michel Foucault called the "insurrection of subjugated knowledges,"[3] a revolt visible in accumulating evidence, and growing awareness, that the oldest divinity perceived by humans was a woman.[4] Black madonnas, like the primordial woman divinity, are believed to nurture all life, all the different peoples of the earth, and all the seasons of life: birth, maturity, death, and regeneration. Ean Begg has counted 450 images of black madonnas in the world. If black women divinities of Africa and dark women divinities of the Middle East, Asia, and indigenous America are added to European black madonnas, then millions of people venerate dark women divinities.[5] This study is concerned with black madonnas of Italy. Why Italy?

A peninsula and islands in the Mediterranean, Italy historically connects Europe, Africa, the Middle East, and Asia.[6] Third-world scholars analyzing Eurocentrism point out that until the Renaissance "Europe belonged to a regional tributary system that included Europeans and Arabs, Christians and Moslems." From the Renaissance on, the capitalist world system shifted toward the Atlantic, and Mediterranean regions became the periphery.[7]

Italy's location on the periphery, and the contradictions of Italian culture and politics, may offer transformative possibilities for the third millennium. The country is the seat of world catholicism, yet widely shared Italian beliefs embodied in black madonnas differ heretically from church doctrine. Italy is fifth among the powerful industrialized nations, yet the large Italian political left identifies with subordinated peoples of the earth.[8] The contemporary Italian political rainbow arcs from left-wing catholics, greens, socialists, and independent radicals to Italy's large independent communist party, Partito comunista italiano (Pci). Early in 1991, this group devolved into the Partito democratico della sinistra (Pds), aiming for the "democracy of socialism," and into Rifondazione comunista, a small party unwilling to give up a name that connotes justice in Italy. Other significant bands in Italy's political rainbow are the pink of what may be the strongest women's movement in the world and the green of large movements for nonviolence and environmentalism.[9]

The new party aiming for the "democracy of socialism" rings with themes of women's cultural and political strength and with notes of men of the democratic left who have seceded from patriarchy. The Pds defines itself as a "party of peace, a party in defense of nature,"[10] a "party of women and men," with values of "liberty, equality, and solidarity," that hopes to overcome the "terrible contradictions between the poor and the rich, between the north and the south of the world, between development and the environment."[11] Grounded on popular, not papal, beliefs,[12] the Partito democratico della sinistra has a logo with the international socialist hammer and sickle resting on the roots of a leafy oak tree. The image recalls l'Incoronata, black madonna of the poor near Foggia, who, for a thousand years, has been depicted in the boughs of an oak tree.[13]

Dalle donne, la forza delle donne, the political motto of contemporary Italian women, rewrites the marxist aphorism, declaring "from women, the force of women," and puts into politics the force of peasant women whose lives and folklore, for millennia, transmitted the values of the civilization of the goddess. To this historical strength has been added the force of Italian feminists, who since 1968 have worked to delegitimate patriarchy and to translate cultural into political power.[14] Before he died, Enrico Berlinguer said that since 1976 women have determined every election in Italy. In the 1990s women hold determining influence in the wide and varied democratic left.[15] Weaving the network that binds contemporary politics, Italian women are intent, not on ascendancy, but on placing values associated with women's experience—justice, and equality with difference—into a good society.

Just as black madonnas differ from the white madonna of church doctrine, the Partito democratico della sinistra differs from historic marxism: "Underneath the oak tree are more women and fewer male factory workers."[16] Women throughout Italy, and Italians south of Rome (whose regions and islands have a percentage of unemployed youth three times that of the north), have enlarged the ranks of the Pds and may be determining the politics of an emerging Italian majority that identifies with the poor and dark peoples of the earth.[17]

The theoretical ground of the spiral of the prehistoric goddess, black madonnas, and vernacular beliefs and politics is found in chapter 2. The actual ground may be seen in archaeological artifacts of the woman divinity located on or near sanctuaries of black madonnas. The civilization of the goddess in Italy is verified by archaeological evidence all along the Ligurian, Tyrrhenian, Adriatic, Ionian, and Mediterranean seacoasts, in regions inhabited by the Etruscans, in the *mezzogiorno* (land of the midday sun south of Rome), and on the Mediterranean islands of Sicily, Malta, and Sardinia.[18]

In 1987 Simona Mafai, feminist communist stateswoman, took me to see a drawing on the walls of the Addaura cave outside Palermo, an image dated in the upper paleolithic age (30,000 to 15,000 B.C.E.) of a horned animal symbolizing the woman divinity circled by sexually aroused men.[19] Close by the Addaura cave is the sanctuary of the black madonna of Milicia; a few kilometers away are sanctuaries of black madonnas of Trapani, Tindari, Palmi, and Seminara.

Ritual scene incised in Grotta dell'Addaura, outside Palermo, dating from 30,000–15,000 B.C.E.

An image of a pregnant earth-mother divinity dated 26,000 to 18,000 B.C.E., whom Italians call Venere Artemide, has been found at Savignano (between Modena and Bologna). Black madonnas near this image are found at Bologna, Florence, Montenero, Siena, Loreto, Spoleto, Padua, Venice, and Rome.

On the island of Malta, where Sicilians migrated about 6000 B.C.E., more than thirty temples were built between 3500 and 2500 B.C.E.[20] representing the goddess as round as the earth, lying on her side,[21] or as the woman colossus at Tarxien. For Elinor Gadon, the "majestic temple ruins at Malta are the most complete survival of the Neolithic vision of rebirth in the body of the goddess."[22] In Sardinia, slender, stylized images of the Cycladic type have been discovered, as well as round figures (e.g., la dea di Olbia).[23] At Megara Hyblaea, founded when Sicily was part of Magna Graecia, the goddess was sculpted as a full-bosomed mother signifying nurturance.

Images of the ancient divinity can be seen throughout Italy: in Sicily, a statue of Isis at Solunto, twelve statues of Cybele at Palazzola Acreide, and many full-bosomed mothers at Megara Hyblaea.[24] In southern Italy at Capua, two hundred statues of mother goddesses, Deae Matres, of the seventh to the first century B.C.E. merge goddess and child. In the archaeological museum of Naples, a nearly seven-foot-tall statue of a black Artemis/Diana of Ephesus melds goddess and all living creatures and suggests the prechristian antecedents of black madonnas.

Symbols, as well as images, of the prechristian divinity have persisted. In Italian folklore of the christian era the belief persisted that caves and grottoes are wombs of the goddess. In iconography the pubic triangle of the woman divinity persisted in the triangular shape of black madonnas, fusing mother and child. Late in the twentieth century, the pubic triangle of the prehistoric divinity, and of black madonnas, reappeared on the placards of Italian, and other, feminists.

The paradox of postmodern Italy, a wealthy industrial nation of the first world sharing liberation beliefs with poor peoples of the third world,[25] may be unraveled by considering Italian pilgrimages to black madonnas of the poor, subversive rituals of carnival, heretical themes of easter in the streets, and a folklore whose themes are justice, equality, and "rights to life of the poor."[26]

After the openings of pope John XXIII and the new-left confrontations of 1968, what is today called liberation theology refers to beliefs of Italians in and out of *comunità di base* (base communities) who declare "we are the church," differentiate themselves from the vatican, and bring "unedited"

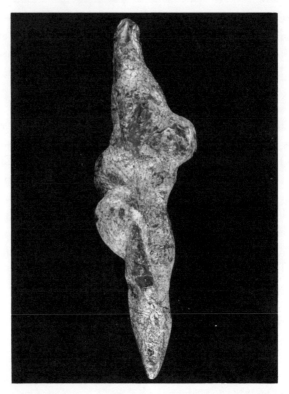

Stone figure of a prehistoric woman divinity, Venere di Savignano, dating from 26,000–18,000 B.C.E., found between Modena and Bologna. Reproduced by permission of the Museo Nazionale Preistorico ed Etnografico "L. Pigorini," Rome.

perspectives to the Judeo-christian scriptures, to popular beliefs, and to marxism in movements for individual and social transformation.[27]

Since 1968 Italian women have been engaged in a *riappropriazione dell'identità* (reappropriation of identity) that puts into the political arena values conveyed for two thousand years in their everyday lives, stories, and rituals.[28] The strength of the contemporary Italian women's movement is apparent in impressive legislation (divorce, federally subsidized nursery schools, family-planning clinics, equal family rights, equal pay for equal work, legal abortion, bill against violence toward women and children, and so on) that women and their men allies have placed into the Italian legal code. This strength also appears in the alignment of the Italian communist party, and the Pds, with nonviolence and with women's historic difference as defined by women. The uniqueness of the Italian communist party was evident in the 1980s in the stipulation that religious beliefs take priority over politics.[29]

The difference is evident today in the identification of the new democratic party of the left (Pds) with left catholics, vernacular beliefs, and the premise that women are protagonists in the movement for transformation. Some women of the Pds declare, "We are the party"; more Italian women, remembering peasant *comari* (godmothers) who helped one another sustain life, weave women's networks across parties to put women's values into politics. Today in Sicily, for example, women in network weave a tapestry of pluralist possibilities created by seceding christian democrats, reconstructed communists, students in resistance, socialists, greens, Rete (a network founded by Leoluca Orlando, former mayor of Palermo, which is open to anybody "honest"), and members of the new Pds.

Autogestione (self-management) is a theme associated the world over with new-left confrontations of 1968. Today the theme is vividly apparent in the breakup of communist nations of eastern Europe. Self-management, central to the concerns of peoples everywhere who have been subordinated culturally, as well as economically and politically, was demonstrated in Italy in the late 1970s during the successful campaign for legal abortion. Standing before parliament, hands on hips, women declared, *"L'utero è mio e me lo gestisco io"*: It is my uterus and I shall manage it. The declaration removes self-determination from abstractions, giving it women's bodily meaning, or what Adrienne Rich has called "the corporeal ground of our intelligence."[30]

Other "denied cultures" of Italy are today reappropriating their identities. It was in Sicily, center of the known world of Europeans in the twelfth century but relegated since 1860 to the "backward" south, that the contemporary Italian student resistance movement began in January 1990. Identifying with the suppressed of the earth, Italian students declared, *"La pantera siamo noi"* (We are the panther), evoking the memory of Isis and Cybele (who were depicted flanked by a feline) and recognizing the militant movement of the Black Panthers in the United States.[31] Sicilian students have named a university building Tiananmen Hall to honor resisting Chinese students of 1989 who held aloft a statue of a goddess of liberty before they were bloodily crushed. The earth-rootedness of Sicilians and other southerners (deprecated by northern Italians, who traditionally called them *terroni*) may be a major source of the transformation today becoming visible in Italy.[32]

In 1993 Italian women and men students call themselves *la resistenza umana* (the human resistance) and identify with the poor, particularly the dark peoples and hungry children of the earth, while self-managed groups of women, left catholics, and environmentalists work for human rights and nonviolence, and hundreds of thousands of Italian men and women of all ages climb mounts in pilgrimage to black madonnas of the poor.

■   ■   ■

AS A FEMINIST cultural historian researching and writing history that tries to include memory, silence, and nonverbal expression,[33] I am postmodern in spirit insofar as I consider the possibilities, as well as the partialities, of all beliefs, including my own.[34] This is similar to what Donna Haraway calls the local nature of all standpoints, and "the priority of partial perspectives over global theorizations,"[35] and similar to the premise of Italian feminists who study fables and believe that "every voice has a right, every subject can put her/himself at the periphery or at the center, every knowledge has its possibilities,"[36] a perspective that reminds me of the early influence of George Santayana on my thinking. Both religion and science are myths, said the philosopher (whose roots were in Spain, early life in the United States, and maturity and death in Italy), but myths are far from signifying nothing.[37]

Chapter 2, the theoretical foundation of this book, suggests the worldview of Italian scholars, one that differs from that of dominant social science in the United States. Chapters 3 and 4 consider continuing myths, stories, and everyday activities of Italian peasant women whose lives perpetuate ancient values as godmothers (an interesting word), midwives, healers, and mourners. A vernacular theology emerges from folklore and rituals of peasant women presiding over life, death, regeneration, and justice. Folk stories, told and enacted, reveal beliefs in a world in motion with a woman at the center, remembering and envisioning a society with values of justice, equality, and rights to life of everybody. I examine a snake festival as a ritual of unconscious/conscious veneration of the goddess and of women's perennial resistance to the church's misappropriation of their gifts. Folk stories about a woman called Giustizia (justice) identify the woman divinity with "almost completely determining" peasant mothers. In Giufà stories, perhaps a metaphor for Italian vernacular theology, the mother has a clown son with a Muslim name who does her errands in the world, subverting patriarchy.

Adapting Mikhail Bakhtin's insights to a feminist perspective, chapters 5 and 6 consider carnivals as the laughter of the goddess as well as texts of contemporary beliefs and primers of how people would like to live. The anthropologists' method of participant observation is borrowed in chapter 7 to study the fifth-century black madonna of Siponto, a woman whose "staring eyes" convey women's historic humiliation, and to consider the black l'Incoronata of the poor, "mother of us all" in a region of peasant communism. I explore multicultural dimensions and prophetic possibilities of black madonnas in chapter 8.

Chapter 9 studies the vernacular theology of easter rituals in the streets, where the centrality of the mother, and other heresies, are enacted. Chapter 10 explores heresies, fables, the peaceful and communal culture of sibyls and witches that was suppressed by authorities, and the continuing story of Lilith. The concluding chapter follows the spiral of vernacular beliefs into the contemporary cultural and political transformation of Italy.

The sisterhood of dark women divinities of the world is suggested in the case of Sicily.[38] The indigenous goddess Ibla, visible in paleolithic and neolithic ruins and remembered today in the folklore of the region of the Iblaean mountains (named for her), was joined by dark images of the goddess brought to the island by Semites (Canaanite Phoenicians) from Asia Minor, Egyptians from Africa, travelers and traders of the Graeco-Roman world, and later by Byzantines and Muslims.[39]

My underlying assumptions are similar to those of the feminist theologians Mary Daly, Nelle Morton, Judith Plaskow, and Marcia Falk.[40] For Mary Daly, black madonnas are powerful figures because they are associated with the fertility of black earth.[41] Symbols, in contrast to signs, "participate in that to which they point." Their meaning, emerging from the unconscious, may be universal, but the meaning takes different forms, since "we belong to different tribes and have great individual diversity."[42] Icons of black madonnas, for Byzantines and for Daly, are symbols that "participate in that to which they point."[43] Metaphor includes symbols, but, taking Nelle Morton's insight into account, Daly states that "metaphors evoke action, movement." By clashing with conventional logic, metaphors connect memory with the future as they transform our perceptions of reality.[44]

"Be-ing," for Daly, is a verb that "cannot without gross falsification be reified into a noun, whether that noun be identified as 'Supreme Being' or 'God' or 'Goddess' (singular or plural). When I choose to use such words as Goddess it is to point Metaphorically to the Powers of Be-ing, the Active Verb in whose potency all biophilic reality participates."[45] While I agree with Daly's ontology, I recognize, as a historian, that Italians have personified their beliefs for millennia; the story I am telling considers black madonnas a metaphor for Italian vernacular beliefs.

Worried about feminist ideas, some conservative white men theologians resort to condemnation of "idolatrous paganism." Judith Plaskow, feminist Jewish theologian, has responded to the assertion that pagans, in their worship of concrete images, "cannot tell the difference between sticks and stones and the living God."[46] Never, states Plaskow, has there been a tradition that "identified the work of human hands with the essence and reality of the sacred. Images serve many functions: they are manifestations of the sacred, they reveal certain of its qualities; they provide foci for worship or meditation. But they are not the sacred itself."[47]

Because "as Jews we only see idols in material terms," states Plaskow, "it is difficult to realize that the identification of particular verbal images (such as the image of God as male) with the reality of the sacred is just as much idolatry as the deification of sticks and stones."[48]

Diverse as the different cultures in which they are venerated, the black madonnas of Italy, Latin America, and other parts of the third world may be regarded as a metaphor for popular hope for liberation of the poor, the marginal, and the suppressed of the earth.[49] In North America, the black Virgin of Guadalupe inspired the Mexican revolution of 1810 and the twentieth-century struggle of the grape workers of Delano. "Today in Texas and Mexico she is more venerated than Jesus or God the Father . . . the single most potent religious, political and cultural image of the Chicano/mexicano."[50]

Black madonnas have drawn me, not because, as Gilles Quispel believes, they may be the only living symbol left of christianity.[51] Although I consider Quispel's insight valid, the image of black madonnas, for me, counters racism and sexism and connotes nurturance of the "other" in contrast to the violence toward the "other" that has historically characterized established religious and political doctrines.

To the tapestry of goddess/mystics/witches now being woven by feminist and other scholars,[52] this study adds the red ribbon of black madonnas as a metaphor for vernacular religious and political beliefs of subaltern peoples of the earth. Influenced by the Italian historian Carlo Ginzburg, I have adopted a binary view that considers history over eons along with history in particular times and places, in this case late nineteenth- and late twentieth-century Italy. In concert with feminist and gender studies, the past is examined to catch a glimpse of possibilities in the future. Vernacular beliefs, in this book, involve men as well as women. Values of justice, equality, and rights to life of the poor were historically taught by peasant mothers telling stories and singing domestic ballads and lullabies to their *bambini* and *bambine*.

I am indebted to Carl Jung for the insights that archetypes, notably the archetype of the earth mother, "were, and still are, living psychic forces that demand to be taken seriously"[53] and that the content of archetypes is expressed in metaphors.[54] The sculptures of Beniamino Bufano prefigure some of the themes of this book. An Italian artist who lived in the United States, Bufano sculpted a black madonna (bare-bosomed, as was Astarte of the Middle East), fusing mother and child, as a symbol of peace at the entrance to the San Francisco International Airport. Along with rounded animals created of black stone, he evoked the African goddess Isis in the black madonna sculpted on an Egyptian obelisk at Timber Cove Inn, California.[55]

Recently, I have been gladdened to learn of a folk opera written by Italians in the United States that resonates with themes of this study. *Il viaggio della Madonna Nera (The Journey of the Black Madonna)* is dedicated to "Mother Earth" and based on "the cult of the Black Virgin in southern Italy." Black madonnas and sibyls are placed in a continuum with the goddess Isis and are associated with carnivals, witches, town idiots, and the dead. In this theatrical representation, the black madonna of the poor of Seminara (in Calabria) and the black madonna of Moiano (in Campania) are bonded with the African-Brazilian goddess of love, Yoruba.[56]

A contemporary efflorescence of women's art conveys the sisterhood of dark Latin madonnas, black African goddesses, and dark women divinities of Europe, the Middle East, and Asia. In Cristina Emmanuele's painting *Meeting of the Madonnas,* in the exhibit of black madonnas brought to Warsaw in 1991 by Dominique Mazeaud, the Virgin of Guadalupe and the black Hindu goddess Kali take tea with the black madonna of Czestochowa.[57] A network created by China Galland in the San Francisco Bay area has formed around images of black madonnas and other dark women divinities of the earth with the hope of building a bridge connecting ethnic groups, movements of deep ecology and feminism, and liberation theologies and politics.

In my journeys in Italy I have studied the black madonna in the national sanctuary at Loreto (whose *casa* in the church depicts sibyls preceding Judeo-christian prophets); the "retouched" black madonna of Montenero (outside Leghorn); dark madonnas of Padua and Venice; the black madonna of Oropa; the dark madonna (as Shulamite woman) in S. Maria in Trastevere in Rome; the gray madonna dell'Arco outside Naples; the whitened Mamma Schiavone (great black slave mother) of Montevergine in Avellino; the very black l'Incoronata near Foggia, venerated by peasant communists; the hidden black madonna in the *duomo* (cathedral) at Foggia, who suggests the invisible church; the Lucan and jeweled black madonna of Bari; the black madonna of Spoleto; the fifth-century C.E. black madonna of the staring eyes of Siponto/Manfredonia; the whitened black madonnas of Lucera and of Chiaramonte

Gulfi; the madonna *bruna* of Matera; the politically important black madonna of red Bologna; the black madonna of the workers of Trapani; the black madonna of Tindari (who at her base carries the inscription from the Song of Songs of Hebrew scriptures: "I am black and beautiful"); the hidden black madonna of the poor of Palmi; and the miracle-working black madonna of the poor of Seminara.

S. Maria in Cosmedin at Rome is black in popular perception (an artist left a black image in the foyer of the church) but white in the church image. The black madonna in the duomo of Siena, the sacristan advised, was not black, but *sporca* (dirty), putting a pejorative meaning on the image. Other clergy told me stories of fires that burned and darkened the images or of candle smoke that blackened the statues. At Oropa, major sanctuary of a black madonna in northern Italy, the priest threw sand in my eyes, misdirecting me when I asked where I could find *la madonna nera*.

Yet there was the franciscan from Asti who had journeyed with his congregation of Gypsies to Stes-Maries-de-la-Mer in the south of France and who advised that many Italians cross the border to this Gypsy celebration of three Marys, one of whom is the black Sarah/Kali. Although the ritual has been condemned by the church, I watched the franciscan priest join in the singing to "santa Sara!" as pilgrims carried their black divinity into the sea.

I have interviewed people and studied what is known about the black madonnas of Cagliari, Anzio, Naples, Moiano, Collechio Parma, Crotone, Florence, Messina, Milazzo, Vicenza, Milicia, and S. Maria Nova of Rome. Many more black madonnas than this list suggests can be found in Italy, some of them hidden, either by the church or by people protecting a beloved figure.

▪   ▪   ▪

NOT A romantic excursion, this study of the beliefs of vernacular, submerged cultures of Italy is in agreement with Antonio Gramsci that folklore can challenge hegemonic culture, and that revolutions are authentic when they tap submerged beliefs of denied cultures.[58] When a woman's optic is brought to the rescue of submerged, vernacular cultures, we find that Italian feminists remember the communal values of "all our grandmothers," sibyls who nurtured all life with the values of good sense, and look to a "good marxist society" that respects women's historical difference, free expression, quality of life, contemplation, times of silence, sentiments, the body, the freely given, care, and diversity.[59]

When Italian women and men students in contemporary resistance (*"La pantera siamo noi"*—We are the panther) add their values to the movement for transformation, the young identify with the feline who accompanied the goddess, with dark and poor peoples of the earth, and with the belief that revolution is genuine when it reaches "the collective unconscious of millions of people."[60]

The meaning of the Italian verb *ricordare* is to sense with the heart,[61] a truth recalled by the Italian historian Giorgio Galli in the folk proverb, "The future has an ancient heart."[62] Remembering an ancient belief, what if the earth, personified by the ancient woman divinity, black madonnas, and other women, is pregnant with possibilities?

What if the memory of an age of peace and equality among all living creatures, a memory embodied in black madonnas and other dark women divinities of submerged cultures, becomes a future celebrating equality with the beauty of differences, and justice?

CHAPTER 2

"folklore is the culture of the

subaltern classes" ▪ theoretical premises

THE DIFFERENT WORLDVIEW of Mediterranean cultures is apparent in writings of late nineteenth-century Italian scholars. Political implications of this different perspective are suggested in contemporary Italy, where folklore is legitimated as the "culture of the subaltern classes" and negated cultures are valorized as *le culture negate,* indispensable to authentic revolution.

The subversive religious and political implications of vernacular beliefs were pointed out by Giuseppe Pitré, a doctor in Palermo in the last quarter of the nineteenth century, who was intrigued by the stories he heard his women patients tell. The physician read and corresponded with British and American ethnographers and psychologists who, at the turn of the twentieth century, were beginning to describe the phenomena of religion in the language of science.

Pitré, a Mediterranean scholar, held another interest. Intrigued by the difference between the doctrines of official religion and the religious beliefs found in folk stories, legends, customs, and rituals, the physician-folklorist noted that papal prohibitions singled out popular saints, erotic elements in folk rituals, and rites that satirized the authority of church and state and implied *rovesciamento di status* (revolution).[1]

The memory of the civilization of the goddess is everywhere apparent in numerous volumes by Pitré recording vernacular beliefs and rituals, many of them cited in subsequent chapters of this book. For a contemporary of Pitré, Giovanni Verga, the aristocratic Sicilian who founded *verismo,* or modern literary realism, in Italy, the memory of the prechristian divinity was an ambivalent one. *La lupa (The She-Wolf),* written in 1880, conveys the fascination and fear that the memory evoked when embodied in some peasant women:

> As in a remembrance from long ago, he stopped cultivating the vines in fertile green fields and went to remove the axe from the elm tree. *La Lupa* saw him come, pale and staring. The axe glistened in the sun. Not hesitating nor lowering her eyes, she went to meet him with her hands full of red poppies. Her black eyes seeming to devour him. "Oh cursed be your soul!" gasped Nanni.[2]

Verga described the *miseria* of *contadini* (peasants), their late nineteenth-century revolt in socialist *fasci,* the suppression of the uprising, and the subsequent emigration of Italians to North and South America.[3] Many of those who remained joined the militant Italian worker movement of the twentieth century, whose militancy was marked by a thrust toward socialist revolution during world war I. Suppressed under the fascist regime, communists, socialists, and feminists went underground, reappearing in the resistance movement against nazis and fascists during world war II, in a women's union in 1944, and in communist and socialist activities after 1945. The hope for a just and equal society was dashed by the cold war, but it emerged again in 1968 in new-left student confrontations and in another spiral of the Italian women's movement, whirls evident again in the Italy of the 1990s.[4]

Believing, at the end of the nineteenth century, that an older world was disappearing, Pitré collected his observations of Sicilian vernacular culture in twenty-five volumes of legends, songs, riddles, games, lullabies, proverbs, and festivals.[5] In an important reminder to scholars, Pitré said that the significant history of a people, not to be confused with the history of their rulers, was to be found in folkloric beliefs and customs transmitted orally or enacted in rituals.[6]

The center of these vernacular beliefs was visible to a cultural outsider, Carlo Levi, an Italian Jew confined, for antifascist activities, in southern Italy in the 1930s. Observing the culture of the peasants of the region, Levi said:

> There is no room for religion because to them everything participates in divinity, everything is actually, not merely symbolically, divine: Christ and

the goat; the heavens above and the beasts of the field below; everything is bound up in natural magic. Even the ceremonies of the church become pagan rites, celebrating the existence of inanimate things, which the peasants endow with a soul.[7]

Black madonnas, Levi noted, were celebrated with wheat, animals, fireworks, and trumpets. A black madonna "was no sorrowful Mother of God, but rather a subterranean deity, black with the shadows of the bowels of the earth, a peasant Persephone, or lower world goddess of the harvest."[8] Neither good nor bad, "This black madonna is like the earth, it can do everything, destroy and make blossom. . . . She withers the harvests and lets them die but also nourishes and protects, and it is necessary to adore her."[9] Peasant revolts, for Levi, surge from "an elementary desire for justice, emerging from the black lake of the heart."[10]

Influenced by Carlo Levi and Antonio Gramsci, Robert Bellah, an American sociologist of religion, adopted the musical metaphor of "ground bass" to describe deep religious beliefs. "Ground bass" refers to a "deep and repetitive sonority," a drone bass "that continues while formal theologies and philosophies send the melody into upper musical registers."[11] Emotional and intense, in comparison with the rationalism of high Italian culture, the ground bass "not infrequently drowns . . . out formal theologies and philosophies."[12]

A religious ground bass "is probably universal," according to Bellah, but its strength varies according to culture, being greater in Japan, for example, than in China, and "greater in Italy than in France or England."[13] For Bellah, southern Italy is a "region in the Italian soul," with "something of the 'south' everywhere in Italy."[14] After the great migration from the south to the north in the twentieth century, there are, indeed, southerners everywhere in Italy.

The significant characteristic of Italian religious beliefs, for Bellah, is that they are "presided over by a woman, an epiphany of the great Mother of the Mediterranean world," who is "only partially and uncertainly" visible in the madonna of the church. In his view, the "real" religion of Italy is based on woman-centered popular beliefs while the "legal" religion is catholicism.[15]

The significance of the folklore of southern Italy and the islands, contemporary scholars have pointed out, is related to resistance to modernization, a resistance evident in the survival of ancient beliefs in everyday rituals, carnivals, and pilgrimages.[16] For the contemporary anthropologist Alessandro Falassi, southern Italians are "authors, often actors, always participants in a sense of the sacred," a sense of the sacred related to a "chthonic" divinity who has little to do with religious institutions.[17]

The Mediterranean islands and coastal areas of Italy, as recent scholarship has demonstrated, resisted invading cultures that brought male-dominant religions. Ancient beliefs held thousands of years before the common era have never been obliterated. Perhaps related to this is the singular fact that the major twentieth-century political thinkers of Italy have come from the south and the islands. Antonio Gramsci, a founder and major theorist of Italian communism, who emphasized the significance of folklore and cultural differences for genuine social transformation, came from Sardinia. Ernesto De Martino, an ethnologist who looked to prechristian beliefs of Old Europe for a new society, came from Naples. Aldo Moro, the martyred christian-democratic statesman of the 1970s who prophesied the "converging parallels" of communism and christianity, came from Bari.[18]

Antonio Gramsci may best be understood if one remembers that he was a Sardinian, a dwarf, and a hunchback. His bodily sense of difference gave him an immediate consciousness of subordinated cultures and the marginality of "others."[19] Folklore was scarcely a dilettante amusement for Gramsci; he called it a vernacular *concezione del mondo e della vita,* a conception of the world and of life that challenged the hegemony of the educated classes. For genuine revolution, and for the necessary organic bond between theory and practice, Gramsci advised the intellectuals who define dominant beliefs that the beliefs of subaltern classes are different.[20]

Deepening marxist thought, Gramsci emphasized the importance of beliefs: "Modern life is made up in great part of these states of mind or 'beliefs' which are as strong as material facts."[21] Differences in beliefs were evident in different versions of Italian catholicism: that of peasants, the petty bourgeoisie and city workers, intellectuals, and women. In Gramsci's view, the catholicism of southern Italians was characterized by magic and paganism.[22]

Believing that "every innovative historic movement is mature" to the extent that it involves women,[23] Gramsci's letters to his mother refer to the unique combination of *forza* (strength, endurance) and *tenerezza* (tenderness) of southern Italian women.[24] Analyzing the beliefs of the *semplici* of the south, whom northern intellectuals (marxist and other) tended to regard condescendingly, Gramsci hoped that intellectuals and peasants would come to the common understanding necessary for creating a socialist society, in theory and practice at once *conservatrice e contestativa,*[25] conservative and challenging. The organic philosophy would resemble traditional folklore in its bonds to the past, yet hold a vision of the future that could constitute a radical challenge to the hegemony of established power.

Published after 1945, Gramsci's writings coincided with Italian ethnologists' insistence that scholars should respect the beliefs of the people they study.[26] For Ernesto De Martino, the beliefs of "primitive peoples" (with whom northern intellectuals aligned southern Italians), far from being exotic superstitions or dismissible as simple notions, may indeed offer a key to overcoming the existential crisis of the twentieth century, one that the ethnologist described as *la fine del mondo*. The end of capitalism and of dominant western culture did not, he said, preclude the possibility of another, better civilization.[27]

Ernesto De Martino may be considered a precursor of contemporary "unedited marxists" of Italy who bypass party and ideology to interpret marxism for themselves. Journeying from the socialist to the communist parties, he early analyzed the compatibility of marxism with popular religious beliefs. With even deeper iconoclasm, De Martino justified the magic in Italian peasant beliefs. For millennia, he said, magic has protected people against the anxiety that accompanies the disappearance of *la presenza* of significant religious figures.

In spite of imprecations against magic by protestant-reformation theologians, criticisms of irrationalism by enlightenment philosophers, and condemnations of superstition and paganism by the catholic hierarchy, magic, said De Martino, has remained an impermeable layer of the beliefs of the subaltern classes of Italy.[28] De Martino points out that after the eighteenth century the party of rationalism may have won, but popular resistance continued in the ceremonials and rituals of the catholics of southern Italy through *magia extra canonica*.[29] At the center of this magic outside the church canon were Mary, other saints, and *gli altri*. These last, "the others," were women who resembled saints in performing acts of magic: *la mammana, la vecchia, la megara, la fattucchiera,* and *la prefica*—the midwife, the old woman, the witch, the healer, and the mourner—peasant women who transmitted the values of the goddess and who are studied in chapter 3 of this book.[30]

The difference of southern Italy, for De Martino, was evident in the fact that Neapolitan enlightenment philosophers did *not* join their northern counterparts in condemning vernacular religious practices. Educated Neapolitan thinkers evaluated the popular practice of the *jettatura* (the belief that a person can project bad luck, or illness, on another)[31] and concluded that the *jettatore* was an individual who actually could, sometimes unknowingly, introduce disorder into the moral sphere. The cosmology of southern Italians, which assumed that humans can interrupt the workings of the world, contrasts conspicuously with the determined clockwork universe of the rationalist philosophers of northern Europe.[32]

Aware of the human need for the psychological protection in magic religious rituals, southern Italian philosophers of the enlightenment were at one with peasants in believing in the reality of a "sense of domination by a force as powerful as it is hidden."[33] In Lucania this force is called *la fascinatura;* in Sicily, *mal'occhio.*[34] Meditating on the crisis of western civilization, De Martino remembered the age of the goddess, when humans were not alienated from nature, and hoped that a society without classes could reconcile humanity with nature once again.[35] In his view, the persistence of nonrational beliefs, or magic, held millennial possibilities for a good society: a remembrance and a vision of a good society grounded on an ethos of human work and covered by the beliefs of Old Europe. De Martino's insight may be a pointer to the postmodern world.[36]

The intellectual path to postmodernism has been traced by Gianni Vattimo as a journey from Nietzsche to Heidegger, from unity to *rottura,* to "adventures among differences."[37] For Francesco Guardiani in 1989, the road to postmodernism seems to veer from Anglo-Saxon modernism to Italian baroque, to a tendency toward excess, seeming chaos, an emphasis on the body, and a future open to many choices.[38]

American anthropologists studying modes of domination and resistance consider enlightenment reason the basis of the modern world. They trace the confluence of this rationalism with protestant civilizing missions intent on abolishing "popish ritual" and "native superstition." The resistance of peoples of the peripheries to enlightenment rationalism, and to the attempts of dominant groups to eradicate "superstition," suggests that the hegemony of modernity has not been total. The south of Italy, and peasant pockets of the north (e.g., all along the Po valley, as Pier Paolo Pasolini pointed out), were never touched by modernity.[39]

Contemporary study of popular religious beliefs was stimulated in the 1960s by pope John XXIII's definition of the church as the people of god in history and by the student and feminist confrontations of 1968.[40] The continuing influence of the thinking of Antonio Gramsci and Ernesto De Martino has converged, in recent years, with Italian feminist theory, whose central premise is women's historical difference.

De Martino held a vision of a good society grounded on beliefs of Old Europe and an ethic of human effort. The civilization of Old Europe dates from 7000 to 3500 B.C.E.,[41] an age when values of the goddess embraced peaceful, egalitarian, and harmonious societies. Marija Gimbutas, an archaeologist at the University of California at Los Angeles, has spent a lifetime documenting the civilization of the goddess of Old Europe in archaeological artifacts.

Before the classical age of Greece, Rome, and Jerusalem,[42] the civilization of Old Europe was based on a "religion in veneration, both of the universe as the living body of a goddess-mother creator, and of all the living things within it as partaking of her divinity."[43] Differing from the account in the Judeo-christian book of Genesis, in the culture of the goddess "the earth out of which all . . . creatures have been born is not dust but alive, as [is] the Goddess-Creator herself."[44]

The culture of Old Europe, according to Gimbutas, was a group of sister societies without forts and without weapons used against other humans, societies of peaceful cooperation characterized by a strong bond between mothers and children. Agricultural societies whose people were creative in their delight in the natural wonders of this world, their tombs, shrines, and houses were organically related to the earth. Father images were unknown, but brothers, uncles, and nephews oversaw trade, crafts, and mining. Old Europeans celebrated the sacredness of everything on earth: life energies of men and women and the cycle of the seasons from birth to maturity to death to regeneration. Symbols of the sacredness of all life in Old Europe were spirals, snakes, whorls, phalluses, and eggs. In these societies without hierarchy, women and men were equal, and different.[45]

Gimbutas's theory is controversial.[46] Some of the unease may relate to the extensive evidence she has amassed that there actually *did* exist an age when there was harmony between the sexes, harmony with nature, and equality and peace among all living creatures in a universe that was alive. Criticism may be related to Gimbutas's implicit judgment on western civilization: the "five thousand years of slavery and wars of our times"[47] that she associates with "patriarchal, stratified, pastoral, mobile, and war-oriented" societies superimposed on the peaceful and harmonious goddess cultures of Old Europe.[48]

For scholars of Italian vernacular beliefs, Gimbutas's evidence cannot be dismissed.[49] Paleolithic and neolithic artifacts of the culture of the goddess can be found all along the seacoasts of the country, pervasively in central and southern Italy and dramatically in Sicily and Sardinia.[50] "The Goddess-centered religion existed for a very long time," states Gimbutas, "much longer than the era of Indo-European and Christian domination . . . leaving an indelible imprint on the Western psyche."[51]

Between 4300 and 2800 B.C.E., invading Indo-Europeans tried to impose male warrior gods, but the values of the goddess have lasted (often obscured and fragmented) for millennia. They can still be glimpsed in vernacular cultures of peripheral areas of Europe: in the Basque sections of Spain and France, in Brittany, Ireland, and Scotland, and in Scandinavia. Resisting male-dominated cultures the longest were the islands of Crete, Malta, Sardinia, and Sicily and the Adriatic coastal regions, where the culture of Old Europe flourished until 1500 B.C.E.[52]

The goddess religion was nearly obliterated in central Europe, yet traces are still visible in art, literature, myths, and archetypes of dreams.[53] Nonverbal layers of religious and political behavior are evident in Poland, for example, where posters of the black madonna of Czestochowa were everywhere visible during the Solidarity liberation movement against what was perceived as unjust soviet communist rule.[54]

The prehistoric earth mother, for Gimbutas, may be understood by studying the deep folk beliefs of Old Europe, beliefs that refer to "the miracle of magical transformation. Everything born from the earth is brimming with the life force. Flower, tree, stone, hill, human and animal alike are born from the earth, and all possess her strength." Leafy trees, meadows, certain groves, rivers, and trees growing together from several stumps "are particularly charged with the mystery of life." A Lithuanian prayer to the earth mother calls her the "Blossomer" and "Bud Raiser."[55] In Poland and Russia, striking the earth is regarded as striking one's own mother. In Italy the earth is called *madre terra;* the custom, observable during pilgrimages to black madonnas, of kissing mother earth endures.[56] In the christian appropriation of the earth mother, she is honored on the feast of the assumption of Mary into heaven in mid-August, a feast of flowers, herbs, and corn celebrated today in all catholic countries from Ireland to Italy, Lithuania to Malta, Mexico to Brazil.[57]

Justice is the central value that emerges from studying the earth mother; Greek, Russian, and Lithuanian goddesses who embody justice are discussed by Gimbutas. This book documents the centrality of the woman figure Giustizia in Italian folk stories.[58] Slavic peasants from time immemorial settled disputes by calling on the earth as witness. "The Earth Mother listens to appeals, settles problems, and punishes all who deceive her or are disrespectful to her. She does not tolerate thieves, liars, or vain and proud people."[59] Folk stories recount that those whom she punished were swallowed by the earth; a lake or mountain would appear on the site.

The regenerative powers of the earth mother are most often symbolized in images of eyes and in spirals, circles, ascending arcs, trees, serpents and snakes, zigzag lines, and meandering water.[60] In the worldview of Old Europe, life was celebrated as in constant motion, as in a spiral or whirl or serpent or in leafy trees and bees; butterflies rose from the uterus of the goddess in tombs and caves. Red ocher was a color of life. Earth-centered and revering life, symbols of the goddess were water, menhirs, tombs, caves, animals, birds, snakes, fish, hills, trees, and flowers.

Unlike the culture of her war-loving successors, in the civilization of the goddess this world, not the next, was the focus of life, an immanent worldview in which existence was characterized by "the sacredness and mystery of all there is on Earth."[61] Like the moon, life is in constant transformation, a rhythmic change of creation and destruction, birth and death. "The moon's three phases, new, waxing, and old, are repeated in trinities, or in triple-function deities who are maiden, nymph, and crone."[62] In Old Europe, the goddess was a life creator; in Greece, Rome, and christianity, she was fragmented into lover, mother, wife, and daughter of the male god.

Popular resistance to the patriarchal christian church, grounded in memories that stretch back to the prehistoric past, may be a central meaning of the black madonnas of Italy. For Gimbutas, the tie between the fertile soil and the earth mother is evident not only in artifacts but also "in the continuous veneration of black madonnas to this day." The color black, which christian iconography associates with death or evil, in Old Europe was "the color of the fertility of the soil." Noting that black madonnas inspire fervent pilgrimages and are believed to have miraculous powers, Gimbutas states that they may be "the most highly venerated of all christian religious symbols." Deepening the iconoclasm, she observes that it is "the blackness" of these madonnas that "still evokes profound and meaningful images and associations for devotees."[63]

Church whitening of black madonnas has occurred in many places in Italy. Franca Bimbi, a feminist sociologist at the University of Padua, referred me to the black madonna of her childhood at Montenero. We traveled to the sanctuary outside Leghorn. Why, I asked a priest, had the church painted her white? Well, he answered, she wasn't really black, she was *bruna* (brown).

In its dark manifestation, the madonna of Montenero may have been too unsettling for the church.[64] At nearby Savignano, the startling artifact of the primordial goddess dated 26,000 to 18,000 B.C.E. suggests women's polyvalent sexuality: "On this Upper Paleolithic pregnant figurine of statite (or serpentine marble) the head is replaced by a figureless phallus."[65]

Political implications of the black madonna of Montenero may also be uncomfortable for the church. Pilgrimages to the site were historically organized by confraternities and artisan guilds who interpreted church doctrine with subversive popular beliefs; in 1921, many of these guilds participated in the formation of the Italian communist party at Leghorn, outside Montenero. Today a significant comunità di base is located in this city in the Piazza del Luogo Pio. In the liberation theology of comunità di base of Italy, marxism is considered compatible with Judeo-christian scriptures, and the history of christianity is researched, not from the perspective of the church, but from the perspective of subaltern classes, particularly women.[66]

The deepening of marxist thought, noted earlier in the works of Gramsci and De Martino, is evident today in writings of Italian anthropologists who consider themselves "unedited marxists." Alfonso Di Nola has pointed out that dialectical materialism by itself is incapable of explaining faith, popular religion, or pilgrimages to sanctuaries of popular saints.[67] Excavating deeply beneath conventional forms of religion, Di Nola has studied the secret Jesus revealed in the gnostic gospels, the medieval cabala, and the survival of ancient beliefs in folklore. Di Nola holds that in peasant religion there is a closer relation to local patron saints than there is to Jesus or to god. In popular beliefs, the madonna becomes many local madonnas regarded as sisters, whose function is protective.[68]

Carlo Ginzburg's works are a landmark in contemporary study of popular religious beliefs. Preferring the plural form, "popular religions," and the term "folklore," he suggests that what is at hand is a conflict between the religion of the hegemonic classes and the religions of subaltern peoples.[69] Evaluating peasant beliefs within their own worldviews,[70] he equates folklore with the culture of subaltern classes and popular religion with *la cultura folclorica*.[71]

In *The Cheese and the Worms*, Ginzburg is struck by the contemporary feel of beliefs of a peasant, Menocchio, on trial for anticlericalism hundreds of years ago: "the air is God . . . the earth is our mother."[72] Jesus was one of the children of God, "because we are all God's children. . . . He was a man like the rest of us . . . born of St. Joseph and Mary, the Virgin."[73] Ginzburg places Menocchio's beliefs in an ancient, and modern, tradition of radicalism,[74] wherein the new world is to come from peasants like Menocchio, a new world in which all peoples, "Turks, Jews, Christians, and heretics," are children of god. Menocchio's beliefs, for Ginzburg, were "fundamentally pre-Christian" and tied to seasonal cycles of nature.[75]

Encouraged by Ernesto De Martino, Ginzburg studied peasant beliefs that were persecuted as witchcraft and magic by the catholic inquisition of the sixteenth and seventeenth centuries. Uncovering an agrarian cult in the Friuli,[76] the historian describes folk rituals of the *Benandanti,* men and women *"nati con la camicia"* (born with the caul), who gathered four times a year (the women in processions, the men armed with stalks of *finocchio,* or fennel) to fight in the presence of their dead against *streghe e stregoni* (witches and warlocks) to save the fertility of their fields. Catholic inquisitors ascribed the rituals to diabolic beliefs and forced peasants to confess thereto. Ginzburg's research has brought to light "a genuinely popular stratum of beliefs . . . later deformed, and then expunged" when educated classes superimposed their ideas on popular beliefs.[77]

In his *Storia notturna,*[78] Ginzburg discovers similarities between the northern Italian cult of the Benandanti and beliefs found in the Pyrenees, Scotland, Sweden, Sicily, the Baltic region, Siberia, and Lapland. In all these cases, the soul is believed to leave the body in the moment of ecstasy and magic is used to secure the material survival of the community, themes found in ancient stories of journeys to the land of the dead. There appears to be something in the human body, Ginzburg states, that suggests rapport with the invisible and with our past.[79] In careful and extensively documented studies, he substantiates the persistence of the belief in a prehistoric woman divinity who was known in Italy by many names, notably *la Signora,* the feminine word for the lord.[80]

Ginzburg's views are significant for historians whose craft has been based on the belief in unilinear time. A historian himself, Ginzburg's binary view alternates the history of short periods with the history of eons, keeps in mind persisting sentient structures of animals and humans, and reminds us that some historical questions are not soluble by reason. Remembering that the ancients regarded historians as poets, Ginzburg recalls that Aristotle said that poets are concerned with that which *can be.* Historians may well "put to use the category of what *can be* to understand what has been."[81]

In a 1989 interview, Ginzburg admitted the difficulties of a binary methodology. How invoke possibility in order to understand the past while not forgetting the principle of reality, which can never be renounced by a historian? How retain the methodology of rationalism while recognizing that in our time rationality has underlain policies leading to death camps?[82]

Ginzburg's studies are an excellent corrective, and substantiation, of feminist studies; he points out that lepers and Jews were killed before witches were burned or hanged and that the feminist focus on "a separate female culture" has tended to ignore the mythical content of the witches' sabbath.[83]

In rituals for the fertility of the fields,[84] "behind the women (and the few men) linked to the 'good' nocturnal goddesses we glimpse a cult of an ecstatic nature."[85]

Inquisition trials of the second half of the sixteenth century in Sicily reveal many women's references to *Donni di fuora* (women from outside), *Donni di locu* (local women), *Donni di notti* (night women), *Donni di casa* (house women), *Belli Signuri* (beautiful ladies), and *Padruni di casa* (house mistresses), who followed "a female divinity who had many names: the Matron, the Teacher, the Greek Mistress, the Wise Sibilla. . . ."[86] Ginzburg's references to Donni di fuora and the like are similar to "the others"—midwives, healers, witches, and mourners—who were significant figures of peasant society. As he describes them, the folk rituals of the Benandanti in the region of the Friuli resemble the ritual processions in Apulia for fertility of the fields that I explore later in this book.[87]

The tangled relationship of vernacular religious beliefs and official religion has been pointed out by Vittorio Lanternari. Only rarely do the views of the people lead to outright revolt: the common pattern is one of absorption or assimilation of vernacular beliefs by dominant classes and institutions. When confronted by subversive vernacular beliefs, religious authority sometimes proscribes, sometimes tolerates. Subaltern classes can submit, change the outward forms of their beliefs, or defy dominant authority.[88] Vernacular rituals and festivals, in this view, reveal degrees of absorption or assimilation, as well as degrees of resistance. Outwardly maintaining church forms, while silently retaining ancient beliefs, appears, in my research, to be the mode used by Italian peasants.

Gustavo Guizzardi cautions against considering popular beliefs a lost paradise. Dominant and subaltern cultures do not, in his view, exist in themselves; what does exist is the rapport that dominant classes have with subaltern classes.[89] Engels said that religious belief generates tension in subaltern classes, a tension that creates a revolutionary egalitarian vision hearkening back to a golden age.[90] Gramsci and De Martino, personally grounded in the cultures they examined, are the theorists who have most deeply influenced contemporary Italian anthropologists who look to popular religious beliefs for their potential to bring a new society into being.[91]

The contemporary positive evaluation of vernacular beliefs contrasts with earlier Italian treatment. When Pitré studied them seriously, a review stated that "Dr. Pitré has published four volumes of *porcherie* [obscene filth]!!"[92] The perspective of an elite culture, until recently, has informed Italian literature. Alessandro Manzoni in his classic, *I promessi sposi,* took a conde-

scending, aristocratic view of the lower classes.[93] Even Verga, founder of a
literature grounded on lives of common people, was not concerned with
them as much as he was with expressing his own pessimistic worldview.[94]
The significant Italian twentieth-century theorist with this aristocratic posture was Benedetto Croce, who wrote a history of liberty that held that
poetry never came from the people.[95]

For the contemporary anthropologists Antonio Carbonaro and Arnaldo
Nesti folk beliefs are traces of a *cultura negata,* a denied culture with beliefs
in an egalitarian and libertarian society.[96] In addition to peasants, mariners,
and shepherds, this denied culture includes industrial workers, often originally from southern Italy, who were deprecated in the north. As Italian
women have insisted since 1968, perhaps the major negated culture is that of
women.[97] Contemporary Italian discussion of denied cultures sometimes
refers to the *diritto alla differenza,* the right to differ from the dominant
culture and to express a collective desire to change one's life.[98] The central
concept of Italian feminists is *difference.*[99]

The recovery of suppressed cultures is proceeding on several levels in Italy.
Women scholars recover ancient values transmitted by women persecuted as
witches.[100] Historians study the "systematic cancellation of peasant culture."[101] Along with historians recovering suppressed peasant culture (who
call its suppression "ethnocide"), a popular ethnic revival in Italy has
stimulated the founding of museums dedicated to vernacular traditions.[102]

The beliefs of the people have been destroyed or deformed by catholic
inquisitors, protestant reformers, and enlightenment rationalists. Catholic
inquisitors carried intolerance and persecution of the "other" beliefs of
Jews, women, and peasants to the point of torture and burning. Protestant
reformers, in addition to burning witches and heretics, attacked and
abolished beliefs that referred to christian martyrs and miracles and directed
particular hostility to the central woman saint, Mary.

Contemporary left catholics in comunità di base throughout Italy believe
that there are many possible interpretations of the Judeo-christian scriptures,
encourage the pluralism of an unedited interpretation of marxism, see a
radically democratic potential in vernacular beliefs, and regard respect for
differences of gender, religion, history, and culture as essential to a healthy
society.[103]

Enlightenment rationalism in Italy, concludes Lombardi Satriani, did not
reach the people; it remained a subject of salon discussion among educated
persons.[104] The efforts of the catholic church to "purify" baroque piety by
condemning indulgences, pilgrimages, and magic, in the hope of eliminating

from christianity every "residue of paganism," came to naught. In the twentieth century, with more scientific progress than in all preceding centuries, the width of the phenomenon of vernacular beliefs in Italy can be measured by the number of widely selling booklets, available in any newspaper kiosk, on the many "sightings" of the madonna.[105] The depth of the phenomenon can be suggested by considering black madonnas as a metaphor for submerged, radically democratic beliefs.

Intrigued by the phenomenon of submerged beliefs, the Italian historian Giorgio Galli has studied the hidden history of western civilization: the bacchantes of Greek culture, the early christian heresy of gnosticism, the persecution of witches in the early modern era, and contemporary feminist and green movements. For Galli, this submerged history represents the possibility of an alternative culture with values of equality, refutation of all hierarchies, and freedom.[106]

In his analysis, women's civilization of the period between 1000 and 700 B.C.E. was suppressed. The story of women's civilization and its suppression was incorporated in Greek myths and transmitted in the Eleusinian mysteries. The civilization of the goddess, wherein all creatures were equal and happiness and peace were the end of life, was overcome by the patriarchal systems of late Greece and Rome and by christianity. Instead of equality, patriarchy imposed the concept of the preferred son and a hierarchical order for society.[107] Although Greek democracy was founded on equal rights, it was flawed at its core, as were later democracies (notably that of the United States), by the equivocation that equal rights did not apply to women and slaves.

Citing the French feminist theorist Françoise D'Eaubonne, who has described the civilization of the goddess as "without classes and without wars," Galli believes that the values of a communitarian, celebratory society endured in dionysianism, which, as I shall demonstrate in chapters 5 and 6 of this book, was never obliterated in Italy. The memory of a peaceful, egalitarian society also endured in Greek tragedy: Aeschylus knew, states Galli, that the subordination of women was the link holding Greek democracy together.[108]

Galli's views coincide with Marija Gimbutas's findings that neolithic agrarian cultures were matrilineal, egalitarian, and peaceful and were overcome by invading horsemen from the Asian steppe.[109] The persecution of christians by Romans, in Galli's view, was a persecution largely of women.[110] Indebted to Elaine Pagels's research,[111] he observes that in the first three centuries of christianity gnostics used christian language bonded to Hebrew scriptures (in the Wisdom literature, as Elisabeth Schussler Fiorenza has pointed out)[112] as a cover for the ancient goddess. Instead of a monistic and male god, many gnostic writings speak of a duality of masculine and feminine elements.[113] Gnostics prayed to a mother goddess who held many names: Grazia, Silenzio, Spirito Santo, Madre lo Spirito Santo, or Sapienza.[114] Among the gnostics, women were equal to men; some were prophets, preachers, healers, and priests. In contrast to the interpretation of christianity that has prevailed (masculine, authoritarian, and hostile to sexuality), submerged beliefs point to an alternative culture at once egalitarian, libertarian, and celebratory.[115]

This book is largely in agreement with Galli's analysis, but my research in Italian folklore suggests that in addition to values of equality, freedom, and celebration of life, the Italian case of submerged cultures points to a potential alternative civilization emphasizing *giustizia*. Justice grounded on equality is implicit in the civilization of the prechristian goddess, wherein the earth was held in common, with everyone having "equal right to the sea, the seashore, the air."[116] People in pilgrimage to black madonnas of the poor of Italy say, "We are all equal because we have the same mother."[117]

The multicultural dimensions of black madonnas have been suggested in recent years by scholars documenting the African and Asian roots of western civilization. Martin Bernal, in 1987, explored the influence of Africans and Semites on Greek civilization. Phoenicians (a branch of the Canaanites) venerated the goddess Astarte, established trading posts in northern Africa, and colonized the west coast of Sicily. Egypt, whose African culture and goddess Isis were integral to the cultures of Greece and Rome, is not far from the south shore of Sicily. "Hebrew Canaanite was not merely the language of a small tribe, isolated inland in the mountains of Palestine . . . it had been spoken all over the Mediterranean—wherever the Phoenicians sailed and settled."[118] Chapter 9 of this book explores easter rituals featuring the black madonna of Trapani on the western Phoenician-Canaanite shore of Sicily. The persistence of the belief in the African goddess Isis is observable today in carnevale on the Greek side of the island, at Acireale.[119]

Recovering the view that the Greeks themselves held, and that was deformed later by racist theorists, Bernal finds that Greek culture arose as the result of Egyptian and Phoenician colonization around 1500 B.C.E.[120] Adding legends, place names, religious cults, language, and the distribution of linguistic and script dialects to the evidence of archaeology, Bernal's study emphasizes Greek cultural borrowings from Egypt and the Levant in the thousand years from 2100 to 1100 B.C.E.[121] According to Bernal, Egypt, on the continent of Africa, was the original source of deities celebrated in Greece, the eastern Mediterranean, and, later, the entire Roman world.

Early fathers of the christian church crushed neoplatonism, the Hellenic descendant of Egyptian religion, as well as gnosticism, its Judeo-christian counterpart. Egyptian religion became a submerged philosophy turning on Hermes Trismegistos, the Greek translation of the name Thoth, Egyptian god of wisdom. In the revival of ancient learning in the Renaissance, Giordano Bruno advocated a return to the original, or natural, religion of Egypt; he was burned by the inquisition in 1600, at the culmination of carnival on *martedì grasso* (Shrove Tuesday). Afterward, authorities continued to fear pantheism, the natural religion that implies an animate universe.[122] Today, a statue of Giordano Bruno stands in a popular Roman market situated a few yards from Al Tempo Ritrovato, Italy's best women's bookstore.

Racism based on skin color in late seventeenth-century England, "alongside the increasing importance of the American colonies with their twin policies of extermination of the Native Americans and enslavement of African Blacks,"[123] accompanied Aryan theorists' replacement of the view that the ancient Greeks themselves held: their civilization was indebted to Africa and to the Levant, and classical Greek civilization was "the result of the mixture of native Europeans and colonizing Africans and Semites."[124]

Many of Bernal's findings regarding a continuum from African and Semitic dark goddesses to Greek and Roman goddesses resonate in this study of black madonnas of Italy. A word for "witch" in Italian dialect is *megara,* a Semitic word in the Greek language that refers to "cave." Megara Hyblaea has one of the largest troves of archaeological evidence of the civilization of the goddess in Sicily. The city was called "cave of the goddess Hybla";[125] the name recalls that the goddess Hybla was venerated in Sicily before Greeks founded Megara Hyblaea in 728 B.C.E.[126]

The syncretism of beliefs in the indigenous Sicilian goddess Ibla, and beliefs in African, Middle Eastern, Asian, and Greek and Roman goddesses, is apparent in Sicily. An image of a seated goddess nursing twins (dated 540 B.C.E.), who appears to be a combination of Ibla and Hera, was found at Megara Hyblaea and may be seen today in the national museum at Syracuse. The museum also houses a depiction of the Anatolian goddess Cybele, dating from the fourth century before the common era, seated on a throne flanked by lions and holding a cornucopia and a serpent, symbols of nature, abundance, and regeneration.[127]

The belief in the indigenous Sicilian goddess Ibla has persisted over the centuries. It is evident today in the folklore of the region of the Iblaean mountains (named for her) in southeastern Sicily, where the madonna of Chiaramonte Gulfi (popularly described as "having come from afar") embodies the bond between African, Asian, and European women divinities. In the Iblaean region the ancient goddess shares her name with the Hellenic goddess Hera in the old name for Ragusa, Ibla Herae. Folklore with themes of justice and equality, and heretical religious and radical political beliefs and actions of this region, are investigated in chapters 3 and 4 of this book.

On the other side of the island, the Canaanite goddess Astarte was brought, via Africa, to the Phoenician coast of Sicily, where Greeks and Romans later venerated Aphrodite and Venus at Erice. Easter rituals in the streets of Trapani, marked by a black madonna who resembles Astarte, Aphrodite, and Venus, are explored in chapter 9 below.

When it has not whitened them, the church has attempted to assimilate dark or black madonnas; this is evident in the many Italian madonnas described as bruna. The usual explanation for the dark brown color is that the icons are "Byzantine." This is often their style, but why do these figures inspire fervent veneration?

Georges Gharib, a lay minister of the Greek Orthodox church who teaches mariology at Rome, has analyzed different Marys of the bible. Matthew calls her the mother of Emmanuel; Mark, speaking of Jesus, says that inhabitants of Nazareth called him son of Mary; and John speaks of the intervention of Mary in the wedding at Cana. Luke may be the most relevant biblical source whose gospel describes Mary as the mother of the son of god; in Acts, referring to her at the last supper, he says that Mary was "already considered the invisible center of the apostolic church."[128]

Black as invisible? The black Mary as hidden center of the apostolic church? Portraits of the madonna said to have been painted at Jerusalem by Luke are all dark. These pictures ended up at Constantinople when that city became the eastern capital of christianity. Italians sometimes refer to the Byzantine images as "the madonna from Constantinople," or *"la greca."* A significant fact about Byzantine madonnas is that it was at Ephesus, the city where the Graeco-Roman goddess Artemis/Diana was venerated, that the church proclaimed Mary the mother of god in 431 C.E., a story whose implications are studied in chapter 10 of this book.

The many black madonnas of Rome weaken the premise of the Byzantine origin of all dark madonnas. Santa Maria in Trastevere is popularly considered to be the black woman of the Song of Songs. The church of the black madonna of santa Maria in Ara Coeli was built on a temple to Cybele. The church of the whitened madonna of santa Maria in Cosmedin was built on a temple to the Roman grain goddess, Ceres.[129] Before the Byzantine era, in the catacombs of Priscilla at Rome, the earliest known depiction of Mary is brown: "Hers is a rich cocoa color that has withstood the centuries. Her skin, deliberately painted so much darker than that of other women painted on these walls, gives pause for thought. The first Virgin Mary is a brown Virgin Mary."[130] Jews and Muslims, as well as christians, according to Gharib, participated in popular veneration of Mary.[131] Consecrated to the mother of god, the church of santa Sophia in Constantinople has an image of Mary in a pose characteristic of the prechristian goddess Hera, seated on a throne. In the Byzantine world, according to Gharib, more churches, sanctuaries, and monasteries were dedicated to the mother than to her son.[132]

Byzantine images of the madonna came to Italy in the eighth and ninth centuries of the common era during the Iconoclastic controversy. To save them from destruction, monks, merchants, and sailors brought the images from Byzantium to France, Germany, Belgium, and, especially, to Italy.[133] In the controversy over icons, women were "among the most strenuous defenders of the images [of the madonna]."[134] Apart from Italy, most Byzantine madonnas are found in the countries of the former soviet bloc.

Ean Begg, once a Dominican priest and now a Jungian analyst, came across a document of 1629 that listed black madonnas in Belgium, Spain, Hungary, France, and Bavaria, as well as in Italy. Counting 450 contemporary images of madonnas "called black, dark, brown, or grey" throughout the world, he points out that the number would be much greater if the naturally black divinities of Africa and the dark women divinities of Asia were included.[135]

The political implication of black madonnas, for Begg, is that they are "in favour of freedom and integrity, the right of peoples, cities, nations to be inviolate and independent from outside interference."[136] The insight seems prescient when one considers that the 1989 nonviolent revolts of central and eastern European countries against soviet communism, and the 1991 declarations of independence of republics within the former U.S.S.R., transpired against a backdrop of many black madonnas.

In Italy sanctuaries of black and brown madonnas are located in areas known for religious heresy and characterized by politics of equality and justice. This is not, as a critic has stated, "geographical determinism," but an instance of what Gramsci and others have pointed out—that religious beliefs may influence political behavior, and that beliefs associated with ancient sites, as Peter Brown has noted, may persist, often on nonverbal levels, over long periods. The area around archaeological sites of the goddess and the

The black madonna of Montenero.

black madonna of Montenero (near Leghorn), as discussed above, combines religious heresy and political radicalism. Pilgrimages to sanctuaries of black madonnas of the Campagna are in a region with abundant evidence of veneration of the ancient goddess and are historically characterized by heresy that the church has attempted to suppress. Bologna, site of a black madonna and a perennially "red" city, was the center of Italian partisan resistance during world war II and was the site of the 1990 conference of the Italian communist party that initiated a radically democratic devolution of the party into its constituent groups.[137] Feminist and antiwar demonstrations of the last three decades culminated at Rome, where (as discussed above) there are many black madonnas with ancient connections, notably santa Maria in Trastevere, santa Maria Nova, with the oldest Lucan image of the madonna, and the church of santa Maria Maggiore.

Black madonnas of Seminara, Palmi, and Capo Colonna are near the place where Joachim of Fiore proclaimed a coming age of the holy spirit that would succeed the ages of the father and the son; more than a thousand years before Joachim, this was where women Pythagorean philosophers analyzed *harmonia*. Many black madonnas are found in Bari, city of Aldo Moro, the martyred christian-democratic statesman, who maintained that beliefs in communism and christianity are "converging parallels." Palermo, near the black madonnas of Milicia, Tindari, and Trapani, is where Rete, the coalition of catholics, communists, and "honest" people led by Leoluca Orlando (the city's former mayor), opposes the mafia and works to save the environment and the future of children. Themes of stories told in the area of the whitened black madonna of Chiaramonte Gulfi emphasize justice and equality, beliefs that took political form in the late nineteenth-century Sicilian socialist fasci and that are visible today in demonstrations on the flanks of the mountain named for the goddess Ibla protesting NATO nuclear bases, the mafia, and imperialist aggression in third-world countries.

CHAPTER 3

a world in motion with a woman

at the center • artifacts, myths,

stories, rituals of everyday life

A SICILIAN peasant ritual of the middle ages that Salvatore Salomone-Marino found still alive in the nineteenth century bonded women's nurturance and life milk with the earth and the goddess. The village *strega* (witch), joined by other women, would lie face down and place bare breasts on the earth. During the ritual, the witch and the women would hold strega beads.[1] Different from christian rosary beads, strega beads that I have seen are a circle of tigereyes.

Some peasant rituals may seem strange to the modern mind and myths and stories more appropriate to children's story time than to historical analysis, yet rituals, myths, and stories are critically important in order to understand the preservation of ancient themes.

Trinacria, symbol of ancient Sicily, was depicted as a woman whose three legs form a circle in motion. Her centrality is visible in artifacts, myths, stories, rituals, and the everyday lives of peasant women.[2] Storytellers melded the indigenous goddess of Sicily with women divinities brought from Africa and Asia Minor, and later with popular, often black, madonnas. On the mount of Eryx/Erice on the west coast of Sicily, Phoenicians venerated Astarte, Greeks worshiped Aphrodite, Romans brought gifts to Venus, and contemporary Sicilians every summer put peace doves in flight for Africa.

In the sanctuary at Selinunte to Demeter Malophoros, apple bearer, there was a special area dedicated to Hekate Triformis, the triple goddess; twelve thousand terra-cotta figurines of the goddess, or of her women followers, dated from the seventh to the fifth centuries B.C.E., were found there. Agrigento, on the south shore of the island, has another trove of goddess figures in the archaeological museum and a sanctuary to Demeter and Persephone that may antedate the founding of Greek colonies in Sicily in the seventh century B.C.E. At Piazza Armerina, in the navel of Sicily, Roman mosaics of African stone depict women who are scantily clad; animals and humans are stylistically similar to Tunisian and Algerian mosaics. At Palazzolo Acreide, where a folklore of justice has been collected, twelve statues of the goddess Cybele are accompanied by a lion and by men in Phrygian caps. "These lions and the tympanum which she sometimes holds, identify the goddess as Cybele, the Magna Mater, a deity of Asiatic origin." Venerated in Athens from the fifth century B.C.E., Cybele's cult spread from Phrygia in northwest Asia Minor to Rome in 204 B.C.E.[3]

Veneration of Demeter and her daughter Kore, or Persephone, may have come to Magna Graecia (southern Italy and the islands) from Africa.[4] In Greek, Demeter means "mother," symbolized by the Greek letter delta, or triangle, symbol of the goddess later repeated in the triangular shape of black madonnas. In Hebrew, the analogous word is *Daleth,* door of birth, death, and sexual paradise. In Asian culture, the symbol for the goddess is "the Doorway of the Mysterious Feminine . . . the root from which Heaven and Earth sprang."[5] Among Demeter's many names are Demeter Chthonia, the Subterranean One, and, in a clue to the origin of black madonnas, Melaina, the Black One. Demeter's daughter, Persephone, was Queen of the Dead; the Italian form, Proserpina, means "First Serpent."

Demeter's cult as virgin-mother-crone and creator-preserver-destroyer was centered at Eleusis in Greece and at Enna in Sicily. A Homeric hymn celebrates "the holy goddess, fair-haired Demeter, and . . . her slim-ankled daughter whom Aidoneus [Hades] snatched away." The daughter was playing "with the deep-bosomed daughters of Ocean," gathering "roses, saffron, violets, iris, hyacinth." She was drawn to the narcissus, "radiantly wonderful, inspiring awe in all who saw it . . . a hundred stems grew from its root, and the whole wide heaven above, the whole earth, and the salt surge of the sea smiled for joy at its fragrance." When Persephone reached out to pluck the narcissus, "suddenly the earth split open wide," Hades "grabbed her, resisting and screaming, and took her below in his golden chariot."[6]

In the tale of the mother searching for her daughter, Demeter often merged with Persephone. For Jung, this merging presages the psychological phenomenon wherein "every mother contains her daughter in herself and every daughter her mother, [so] that every woman extends backwards into her mother and forwards into her daughter."[7] This gives rise to a sense of time reaching backward and forward, suggested in the phrase "remembering the future." In the christian age the merging of mother and daughter became the fusing of mother and son evident in images of black madonnas. Persephone as queen of the underworld was worshiped as goddess of the dead, holding the keys of heaven and hell before they were given to saint Peter in the christian age.[8]

Demeter and her daughter were celebrated in the Eleusinian mysteries. Merlin Stone wonders, "Did they tell of Demeter as Thesmophorus, the Giver of the Law, and explain that it was She who first established the law of the land? Did they speak of the gift that She gave, the knowledge of the seeds and the growing of the wheat, so that the fruits of Demeter's harvest might feed the people?" Did the mysteries reenact the abduction of Persephone?[9]

In Italy, the myth of Demeter and her daughter continues to be told to this day as the story of Cerere and Proserpina. Cerere hid her daughter, in the Sicilian version, to keep her from being married to Apollo, or Mars. While Proserpina was plucking flowers with women friends on the banks of Lago di Pergusa in the center of Sicily, the earth suddenly opened and Hades/Pluto in his chariot kidnapped her and took her below the earth. Cerere looked for her daughter all over Mount Etna. When lupin bushes impeded her search, the mother goddess vowed that their beans would forever be bitter, which they are. After several days of futile search, the mother in her grief withered all vegetation on earth. Zeus/Jove sent his messenger Hermes/Mercury to persuade Pluto to release Proserpina. The god of the underworld had her eat six pomegranate seeds, symbols of marital fidelity, so that she would return. Jove adjudicated that for one-half or two-thirds of the year the daughter could stay with her mother on the earth, but that for the remaining part of the year she would have to stay with her husband under the ground.[10]

Demeter, often depicted carrying a wheat sheaf, harks back to an earlier grain goddess who became the Roman goddess Ceres, and later the christian madonna, particularly in her black manifestation. Yet, as Pamela Berger has demonstrated in her study of this transformation, "The Greek grain goddess Demeter is only a shadow of the earlier great vegetation goddess."[11] However, traits of the prehistoric goddess did remain in the figures of Demeter and Hera among the Greeks and in Ceres and Juno among the Romans, merging with the worship of the Anatolian Magna Mater, Cybele, and the African goddess Isis.[12]

Cybele was honored in the Graeco-Roman world as mother goddess of fertility. In forests and on mountaintops, her special places, the goddess, holding a tambourine, inspired wild dancing; as mistress of wild animals she was always accompanied by lions.[13] Cybele's son Attis was the prototype of the *galli,* who have been described as followers of the goddess who castrated themselves. Will Roscoe, a gender-studies scholar, has challenged this interpretation, considering the galli as men who renounced patriarchal society. Neither distinctively male nor female, the galli resemble the *Berdaches* of the Navajo tradition, "who combined the traits and skills of women and men in a distinct third gender status."[14]

The cult of Isis came to Rome about 80 B.C.E., after that of Cybele. Isis, in Egyptian scriptures, was described as the "Oldest of the Old . . . the

Statue of Isis/Cybele/Demeter/Cerere, Piazza San Marco, Rome. Photograph by Wallace Birnbaum.

Goddess from whom all becoming arose." Considered "Giver of Life," Isis was invoked by Lucius as "the One Who is All" and "Savior of the human race." Apuleius said she was "Nature, the parent of all things, the sovereign of the elements, the primary progeny of time, the most exalted of the deities, the first of the heavenly gods and goddesses."[15]

In Greek and Roman cultures the many dimensions of the primordial goddess were splintered and assigned to many women deities. Church fathers eliminated feminine images of the deity from the bible, but art historians have uncovered many instances of pagan images used for christian figures. Pamela Berger has suggested the continuation of traits of the primordial goddess in characteristics of the madonna and other saints and in folk stories, paintings, and sculpture in the British Isles, Germany, and the Low Countries. The catholic church retained the figure of the mother but reduced the madonna to a great saint embodying virginity and obedience. Yet the memory of the ancient goddess appears to have persisted in the christian era in black images of Mary, in vernacular beliefs and rituals, and in political activities enacting beliefs in justice and equality.[16]

Like the prehistoric goddess, the madonna has many names, many manifestations. In Sicily, as the madonna Odigitria, she who shows the way, she is the protectress of the island. Veneration of the madonna in Sicily dates from the year 42 C.E. when, according to popular tradition, she sent a letter to the people of Messina blessing them and their city, a blessing inscribed at the base of the statue of the Madonnina (the diminutive, affectionate Sicilian term for "madonna") that travelers see while crossing the Strait of Messina (home of Scylla and Charybdis) from the Italian mainland to the island. Sicilians regard their island as the homeland of the mother goddess Demeter/Ceres and her daughter Persephone/Proserpina. Passengers aboard the ferry rush out of cars and trains to eat *arancini,* rice balls shaped like oranges sold to travelers as the boat approaches the island. The madonna of Messina, as I shall indicate in chapter 11, is bonded with the Calabrian black madonnas of Palmi and Seminara.

In Sicily, the black madonna of Tindari, santa Maria Sacratissima, is a few kilometers from the paleolithic drawing of the divinity in the Addaura cave outside Palermo and near the black madonna of Milicia. The Tindari wooden icon is a black mother and child merged into one triangular figure; the mother carries a wheat sheaf. The triangle, connoting the vulva, is a sign of the ancient goddess; the wheat suggests Demeter; and the Black woman of the Song of Songs of the Hebrew scriptures is recalled in the inscription at

The black madonna of Tindari.

the base: *Nigra sum sed furmosa* (I am black and beautiful), a Semitic connection explored in chapter 7 of this work.

Why, I asked a priest, was the statue black? The paint on the wood, he answered, had darkened over time. Perhaps, but the color black may have something to do with the popular belief that the sanctuary at Tindari is the most sacred place of Sicily. The remembrance of Tindari assailed the poet Salvatore Quasimodo when he was far from his native Sicily.[17] The memory also remains in the consciousness/unconscious of an Italian American who remembers the stories his Sicilian grandmother told. Gian Banchero is an artist and poet who paints black madonnas of Italy. He describes the blackness of "Nostra Signora di Tindari" as "Indian-Brazilian, Ethiopian, Spanish, Gypsy, Southern European, but yet [she] could be of India." Different from the "standard Madonna, meaning . . . nothing, representing the attitude of the handmaiden of God," Banchero describes this madonna as "joyous as if she is really glad to see you . . . a slight hint of concern . . . comes through after a moment or two." The black madonna responds, he says, to "Mariachi, Indian, Afro, and Asian music . . . Mambo." "She is Third World but mother of all . . . a visage that could be said to be eternal . . . a face familiar enough to be Mamma."[18]

▪   ▪   ▪

"*Black Madonna of Italy,*" *by Gian Banchero, Italian-American painter, based on stories his grandparents told him as a child. Reproduced by permission.*

IN THE ENVIRONS of the black madonna of Tindari, people resist the church image of the madonna, and their folk art indicates resistance to secular authority. At Santo Stefano di Camastra, Sicilians make ceramic eggcups that depict their former kings as comic idiots whose heads have been removed to make space for eggs, symbol of the goddess. Images of the prechristian woman divinity are everywhere in the Museo Mandralisca at nearby Cefalù. Figures of Demeter, which the museum literature states were diffused throughout Sicily in the fourth century B.C.E., carry a little pig, an animal signifying regeneration, while the mother holds a torch to look for her daughter. Images of Demeter/Persephone are often accompanied by women dancing and playing flutes, perhaps celebrating the Eleusinian mysteries.

At Altavilla, very close to the paleolithic drawing at Addaura, the black madonna of Milicia, like her sister figure at Tindari, is shown in triangular form fusing mother and son.[19] The painting, dating from the seventh century C.E., was placed in a church built in 1077 by the Norman conqueror Robert Guiscard. Frank Fricano, an Italian American, sent me a photograph of the black madonna of Milicia that his parents brought from Sicily and that he keeps in his office in East Liverpool, Ohio.

The church of the black madonna of Milicia is situated with a superb view of the panorama from Capo Zafferano to the Rocca di Cefalù and is not far from the renowned mosaics of Monreale crafted by Muslims during Norman rule of Sicily after 1060. Henry Adams, an American historian who

Vernacular art at Santo Stefano di Camastra, Sicily: eggcups depicting kings of Italy as imbeciles; their heads have been hollowed out to make room for eggs—which are a symbol of a goddess. Photograph by Wallace Birnbaum.

pondered the meaning of the madonna, contemplated Norman France and
Norman Sicily, symbolized by Mont-Saint-Michel and Chartres, and by the
mosaics of Monreale near Milicia. "No art—neither Greek nor Byzantine,
Italian or Arab—has ever created two religious types so beautiful, so serious,
so impressive, and yet so different, as Mont Saint Michel watching over its
northern ocean, and Monreale, looking down over its forests of orange and
lemon, on Palermo and the Sicilian seas."[20] Different, yet the people who
put stone and mortar together for French and Sicilian churches shared a
passion for black madonnas. The figure behind the altar at Chartres inspired
Joseph Campbell to a lifelong study of myths. The black madonna of Milicia
remains in the memory of emigrants to the United States.[21]

According to the legend of the black madonna of Milicia, townspeople
saw a ship experiencing difficulty as it sailed toward Palermo.[22] The ship's
crew of Saracen pirates believed the trouble was caused by a painting of a
black madonna that they had used as a porthole lid, and they gave it to
christians on shore. Resembling stories of other black madonnas, in the
account of the black madonna of Milicia her statue was drawn in a cart by
two bulls to the sanctuary site outside Palermo. Bull horns, according to
Gimbutas, are a sign of the goddess.

Stories about the black madonna of Milicia merge madonnas and other
saints. This madonna is celebrated for saving the area around Palermo from
pirates; santa Rosalia, patron saint of the city and sometimes depicted as
black, is venerated for saving Palermo from the plague. During the procession
of the black madonna of Milicia in September, the painting is turned toward
Palermo, indicating that Milicians share the black madonna's protection with
that city.

Black madonnas near Palermo, at Milicia, Tindari, and Trapani, have
multicultural origins. Considered an outpost of North Africa, Palermo
became a world capital after the Saracens took the city in 831 C.E. The
center of a trading empire that reached from Spain to Syria and rivaled the
riches of Baghdad and Constantinople, the population of Palermo when it
was an Arab capital, Denis Mack Smith has noted, "included Greeks,
Lombards, Jews, Slavs, Berbers, Persians, Tartars and Negroes." A Baghdad
merchant noted "hundreds of mosques in Palermo, more than he had seen
in any town except Cordoba."[23] When the Normans took Palermo away from
the Arabs, they made it the capital of a kingdom that extended from
southern Italy to Tunis and Tripoli in northern Africa.

Many cultures were superimposed on the indigenous goddess culture of
Italy, yet the valence of the original goddess appears to have retained its

power. In a list of popular madonnas of southeastern Sicily (la Madonna delle grazie di Modica, la Madonna di Alemagna di Terranova, la Madonna della Neve di Francofone, la Madonna dell'Orto di Gran Michele, la Madonna Addolorato di Monterosso, and la Madonna del Mazzaro), the madonna of Chiaramonte Gulfi holds first place. This madonna, of Byzantine origin, was whitened by Normans and counter-reformation clerics, yet the older darkness appears to be related to its cult site in a mountainous region named for the goddess Ibla.[24]

The whitened black madonna of Chiaramonte Gulfi fits the lineaments of a divinity of a submerged culture. In the drive of the counter-reformation clergy to eradicate popular superstition, the divinity was sculpted in an unearthly white marble and painted a whiter white than that of people around her. Papal and secular authorities may have hoped that whitening would dampen the radicalism that has characterized this region from the Sicilian Vespers of the thirteenth century to the socialist fasci of the nineteenth century to international pilgrimages and a women's camp protesting the violence of nearby NATO nuclear bases in the twentieth century.

Sometimes a characteristic of the primordial goddess was put into the protective custody of a christian saint. This appears to be the case with santa Lucia. A franciscan friar advised me a few years ago that the most beloved saint of southern Italy and Sicily—after Mary—is Lucia, evident in the popularity of the songs "O Marie" and "Santa Lucia." The iconography of santa Lucia suggests a continuum with the goddess. Eyes, as well as circles, spirals, and labyrinths, as discussed in chapter 2, were symbols of the prechristian divinity. The church appropriated the eyes of the goddess and attached them to the story of santa Lucia, a figure who recalls the goddess as maiden. Lucia, according to the church story, plucked out her eyes rather than yield her virginity to a Roman soldier. Older memories remain in the vernacular culture. Lucia is celebrated by Italians at the time of the winter solstice (in the Julian calendar, on December 13), when they eat couscous (whole-grained wheat) from Africa. The folk story, recounted by Mary Taylor Simeti, is that Sicilians were once saved from starvation when santa Lucia sent ships with grain that hungry Sicilians boiled and ate immediately.[25]

Regarded as the saint of light in Sicily, southern Italy, and Sweden (where her cult may have been taken by the Normans), Lucia is celebrated on December 13 with bonfires and torches expelling the winter darkness. In the vernacular tradition, the presence of santa Lucia is believed to counter the *mal'occhio* (evil eye). Lucia brings gifts at the time of the winter solstice, just as *la befana,* the popular image of the goddess as crone, brings gifts to children on the feast of the epiphany on January 6.[26]

In spite of church interpretation of Lucia as a pious virgin, popular customs tap submerged beliefs that remember her as the pagan Sabine mother goddess, Juno Lucina, "mother of light." As late as 1890, "Tuscan witches still used Lucina's healing charm, a wreath of rue tied with red ribbon, making the patient spit three times through the wreath, calling on St. Lucy for protection against the evil eye."[27] In the 1960s, the Beatles sang "Lucy in the sky with diamonds."

Folk stories became a repository of the values of the prehistoric goddess. The heretical and radical implications of the stories are visible in a collection by a nineteenth-century folklorist, Serafino Amabile Guastella, who lived in the area of the madonna of Chiaramonte Gulfi. An 1884 compilation reprinted in 1968, year of new-left radical confrontations in Italy and the world, offers evidence of the persistence of themes of justice and equality, as well as of a theme with contemporary resonance, "rights to life" of the poor.

Folk stories may be timeless, Carlo Lapucci has pointed out, because people continue to respond to conscious or unconscious themes of the tales. Stories collected by Pitré, Guastella, Salomone-Marino, and others may be studied for beliefs of nineteenth-century Italian peasants; Lapucci's contemporary collection of folklore suggests that earlier southern Italian folk beliefs remain alive in Italy's urban society of today. In the twentieth century, the beliefs were diffused throughout the country by southerners who migrated north, converging with similar beliefs of northern peasants. Today a southern Italian may be a communist worker in an automobile factory in Turin, and his wife may be a feminist, but ancient beliefs, not entirely conscious, appear to determine their views. Themes of justice, equality, and rights to life of the poor, woven by nineteenth-century southern Italian peasants into moral analogies, are themes today of an Italian left that includes socialists, independent radicals, left catholics, "refounded communists," greens, and feminists, the wide swath encompassing what is called the "democratic left" of Italy.[28]

In the vernacular morality implicit in Guastella's collection of stories, one belief is that poor people cannot depend on the church for their salvation. In the story "St. Paul first does his own beard, then he does yours," Romans tracking down early christians learned that they could be identified by a certain cut of beard; whereupon the authorities promulgated a decree that persons with such beards were to be arrested. Two poor christians approached saint Paul, "who could do anything, had read every book, and was so knowledgeable he could even shave a beard," and asked him to save them.

The saint prepared soap and began to shave himself. Why, asked the christians, was he shaving himself when it was they, not he, who were being followed? Saint Paul responded that it was true that he was in less danger because he was a friend of the authorities, but he would first see to his own safety, and then, if he had time, he would shave them too. The story has been distilled into a proverb: the church, personified by saint Paul, will first see to its own safety, and then, if it has time, to the salvation of the people. The moral appears to be that the people, in brotherhood and sisterhood, without the assistance of the church, will have to see to their own salvation.[29] The parable held considerable resonance in early twentieth-century Italian socialism and communism.

Resistance is evident in folk stories, whose frequent theme is the sardonic wit and shrewdness of peasants. Resistance periodically exploded in rebellions. Today an upswell of resistance is evident again in nonviolent actions against NATO military installations, opposition to the mafia, and demonstrations against imperialist aggression in third-world countries.

Sardonic wit is evident in the story of a poor peasant who consoled himself in his poverty with the example of Jesus: if everyone were rich, nobody would grow any *fave,* or broad beans. Rich people have a hundred misfortunes, from gout to poor teeth, while poor peasants, in spite of hardships, enjoy good health. The rich also had many worries, the peasant only one: how to cheat the *padrone.*[30]

Nineteenth-century peasants did not need to read the writings of Karl Marx to be conscious of classes: they put the theme of class differences in vernacular versions of the story of creation. When *domineddio* (diminutive, affectionate term for god) created man, the devil found one of god's discarded models and breathed life into the mud. As a consequence, there are two kinds of people. Peasants and workers, who wear berets, are descended from mud animated by god. People in authority, who wear hats, *i cappelli,* are made of mud animated by the devil. Addressing i cappelli, a peasant said, "You are gifted, but without fear of god, and without compassion for the miseries of the poor."[31]

The origins of injustice can be found in the story of how god, wearied by human complaints, decided to distribute good and evil equally. First to present themselves were the *cavalieri* (the nobility and the authorities), who took all the riches, the lands, the honors, and all the world's amusements, grasping everything but good health. Next came the priests and the monks, who said to the lord that all they wanted was the spiritual happiness of paradise. Then, realizing that all the glories of paradise *"non bollische la pentola"* (do not make the pot boil), the clergy took the leftovers of the cavalieri. For their allotment of misfortune, the clergy had to renounce women, the clerical gown reminding priests that women are sisters, not lovers and wives. Last came the peasants, who discovered that the male divinity (scarcely a just god in Italian stories) had already distributed everything to the rich and the clergy. Finding they were even poorer after redistribution, peasants asked why. He who does not hurry, advised the male god, does not eat.

The only good that remained was the donkey, whom god gave to peasants to help them in their work. And what, they asked, is our misfortune? The lord responded that they already had several, but he would give them another, *lo sbirro*. The word means "police," but connotes all agents of the authorities: customs officers, judges, tax collectors, and the like. And women? In an analogous peasant story about women, the lord had already given everything away to the nobility, the clergy, and the men before women presented themselves. So the lord, and millennia of catholic clergy invoking the model of the white madonna of the church, advised them to have *pazienza,* patience.[32]

The donkey being his only good, the peasant loves him and takes him to church on new year's day, the day of san Silvestro, to be blessed to protect the donkey from wolves. His children may cry because they are hungry, said Guastella, but the peasant always sees to it that his donkey has hay.[33] Sardonically, a peasant would say that after his donkey he loved his wife. He loved her *squaciata* (in the succulence of full bloom), not delicate and "pale as a codfish." Women "who looked like renaissance madonnas" belonged to the cavalieri: they did not warm the blood. Delicate, fair women were too fragile to carry sacks of grain and bundles of firewood. Furthermore, a dark and full-bodied peasant woman was more likely to be faithful.[34]

In the late nineteenth century, popular beliefs in equality, visible in the rituals of carnival, and beliefs in justice, informing folk stories, easily melded with the marxist movement of the fasci siciliani. Among peasant movements of western Europe, the fasci were almost unique in being organized "with a leadership, a modern ideology and programme," the "first peasant movement as distinct from spontaneous peasant reaction."[35] Another distinctive characteristic of the Sicilian socialist movement was that it involved "masses of peasant women."[36]

The peasant woman, who was the martyr of the family, caring, cooking, and cleaning in conditions of miseria, has been described elsewhere.[37] Yet, except for her husband (and she had to take care of him), male authority figures were nearly irrelevant to the everyday lives of peasant mothers and wives. Priests could preach what they would, but women put their own beliefs into stories and songs that were repeated by *cantastorie* (storysingers), who traveled from village to village. As Linda Barwick has pointed out, the songs women sang as they made bread, looked after the children, comforted the sick, and worked in the fields were the main transmission channel for vernacular beliefs.[38]

In lullabies, Italian women communicated deep and ultimately subversive messages to their children. In the many versions of "La malmaritata," there is an unmistakable message discouraging girls from entering patriarchal marriages. Lullabies, for Piera Carroli, are "the most archaic form of popular culture and the only direct documents in which women expressed their most intimate feelings."[39]

Peasant women, resembling the primordial goddess and formidable black madonnas, were fiercely nurturant, teaching their children the realities of life and death early on. "Universal dissatisfaction with patriarchy" may have been the most pervasive theme of traditional Italian lullabies. Carroli's conclusion converges with my finding that contemporary Italian feminists and men of the Italian democratic left owe a great deal to seeds "planted by peasant mothers . . . singing lullabies."[40]

In a collection of tales about madonnas and pirates told by traveling storytellers, peasant women are described as astute and shrewd, characteristics, according to Claudia Angeletti, that were the "deposit of the natural diffidence the peasant woman held before institutionalized religion and the hierarchy of the church."[41] Tales of cantastorie often recounted stories about women peasants who found themselves deceived or in threatening circumstances. Called upon, the madonna would appear, "covered by stars and light." Telling the women to follow her out of the dark forest, she would say, *"Son madre di Gesù, sposa di Dio"* (I am mother of Jesus, wife of God).[42] There is no wife of god in catholic doctrine. Reaching back into pagan history, the stories merge the christian madonna with African, Middle Eastern, and Graeco-Roman married goddesses.

Popular exclamations also deviate from church doctrine. The outcry *"Santamariagesù!"* invokes Mary first and then merges her with her son, who is not called the christ but addressed by his popular name, Gesù. Sometimes Mary is called Madre del Signore (mother of god the father? or mother of god the son?). Comari, or godmothers, were peasant women bonded to Mary as mother of god and to one another as mothers of god. The popular outcry *"Bedda Matri!"* (beautiful mother!) refers to the "queen of heaven without equal," "queen and protectress of sinners," invoked as *"siete per noi"* (you are for us).[43] Sometimes she is called la Signora, a name that signifies the feminine version of "the lord," a figure in popular culture whom Carlo Ginzburg has identified with the prehistoric divinity.[44]

In popular stories, the madonna often comes to the rescue of a wife put in perilous straits by a husband and confounds the devil, with whom the husband has made a pact.[45] Folk stories of peasant women encountering false clerics reveal a good deal of distrust, verging on hostility, toward the clergy. In "Storia di un falso frate," Assunta, Beppa, Rosa, Maddalena, and Catarina suggest the identification of peasant women with the many dimensions of the primordial woman divinity and her preservation under christian names in the historic era. Santa Catarina was historically adopted by women as church cover for noncanonical beliefs. Maddalena, the fallen woman of the canon, is often merged with the virgin mother in popular stories. Rosa is the medieval symbol of the madonna. Assunta is the popular name commemorating the assumption of Mary into heaven. Beppa is the feminine form of san Giuseppe, Mary's earthly husband.

In the story of a false friar, women had been left alone by their menfolk, who had gone to work for their padrone. A monk came by and asked for lodging. Not knowing he was a thief, the women gave him food and put him up for the night. Beppa, feeling he was a *"falso religioso,"* hid under the bed and discovered that robbery was the monk's aim. The women disarmed and bound the cleric. Beppa, storytellers would tell audiences, because of her candor and courage had *"mise tutto in salvazione,"* put everything in salvation.[46]

The moral of this and other popular stories appears to be that the madonna, merging with the candor and courage of peasant women, rescues wives whose husbands have made a pact with the devil. Women confound false clerics whose aim is to rob them. Of their beliefs?

The mother was the center of the economic, social, and religious life of the peasant family. She may have played the patriarchal game of addressing her husband as *voi,* while he called her *tu,* and she may have suffered the abuse of a man constricted by poverty who descended into violent rages, but everyone in the family was ultimately dependent on the mother. The strong southern Italian woman has become a stereotype, but there is truth in the portrait.[47]

Her strength was related to a good deal of help she received from her friends. In addition to the particular madonna to whom she was devoted, and to her comari, or close women friends bonded together in Mary in godmotherhood, the peasant woman depended on *mammane* (midwives), *fattucchiere* (healers),[48] *streghe* (witches), and *prefiche* or *reputatrici* (official mourners). The continuity with the prechristian goddess is visible in the responsibility of these women for life, death, and regeneration.

Mammane helped peasant women during childbirth and gave them herbs for an abortion if one were needed. The old woman of the village, *la vecchia*, the ultimate resident authority, would be called in to see to someone seriously ill; she often advised a pigeon broth instead of the medicine the doctor had prescribed. The village fattucchiera would be summoned to exorcise the mal'occhio. After searching for signs, *la Stefanu* (village witch) would exclaim *"fattura!"* or *"mal'occhio!"* and would exorcise the illness or misfortune with rituals using salt, oil and water, and incantations. Placing a christian cover on the pagan ritual, the women would say, *"Gesacca Maria,"* Jesus and Mary are here.

Mixing pagan and christian beliefs, women were responsible for the healing arts in peasant society. Whether a fattucchiera or a strega presided over a recovery, or it was believed that a particular saint had intervened, peasants would exclaim, *"un miracolo!"*[49] In nineteenth-century Italian peasant culture, there was little difference between a fattucchiera and a strega, and they each had considerable resemblance to saints: the people believed that both saints and witches could effect miracles.

Feminists today are recovering the stories of these "other" women who were central to peasant society. Orazia Torrisi, a healer born in southeastern Sicily in the time and place my own *nonna* Lucia lived, was considered a saint; she had not been beatified, women said, because she had performed an abortion or two.[50] A healer, whose wisdom she had learned from other women, Orazia carried out exorcisms with symbolic rituals that blended pagan practices with invocations to saints and that adapted church ritual to rituals outside the canon (e.g., making three signs of the cross while cutting garlic in a special manner).[51]

Wives and mothers, lemon pickers, fruit packers, carters, and washer-women, who did not have money for a doctor, came to Orazia. A gynecologist concerned with all aspects of women's lives, she often acted as matchmaker and marriage counselor as well as chiropractor. People described Orazia as a "figure of the greatest prestige,"[52] with a long memory and "strong as an oak tree."[53]

Witches, and other women with occult powers, were considered good to have around in peasant society. It was a good idea to adhere to prescribed convention: *"Aver Dio e i Santi per amici e protettori; ma non è male ricordarsi anche di quegli altri . . . Non si sa mai!"* (The lord and saints were fine as friends and protectors, but it wasn't a bad idea to remember "those others" . . . "one never knows!").[54] If a sick person continued to deteriorate, godmothers would ask la vecchia whether to summon the *megara* (witch) to perform rituals of *contrafuoco* against the diabolic fire and *contromina* against the diabolic tendency. Witches would take dried herbs, incense, and crosses made of palm leaves dipped in water and put them on the roof and in the corners of the house where someone was ill. With a little scissors, a strega would cut a cross of palm leaves atop the patient's chest and then say an Ave Maria, the church prayer to the madonna, in which all the women present would join.

As the mammana was responsible for birth, the reputatrice, or prefica, was responsible for death. These women, dressed in black, led the cries and praises of the dead in a *lutto* (mourning period) that lasted nine days. The church considers black the color of mourning; in unconscious layers of vernacular belief, peasant women who wear black most of their lives may be honoring the ancient goddess and her values of life, death, and regeneration.

Antecedents of Sicilian prefiche are thought to have been followers of the primordial goddess Ibla of the Siculi.[55] Tear sellers, or *vendilacrime,* represent a very old practice that may be found among ancient rites of Hebrews, Etruscans, Greeks, and Romans.[56] Prefiche were among the first to be persecuted after christianity was established. Christian councils and synods condemned the mourning practices (such as hair pulling and face scratching) of reputatrici as "false beliefs of ancient cults." In spite of denunciations by synods, sovereigns, and archbishops, mourning rites led by women persisted until the latter part of the nineteenth century,[57] and traces of them remain today, as anyone who has attended a traditional Italian wake can attest. The name "reputatrice" suggests the repetitive monotony of the *cantilene* that women sang to the beat of a tympanum and the repetitive clapping and chorus of other mourners, who for nine days repeated chants of the dead person's worthy characteristics in front of the bier in the home, before the body, accompanied by torches, was carried to the church and the grave.[58]

The sight of women with loosened hair screaming words considered provocative and *"all'ingiuria dell'omnipotente Iddio"* (to the injury of omnipotent god) disturbed clerical authorities.[59] In one description, a woman in mourning accompanied by one hundred women covered in black from head to foot, screaming and crying, beating chests and clapping hands, turned the town of Sciacca on the west coast of Sicily, near many sites of the goddess and the black madonna of Trapani, into "a city of grief and of death."[60] Prefiche may have symbolized the goddess as an old woman who connotes death and in whose honor Italians, at all *feste*, eat *semenze* (seeds), signifying regeneration.

At Trapani, where easter mysteries, as I will indicate in chapter 9, are full of echoes of the goddess, there was a funerary custom that referred to an *ambasciatrice*, a custom that lasted until the first third of the nineteenth century. A woman ambassador would go to the house where someone had died. Covered entirely by a black mantle and addressing the oldest woman of the family, she would throw herself on the earth and announce that she had come in the place of "a distant relative" to mourn the dead person.[61]

Mourners, in popular culture, were often paid with beans, chickpeas, and lentils, germinating legumes that connect death with regeneration,[62] in contrast to the christian custom of distributing crosses, symbol of resurrection, on the day of death. Another custom linking death with the grain goddess and with regeneration was the funerary ritual of distributing cooked wheat, or couscous, on the day of death.[63]

Mourning rituals with *prefiche* were characteristic, according to Salomone-Marino, not only of Sicily but of Apulia, Calabria, Sardinia, and areas of northern Italy on the Ligurian coast and in the Friuli.[64] The nineteenth-century folklorist could not have known this, but these are the areas where contemporary archaeologists have found a great deal of evidence of the civilization of the primordial goddess.

In ancient and contemporary funerary rituals of southern Italians, mourners speak to the dead person and invite her or him to return to visit the living. This ritual is related to the cult of the dead, which in southern Italy merges with the cult of the saints.[65] Dead relatives are regarded in the same light as saints, as intercessors and guardians and part of the living landscape: in contemporary Italian cemeteries the dead are put in little structures that resemble houses. The dead, represented by la befana, come to visit the living on the night of the first of November and stay until January 6, the day of la befana, which often commences carnival in Italy. Venerated in religious niches in the homes of my Sicilian and Sicilian-American aunts are icons of the madonna and a special saint, along with photographs and symbolic possessions of relatives who have died.

The main threads of peasant women's networks were woven by *comari*, women as godmothers pledged to Mary and bonded in solidarity with other women. Comari and "the others" (la mammana, la vecchia, la strega, and la prefica) constituted a network in which women assisted each other during pregnancy, birth, weddings, sickness, and death, participating in crises as well as celebrations of life, and helping with the children.[66]

In addition to godmothers, midwives, healers, mourners, saints, and the dead, peasant women had an ultimate resource: the madonna. Believed able to effect miracles, she was, and is, considered women's "special advocate."[67] The centrality of the madonna in everyday life during the nineteenth century may be glimpsed in the number of times she is called on in the peasant dialogue of Verga's novels. Her centrality in contemporary Italy is evident in the large number of marian sanctuaries and in the fervor of pilgrimages to her.

Pilgrimages to popular, often black, madonnas were, and still are, integral to Italian life. Participants in a social as well as a religious event, contemporary pilgrims are men and women, and sometimes more men than women, as in the pilgrimage to the black madonna dell'Arco. In the nineteenth century pilgrims would depart before dawn, journeying on foot with wicker baskets containing wine and food.[68] Today they may still travel on foot, but the usual pattern is to pack the whole family in the car and on arrival to climb the hill to the sanctuary of the popular madonna.

Local vendors sell cassettes of popular love songs, toys for the children, and seeds, nuts, and dried fruit connoting birth, maturity, and death, the three ages of the goddess. In pilgrimages to black madonnas that we observed in 1990, grandparents, married couples holding hands, sweethearts, and many children participated in a festa that seemed to be a celebration of life.

The festival of snakes in Italian popular culture may be interpreted as a celebration of regeneration. The ritual may also convey women's perennial resistance to the church appropriation of a gift of the goddess and ascription of it to a male saint. The *festa dei serpari* on the first Thursday of May at Cocullo in the Abruzzi attracts thousands;[69] in 1990 we joined the throng of people who scaled a hill to observe shepherds and children fondling serpents.

In the culture of the Old Europe, the snake was a symbol of life and death and of rebirth, a sign of the regenerative and transformative power of the goddess. Christianity obliterated this side of the symbol, emphasizing solely the "death wielding aspect of the goddess when the snake is poisonous and appears in the guise of a woman with some features of a snake." This church view may be seen in Michelangelo's painting of a snake with a woman's head in the Sistine Chapel. The snake as the negative image of the goddess is implicit in church beatification of saints Michael, Patrick, and George, who are venerated for killing snakes.

Artifacts of winding snakes, snake coils, snake figurines, and snake-woman hybrids are abundant in southern Italy and considered "epiphanies of the goddess" and symbols of regeneration by Gimbutas.[70] A young woman scholar studying the symbolism of the spiral finds "the serpent . . . the single most powerful image in history."[71] Scratched on the walls of the cavern of Porto Badisco in Apulia is a snake goddess with limbs ending in snake spirals.

In the Greek and Roman eras the benign serpent associated with the goddess became the snake as phallus and symbol of the Graeco-Roman god Hermes (Mercury); the snake as symbol of medicine and healing was attributed to the male savior-healer Asclepius. In christianity, the snake was adjudged evil, healing was attributed to another savior-healer, and the specific gift of healing snakebite was given to saint Dominic.

Yet in European folklore the crowned snake queen, mother of snakes, persists to the present. This figure connotes the goddess as life giver, wise and prophetic; in her gift of foretelling the future she resembles her sister, the bird goddess. As snake queen, "she is the owner and guardian of life water and life milk and of magical healing herbs."[72] For Gimbutas, the life energy of the snake symbolizes nature; the ability to shed its skin links the snake with the souls of the dead and with well-being in life.[73] This powerful image is further described in Buffie Johnson's authoritative study: "Grace and beauty, silent speed of movement, mesmerizing eyes and often fatal bite all contribute to the creature's aura of wonder. Its ability to slough its skin and arise renewed places the serpent in the forefront of the animals of rebirth."[74]

The Marsi, native peoples of the region around Cocullo, the town with the snake festival that we attended, were named for Marso, son of Circe. This siren was believed to transform men into sacrificial swine, an example of Greek fracture of the primordial goddess into negative images.[75] Sirens appear as the winged feminine figures on Greek pottery, as well as the mermaids of many cultures.[76] Enchantresses who could foretell the future, they connoted "dream, water, birth, vagina, death. Attraction and anxiety."[77] In positive form, sirens became angels; in negative image they became succubi and other creatures of the medieval bestiary. Renaissance alchemists were fascinated by sirens. Varying according to culture, the siren was gorgon in the Hellenistic era, the mandrake/siren of the Renaissance, and undine in Germany.

Italy, particularly in the south, is the "land of sirens," according to Meri Lao, a major interpreter. Writers and poets are said to have heard the music of sirens (symbol of Neapolitan culture) at Capri. The ancients located sirens on an island near the Strait of Messina and named the channel between Sicily and the Italian mainland for two sirens, Scylla and Charybdis. Scylla is believed to be a mermaid dwelling in a cave on a high rock who waits to pull sailors from their ships. Charybdis is believed to be a siren whose form as a whirlpool threatens ships and sailors. The statue of la Madonnina is believed to guard people who pass through the strait.[78] Strabo puts sirens in the bay of Naples. Others put them in the center of Sicily and recount that after the rape of Persephone sirens fled to the bay of Naples. "More than one observer has noted that Italian sirens are represented in popular art in the same manner as the Madonna."[79]

Near the site of the snake festival at Cocullo is a village called Cerchio (circle), where an ancient temple had been dedicated to the siren Circe, fate spinner of the destinies of humans. The circle was the symbol of sirens as well as symbol of the goddess.[80] Around 951–1031 C.E., old legends of Cocullo were *"cristianeggiate"* (christianized).[81] The church replaced the siren Circe with saint Dominic, whose specific healing power was the ability to pacify snakes and to cure snakebite.[82]

On the first Thursday of May, the festa of saint Dominic at Cocullo, and elsewhere in the mezzogiorno, attracts thousands of people to a celebration where they eat *ciambelle* (circle-shaped bread) and watch shepherds and children caress snakes. Afterward, in the church ritual, snakes are brought to the altar, where they circle around; after the mass, saint Dominic comes out of the church draped with somnolent snakes. The snake festa may be interpreted as a case of the church replacing the goddess and her regenerative powers, and replacing her descendant, the fate-spinning Circe, with a male saint whose relics can pacify snakes (women?) and cure snakebite.

Women's historic subtle and overt resistance to church doctrine may be glimpsed during the snake festival at Cocullo. In a variant of the prechristian custom of baking cakes for the queen of heaven, women of Cocullo bake a circle bread for the snake festa; a ciambella in the form of a circle, or of a serpent biting its tail.[83] The bread may recall the circle of the prehistoric goddess and the siren Circe, as well as the wheat of the Graeco-Roman mother goddess Demeter. I asked an old woman in the piazza the significance of the bread. She responded, "It's good—have some!" and told me that she lives alone in the mountain hamlet; all of her children and grandchildren are in America. The circle bread is indeed good and is a favorite throughout Italy.[84]

At the festa at Cocullo, before the serpents entered the church and before saint Dominic, draped with pacified snakes, left it, we watched women in folk costume take the lead in the ritual. They carried a large triangular construction to which they had fastened circle breads. In a women's ritual conveying a primordial sense of self and historic resistance, contemporary women of Cocullo put the vulva symbol and their great circle breads atop their heads and precede the men going into, and out of, the church.

Today christian-democratic and communist women of the Abruzzi work in politics. Carrying on women's ancient vocation as healers, they support public medicine and public health. Transmitting the values of the goddess and black madonnas, Rosina Giffi, a christian democrat, campaigned in 1990 "in favor of the young, of the old, of the handicapped, and the sick."[85]

CHAPTER 4

stories and politics of justice,

equality, and rights to life

of the poor

THE IMPLICIT liberation theology of black madonnas of Italy is suggested in the folklore of the region of the Iblaean mountains in Sicily. The theme of justice of the age of the goddess became a popular religious belief in universal salvation with a political corollary of distributive justice, a people's decalogue in which stealing from the poor is the worst sin, and a politics of resistance.

The soft folds of the Iblaean mountains suggest the body of a woman clad with plants brought by many peoples. Arabs from the Near East and Africa brought the carob tree, date palm, mulberry, bitter orange, and lemon tree. Asians brought pistachio, Portuguese the sweet orange, and Italian emigrants returning from Central and South America have planted cactus, agave, araucaria, acacia, and locust alongside native laurel, myrtle, oleander, almond, pomegranate, and balm mint. Poets, ancient and modern, have celebrated the honey that bees draw from the flowers of Monti Iblei.[1]

Stories of the origin of the very popular madonna of this region refer to the eighth century of the common era, when a controversy over the nature of the holy erupted in the Byzantine empire (which included southern Italy and Sicily). For iconoclasts, only the eucharist, church buildings, and the sign of the cross qualified as holy.[2] Iconodules, who favored icons, considered certain of them holy because they were believed to be in continuity with the gospel. "St. Luke had sent to Theophilus not only his gospel, but his portrait of the Virgin, painted from life, and copious illustrations of scenes from the life of Christ as they had happened. Icons of the Virgin, therefore, could well be thought of as continuations of St. Luke's original."[3]

A tendency to worship icons "had always existed among Mediterranean people," a practice frowned upon by the church hierarchy, which opposed the "naive, animistic ideas of the masses."[4] Yet, as the historian Peter Brown states, people preferred religious icons to imperial images, a great many people believed in intercession, and this was "the lever that shifted the religious art of the early Byzantine world."[5] Icons of Mary "represented the acme of a mortal's intercession in heaven. She was invariably portrayed with Christ sitting on her lap. For her intercessions had the infallible efficacy of a blood-relative."[6] For Brown, "Icons were invested with holiness in the late sixth and seventh centuries because they still expressed the continuing needs of the ancient city; they were backed up by continued loyalty to particular cult-sites."[7]

The story of the madonna of Chiaramonte Gulfi is found in a pastoral letter written in 1875 by a monsignor of Messina: God had given to Mary the divine mission of being the mother of the living, comfort of the unfortunate, solace of the oppressed, and mediator between man and god.[8] To thwart the attempt of iconoclasts to destroy holy images, the lord put two statues, one of the madonna and one of Jesus, on a ship without sails that landed in 732 C.E. at Camarina, on the African shore of Sicily. Pulled by wild oxen, the cart carrying the statue of Jesus stopped at Vittoria, where it was later highly venerated by the Normans, who, said the monsignor, were very taken with "the cult of the male savior." The cart carrying the statue of the madonna came to a stop at Chiaramonte Gulfi, where a sanctuary was built and where veneration of the madonna has increased from the eighth century to the present.[9]

Nineteenth-century folk stories of this region transmitted the memory of the civilization of the goddess, when all creatures were equal, in tales with moral and political messages. The legitimate proprietor of the earth, in these stories, is the person who cultivates it, "not the person who profits from the sweat of others."[10] Stealing is a sin, but the greatest theft is property. Stealing from the rich should be judged in the context of the hunger of the poor.[11] Stealing from the poor is the greatest sin.[12]

One day an old man discharged from his post accused the lord of being unjust: the nobleman who had dismissed him lived in extravagant luxury, while the old man had nothing. The lord told him to take whatever he needed from the padrone. He did. Another day, the old man watched a peasant woman bring an egg to a poor hermit who lived in a grotto. While the hermit was sleeping, the old man stole the egg. Whereupon he heard the voice of the lord say that he had robbed from the poor and was now accursed. And the earth opened and swallowed him.

The hermit asked the lord to have mercy on the old man. The lord responded that he was a lord of mercy, but *"sono anche il padre della guistizia"* (I am also the father of justice). In this story, merging pagan and Judeo-christian prophetic themes, the significant child of god is Justice, who in folk stories of Sicily and southern Italy is a woman. In this vernacular view of justice, those who steal from the poor can expect no mercy, but the poor person who steals out of hunger has not committed a sin: this is a *"diritto alla vita,"* right to life, of the poor, a right guaranteed by the lord.[13]

A belief bonding universal salvation and equality to the mother is visible in folk stories. Pitrè recounts a tale about the opposition of Jesus to allowing souls who were damned into heaven. His mother intervened: if he did not extend grace to everyone, she would leave paradise and would take her entire entourage with her. Whereupon, as queen of heaven, she began calling the angels, the patriarchs, the apostles, the martyrs, and all the saints. Whereupon Jesus conceded universal grace.[14]

In folk stories, mother figures in continuum with the earth mother held higher authority than the moral law; for example, saint Anne, mother of Mary and grandmother of Jesus, who recalls the earth mother as patron saint of fields and harvests.[15] One day saint Joseph took the child Jesus to an orchard to steal figs for sant'Anna, who was ill. When saint Joseph was caught he was beaten, but he brought the figs to saint Anne. The story of san Giuseppe stealing figs with bambinello Gesù became a *ninnananna* that suggests the radical morality conveyed in lullabies. "San Gisipuzzu jiu a rubari ficu. Tutti la notti fu vastuniatu . . . E l'he purtatu a la Matri Sant'Anna"[16] (Saint Joseph went to rob figs; he was beaten all night, but he brought the figs to "the Mother sant'Anna").[17]

Recalling the age of the goddess, when humans and animals were equal, Italians give human names and extend brotherhood, sisterhood, and godparenthood to animals. The origin of injustice in the world is conveyed in a fable, "La parità di Giovanuzza," about comar Giovanuzza, godmother fox. When the lord created animals he asked each of them to choose a virtue. Comar Giovanuzza presented herself to the lord and said she wanted strength, whereupon Silvestro, the wolf, said that strength belonged to him. So comar Giovanuzza asked the lord for impudence, whereupon a fly lit upon her head and said that was *her* virtue. The fox, having watched the strong and the impudent appropriate the virtues she wanted, asked for shrewdness. The fable concludes with a statement of peasant resistance to an unjust society: "You with the hats have taken over by force and impudence; we who wear berets will survive with shrewdness."[18]

Recently, Dacia Maraini, a major feminist writer and poet of Italy, has written a book of poetry in which she takes the symbol of the fox for herself. Remembering the Japanese fable wherein an enchanted woman has been transformed into a fox, Maraini likens herself to a fox who travels with light foot in unknown forests by the light of the moon.[19]

In peasant stories, saint Peter, symbol of the catholic church, is described as an "ingenious shrewd flatterer, glutton, clown deceiver, and backbiting grumbler."[20] Jesus asked Peter to go to the sea and catch a fish, which he did, and then asked him to take it to his mother, Mary, in Jerusalem. Alluding perhaps to the popular belief that the church does not attend to the mother whom peasants love, the story recounts that Peter wanted to keep the fish for himself and the other apostles. Jesus, becoming angry, told Peter to take the fish to his mother, or he would take the keys of heaven away from him. He went reluctantly. Peter (the church?) is popularly regarded at best as a buffoon, at worst as greedy and gluttonous. For Peter's mother, peasants created a pejorative epithet, *"Pari a matri di san Petru!"* (Just like saint Peter's mother!), considering her *"avida, avara ed egoista"* (greedy, stingy, and selfish).[21]

Justice is the theme of a story about saint Peter's mother. Exerting herself one day, she made a charitable gift of one onion leaf to the poor. When she died she went to hell, where she shrieked to her son to go to the lord on her behalf. The lord sent an angel with one onion leaf so she could pull herself out. As she pulled, many of the damned tried to attach themselves to her clothing. Brushing them away, she tore the onion leaf, and *"l'egoista madre di san Pietro ricadde definitivamente nell'inferno"* (the selfish mother of saint Peter fell back, permanently, into hell).[22] Peasants do not care for saint Peter, and they heartily dislike his mother. As to their own mother/madonna, Sicilians call her, in their favorite outcry, "Bedda Matri!" (beautiful mother!).

Giustizia, or justice, in stories seems to be a lightly disguised figure of the goddess. "When the lord came into the world," he brought with him the woman Giustizia. Genuinely just, she gave audiences to everyone, listening to the rich with her right ear (the ear of the intellect) and to the poor with her left (the ear of the heart). Giustizia dispensed so much justice that devils became worried that the number of sinners would decrease and they would have to close down hell. So they thought up a ruse, gave the scribes and the pharisees the key to Giustizia's tower, and told them to find a way to change her to Ingiustizia (injustice). The scribes made her deaf in the ear that listened to the poor, and thereafter Giustizia listened only to the rich.[23]

Peasants indicated in their folk stories that they did not believe that theirs was the only true faith, and they did not, as did institutional christianity, demonize the "other." When saint Anthony fell ill he asked the lord to make him well, vowing he would go on foot to Turkey to convert the infidel. The lord restored him to health, and the saint thought about his vow. Dismayed at what he had promised, he asked the lord if instead of converting the Turks he could stay home and convert *"questi nostri cristiani che son peggiori dei turchi"* (our christians who are worse than the Turks).[24]

Resistance, the chief political strategy of peasants, is evident in the poetic satire of injustice declaimed by women, shepherds, shoemakers, farmers, barbers, and poets at carnival time,[25] as well as in proverbs and stories reinterpreting political and church doctrine. Preferring realism to abstractions, a peasant responded to a question about *libertà*. "There is," said the peasant, "the liberty to assassinate the poor." Skeptical of the universalist abstractions of church doctrine, peasants preferred a realistic rendering of the golden rule: *"Quello che non vuoi fatto a te, ad altri non fare"* (That which you do not want done to you, do not do to others).[26]

Echoes of the world of the goddess, in which the earth is alive and all creatures equal, can be heard in Lapucci's collection of contemporary folk stories, *La bibbia dei poveri* (The bible of the poor). Animals participate in revelation in the world; a rose is a metaphor of human life, blooming in the early morning and fading at nightfall.[27] The divinity to whom contemporary folk stories refer, Lapucci says, "precedes christianity." This is a divinity of justice implicit in the implacable sequence of the seasons, in the irrevocable nature of time that is conveyed in the proverb *"L'orologio di Dio va lento, ma non va indietro"* (The clock of the divinity goes slowly, but it does not go backward),[28] and in carnival rituals personifying the months and the seasons. This divinity of justice, for Lapucci, has none of the trappings of the church, no halo, and no serving angels; it is a divinity who talks with animals and loses patience with human beings.[29]

Differences between women and men are suggested in folk stories about the moon goddess and the sun god. In a tale about the argument of the sun and the moon as to whose light was better, the sun said his light was stronger and more splendid, while the moon said that her light was clear and pleasing. The wind was called in to mediate. The sun put forth all his power, and soon parched animals went searching for water and shade, plants drooped their leaves anxiously awaiting nightfall, and humans wilted in the heat. The next night the moon diffused her clear light on earth and was blessed by travelers, mariners, and fishermen. Herbs and plants revived, and animals came out of their caves.

The moon had won, but the sun, enraged, grasped a fistful of mud from the sea and threw it at the face of the moon. *"La luna rimase macchiata, ma da quel giorno tutti i viventi, a cominciare dagli innamorati, preferiscono la luce della luna"* (The moon remains with a dirty spot, but from that time on all living beings, beginning with lovers, prefer the light of the moon).[30]

Riddles, conundrums, and enigmas wrap folk wisdom in short pieces easily memorized. *Indovinelli* in the area of Chiaramonte Gulfi describe fruits and vegetables with sensual characteristics, consider humans and animals equal, and suffuse rituals of everyday life with meaning.[31] "When Jesus and the saints were on earth," the plant salvia offered her leaves for a bed for the infant Jesus on the flight into Egypt. Thereafter, salvia was blessed by the madonna as an herb that can cure many maladies.[32] The olive tree, beloved of the madonna, has long life, and its fruit produces holy oil. In ancient and contemporary vernacular lore there is an herb for every malady.[33]

Animals, in Italian fables, have secrets. Do the oxen who pulled the carts of black madonnas to sanctuary sites know the true mother? Women, too, have secrets. In one story, a young woman wants the freedom not to marry. Someone behind a statue of Mary urges her to wed, whereupon the maiden addresses the madonna with candor, saying *she* was scarcely in a position to talk to her about virginity and marriage.[34]

The story of Piovano Arlotto hints that parish priests may teach the doctrine of the immaculate conception, but people believe that clerics also have secrets. A rich citizen of Florence invited Piovano Arlotto (a name that means "clownish parish priest") to drink with him, asking if his guest wanted to drink the excellent *malvasia* before or after the meal. Piovano Arlotto responded: *"Tu sai che Maria fu vergine prima, durante e dopo il parto!"* (You know that Mary was a virgin before, during, and after childbirth!).[35]

Class consciousness is a major theme of nineteenth- and twentieth-century Italian folklore. In the story of thirteen piglets and a padrone, the "boss" encountered a peasant and asked how things were going. The peasant responded that his sow had delivered thirteen piglets. The padrone asked, How many teats did the sow have? Twelve, said the peasant. And what did the thirteenth piglet do? The peasant responded, *"Quello che faccio io che sto a guardarvi mangiare!"* (What I do when I watch you eat!).[36]

In stories, scholars are regarded in the role of padroni who do not see the ground beneath them, a vernacular version of Gramsci's view of intellectuals. One day a philosopher who studied the stars asked a serving girl to leave the door open during the night because he wanted to observe the stars. She did so. A squall came up and left a large puddle by the door. When the philosopher stepped outside he did not see the water and fell in. As the servant girl helped him up, she asked, How can you understand the stars, if you do not even see the earth under your feet?[37]

▪   ▪   ▪

GIUFÀ, the popular fool figure invented by Muslims to satirize christians during the period they held the southern mainland and Sicily, is beloved all over Italy. Muslim towns in Sicily were founded at Alcamo, Marsala, Calascibetta, and Regalmuto. After Normans displaced Muslims in the eleventh century, Arabic continued to be spoken, along with Greek and Latin, at the court of Frederick II. The collision of Muslim and Norman cultures is still visible in Palermo, where catholic churches built by Muslim workmen look like mosques.[38]

In Giufà tales, the mother resembles la Giustizia and the son has a Muslim name, not Gesù. Set in the area of Chiaramonte Gulfi, Giufà stories suggest a continuity from the primordial goddess, powerful madonnas, and Giufà's peasant mother (Hagar, mother of Ishmael?), with the shared value of justice. In the tales, the son Giufà is a clown who, like Arlecchino (Harlequin) during carnevale, erodes the hypocrisy of patriarchal institutions and beliefs. Considered an example of the truth of the proverb *"il savio fa la festa e il pazzo se la gode!"* (a wise man organizes the festa and the fool enjoys it!), Giufà embodies the ancient belief in the divine wisdom of the fool/clown/trickster.

A startling personification of Elisabeth Schussler Fiorenza's thesis that Mary sent her envoy to do her errands,[39] Giufà does what his mother tells him and wreaks havoc on patriarchal institutions. His mother told her son to shoot a "red breast," meaning a bird, for dinner, whereupon he shot the red breast of a church cardinal. His mother, before going to the river to do the wash, told Giufà to cook *causunedde* (pasta shaped like stockings) while she was gone, whereupon he cooked his father's stockings.

Giufà is older than saint Francis, the patron saint of Italy. The franciscan order of *cappuccini* is respected by southern Italians because friars do not have anything to do with money. The Francis they love is *"il poverello Francesco,"* who is *"un 'pazzo' da slegare,"*[40] the poor little saint who believed that the lord wanted him to be a madman in the world, and whom contemporary Italians, interested in the potential of franciscan values for individual and social transformation, consider a "madman to untie."

More subversive than saint Francis, Giufà harks back to the unconscious trickster who has existed in the vernacular tradition since ancient times.[41] Visibly ambivalent about his own father, as well as about the ultimate father and the father's institutions in church and state, Giufà adores his mother, who, according to the Iblaean writer Mario Agosta, had "the moral characteristics of mother and father together." She guided her son in everyday life with the authority of her presence. Her influence, and her intervention, are "almost always determining."[42] If folklore reveals ultimate attitudes, Giufà stories may be read as vernacular theology wherein an almost completely determining mother sends her child to do her errands in the world.

Madonnas and saints who inhabit folk stories resemble peasant women and men. In its co-optative embrace of popular saints, the church has redesigned them to fit catholic doctrine. In the vernacular world of madonna and saints, however, closeness to the church signifies distance from goddess/god: *"Vicino alla chiesa, lontano da Dio."*[43] Stories about saint Peter and Jesus convey Peter's institutional anxieties, in contrast to the willingness of Jesus, regarded in the folk tradition as his mother's son, to leave people to their own beliefs.[44]

In the vernacular perspective, the priest can preach what he wishes and the "faithful" will do as they wish (*"Il parroco predica quanto vuole e i fedeli fanno come vogliono"*).[45] The difference between what the church may decree and what the people (including many priests and monks from poor families) believe and do is suggested in a story about a friar. One day, carried away by zeal, he preached that the madonna could liberate the damned from hell. Afterward, he worried that he had uttered a heresy, and the next day he said that he had exaggerated. In a revealing explication of vernacular theology, the friar said that the madonna had the power to liberate from hell "only those damned that the lord had condemned unjustly."[46]

Avarice, in the vernacular decalogue, is the greatest vice,[47] the school of every iniquity, and personified in the mother of saint Peter, who, in popular belief, is considered the chief link in the great chain of woes. Saint Peter's mother, sometimes called Donna Bisodia, may be a parody of the Latin phrase *"da nobis hodie"* in the Pater Noster, the church prayer to the father.[48]

In peasant stories, the devil is rendered so fallibly human that the *povero diavolo* (poor devil) receives a good deal of popular empathy.[49] Theologians may allocate evil to the devil, but in vernacular Italian belief evil is an everyday phenomenon with which ordinary people have learned to live.[50] In the Iblaean region, the devil is affectionately referred to as santo Diavoluni.

The pretensions of church doctrine are popularly satirized in the story "Il freddo," the cold. A little old man presented himself to saint Peter at heaven's gate; saying he was very cold, he asked to go to purgatory for a while. Later, Peter went to purgatory to see how he was, only to discover that the little old man, still cold, had asked to go to hell for a while to warm up. Saint Peter went looking for him, retracing the old man's stays in all the rims of hell. When he finally found him among the flames of the last rung of hell, he heard the old man say, "Please close the door."[51]

In the popular perception of male saints, Paul is regarded as too learned and self-interested and Peter is something of a buffoon (his mother is considered very greedy). Saint Christopher may be the most popular, not only because he helps poor people who deal in contraband but because the church unsainted him a few years ago. Very high in popularity is san Giuseppe (saint Joseph), earthly husband of Mary. Not only did Joseph put up with a wife whose attention was elsewhere, he reared a son whom the church said was not his child, and he helps anyone who asks. Father of the popular holy family, saint Joseph is considered the patron saint of the very poor, the defenseless, orphans, and the homeless.

Subordinated people of Italy celebrate san Giuseppe on March 19 and the first of May, associating the saint with the spring equinox, the goddess, and workers of the world. At the time of the spring equinox, women bake great rounds of bread five feet in diameter, and food is distributed to family, friends, strangers, and the poor, a ritual that historically became a way of feeding the hungry during famines. Another connection of the saint with the primordial divinity is suggested in the pine cones placed on saint Joseph tables; wheat seeds are put in the crevices of the pine cones to sprout, a ritual of regeneration.[52]

Once when saint Peter was busy, he asked saint Joseph to be gatekeeper of heaven for a while; he let everyone in. A carpenter by trade, another time he made a ladder so that souls whom saint Peter would not let into heaven could come in by a window. Summoned in front of the lord, saint Joseph pled that he understood sinners because of his own family troubles: in popular belief, saint Joseph is affectionately regarded as having been cuckolded by Mary.

The story in which Mary delivers an ultimatum to Jesus that she will leave heaven with all of her entourage unless he concedes grace to all human beings has an analogue in a tale about saint Joseph. In both cases the stories satirize church doctrine. When the lord told saint Joseph he must leave paradise because he had broken the law by making a ladder for sinners, Joseph said, I'll leave. And since he's my son, I'll take Jesus. And since the bible says that the wife goes with the husband, I'll take Mary with me. And since the church proclaims that she is queen of the martyrs, I'll take all the martyrs with me. And since she is queen of the virgins, all the virgins. And since she is queen of the patriarchs and prophets, I'll take them also. And since Mary is the greatest of the saints, I'll take all the saints. The lord, taken aback, let saint Joseph stay in heaven, asking him to be more discreet dispensing grace.[53]

Significant for an understanding of the radical potential of vernacular religious and political beliefs, saint Joseph is a father and husband in a nonpatriarchal family. The popular trinity of Joseph, Mary, and Jesus is celebrated on March 19 at the time of the spring equinox. On May 1 he is honored again, this time along with celebrations of the prechristian woman divinity and workers of the world.

For the spring holiday of saint Joseph and the vernacular holy family, a woman may ask for something she devoutly wants and vow to cook a banquet for the poor. A poor man, a poor woman, and an orphan are asked to play the roles of Joseph, Mary, and Jesus at the feast. In contrast to the church trinity (the father in heaven, the son, who sits on his right, and the holy ghost), in the vernacular holy family saint Joseph is a workman father who cares for everyone, Mary is mother and ultimate advocate of all peoples, and Jesus is their child. Saint Joseph the workman is highly respected by the male left of Italy. In the 1970s, when feminists carried banners identifying themselves with witches—*"Tremate, tremate, le streghe son tornate!"* (Tremble, tremble, the witches have returned!)—they twitted male communists for *their* attachment to saint Joseph.

In the first years of christianity, Mary, Joseph, and Jesus were considered a Jewish family. A study of the cult of the holy family in Ragusa notes that a bas-relief of the fourth century C.E. found in a house in the Jewish quarter of the old town describes the flight of "a Jewish family," Joseph, Mary, and Jesus, into Egypt.[54] Rituals associated with saint Anne and saint John, both associated with the vernacular trinity, also have prechristian elements. Saint Anne, mother of Mary and grandmother of Jesus, is patron saint of fields and harvests. Saint John suggests an apostolic community that includes women, in contrast to saint Peter, who in popular understanding symbolizes the male hierarchy of the catholic church. Saint John is celebrated with practices outside the church canon on June 24 at the time of the summer solstice.[55]

A uniquely Italian vernacular liberation theology is implicit in the people's celebration of the seasonal change from spring to summer. The fertility of the earth, not the resurrection of Jesus, is associated with salvation. The custom on saint John's day is to eat new *fave* (broad beans). In the Iblaean region, the popular belief is that for each new *fava* eaten one sin is forgiven.[56]

Prechristian women figures in the folklore are associated with saint John the baptist, who preceded Jesus, perhaps implying a message similar to that of the sculpture at Loreto where ten sibyls precede ten Judeo-christian prophets.[57] At Marsala, whose old name commemorated the sibyl Lilibet, the church of saint John was built in the grotto of the sibyl Lilibetana.[58] Another church was built in a grotto on Mount Etna where Persephone was believed to have been kidnapped by Hades.[59] The prechristian John the baptist is popularly merged with John the evangelist, to whom Jesus entrusted his mother. The pilgrimage to saint John the evangelist originated in the thirteenth century and lasts from the Monday after easter until August 29, when saint John the baptist was beheaded.[60]

In the Galleria d'Arte Sacra Contemporanea, at Assisi, there is a sculpture by Manuel Bordogna, *Le tre Marie e San Giovanni*. The popular ritual of the three Maries has been banned by the church, but it is still celebrated at Stes-Maries-de-la-Mer in France on May 24 and 25, when Italians cross the border and Gypsies converge to venerate three figures who symbolize Mary. One of the three Marys is Sarah/Kali, a small black figure whose fervent veneration culminates in a ritual of taking her into the sea. Two paler Marys, considered Mary's half sisters, are celebrated the next day.

Folk celebrations of saint John indicate that his veneration does *not* include the church. Historically on his feast day in the Iblaean region there was a great fair celebrating the summer solstice when peasants sang yes to John, no to Peter: "*San Giovanni sì, San Petru no.*"[61]

John's feast day on June 24 celebrates the goddess, the summer solstice, and bonds outside the patriarchal family. These last are embodied in the southern Italian practice of *comparatico,* bonding godfathers and godmothers, a custom the church considers threatening to patriarchal family and society.[62] Catholic synods of the eighteenth century threatened people with excommunication if they persevered in believing in customs of godparenthood and extrafamilial sisterhood and brotherhood. But Italians have continued celebrating san Giovanni and vows of *comari* and *compari* on the summer-solstice night of saint John on June 24. In the nineteenth century, the celebration, described by Verga in his novels, was a great feast day flawed by one worry: this was the day saint John severely judged anyone who violated the vow of sisterhood or brotherhood.[63]

The prophetic strand in Italian popular beliefs appears to relate to the mother, her child, and to both Johns. John the baptist, who baptized Jesus, is regarded as a member of his family, as is John the evangelist, to whom Jesus entrusted his mother. The cult of the Precursore di Cristo dates back to the first years of christianity; the first church of saint John was erected over catacombs in Syracuse, Sicily. From there the cult spread inland to Ibla Erae (Ragusa). The first christian churches built in that city venerated women; the church of the Madonna della Luce was built on a pagan temple to Juno Lucina, the Roman mother goddess of light.

In the middle ages the cult of saint John the baptist competed with the Norman cult of saint George (who slew the dragon, symbol of the goddess). After the earthquake and destruction of 1696 in Sicily, churches were rebuilt, and John became patron saint of the upper city of Ragusa and George of the lower. Subterranean, ancient loyalties were associated with the cult of saint John, church loyalties with the cult of saint George. Tumult during their festivals was related to competition between followers of the two saints, and perhaps to different ultimate beliefs.

If anyone violated the folk ritual of godmothers and godfathers, san Giovanni (in a merging of the two Johns) acted like an angry Jewish prophet. In one story, two comari argued over a fig tree that grew on the boundary between their houses. A disputed tree (perhaps referring to the tree of life, symbol of the goddess in Hebrew popular belief) is the theme of many Italian folk stories. In punishment for violating the vow of sisterhood in the ritual of comparatico, saint John put a large cooking pan atop the disputed fig tree and lit a fire beneath the pot that burned for a week.[64]

Feasts for saint John the baptist after 1600 were very lively. In the *sangiovannaro* neighborhood of old Ragusa the festa was a great fair heralded by trumpeters on horseback who were followed by people walking with candles. Merchants came from all parts of Sicily, people dressed in ancient costumes, tailors, shoemakers, and other artisans put out their best wares in sidewalk stalls,[65] and women made *cuccidati,* crescent-moon-shaped pastries filled with figs that recalled the goddess.[66]

The summer-solstice celebration of saint John the baptist had, and continues to have, the flavor of a counterculture festival. In foil to the church story of Jesus at eastertime, the significant events of saint John's life are enacted: his birth, circumcision, retreat to the desert, baptism of Jesus, appearance before Herod's court, and his beheading.[67] Popular veneration of John seems to suggest a belief in the equality of Jewish prophets, and specifically the equality of John and Jesus, who are considered members of the same family. In one festival enactment the cousins John and Jesus are infants in the same room with their mothers, Elizabeth and Mary.[68]

▪   ▪   ▪

THE POLITICAL IMPLICATIONS of folk stories of madonnas and saints are radical. Long before the socialist diagnosis of the problems of modern society, Italian peasants told stories with themes of justice, class consciousness, vindication of the poor, and strategies of resistance. The tales were considered as true as stories of the Norman conquest, stories about bandits, or stories about Giuseppina la brigantessa (Josephine the woman pirate).[69]

In Sicily, christians built churches on sites of the goddess, Byzantines built castles that were taken by Muslims, Normans (commissioned by the church) expelled or absorbed Muslims, and French Angevins replaced Normans. Following unification of Italy after 1860, the Bourbons were run off and northern Italians took on the governing role of preceding rulers.

In this history of invasion and cultural, political, economic, and physical rape of Sicilians, the Iblaean mountains remain a timeless reminder of the original Sicul goddess Ibla, who was joined by the Asian great mother goddess, Cybele (still visible hewn into the rock and in a dozen statues at Palazzolo Acreide), and by Isis, Egyptian goddess from Africa, whose presence continues to be palpable in the folklore. Sicilians have turned Isis's headdress of bull's horns into a finger symbol of the goddess to exorcise evil when pointed downward and a finger symbol of a cuckold when pointed upward.

Artifacts of Demeter and Persephone and of Graeco-Roman goddesses can be found in all Sicilian museums. Spaniards left baroque architecture and veneration of santa Teresa, the popular saint of Jewish and *converso* ancestry who initiated the reform of "mental" (instead of oral) prayer so that women, and others, could keep their different beliefs to themselves with a covering of conformity to the church.

Black madonnas, since the early years of christianity, have been believed to have magical power to overcome *la peste, la fame, la sete* (plague, hunger, and thirst) and to succor the poor "thirsting for justice."[70] Sicilian peasants "thirsting for justice" at Ragusa in 1820 divided the land equally among themselves until Austrian troops arrived.[71] At Monterosso in 1830, peasants elected a king from among themselves. Nineteenth-century Italian peasants believed, and many Italians believe today, that *"chi ruba al Re non ruba a nessuno"* (he who robs the king robs nobody),[72] a version of anarchism translatable as a belief that it is not necessary to pay taxes to illegitimate government.

In 1893–94, socialist *fasci siciliani* erupted in a rebellion considered "the first proletarian act in Italy."[73] How was it possible, wondered Benedetto Croce, liberal philosopher of Italy, that the first region of the country to display a genuine revolutionary marxism was its least industrialized, least progressive, and physically most detached?[74] Catania and Palermo, cities near archaeological sites of the goddess and sanctuaries of black madonnas, were centers of the uprising of socialist fasci, a rebellion that encompassed agricultural workers, city artisans, miners, women, and young people.

The earth-rootedness of socialist uprisings of Sicilian fasci (eventually totaling 250,000 peasants and 100,000 workers and artisans) is suggested in that most of the rebels were peasants, the movement included women, and the significant revolutionary activity was occupying the land, a legacy reenacted and led by women after both world wars of the twentieth century.

The authorities, on January 3, 1894, declared a state of siege, arrested leaders of socialist fasci, and put their organizations under the ban. The court trial of socialist leaders from the area of the Iblaean mountains revealed vernacular political beliefs. Sicilian socialists defended themselves against charges that they had attacked the government, incited class hatred, and engaged in "conspiracy, public instigation to delinquency, and excitement leading to civil war."[75] Giuseppe De Stefano Paternò of Catania, lawyer and socialist leader, said that he had distributed literature encouraging the creation of cooperatives. Nunzio Caruso of Regalbuto said that he had worked for political candidates who were "champions of democracy." The aim of socialist fasci, said the defendants, was the creation of a great agricultural cooperative of producers and consumers to cope with *"la grande miseria"* that had fallen on Sicily with the disease that had destroyed the grapevines and caused a sharp fall in agricultural prices. They advocated the electoral process to attain a socialist commonwealth.

The barons, however, were worried about cries for *"pane e lavoro"* (bread and work), shouts of *"viva la rivoluzione sociale,"* and "down with the local government and the robbers."[76] Leaders of socialist fasci urged *"unità, fratellanza, mutuo soccorso,"*[77] but unity, brotherhood, and mutual aid with cooperatives seemed "anarchism" to property owners, an anarchism they felt would lead to redistribution of property.

Sicilian socialist fasci were suppressed, but they bequeathed a continuing legacy of a nonviolent and democratic path to socialism emphasizing cooperatives, responsibility, democratic methods, and nonviolence. "We are revolutionaries of thought; to win we do not need war that kills."[78] Instead of educating a boy to become *"un buon soldato"* (a good soldier), he should be taught to be *"un buon cittadino ed un onesto padre di famiglia"* (a good citizen and an honest father of a family).[79] Education should be directed to brotherhood, union, peace, work, saving, and mutual aid. Echoing the principle in folk stories of *diritti alla vita,* or rights to life, socialist leaders said that the first step toward a good society was to create agricultural producer and consumer cooperatives and to enact social legislation guaranteeing "the right to existence" to everyone.

Like contemporary liberation theologians, leaders of socialist fasci said their ideas were religious as well as indebted to marxism.[80] Before being condemned to prison, they invoked the freedom of thought of the risorgimento, using a metaphor that recalls black madonnas who appeared in oak trees. Their ideas, said Sicilian socialists of the 1890s, would grow "like an oak in the forest, never dying nor losing its leaves, nor losing its branches to lightning because the oak signified life." They believed their struggle for giustizia in a society with *uguali diritti e uguali doveri* (equal rights and equal duties)[81] would eventually be vindicated.

In the first decades of the twentieth century, after suppression of the socialist uprisings, many Italians emigrated to the Americas. Those who remained were confronted with continuing social and economic depression, thwarted socialist hopes during world war I, and suppression under fascism. Near the end of world war II, in the civil chaos that attended war and Allied disembarkation in Sicily, peasants rose again. At first Allied troops were welcomed by Sicilians (who had many relatives in the United States), but when they began behaving as had preceding invaders Sicilians resisted a draft to fight in the north: *"Siamo stanchi della guerra."*[82] Shouting "We are tired of war," demonstrators at Chiaramonte Gulfi attempted to take the city hall.[83]

A nonviolent anarcho-communism has come to characterize political struggle in this area whose mountains are named for the goddess and whose madonna retains her deep, dark power even though the church has painted and sculpted her white.[84] A contemporary analysis of continuing southern Italian subordination to northern capitalism points out that reform measures like the Cassa per il Mezzogiorno have not stanched a hundred years of emigration by southerners hoping to find work. In the cultural as well as economic analysis, capitalism is viewed as having colonized the rural and urban subproletariat, subjecting them to the exigencies of capitalist expansion and accumulation. Socialist politicians, in southern Italian vernacular belief, have subordinated rural and subproletarian populations to the needs of the industrial north, and a reformist bureaucracy, allied with capitalist development, has ruined the environment.[85] For Sicilian and other southern Italian anarcho-communists, analysis of the class struggle must be deepened to include a cultural analysis of "negated cultures" whose beliefs must be recovered before transformation can happen.[86]

For anarcho-communists of southern Italy, cultural and economic exploitation is very old. In the modern era, it dates from Italian unification in the last quarter of the nineteenth century when the north colonized the south. They remember the Spanish civil war of the 1930s, when communists suppressed anarchists and popular initiatives, and world war II, when stalinist directives forbade socialist revolution in Italy.

The contemporary Italian belief in transformation may be traced to a nineteenth-century peasant story, "Breaking the chain of woes."[87] When Jesus "was on earth" removing people from the devil's reach, Lucifer, thirsting for revenge, devised *la catina di guaj,* a long chain of woes that strangles all humans. Strangled by the chain, humans become violent toward one another, killing, robbing, committing all kinds of crimes.

In the nineteenth-century peasant version of nonviolent revolution (a vernacular tradition that lives today in the large audience that reads the periodical *Azione nonviolenta*), every human being must take personal responsibility to break the chain of woes, so that everyone can live together as sisters and brothers. In the great family that will be formed, each person will have responsibilities and regard for the rights of others in a society of equality, justice, and "rights to life" of everyone.[88]

Today in southern Italy and the islands, there is a sense of a long history stretching back before the christian era, a long history that must be remembered to build an alternative society concerned for all life and concerned for the earth. A book whose title translates as "A society to the measure of nature," published in Catania in 1981, prints a statement made by Amenhemet I of Egypt, 1,996 years before christ, revealing the values of the civilization of the goddess Isis:

Struggle for happiness
like people with little struggle for bread
and remember that love is the seed and the
fruit of joy

Love one another and love yourselves
Be born without fear
because she who gives you life gives you a
fertile earth

Do not be fearful of hunger, or of the years,
or of growing old
because at each season of life you will find
new wisdom.[89]

In Comiso in the Iblaean area, Gesualdo Bufalino, a contemporary Sicilian writer, considers the Monti Iblei "an island within the island, the banner of our solitude."[90] In the late twentieth century, the island within the island at the feet of Monti Iblei became the destination of thousands of Italian and international pilgrims for peace and the campsite of women from many countries who wove a spider's net (*la ragnatela*) of resistance to nuclear missiles that endanger the earth and all its creatures.[91]

In the 1983 women's day demonstration against nuclear missiles at Comiso, placards declared values ultimately rooted in the civilization of the goddess:

Against hierarchy, militarism, exploitation, sexual violence, ecologic disaster, and delegation of life decisions.

For self-determination, denuclearization, liberated work, clean seas, and every person's responsibility for life.

CHAPTER 5

carnevale: the laughter of the

goddess ▪ festival defying the powers

that be, ritual of how people

would like to live in freedom,

equality, and abundance

ARNIVAL, for the Russian theorist Mikhail Bakhtin, "preexists priests and kings and its theme is freedom." Festivals of Italy closely tied to "fertility rites" (the academic term referring to the civilization of the goddess) are new year's day, carnival, and May 1. Although christmas, epiphany, and easter are festivals of renewal, the church imprimatur on these holidays has obscured earlier origins. The Italian festa most clearly bonded with the goddess is carnevale.[1]

Bakhtin, major theorist of the folk custom of carnival, was a soviet scholar whose works became known in the west after 1968. In part a critique of the stalinist prohibition of satire, Bakhtin's study of carnival stresses the challenge of "low" culture to laughterless "high" culture. In his study of Rabelais, Bakhtin found carnival customs and rituals to be the "indispensable component" of folk culture.[2]

Carnival, in Bakhtin's theory, is other than the somewhat seamy scene of barkers, cruel displays of human oddities, and traveling Ferris wheels familiar in the United States a few decades ago. It is also something other than carnivals sponsored by the catholic church, whose roulette wheels and sausage sandwiches cover the co-optation of a genuine people's festival. Authentic carnivals were, and still are in some places, spontaneous explosions of vernacular culture that defy the powers that be in radical satire of the dominant culture and politics. In its authentic manifestation, particularly in moments of rapid change, carnival behavior has serious political and cultural implications. In the United States of the late 1960s, the laughter and antics of antiwar protesters, before hilarity turned to bitterness, had more than a little to do with eventually stopping the U.S. invasion and merciless bombing of Vietnam.

In his undeveloped premise that carnival "preexists priests and kings"[3] and that its theme is freedom,[4] Bakhtin is not referring to liberal bourgeois freedom: peasants in carnival freedom are blasphemous, cunning, coarse, dirty, and physical, "reveling in oceans of strong drink, poods of sausage, and endless couplings of bodies."[5] World history, in this perspective, has a laughing chorus of people for each event; for Bakhtin, it is the historian's task to search for this laughing chorus, rather than hasten to lifeless official statements.

In the long history of peasant culture, carnival spirit was not limited to pre-lenten processions culminating in the revelry of Fat Tuesday. All official events were infiltrated by laughter, every agricultural festival had its merriment, every church celebration its comic counterpart, every civil ceremony its clowns. "All these forms of protocol and ritual based on laughter and consecrated by tradition existed in all the countries of medieval Europe."[6] Acting out subversive vernacular beliefs under the canopy of festival, peasants in carnevale shed subjection to the authoritarian rule of lords and bishops and creatively expressed their desire to turn the existing order upside down.

For Barbara G. Walker, the origins of carnival are the *ludi,* or games, celebrated in honor of Cybele, great mother of the gods brought to Rome from Phrygia in Anatolia. "Her temple stood on the Vatican, where St. Peter's basilica stands today, up to the 4th century A.D. when Christians took it over." Greeks celebrated Dionysus and his court of satyrs and fauns. Romans feted Bacchus around the first of the year with drunken revelry and mad dancing.[7] One bacchic rite featured the myth of Ceres and her daughter Proserpina, who personified the growth, maturity, death, and renewal of grain, flowers, and all life. The continuity of all life is celebrated at carnival time in Italy with seeds, nuts, flowers, and fruit. *Coriandoli,* Italian symbols of carnival, are bits of colored paper representing coriander seeds.

Radical democracy is implicit in celebrations of Dionysus/Bacchus and carnivals: everybody participates. The December and March dates of Roman saturnalia celebrated the death of vegetation and the renewal of plant and animal life. Political corollaries of this celebration of the seasons of nature were subversive. During saturnalia, slaves became masters and the people elected a king of the festival, *Saturnalicius princeps,* who ensured their liberty to do what they wanted in the piazza while the nobility reveled in orgies in their villas.

Celebration of all life in dionysian and bacchic rites included the loosening of marital bonds, alarming conservatives, who feared that loosening patriarchal familial ties would lead to loosening patriarchal social stratification. A story has it that once during a saturnalia "160 women in order to unite with other men poisoned their husbands,"[8] a story that may have titillated, as well as alarmed, misogynists.

Lupercali, the Roman "fertility" holiday honoring the wolf who nursed Romulus and Remus, founders of Rome, may have commemorated a Roman version of the prechristian woman divinity, who nurtured animals as well as humans and who is later remembered in Verga's *La lupa* (*The She-Wolf*). Continuity with the goddess is also visible in Juno, the Roman mother goddess who was mistress of fate, preserver of life, queen of heaven, adviser and admonisher, virgin mother of Mars, goddess of erotic love, and mother of the people.[9] As Juno Lucina, she was goddess of celestial light and fertility; a male ritual honoring Juno involved carrying women to the sacred forest of the Esquiline to become fertile.[10]

Bacchanalia were festivals described by a Roman writer as dear to "proletarians, women, and slaves." After Roman prohibition of bacchanalia, there were public massacres of men and women accused of promiscuity.[11] After the official establishment of christianity in 323 C.E., the church began a long campaign to ban carnival revelry as the work of the devil. Popes in the ninth and tenth centuries censured carnivals as *feste dei pazzi,* or holidays of mad people; in a revealing phrase, they were called festivals *"della libertà."* Celebrating liberty, carnival satire erodes the pretensions of the patriarchal church and state and tears away the deferential masks of subordinate people.[12]

Carnivals, for Bakhtin, are utopian projections of how people would like to live in a community of freedom, equality, and abundance,[13] in a society hostile to dogma of all kinds and inimical to views that close off possibilities. As dynamic as the spiral of nature, carnevale can be regarded as a feast of becoming, change, and renewal.[14] The ultimate egalitarian festival, in authentic manifestation carnival turns everything inside out, bottom to top, front to rear, and unveils, unmasks, and uncrowns. A rite of renewal, and potentially of transformation, carnival laughter is directed not only at authority but at one's self.

In Bakhtin's analysis, the seventeenth and early eighteenth centuries marked the rise to dominance of the classical canon in art and literature.

With consolidation of the nation-state, spontaneous festivals became arranged parades. An insight into the dynamics of the suppression of popular
culture is offered by Mary Ryan's analysis of the institutionalization of the
parade in the United States in the nineteenth century.[15]

The nineteenth-century romantic rebellion against classicism and the
enlightenment held echoes of medieval festivals, yet romanticism differs from
carnival spirit in being fearful of the world. For the peasant, the devil was a
fellow similar to himself and in kinship with saints: a common expletive in
southern Italy is *"santo diavolo!"* In the perspective of romanticism, the devil
is terrifying. Romantic humor has an edge of bitterness and does not, like
carnival hilarity, erode authority while transforming the individual.

The protestant reformation and the catholic counter-reformation, along
with other efforts to suppress peasant culture, tried to put a stop to carnival
revelry, regarding it, accurately, as dangerous to the patriarchal family and
society and to the authoritarian state. In carnivals clowns riddle arbitrary
rule, making fun of authority and official truth. In the middle ages, and in
authentic carnivals today, comedy disperses anxiety by turning the awesome
into comic monsters, the terrifying into the grotesque. Profound in its gaiety,
carnival laughter has multiple meanings, coupling mockery with praise,
denial with affirmation, and satire of self with hope.[16]

Tracking the common origin of carnevale and the Italian theater to
prehistoric "fertility rites," Paolo Toschi describes the convention of a male
protagonist countered by a woman figure, a duality that, in the double
standard of the church, became carnival as male expression of sexuality and
lent as female abstinence from sex.[17] In vernacular culture, the duality is
expressed as difference with equality in the ritual of *comparatico* (brotherhood
and sisterhood), celebrated near the time of the summer solstice.[18] Women
and men pass a stick back and forth through a great bonfire,[19] implying
equality in the love act.

Carnival is a festival of life; the end of it is symbolized by the old woman
as death. For millennia of peasant history, old women of the village
performed useful functions.[20] Hostility to *la vecchia,* and the carnival custom
of sawing her in two, may date from the period of the reformation and
counter-reformation, when male authorities of church and state expressed
murderous fear of women and burned them as witches.

Continuing hostility was implicit in a nineteenth-century custom at
Verona: a puppet of la vecchia would be put on a cart and taken through the
streets to a judge (the inquisition?), who would condemn the old woman to
death. Ambivalence, rather more than hostility, is suggested in the contem-

porary carnival or lenten custom of *segare la vecchia:* a puppet of the old woman is stuffed with bread, fruit, and sweets, and after the figure is sawed apart the sweets are given to the children.[21] In a variant of this ritual, the old woman is sometimes adorned with necklaces and bracelets of dried figs, prunes, and chestnuts. In another version, which suggests her continuing sexual attraction, the figure of la vecchia is stuffed with phallic foods like sardines, codfish, or a red pepper.[22]

A clue as to why authorities regarded the manifestation of the goddess as old woman or witch as dangerous to patriarchal church and state may lie in a traditional custom on the first day of lent in Italy: a procession of people carried a poster demanding *diritti antichissimi* (ancient rights).[23]

In Bakhtin's view, carnival consciousness always precedes great change. Carnevale in Italy today presents a spectacle that may be read as a text to study a culture and polity in rapid transition, offering glimpses of what kind of society, state, and world Italians would have if their submerged beliefs came true.

Italy today is a highly industrialized nation that has overtaken Great Britain in productivity. Yet it is also a country with striking similarities to the third world in the persistence of economically "underdeveloped" regions and in having liberation beliefs with ancient roots, beliefs that illumine an arc stretching from feminist theory and politics, to beliefs of left catholicism, to transformed communist beliefs in the "democracy of socialism."

Marx and Gramsci pointed out that the past is always present in new beginnings. Ancient themes mingle with the new in Italy today and offer a glimpse of possibility. Alfonso Di Nola, a Neapolitan cultural anthropologist, thinking about the 360 days in the lunar and the 365 days in the solar year, considers the time in between "a situation of risk, of emergency, of a moment of trespass between the old and the new,"[24] a time *in between* that can be felt at the end of the old and the beginning of the new year.

Between christmas and epiphany (December 25 and January 6) the days are blanketed by domestic warmth; but there is something "unquiet" about them, states Di Nola, because they belong to the "archaic culture of Europe." In spite of secularism and commercialism, the ancient culture continues to exist in "residual memory." In Anglo-Saxon countries, the "unquiet times" come to an end on Twelfth Night, January 6. In Latin countries, the tensions of the season are released in the explosive gaiety of carnevale.

La befana, vernacular personification of the goddess as old woman, who parodies the church festival of the epiphany, lives in the midst of Italians during the first week of January. Like the nurturing earth mother, la befana brings sweetmeats to the young. Like the sibyls, who succeeded the goddess and prepared calming medicines and murmured soft incantations, la befana practices the magical arts of giving and punishing, bringing *dolci* to good children and coal to the naughty on January 6.

For the church, this day commemorates the arrival of the three wise men from the east bringing gifts to the christ child, an event considered the manifestation of the divine nature of christ, or epiphany. For the people, January 6 marks the visit of la befana and the commencement of carnevale, when the laughter of the goddess subverts church doctrine.

For Di Nola the period from christmas to epiphany may be considered the difference between solar and lunar time, a transition from dead time to time aborning, and a reversion into chaos followed by the return of order. In Babylonian times, priests celebrated a metaphorical destruction and re-creation of the world in the five days between the solar and lunar calendars: statues of the gods were covered while priests rhythmically read the story of the origin of the cosmos. The recitation held the function of magic, reconstituting the old into the new. Carnevale, in this light, may be regarded as a festival when statues of the gods are covered and people play out the death of the old and the birth of the new in a festival of regenerative laughter.[25]

In the Italian vernacular calendar, the time of transition from old to new has several beginning dates: the day after christmas (the church festival of santo Stefano), Capodanno on January 1, and the day of la befana on January 6. The official church date for the commencement of carnevale is January 18, when a church figure, sant'Antonio the abbot, co-opts a popular festival with prechristian roots. The end of carnival, according to church and secular authorities, is the Tuesday (martedì grasso in Italy) before Ash Wednesday, when lent begins. In Italian vernacular culture, the spirit of carnevale is extended forward to the summer solstice on June 24, when the people celebrate the church festival of saint John with pagan rituals.

In the carnival period, subaltern classes tend to "exceed customary behavior."[26] At Naples, on New Year's eve at midnight, people throw old things out of windows without caring on whom a sofa may fall. Vittorio Lanternari has suggested that this *empty time* when the old passes to the new is the eternal game of eros and thanatos, or love and death.[27]

In the people's calendar, the beginning of carnevale is pushed back as far as possible. In vernacular belief, the dead visit the living on the night of November 1–2, leaving dolci and toys for the children; they are required to return to the land of the dead on the day of la befana, January 6, the day popularly regarded as the boundary between the dead and the living. At some point in the period when the dead are believed to be among the living, carnevale commences in Italy.

The ancient origins of carnevale are visible at Putignano, in Apulia, where the festa begins on December 26, the feast day of the town's patron saint, Stephen. On this day, in the ritual of *le propaggini,* peasant men plant a "mother" grapevine to start new growth. After the vine branch puts down roots, it is detached from the mother to begin its own life.[28] In the long peasant past, groups of men would blacken their faces with kitchen smoke for these rites of propaggini. Sometimes they would be accompanied by the padrona, wife of the landowner, a figure who gives one pause. Is the padrona the woman divinity, who symbolizes the earth? In later peasant rituals of the propaggini, men took over the role of the padrona, pulling a cart festooned with ivy, grapevines, bunches of grapes, and the branches of fig plants, to which oblong zucchini were appended.

Pulling the cart decorated with symbols of female and male genitalia around the farm, peasant men performed a ritual that recalls the prechristian woman divinity as the fertile earth. Men would stop three or four times to make a circle and then plant the vines ritually. Pushing their work tools up and down, "with evident obscene allusions," peasant men sang work songs accompanied by repetitive melodies from a mouth harp in this ritual enactment of planting new growth.

Sedition accompanied the planting of the vines, with participants taking turns reciting short rhymes satirizing the powerful in their midst.[29] Phallic allusions were evident in the chant "to plant—or to put the vines inside."[30] Donato Morelli's study of the ritual of le propaggini states that the double entendre of this phrase, alluding to the sexual act, was understood by everyone. Political targets of peasant satire included the *domini* (gentlemen), urban artisans, and political authorities of the city.

Interpretation of the ritual of le propaggini varies according to gender. For a woman philologist, R. Lamacchia, in olden times an old woman followed by young women preceded the men who planted the vines. Implying women's control of their own sexuality and reproduction, Lamacchia states that the women, like the men, also carried vines and farm tools.[31] Salacious verses of rites of propaggini, in her view, recall ancient rituals when the planting of the vines was accompanied by "free coupling," or "natural weddings in the open fields."[32] Male interpreters of the ritual of le propaggini prefer to trace it, not to the culture of the goddess, but to Roman bacchanalian rituals, when fertility was personified by the male god Bacchus.[33]

Carnevale as a satire of conventional religion harks back to the continuation of pagan saturnalia in the first centuries of christianity, when a buffoon bishop would be elected, a *papa dei folli,* or pope for mad people. The reign of the papa dei folli, in the words of church synods, permitted "every oral and behavioral indecency, from nude dancing, to sexual acts normally forbidden, to depraved poetry, dances and fornications."[34] Saturnalian defiance of church morality is documented in the many prohibitions of Italian, German, and French churches and in the continual condemnation by synods. Later the buffoon bishop was replaced by clowns, who personify carnevale today. Clowns lead the revelry that not only desacralizes authority but pulls off everyone's everyday mask.

Benedetto Croce banished carnival figures and improvisational comedy to the category of nonart.[35] In contemporary Italian appreciation of the significance of vernacular culture, Giuseppe Balestra, a sculptor from Apulia, has created beaten-iron carnival figures that symbolize the Italian festival. They suggest that the protagonists of carnival are peasant men and women and other subordinated groups.

Arlecchino (Harlequin), mascot of carnival in Italy, is a lower-class figure with aspirations, manservant from Bergamo with a Venetian accent, a peasant figure who has come to the city bringing ancient lore symbolized by a black mask and a tail.[36] Italian symbol of subversion by scurrility, Arlecchino may be at least nineteen centuries old, a descendant of the Samnites, indigenous peoples of the Naples area who were continually invaded but never spiritually conquered, and whose passion is evident in pilgrimages to the black madonna dell'Arco and to the great black slave mother, la Schiavone of Montevergine.

Pulcinella, almost as well known as Arlecchino, also originated in Naples. Black-masked Pulcinella, symbolizing the Neapolitan and Roman theater from the seventeenth to the nineteenth centuries, represented peasants and servants and, later, the Neapolitan middle class.[37] Gianduja, peasant of the piedmont, has a face that combines ignorance and malice, and a great heart; he loves wine and women and is today mascot of the carnival at Turin.[38] Balanzone, symbolizing the foolishness of a doctor from Bologna, makes fun of the conceits of the learned.[39] Colombina is the young peasant serving maid who flirts, gossips, and knows everyone's secrets.[40] Scaramuccia is the Neapolitan character always engaged in uncertain skirmishes, vain and clever, poltroon, thief, and womanizer.[41]

Venice has the most splendid carnevale of Italy, an aristocratic version of the popular festival.[42] At its most brilliant, in the cinquecento and thereafter, the carnival of Venice began on December 26, the day of saint Stephen, with a great burst of spectacles, concerts, balls, masked *sfilate,* and gondola processions. Great artists of Europe vied for Venetian carnival engagements, great families in ornate gondolas glided majestically along the Grand Canal to the sound of tambourines and trumpets, and carnival animal games vied for attention with the brilliant comedies of Carlo Goldoni. The link between the brilliant Venetian carnival and the culture of established authorities is suggested in the theme for the 1992 carnival, celebrating Columbus's "discovery" of the new world. This position is opposed by the entire Italian left, which considers the Columbian expedition an "invasion" that initiated the genocide of native peoples.[43]

For the scholar searching carnevale for ancient themes and vernacular beliefs, the Ligurian and Adriatic coasts of Italy, as well as the islands of Sicily and Sardinia, beckon; in these regions, evidence of the civilization of Old Europe is visible in archaeological sites, black madonnas, and in folklore.[44]

Carnevale at Naples, the luminous capital of the Kingdom of the Two Sicilies, has always held visible ties with the prehistoric goddess. The symbol of the Neapolitan carnevale is *la vecchia o' carnevale,* a homemade puppet of an old woman with a young body, large breasts, and a widow's hump, an evocation of the three ages of the woman divinity. The meaning of carnevale as a rite of death and regeneration is symbolized at Naples with la vecchia o' carnevale and Pulcinella, peasant servant who wears a white shirt (symbol of death) and a black mask (symbol of the earth and of regeneration). Pulcinella is carried around town by peasants and city workers to the music of a fife and bass drum. In the Campagna, *"magare"* is the dialect word for healers and witches, and people still wear amulets to protect against la fattura, or the mal'occhio,[45] in the belief that a malevolent gaze of the goddess as old woman bringing misfortune can be countered by a ritual invoking the healing power of the goddess.[46]

During the cinquecento, when Naples was the capital of the Aragonese court of Spain in southern Italy, cavaliers and ladies in elegant costumes participated in theatrical tourneys while the common people circulated in the streets, performed in the piazza, and sang ribald songs. The most renowned popular comedy was the *Zeza,* whose origins date back to Muslim rule of southern Italy. Scurrilous jests, erotic play, and satire of the clergy were the vivid lower-class counterpoint to the elegant carnival balls and banquets of the nobility.[47]

The way the festival must have existed in peasant culture for millennia is conveyed in Salvatore Salomone-Marino's description of an 1879 Sicilian carnival in the countryside. For peasants the three most important festivals of the year were the day celebrating one's patron saint, the day of the *santo padrone* of the town, and carnevale. Today, the festival stretches for the three or more weeks between la befana and martedì grasso, but traditionally carnival in Sicily lasted only three days, the Sunday, Monday, and Tuesday before Ash Wednesday. These three days, for the peasant constrained by poverty the rest of the year, were time out from a life of miseria.[48]

On the three carnival days, nobody worked, everyone gathered in the streets laughing, joking, teasing, in the words of a conservative spokesman, with "no respect for sex, age, class, or authority."[49] Some limericks and practical jokes when directed at figures of authority were truly "brutal and ferocious." As the proverb put it, *A carniliviari semmu tutti aguali!* (At carnival we are all equal!).[50]

Everything short of major crime was permitted. Peasant men pelted upper-class gentlemen and clerics with rotten eggs, dust, ink, mud, and urine to the whistles and applause of the crowd. Peasant women leapt out of church stereotypes and declaimed "insolent, brazen, and downright obscene" poetry, seizing the carnival prerogative of peasant men to denounce in satire the injustices and abuses of the powerful.

Costume, in nineteenth-century Sicilian carnevale, was a simple matter of painting one's face, turning one's jacket inside out, and playing instruments adapted from kitchen utensils. Young men in packs would roam through the town singing and playing practical jokes. Sometimes a puppet of straw was made to play jokes on others. A *cantaru* (slop jar) was often taken along for merriment.

An old couple was the symbol of carnevale for nineteenth-century Sicilian peasants: a *nonnu,* an old, fat grandfather puppet, and his spouse, a *nonna,* an old, thin (yet pregnant) grandmother. In this and other rituals of Italian folklore, the goddess is personified as married; even in her crone form as nonna, she is still considered fertile, signifying, in becoming pregnant, regeneration.

Besides Arlecchino and Pulcinella, Gypsy fortune-tellers are also significant figures in Italian carnivals. As nonchristians, Gypsies have a tradition of pagan lore, including the veneration of Isis. In their pilgrimage in the south of France to les Saintes Maries, Gypsies venerate three Maries, one of whom is Sarah/Kali. Sarah, a black servant maid, is venerated in an underground crypt of the church where she draws a multitude of fervent pilgrims; her two white half sisters (both of them Marie) are in the upper part of the church. Of the three, it is the small black figure called santa Sara (identified with the black woman divinity Kali of India) who is the most powerful figure. Gypsies, according to Barbara G. Walker, are the last active worshipers of the goddess in Europe. They believe that "the earth is our mother, and so is woman. The secret of life comes from the ground."[51] Among their millions of Jewish, and other, victims, the Nazis murdered more than 400,000 Gypsies.[52]

Dwarfs, in Italian carnivals, are humble figures symbolizing the lowly, in counterpoint to the giant figures, often on stilts, of vernacular feste. Carnival processions in the nineteenth century enacted the social structure: courtiers and peasants, generals, judges, doctors, gentlemen, and serving girls. At the one time of the year when it was permissible to speak and act freely, peasants blew whistles, banged cymbals, danced, and feasted. Doors of houses were thrown open so that young men making a raucous tour of the town could stop and dance the *fasola* (similar to the tarantella) with women of the house. On martedì grasso there were family banquets of pasta with tomato sauce, stuffed pork, and sausage, as well as the legumes (chick-peas and *fave*) and nuts that suggest regeneration.

Carnivals celebrate life and always end with death. In traditional villages the custom endures of sawing the old woman, la vecchia, who connotes death, in two.[53] An Italian-American woman has pointed out that *"segare"* in its folk meaning refers to the sexual act.[54] Rape? The death of Nonno Carnevale (Grandfather Carnival) in Sicilian villages of the last century was mourned in a midnight funeral (the disappearance of Padre eterno?). Today, bonfires at midnight on martedì grasso burn a younger symbolic male figure, the king of carnevale.

Mario Colangeli and Anna Fraschetti, in their study of the festa, state that the burning of this figure symbolizing carnival indicates the ambivalence inherent in the holiday, the fear beneath the gaiety. All carnivals have in common cross dressing, frenetic dancing, ribald satire, and crowd madness. Contemporary Italian carnivals are characterized by costumed figures and processions of allegorical carts satirizing the church and the clergy and local, national, and international politicians. For Colangeli and Fraschetti, the most authentic aspects of today's carnivals are the traces of prehistoric "agrarian rituals" containing pagan and magico-religious elements.[55]

Although satire and gaiety are characteristic of all carnival celebrations, there are regional and local differences. In the Ligurian coastal town of Ameglia (La Spezia), the festival committee chooses a person to interpret carnevale in the neighborhoods. Afterward, he is brought before a tribunal of elders to be judged on the accuracy of the interpretation. The elders, as proprietors of tradition, fine the interpreter for his mistakes, throw him into a ditch, and then permit him to go to the grand carnival ball to dance with any woman of his choice.[56] This version of the festa suggests that elders know the meaning of carnival and enforce a double standard limiting sexual freedom to men.

When carnivals are authentic, the lower-class nature of the festival is apparent; peasant rabelaisian humor is omnipresent. In Anghiari (Arezzo) masked paraders carry a night jar full of chocolate to be distributed to onlookers.[57] Class differences are apparent in the two festivals of Bagolino (Brescia), a "gentlemen's carnival" and a carnival for the poor. In the poor people's carnival of Bagolino, there are no rules, all is spontaneous, and there is a great deal of erotic play.[58]

At Biccari (Foggia), scholars trying to analyze popular customs are satirized: the puppet figure representing carnevale is taken to the piazza, put over a barrel, and operated upon by strange doctors who pull sausages, salami, and pieces of pork from its stomach. Women's diffident attitude toward what has become a male-organized festival is suggested in the carnival of Foggia (near the black madonna l'Incoronata), where two women take turns singing songs, in dialect, of love and of women's disdain for marriage and other socially enforced forms of love.[59]

In the north, at Biella (Vercelli), carnevale is opened by Gipin, a figure who represents the shrewd yet good-hearted mountain peasant characterized by a peaceful nature and common sense. He is accompanied by his wife, Catlina, and son, Gipinot. The peasant trinity is followed around town by bands, and the festival culminates in a grand peasant meal of *fagioli* (beans).[60]

During carnevale at Bosses (Aosta) in northern Italy (near the black madonna of Oropa), streets and houses are invaded by people playing devils and hobgoblins.[61] In southern Italy at Capua, near the many black madonnas of the Campagna, the mayor gives the keys of the city to King Carnival who governs during the festival.[62] At Castellero (Asti), in the ritual of "the goat and the beard," everyone tries to discover who is disguised as the (scape?) goat.[63] A memory of the prehistoric goddess is evident at Castelletto Stura (Cuneo), where carnevale ends with dancing around a maypole.[64]

At Castelnuovo al Volturno (Isernia), while everyone attends church a man dresses himself in a goatskin, blackens his face, puts on a pair of horns, and becomes the *cervo-Carnevale,* or carnival scapegoat for evil.[65] At Cirigliano, near the madonna bruna of Matera, there is a personification of the earth cycle of birth, maturity, death, and regeneration, and attempted escape from the irrevocable sequence of time in the mad dancing of the tarantella. The death of carnevale in the south resembles easter-week processions: lamenting women follow the funeral bier of carnevale.[66] For whom are the women mourning?

The festival at Ivrea (Turin) enacts the medieval custom of *jus primae noctis* (the patriarchal custom that remained in some places until the nineteenth century in which the lord of the castle exacted sexual favors from brides on the first night of a peasant marriage). This ritual exemplifying women's reduced condition in the christian age is accompanied by evidence of their resistance. Along with the enactment of women's humiliation, the carnival at Ivrea holds a procession in honor of Diana, Roman goddess who had complete control of her sexuality.[67]

Christianity identified carnival pleasures with the devil. The devil and saint Martin is the theme of carnevale at Pont Saint Martin (Aosta), where the devil is burned on the last night of the festival.[68] At San Nicola da Crissa (Catanzaro), a farce of masked men with stomachs full of sausages is enacted, suggesting that gluttony has today become the chief carnival freedom; the festa ends with a grand peasant banquet of roast pork.[69]

Carnival satire of christianity is sometimes enigmatic, as in the ritual of an old woman with a child and two husbands, *la vecchia col bambino e due spose*. Is this an allusion to the ancient earth mother, who became a young christian mother with a child of two spouses, one earthly and one nonearthly? Parody also extends to the easter story: one carnival enactment merges husband and son, while another enacts a wedding ceremony of mother and son in which the son is killed.[70]

The religious implications of carnevale, perhaps because they touch very deep layers of the unconscious, may be enigmatic, but the political thrust of the festa is clear. Sicilian peasants of the last century said that during carnevale "we are all equal." In Germany, the carnival at Cologne features a "Thursday of the Women," when they take over the city and permit every liberty. Women catch men and cut off their ties, a rite susceptible to freudian interpretation.[71]

In Greece, at Naoussa, Dea Carnevale, the carnival goddess, has a cart full of poets declaiming satirical pieces.[72] The long arm of the church is apparent in the carnival at Fort-de-France in Martinique, where *"Vaval"* is a festival of women devils dancing madly;[73] at Oruro in Bolivia, everyone dances the *Diablada* (devil's dance), and in the joust between good and evil, devils are opposed by angels.

Italy has close ties with Latin America, not only because hundreds of thousands of Italians emigrated to Central and South America in the twentieth century but because of shared liberation beliefs. Themes of liberation are vivid in Latin-American carnivals, which often recall that the last Inca king was killed by the Spanish invader Pizarro.[74] Native Americans and African slaves are essential carnival figures of Central and South America.[75] In the festival at Port of Spain in Trinidad, Blacks, mulattoes, and Amerindians dance with Afro-Spanish rhythms and satirize international figures.[76] The greatest of all carnivals, at Rio de Janeiro, has given the samba dance to carnivals throughout the world, notably to Italy. The Rio carnival originated in the struggles of Angolan slaves for liberty.

Carnevale in Sicily is analyzed in chapter 6. Sardinia, the other large Mediterranean island of Italy, where archaeological evidence of the culture of the goddess is impressive, offers a revealing example of the festa.[77] At Cagliari there is a black madonna in the Santuario di Bonaria. Artifacts of the original peoples of Sardinia, who came to the island from Corsica about 6000 B.C.E., suggest that prehistoric Sardinian civilization resembled that of Liguria in Italy and Provence in France: all these regions share an abundance of prehistoric "mother" statuettes. Sardinian figures of a woman divinity resemble the well-known Greek images of the Cyclades, but they are much older.[78] Middle Eastern and African influence in Sardinia arrived with the Phoenicians based in Carthage. The supercession of a great-mother civilization by a male-warrior culture is evident in the age of the *nuraghe* (earth and stone structures) of Sardinia.[79]

In the age of the great mother, neolithic tombs of Sardinia are uterine.[80] A late-neolithic wall drawing in a cave at Bue Marino (Dorgali) represents the goddess as a bee.[81] Snake heads on the rim of a neolithic vase at Tintirriolu, Mara, are dated at the end of the fifth century B.C.E.[82] Among the arresting prehistoric images of the goddess in Sardinia is one at Oristano from the fifth century B.C.E.: "She is rotund, not obese, and the treatment of the upper and lower parts of her body displays an amazing sculptural harmony. In the center is the pubic triangle fused with the belly."[83]

Among Sardinian treasures of the civilization of the goddess is a terra-cotta figure with breasts as eyes.[84] The meaning of pervasive images of bull's horns in the civilization of Old Europe may be discerned in a Sardinian tomb where three vulvas painted red are situated above bull's horns.[85] Confirming Gimbutas's theory that horns are a sign of the goddess, the bull's horns have a vivid resemblance to fallopian tubes.

Double triangles, connoting the fecund power of the vulva, are painted on the walls of Sardinian tombs.[86] In northern Sardinia there are images of a bird goddess[87] and of a neolithic ram-bird hybrid with spiraling horns and an owl's beak.[88] Stiff nude goddesses carved of bone have incised eyes, and no mouth.[89] An alabaster goddess of the fourth millennium B.C.E. has folded arms, a long neck, and a blank face.[90]

The laughter of the goddess may be heard during carnevale at Bosa (Nuoro), when Sardinian peasants sing satirical verses in front of the homes of the *prominenti* and play all-night games of looking for treasure in the genital areas of both sexes.[91] More elusive is the meaning of the Sardinian carnival rite of men dressed in long black gowns, corsets, and shawls.

A carnival rite at Mamoida at Nuoro in Sardinia sends the senses spinning. In the procession of *mamuthones,* masked figures dressed in black carry large bells on their shoulders, rattles around their necks, and tragic facial expressions. In this heavily valenced rite, the black figures move in cadenced gait—in absolute silence, the absolute silence of a Sardinian image of the goddess with no mouth.

CHAPTER 6

"a carniliviari semmu tutti

aguali," at carnival we are all

equal ▪ *Viareggio, Putignano, and Acireale*

NINETEENTH-CENTURY carnivals in Sicily, acting out the belief "We are all equal," may be regarded as cultural precursors of socialist uprisings at the end of the century. Contemporary carnivals of Italy may be read as texts of vernacular religious and political beliefs that offer signs of the third millennium.

Whether the satire is cultural or political, carnevale suggests subversion. The early church fathers Tertullian, Ciprian, and Augustine fulminated against the saturnalian excesses of the people. Leaders of the catholic counter-reformation imitated protestant reformers in condemning sensual pleasure, excessive ornaments, music, masquerading, sensual body movements, and suggestive dancing. The counter-reformation papacy called these acts *libertà della carne*. Acts of "liberty of the flesh" were considered "acts of disobedience," disturbing not only to the church but to social order.[1]

In February and March of 1989 I observed carnivals at Viareggio in Tuscany, Putignano in Apulia, and Acireale in Sicily. There are regional differences. In the north, carnival satire is close to Roman saturnalian origins and commedia dell'arte, anticlerical and pungently political. In the south, where the festival reaches farther back in time, carnival satire is more deeply subversive, culturally and politically.[2]

For Annabella Rossi, a perceptive interpreter of the festival at Naples,[3] carnival rituals of southern Italy connote not only affirmation of life but passage from life to death and from death to life, themes of the civilization of the goddess.[4] In Putignano, carnevale is symbolized by Farinella, an enigmatic male figure whose name is feminine and whose face, covered with white rice flour, suggests the white of semen, or the white of death.[5] Carnival dancing everywhere is characterized by back-and-forth movements that musicologists consider sexual. The three places selected for study of carnevale in Italy are on the Ligurian and Adriatic coasts and in Sicily; all are close to archaeological sites of the goddess and sanctuaries of black madonnas.

▪ VIAREGGIO

This city, on the Ligurian coast, is close to paleolithic evidence of the culture of the goddess at Arene Candide and Barma Grande, to the paleolithic figure of a pregnant earth mother at Savignano, to neolithic ruins of the civilization of the goddess in the Genoa area, and near the black madonna of Montenero outside Leghorn. Home of sailors, fishermen, farmers, marble excavators,[6] and townspeople providing services for carnevale and seaside holidays, Viareggio has a continuing radical spirit that may be related to its religious "ground bass" and to its radical history and politics.[7] Left politics and the artisanry of its craftsmen characterize the contemporary carnival of Viareggio. Sailors and shipmakers of the area create carnival floats that are considered the best in Italy.[8]

Located near the northern boundary of old Etruria, Viareggio is in the land of the Etruscans (comprising modern Tuscany and Latium), whose civilization extended north to the Po valley and south to the Campagna. Old Etruria, a region of the goddess civilization of Old Europe, was not invaded by Indo-Europeans, who elsewhere imposed male-dominant warrior cultures. Etruscan reverence for all life is suggested in the pervasiveness of the symbol of the egg. The harmony and equality of the culture of Old Europe is visible in statues of Etruscan couples who startle because they seem so content. The spontaneous art of the Etruscans depicted independent women and loving couples.

Simultaneously spiritual and sensual, in a civilization where women were equals, the Etruscans have fascinated observers from D. H. Lawrence to contemporary feminists. The married couple on the sarcophagus in the Villa Giulia, and many Etruscan sculptures of smiling couples holding hands, are evidence that there was no war between the sexes in the goddess civilization of old Etruria.[9]

Contemporary carnevale as a procession of floats commenced here in 1873, organized by young men shortly after the unification of Italy. Carts festooned with flowers carried masked celebrants throwing *coriandoli* (confetti) at bystanders. People danced in the streets all night, and revelers masked their faces with flour and coal and played tricks on prominent authority figures. Gendarmes were posted by the state to prevent the people from indulging in "excessive dangers."[10]

The sharpness of the political satire at Viareggio's contemporary carnival may relate to the city's radical history. In the last years of the nineteenth century, women threw themselves across railroad tracks to oppose the Italian war in North Africa. In 1908, carnival satire of the catholic church was enacted by a group of young men dressed as priests in a parody of catholic religious rites; they were fined for the "indecent spectacle."[11]

In the early twentieth century, worker struggles and a strong antiwar movement before world war I culminated in postwar *giorni rossi,* red days, aiming for socialist revolution. During the first week of May 1920, workers and farmers occupied factories and the land, and mariners occupied the docks, in a popular revolution with anarchist overtones. The people of Viareggio declared a general strike and installed a socialist government.

In what became the characteristic pattern of fascist suppression, socialist initiatives at Viareggio and elsewhere in Italy were destroyed. Fascist squadrons arrived, wrecked worker organizations, and killed townspeople indiscriminately.[12] In the fascist period, the authorities tried to suffocate the libertarian spirit of the city, remanding carnival activities to the supervised recreation of their own *dopolavoro.* Antifascists of Viareggio went underground; carnival cartmakers constructed floats of *cartapesta* (papier-mâché) and adopted metaphor and allegory to disguise political criticism.

In 1930 Burlamacco, mascot of the carnival of Viareggio, was born; he was a synthesis of Arlecchino (Harlequin) dressed in patches, Doctor Balanzone with a black cape, and Rugantino with a nautical cocked hat. Women carnival figures became watered-down images of the goddess, like the nymph Ondina, or Colombina, or patriotic figures, like queen Isabella, who pawned her jewels so that Columbus could sail to America.[13]

Fascists tried to dampen the carnival spirit with sober sayings like *chi dorme non piglia pesci* (he who sleeps does not catch fish) and attempted to deflect criticism of politicians into mockery of women. The fascist version of carnival at Viareggio in the 1930s is suggested in photographs of mayors launching flowered floats of *Le Sirene, Il Decamerone, Orlando Furioso,* and *I Promessi Sposi.* Darts of indirect political criticism were directed at fascist bombast; one float was entitled *Tanto fumo e poco arrosto* (So much smoke, little roast to eat). In 1938, when Mussolini had allied with Hitler, another float, *I pagliacci tragicomici,* depicted tragicomic clowns.[14]

During world war II, Viareggio, the center of Tuscan resistance to nazis and fascists, suffered nazi occupation, reprisals against partisans, and aerial bombardment by the Allies. Memories of the heroic partisan resistance have been kept alive by the monument outside Viareggio in the adjoining village of Sant'Anna that commemorates the nazi massacre of noncombatants and babies.[15] Resistance to fascism continues to be felt today in the carnival satire at Viareggio.

After the defeat of fascism in 1945,[16] postwar hope for a communist-socialist government suffused the festival, a hope suffocated by international cold-war politics and the hegemony, for the next four decades, of conservative christian-democratic governments. During the cold war, a float was entitled *Zona del silenzio,* and carnivals became diversions featuring bathing beauties and American jazz.

Silence and apathy continued until 1968, when left political confrontations in Italy and across the world gave new life to carnival.[17] In the 1970s when Italian left politics became deadly serious with electoral gains by communists, women intent on their rights, and the rise of the red brigades, a revolutionary spirit characterized carnevale, particularly in the neighborhoods of Viareggio. Red became the dominant color of the *carri,* Mao a favorite subject,[18] cartapesta floats sailed into utopian hopes, and *rioni* (neighborhoods) burst into wild dancing, eating, roistering, and people knee-deep in coriandoli in front of the churches.

Subsequently, revolutionary carnival spirit in the neighborhoods has toned down, but anyone who tried in 1989 to walk across a street in carnival in the rione of Marco Polo was swept up into singing, swaying, playing, dancing masses of people. For a contemporary chronicler of Viareggio, the festa sweeps away all that is static into a hope that everyone will be inspired, not by dreams, but by the real possibility *di vivere meglio* (to live better).[19]

Exuberance is characteristic of the early stages of revolution. In 1989, carnival celebrants at Viareggio arranged a futurist exhibit of Filippo Tommaso Marinetti's art, awarded a journalism prize for courageous reporting, and held a soccer match, a swim meet, a sailboat regatta, an automobile rally, poetry readings, several theatrical spectacles, and many masked balls. Artists and artisans created and organized *sfilate di carri* and afterward ran off to spontaneous neighborhood carnival celebrations in Croce Verde, Torre del Lago, Marco Polo, Varignano, Vecchia Viareggio, and Darsena.

Pride in the "desacralizing" Tuscan spirit was reflected in floats of 1989.[20] One celebrated *Libera stampa in libero stato,* a free press in a free state, a theme that has become urgent in Italy, and elsewhere, as a few financiers, and governments in wartime, control the news.[21] This issue has become a vital concern of the Italian student-resistance movement of the 1990s.

In 1989 a float entitled *L'impero del male* punctured the hypocrisy of Reagan's description of the Soviet Union as an evil empire and laughed at Gorbachev's top-down program of *perestroika.* Five angels of the west were parodied for hypocrisy: Reagan dangled a rope around a Native American and a Latin-American peasant, the Italian prime minister displayed a fascist symbol, the German prime minister held a picture of Hitler in one hand and an imprisoned Jew in the other, François Mitterrand tortured an Algerian, and Margaret Thatcher was portrayed hanging an Irishman.

Older oppressors were speared with ribald humor; a float of Napoleon at Waterloo was renamed "watercloset." Perennial christian-democratic politicos were put away as old clothes in a chest of drawers, *Carnevale nel cassetto.* Another float, *Europa '92,* made fun of the economic consolidation of Europe as an unequal union of countries, some depicted as snails, others as hares. *Fermiamolo* (Let's stop it) portrayed industrial pollution as a monster menacing Italy's life and art treasures.

Carnival satire cuts deep and wide. Italians, who courageously saved most of the Jews of their country during world war II, are critical of Israel today for oppressing Palestinians and of the United States for inserting its geopolitical interests into Middle Eastern politics. In the float *Davide e Golia,* a King Kong monster holding a can of Coca-Cola was the oppressor at whom the Palestinian David threw a rock.

All politicians, including the president of Italy, were satirized as *fanfaroni,* braggarts. Another float, *Non sono una trottola,* criticized media manipulation of children that robs the young of the freedom to fantasize.[22] *E le stelle stanno a guardare* depicted the stars watching humans destroy the ozone layer, generate ills that have become plagues, and pollute outer space with nuclear warheads. *Il mondo è così* portrayed a diabolic marriage of politics and money. *Il piatto ride, il piatto piange* depicted two faces, a first-world adult in an orgy of eating and a third-world child dying of hunger. The float was engineered to move in a way suggesting that the dish that laughs can easily become the dish that cries.

A critical view of the traditional emphasis of the left on economic development was implicit in *Nella vecchia fattoria,* depicting the dubious progress from a peaceful farm of pigs and donkeys to a capitalist jungle of crocodiles, tigers, and lions. All the political leaders of Italy were scurrilously presented seated on toilets, *Sedute nel gabinetto.* A woman's dart was apparent in Maria Angela Rugani's float, *Servi e padroni, ingenui e furbacchioni?* It asked: Who are the servants? Who are the bosses? Who are the ingenuous ones? Who are the shrewd ones? Carnival satire turned back on itself was evident in *Le nuove maschere,* in which real clowns manipulated mechanical carnival clowns and an X-ray photo of a masked ball revealing death beneath the gaiety.

▪ PUTIGNANO

Here we had arrived in the mezzogiorno of Italy, land of the noonday sun south of Rome. Compounded with contradiction, the south of Italy has thousands of churches and a great deal of recent economic development, along with byways that seem untouched by two thousand years of christianity and progress, a dominant catholicism, and traces of continuing ancient beliefs visible in many sanctuaries of black madonnas and in rituals of carnival.

In this Apulian agricultural and commercial town in the hills of the Murge, we were close to the locale of Carlo Levi's *Christ Stopped at Eboli;* near the lands occupied after each world war of the twentieth century by women carrying babies, statues of madonnas, and communist banners; and in a region of peasant communism whose center is Cerignola. The "ground bass" of this area is suggested by two notable black madonnas, the fifth-century black madonna of Siponto and l'Incoronata, black madonna of the poor outside Foggia. Also nearby are the Lucan black madonna at Bari, the black madonna of Lucera, the great black slave mother (la Schiavone) of Montevergine, la Madonna bruna di Napoli, la Madonna bruna di Matera, la Madonna di Capocolonna di Crotone, the black madonnas of Palmi and Seminara, and many dark Byzantine madonnas.

Carnevale at Putignano is often called the most ancient of Italy because the archaic ritual of the *propaggini,* discussed in chapter 5, initiates the festa on the day after christmas. The tie between ancient rituals and radical politics is suggested in the verb that has emerged from the ritual of the propaggini. *Piantare,* or to plant the vines with sexual allusions, has become an Italian word meaning to spear authority figures with satire.

The ritual of transplanting the vines harks back to the age of the goddess and has been given a christian overlay with the festa of santo Stefano on December 26. Saint Stephen's bones were removed from the coast in 1394 and installed in a Norman monastery at Conversano. Today the actual transplanting of the vines has been discontinued (they are now imported), but poets of Putignano still gather before the *municipale* (the city hall) on December 26 and recite poems satirizing authority.

In addition to archaeological sites of the goddess in this region mentioned earlier, there is a 4000 B.C.E. cylindrical woman figure found near Lecce in an oven-shaped tomb whose triple chevron marks denote the goddess, as does the owl mask.[23] The owl, in the civilization of the goddess, was a symbol of wisdom, with the ability to avert evil and to foresee the future. In its negative meaning, the owl evoked the goddess in her form as death.[24]

Apulia marks the northern boundary of ancient Magna Graecia, whose cult of Dionysus, Greek god of vegetation, celebrated Demeter and Persephone. In dionysian festivals there was open sexuality and a pervasive sensuality in which vegetables like oblong squash and figs signified genitalia. Although the Romans prohibited the festivals, cults of Dionysus and Bacchus never died in the south of Italy and were celebrated with eating, drinking, and free sexuality. The legacy is visible today in the everyday conversation of southern Italians, who adopt names of vegetables to make sexual and satirical statements about people in authority.[25]

Putignano is a few miles from Bari, place of a jeweled Lucan madonna and home of Aldo Moro, christian-democratic minister who in the 1970s tried to effect a "historical compromise" between catholicism and communism. He was kidnapped and murdered by the red brigades in the "years of lead" of the late 1970s, when the fanatic Italian left pushed toward violent revolution. Moro's belief that communism and catholicism are "converging parallels" remains alive among left catholics throughout Italy and was inflamed in the 1990s by revelations of bad faith on the part of Moro's christian-democratic colleagues.

Putignano is in christian-democratic country, but at carnival time the party's icons of family and church are harpooned with satire. In the small hill village of Santa Maria in the Alta Irpinia, a few miles from Putignano, satire of *la famiglia* is enacted at carnival time. Paola Sensi-Isolani, an anthropologist, has analyzed a ritual of a mock wedding procession with a bumbling priest marrying Signor Carnevale and his unattractive bride. Marriage, a sacrament of the church, is lampooned as the priest drunkenly marries the mismatched pair.

The consummation of the marriage occurs on the following Sunday when the *pignatta,* a pot filled with ashes, garlic, and sweet meats for the children, is broken by men wielding phallic sticks. The ritual, Sensi-Isolani has suggested, implies male criticism of marital sexual relations: the contents of the pot are rather more bitter than sweet.[26] Anthropologists refer to the ambivalence southern European men feel about their dependence on their mothers, and later their wives,[27] and connect the transvestism that is strikingly characteristic of southern Italian carnival customs to this ambivalence.[28] Another interpretation is possible: Is male love of the goddess expressed in the bodily imitation of wearing padded breasts and women's clothes?[29] Or, are men dressed as women enacting a third sex neither distinctly male nor female, in memory of Cybele and Attis, as Will Roscoe has pointed out?[30]

For five Thursdays before martedì grasso, priests, matrons, and widows are singled out to be "honored" in satire, culminating on giovedì grasso, fat Thursday, when cuckolds are honored.[31] Folk sayings refer to an abundance of men with unfaithful wives in southern Italy. The finger symbol that connotes the cuckold is pervasive in the vernacular culture of the Mediterranean.[32] Formed by holding the second and fourth fingers upright, the finger sign resembles bull's horns, an emblem of the goddess. Unlike a woman subordinated to patriarchal institutions, whose sexuality is controlled by the church, the state, and her husband, a woman in the tradition of the goddess manages her own body. The two-finger cuckold gesture directed at a man implies the ultimate dishonor of the patriarchy: not being able to control the sexuality of one's wife.

Farinella, the Apulian mascot of carnevale, is not a hero; he is a meschinu, or peasant wretch of the south, who whitens his face with a flour of ground chick-peas and roasted rice and leads revelers in dancing in circles. In 1989 young men dressed as priests reading Playboy mocked the fantasies of the celibate clergy and satirized all forms of institutionalized coupling. Homosexual marriage was lampooned in a skit with young men dressed as brides in white, carrying signs that read Marriage without Frontiers.

Underneath the gaiety lies anxiety. A 1989 article in the carnival literature of Putignano points to the number of suicides and homicides at carnival time in the world.[33] A special fear has overtaken some Italian men because of the rapidity of political and cultural change in the country since 1968. Contemporary advanced feminist legislation (equal access to education and the professions, divorce, equal family rights, equal pay for equal work, legalized abortion, bill outlawing violence against women and children, and so on) offers a sharp contrast to nineteenth-century themes of ninnenanne, lullabies in which Italian women lamented having to live with overbearing husbands.[34] In centuries of resistance to male domination, the southern Italian woman has always known who she was; today, she lets others know.[35] And some of the men have become anxious.

The unease may be deeper in the north than in the south of Italy,[36] where men have lived with strong mothers and wives for millennia and openly acknowledge the power of women. This was apparent in the most audacious carnival float that we saw in 1989, one designed by a man that satirized men who try to control women's sexuality.

The float depicted a feminist riding a phallic motorcycle while holding a Stop sign. In her other hand she held aloft three condoms blown up as balloons. Painted on the condoms were the faces of the male leaders of the christian democrats and the communists, and the face of pope John Paul II. The power of the ancient woman divinity could be felt in this float: men, whether christian-democratic, communist, or catholic, were portrayed as equally ridiculous when they interfere with women's sexuality.

No significant political or cultural figure remained unscathed in the carnevale at Putignano. Socialist leader Bettino Craxi was shown as a grinning sun god shining splendidly while putting all the ills of Italy out of sight. Gorbachev was caricatured as an American sheriff riding a Russian bear trying to reform the soviet system. Italy's large public debt was depicted as an enormous monster against which politicians threw tiny pitchforks. In only slightly disguised criticism of the United States, the pollution of the earth, the atmosphere, and the sea was attributed to a monstrous greedy cowboy shoveling in money from the petrochemical industry while ecologists vainly try to stop him. Another polluting monster, formed of all kinds of garbage, had a Coca-Cola can for a body.

A carro entitled "empire of vampires" was inhabited by vendors and consumers of drugs. A float fashioned by elementary-school children criticized the racism of the north of the world toward the less developed south, a racism replicated in northern Italian attitudes toward southern Italians and, more recently, in Lombard racism toward immigrants from Africa, an attitude schoolchildren found shameful for a nation that officially declares itself opposed to racism.

Enormous cardboard eggs enclosed carnival participants at the end of the 1989 procession at Putignano, eggs that suggested fecundity, regeneration, and the ancient woman divinity. The social and political values of contemporary Apulians may be found in a collection of popular stories that the editor said referred to the "other" literature of vernacular beliefs. The stories are about equality, better relationships among humans, and values of everyday life, "with no space for flight from the earth or from society."[37]

Carnival image, Putignano, 1989: a laughing feminist holding condoms on which are drawn caricatures of male politicians and the pope, who try to control women's sexuality. Not visible here is her phallic motorcycle. Photograph by Wallace Birnbaum.

▪ ACIREALE

Carnival in the Kingdom of the Two Sicilies, a region that comprised southern Italy and Sicily, historically reached peaks of surrealism. Ernesto De Martino points out that the popular culture of the south, with cults of saints and the dead, obsession with the malevolent gaze of *il mal'occhio* or *la fattura,* and the vertiginous dancing of the tarantella, was a magical world.

Annabella Rossi, in *Il carnevale si chiamava Vincenzo,* analyzes the porous wall in the south between "archaic, preclassical, and classical cults." In her interpretation, carnival rites signify death and regeneration and remember the great mother of many names: Cybele/Demetra/Iside/Hera/Cerere/la Dea Syria/la Mater Matuta di Capua/la Dea Marica, and others. They also remember her children, Persephone/Proserpina and Adonis/Dionysus/Horus.[38]

At Capua in 1989 we visited the *Museo campano* that houses ruins of a Roman sanctuary of Mater Matuta, protectress of fecundity and maternity. Given the ambiguity that presides over the subject of the goddess, the museum guide and I were not sure whether two hundred sculpted images of mothers with infants in the sanctuary of la Mater Matuta were images of the goddess or of her women followers. These Roman depictions of mother and child, dated from the fifth to the third century before the common era, resemble the Egyptian goddess Isis and the Greek goddess Hera, who, like these mothers, were characteristically depicted seated on a throne. The similarity to the christian madonna and child is striking.

Near the carnival of Acireale is the Chiusazza Cave outside Syracuse. In evidence dated 3500–3000 B.C.E., signs of the goddess are hourglass (or double vulva) figures and elongated triangles with winding snakes. Maidens in ritual dances have an hourglass shape. On Sicilian vases dated the early fourth millennium B.C.E., young women dance in a circle, one hand on head, the other at the hip, in a posture remarkably similar to contemporary Sicilian folk dancers.[39] At Agrigento, river pebbles sculpted into stiff nudes have been found in graves dated 4000 B.C.E.[40] At Castelluccio Noto there are tombs with egg-shaped side chambers dated 3000–2500 B.C.E. whose outlines are similar to the body of a woman.[41] These tomb entrances are decorated with snake coils or ram horns.[42]

In southern Italy, cities and temples of Magna Graecia were larger than those of Greece. The coming of Greek goddesses, however, marked a decline in women's status. Unlike the earlier egalitarian civilization of the earth-mother goddess, in the Greek era women divinities were molded by male perspective. Athena, for example, was said to have been born without a mother from the forehead of Zeus; she was changed from a goddess of wisdom into a goddess of war.

Acireale's name recalls the Greek myth of Galatea, a sea nymph who fell in love with Acis. Polyphemus, the ugly giant whom Galatea had spurned, became enraged and crushed Acis to death under a rock. Galatea threw herself into the sea, and Acis became the river bearing his name and remembered in the names of the towns Acireale and Aci Castello. The patron saint of Acireale is santa Venere, an example of the catholic custom of transforming a pagan goddess, in this case the Roman goddess Venus, into a saint.

Perhaps more so than in other regions, carnevale in Sicily evokes ancient themes and the sense of transition between dead time and time aborning. On this island of the mafia, drugs, corruption, and poverty, evil is so palpable it can almost be tasted. Yet there are also sudden examples of courageous *good* actions that are visible in demonstrations against nuclear bases at Comiso a few years ago, in women in unison putting sheets out the window to defy the mafia, and in men's shouts of *"giustizia!"* at funerals of investigating judges killed by the mafia.

As midnight of martedì grasso approached, flying *porcellini* circled high over my head, over and over and over, enacting the story of animals besieging Jesus for more gifts. Pigs, dear to the goddess Demeter, thought Jesus should give them wings. Losing patience, he said *"Mai ali!"* (Never wings!), thereby depriving pigs of the sacred character they held in the culture of the goddess. That, mothers tell their children, is why pigs are called *maiali*. And why flying pigs are characteristic of Sicilian carnevale.

Sicilians say that carnival on their island is redundant because reality itself is so grotesque. This is similar to the exasperation of Italian women in February 1989, so immersed in the grotesque reality of trying to secure a law prohibiting violence against women and children that they marked the season in their women's journal, *Noidonne,* with photographs of carnival-masked sexual abusers of children.

Hope and bitterness collide in Sicily, an island Goethe called the soul of Italy. Acireale is a sea city, swept by breezes from the Ionian. It is not far from the *superstrada* that streaks through the island's harsh interior to Palermo, and it adjoins Catania. In these two large Sicilian cities the bitterness of Italy's *sottoproletario* over dreams too long thwarted has turned to hatred and crime.

Sicily has been invaded and looted and its women raped from time immemorial by Phoenicians, Greeks, Romans, Germanic tribes, Byzantines, Lombards, Saracens, Normans, Angevins, Swabians, and Spanish and Austrian Bourbons. Sicilian *contadini* have risen up against oppressors many times. At the end of the nineteenth century, the defeat of socialist hopes propelled the large migration of southern Italians to the new world; for those who remained, hopelessness sent Sicilians to find work in the north. A bitter history, yet the other side of bitterness is the hope embedded in the folklore promising a new time when there will be neither rich nor poor, everyone will have plenty to eat, and fountains will splash olive oil instead of water.

Predominantly christian-democratic, but with significant communist, socialist, feminist, student, and nonviolence groups, Sicily's politics are like those of the rest of Italy—only, like Sicilian sunsets, more vividly so. Greek drama, baroque taste, and Sicilian history have left monstrous, gaping stone faces sculpted on civic buildings—yet sculpted angels are everywhere among the monsters.

In the Acireale carnival procession of 1989, a figure symbolized Sicilian bitterness at the church version of christianity: an illuminated devil with a body shaped like a heart held a christian star as scepter. Yet beneath the bitterness is a love of innocence: a float designed as a picnic basket held beautiful real children nestled among pears and apples created from flowers.

Male ambivalence toward the goddess was apparent in a float constructed with more glaring neon lights than are probably found on the last rim of hell, merging with drifts of flower petals from the elysian fields, fashioning an enormous cat: the goddess Bastet, familiar of the African goddess Isis.[43]

Known as Au Set to Egyptians, Isis had a myriad of names: mistress of the cosmos, ruler of the house of life, sovereign of all that is miraculous, almighty lady of wisdom, mother from whom all life arose, establisher of justice, giver of the gift of abundance, inventor of agriculture, designer of the first sail, inventor of the loom, source of healing herbs, restorer of life . . .[44] Her daughters dispensed healing and protecting medicines and herbs. Source of equity and law of the heart, Isis meted out justice to all people and taught that "they must dispense it to each other."[45]

In the surreal carnevale of Acireale in 1989, faces of politicians, portraying the dark side of the goddess, resembled birds of prey. The laughter of the goddess at patriarchy could be heard in scurrilous, seditious humor portraying the christian-democratic prime minister in bed with a sign, *Mi kappa la pipi, papa,* asking the pope's permission to urinate. The float mocked deference of christian-democratic politicians to papal policy on issues related to women and liberation theology.

Removing sentiment from everything, floats inhabited by popular American icons (Walt Disney ducks and pigs) cozied with vultures, symbol of the goddess in her manifestation as death. Human figures with enormous noses, distended heads, and claws for hands were densely packed together and edged the scatological: a platoon of politicians was entitled *Rompipalle* (balls breakers). Death's heads pushed out of soccer balls. The socialist leader Bettino Craxi, commonly regarded as an opportunist, was portrayed naked, with a neon rosary. A lucullan carnival menu served up *Plasma di popolo amaricante* (blood of the people with a dash of bitters) and *Macedonia di disoccupati* (fruit cup of unemployed people). Grotesquely grinning politicians nested with malevolent monsters, all horned, in this part of the world where

The Egyptian goddess Isis, at right, with Osiris and Horus. Reproduced by permission of the Louvre Museum, Department of Antiquities, Paris.

"horned," or *cornuto,* refers to the ultimate patriarchal dishonor: a husband betrayed by his wife.[46]

The winding procession of monsters went past churches with garlanded angels, passed in front of *palazzi* protected by gargoyle friezes, and proceeded through narrow alleys with open-air markets of fruit, vegetables, and flowers. A simple float came by—a woman holding a heart with a sign: "The heart is the foundation of life. Let us give a healthy heart to the person with a sick one." Long before Jesus proclaimed a similar message, Isis was believed to be the source of justice and of the law of the heart.

In December 1989 the student movement of Italy exploded. Clues as to why this first happened in Sicily are visible in the carnival edition of a university publication from the spring of that year. It points out that scholars have found the origins of the Acireale carnival in the celebration of the goddess Isis. Student editors of the carnival booklet satirized local politicians as robbers and "the last emperors"; they depicted a peasant with a bodily gesture of query in front of the archbishop and the "omniscient and all-powerful Dicci," party of the christian democrats.

Students felt that carnival in Italy was scarcely a laughing matter. Corruption in politics and the passage from an agricultural economy to an industrial economy meant that craftsmanship was replaced by plastic, attended by "drugs, organized crime, the mafia, and dirty politics. . . . All the religious myths have fallen . . . not only in Acireale, but in all the world."[47]

A sudden opening of possibility on this island of drugs, organized crime, the mafia, and dirty politics is embodied in Leoluca Orlando. His book, *Palermo,* states that one's first sensation on arrival in that city is a triple blast of the sirocco, murder, and sensuality. A postmodern vision of horror, eleven-year-olds in this city sell heroin. Yet it is in Palermo that a significant break in Italian politics is visible. Of the generation of 1968 (and a christian democrat), Orlando was mayor of Palermo from 1985 to 1990 in coalition with communists and greens on a platform opposing the mafia. In 1991 he was the runaway victor for mayor, but elders of the christian-democratic party installed the person who placed twenty-third in the race. Orlando challenges the alliance of christian democrats and the mafia and has incurred the enmity of party leaders. In 1991 he formed a new party, Rete, a network of seceding christian democrats, communists, greens, and others, whose only qualification for membership is "honesty."[48]

At Palermo, women have woven their concerns into their own network that also crosses parties, coming together as "ex-communists and greens, Orlando catholics, women of the left of many derivations, women students of *La Pantera* . . . the entire class of women's politics of Palermo," so that "each person's choice can be heard politically." The editor of *Noidonne* calls the Palermo example of a women's political network that has been woven by Simona Mafai, feminist communist stateswoman, and her friends in other parties "a school for politics for women."[49]

CHAPTER 7

black madonna of Siponto: a woman

humiliated • black madonna and sibyls

of Loreto: women prophets • black

madonna of the poor of Foggia

T HE HIGHLY VENERATED goddess vividly described in Apuleius's ode of the second century C.E. descended sharply to become the subordinate mother of Jesus in christian doctrine. Demoted from goddess to saint, left out of the trinity, her many characteristics reduced to obedience and patience, humiliation seems to be reflected in the staring eyes of the black madonna of Siponto, whose sanctuary was built in the fifth century of the common era.

The valence of the goddess may have persisted in the role of black madonnas in the prophetic tradition of Judeo-christianity and in the sibylline prophetic tradition transmitted by women peasants. These themes are suggested in the art of the sanctuary of the black madonna at Loreto, as well as in the implicit liberation theology of black madonnas of the poor.

The very black madonna at Siponto in Apulia is popularly known as the madonna with *gli occhi sbaratti,* or staring eyes. The image, in this "first medieval church" built to Mary,[1] is attributed to saint Luke, and was said to have been drawn at Jerusalem from life. The story is curious, since faces of the several dark Lucan madonnas vary considerably. Of the thirty-four images attributed to saint Luke, one is in Syria, two in Egypt, one in Poland, ten in Russia, several at Mount Athos in Greece, eight in Rome, and others elsewhere in Italy.[2]

Located on the Gargano peninsula in the Adriatic sea, the area around the sanctuary of la Sipontina attracts students of prehistory because it was submerged for eons. Humans have lived here "since their first appearance on earth."[3] In the pebble culture of the original inhabitants, humans depicted themselves with pyramidal bodies (the triangle of the goddess?) and three or four faces.[4] The sanctuary of the black madonna of Siponto is located near prehistoric evidence of the goddess at Grotta Paglicci, Castelluccio dei Sauri, and Grotta Scaloria. At Porto Badisco there are cave drawings of a woman with serpent limbs. Signs of the goddess—dots, triangles, semicircles, circles, and spirals—are incised on neolithic pottery of this region.[5] In the museum reconstruction of a neolithic village at Passo di Corvo, the communal way people lived in the civilization of the goddess may be viewed. The sanctuary of la Sipontina was built on the site of a temple to the Roman goddess Diana.[6] Near seaports on the Adriatic, the local indigenous goddess was joined by the divinities of peaceful and nonpeaceful peoples: Dauni, Greeks, Romans, Byzantines, Slavs, Jews, and Lombards.[7]

In spite of the hostility of the church, veneration of the woman divinity in her many forms persisted into the early years of christianity. Apuleius's description, in the second century of the common era, suggests the fervency of her veneration. Invoking her as "Queen of Heaven, whether you are fostering Ceres the motherly nurse of all growth"; or as "celestial Venus who in the first moment of Creation mingled the opposing sexes in the generation of mutual desires, sowing in humanity the seeds of indestructible continuing life"; or as "the sister of Phoebus, who by relieving the pangs of childbirth travail with soothing remedies have brought safe into the world lives innumerable and who are now venerated in the thronged sanctuary of Ephesus"; or as Proserpina, "whose triple face has power to ward off all the assaults of ghosts . . . nurturing the glad seeds in the earth with your damp light, and dispensing abroad your dim radiance when the sun has abandoned us"—by "whatever name, and by whatever rites, and in whatever form it is permitted to invoke you, come now and succour me in the hour of my calamity."[8]

This passionate feeling evidently threatened the early church fathers, who tried to extirpate veneration of the three great pagan goddesses, Isis of Africa, Cybele of Anatolia, and Diana of the Middle East, in the years before the Siponto church was built. The staring eyes of the black madonna of Siponto seem to reflect a woman spurned and the dramatic decline in the fortunes of the goddess by the fifth century of the common era.

The tension of established religion confronted by passionate popular beliefs was apparent as early as 186 B.C.E., when, as Raffaelle Pettazione points out, Romans prohibited the popular religious movement of the bacchanals.[9] When Constantine, in 323 C.E., resolved the problem of subversive popular beliefs by establishing christianity, he did so at a cost to women. The memory of the prechristian woman divinity persisted in folk culture, but church fathers at the second Council of Ephesus in 431 C.E. reduced her many dimensions to the virginal, obediently submissive mother of god. Identification of early christianity with slaves and outcasts was replaced, after its establishment as a state religion, by the Roman imperial policy of suppressing beliefs considered pagan, a word that originally referred to beliefs of people in local villages. The main reference of the word "pagan," given negative connotation after the establishment of christianity, was to the goddess and her culture.

In the first centuries of christianity, church fathers negatively interpreted the life-enhancing values associated with the goddess and deduced the necessity of conservative political institutions. Augustine declared that "spontaneous sexual desire is the proof of—and penalty for—universal original sin."[10] The transgression of Eve and Adam in the garden of Eden meant that government, even when tyrannical, was a defense against human sin. "Male domination of women, coercive government, and slavery," Elaine Pagels has pointed out, became "necessary evils—because of original sin."[11] The belief that human nature is inherently evil became the main source of subsequent conservative political thinking.[12] The checks and balances of the constitution of the United States are grounded on this pessimistic view of human nature.[13]

About the time the sanctuary of la Sipontina was built, Lombards from the north made themselves "untiring propagators" of the cult of saint Michael, who was beatified for stamping out pagan cults of women divinities.[14] The first sanctuary to Michael was built on Monte Sant'Angelo, a few kilometers away from the church of la Sipontina. In Italy the cult did not have the fervor it held in northern Europe, where Michael "was considered the national protector of all the germanic peoples,"[15] but this sanctuary became the destination of Normans who came to pray and stayed to conquer southern Italy, Sicily, and England in the eleventh century.

Normans were Scandinavian adventurers who settled in the Loire valley of France. Among their descendants were the English Puritans who came to New England in the seventeenth century and helped found what came to be the United States. In Italy, the Normans were called "sackers of churches."[16]

In the region around Siponto, Normans and bishops supported the cult of saint Michael, while the people venerated the black la Sipontina. A recent study found that santa Maria Maggiore of Siponto is the most venerated of several beloved madonnas of the area: santa Maria di Pulsano, santa Maria dell'Orto nel Monastero di S. Chiara in Manfredonia, santa Maria della Pietà and santa Maria della Spiga at Lucera, santa Maria della Valle of Signano, santa Maria della Pietà in San Severo, santa Maria dei Carmini in Torremaggiore, and santa Maria delle Isole di Tremiti.

The ancient black santa Maria Maggiore of Siponto is also first, according to Apulian archives, on a list of black madonnas: santa Maria di Costantinopoli (the Lucan black Iconavetere in the duomo, or cathedral, at Bari), the Madonna delle Fonte of Trani, the Vergine dei Martiri in Molfetta (said to have been brought by crusaders in 1188), Madonna della Guardia of Bologna (said to have arrived from Constantinople in 1160), the miraculous image of santa Maria di Valleverde in Bovino (believed to have appeared in 1253), the madonna of Grottaferrata (said to have appeared in 1230), the madonna of Conversano, santa Maria di Costantinopoli of Venezia (a dark Byzantine madonna that arrived in Venice, according to some authorities, from the sea of Siponto),[17] and the very black madonna dell'Incoronata of Foggia, discussed later in this chapter.

The black madonna of Siponto is considered Mater Dei Genetrix, generative mother of God, whose veneration ascended after the fifth century to a peak in the thirteenth century.[18] Called Odigitria, or guide, she is thought to be deeply revered because she holds, not *cristo bambino,* but christ with the face of an adult, the christ of the apocalypse.[19]

On the spring day in 1990 when we visited the ancient church of Siponto, we found that the statue had been removed, for "security reasons," to the cathedral at Manfredonia. Alongside the picture of the black madonna that remained, a church organization had left a leaflet entitled "Maria: Donna Obbediente," with a photograph of an image of a white, presumably obedient, madonna.[20] Do black madonnas connote, for the church, the disobedience of Lilith and her daughters?

At the altar of the upper part of the old church of Siponto is a painting of a dark Byzantine madonna. A pattern, reflecting the relationship of church doctrine to vernacular beliefs, was becoming clear: on the subterranean level of the early church, a black woman divinity; adjacent to the fifth-century church, ruins of a pagan temple to the prechristian goddess Diana;[21] and on the upper level of the church, a painting of a dark Byzantine madonna.

In search of the black madonna of Siponto, we went to the duomo at Manfredonia, passing in the churchyard a large ecology exhibit protesting the company Enichem's pollution of the Adriatic sea, a political statement that seemed appropriate to the residence of a black madonna. Inside the church in a side niche, we found the icon, whose severe face is untouched by any idealization.

The mosaic façade of the duomo, constructed in the 1960s, depicts pope John XXIII presenting a crown to a very black madonna. The only pope to whose crypt people bring flowers every day, John commended the women's movement and the struggles for colonial independence as "signs of the times" and gave a large impetus to contemporary liberation theologies.[22]

Today the mainstream church (and its supporters) is uneasy with black madonnas. A friendly young priest approached while we gazed at la Sipontina and offered to show us something else, taking us to a statue of Jesus crucified without nails. At the University of Padua, where I presented a paper on black madonnas in May 1990, women scholars offered helpful bibliographical suggestions, but some male professors appear to have drawn defensive fortifications around the subject in this city where there is a dark santa Maria dei Servi (saint Mary of the serfs) and students are radical.[23] At the university where Galileo initiated modern science and where, in the 1970s, students joined revolutionary red brigades, male sociologists of religion said that I should look to what was empirically verifiable: black madonnas are black because they are "Byzantine"; they had been whitened because the skin of the parishioners was white. A woman art historian helped shore up the male bastions, saying that the *simplest* answer for dark and black madonnas was that they are "Byzantine."

Black madonnas may symbolize women's prophetic tradition—beginning with Miriam, sister of Moses,[24] and continuing through the sibyls, who were prophets before and after the christian era. At Loreto, the national sanctuary of a very black madonna that we visited in 1989, ten sibyls stand before ten Jewish prophets on the marble facing of the *casa* that encloses the black madonna inside the church. According to christian interpreters, sibyls were prechristian women who prophesied the coming of christ. According to feminists, sibyls may be regarded as peasant women who kept the memory and the values of the prechristian woman divinity.[25] A clue to the continuity between the earth-mother goddess, sibyls, and black madonnas is the black *sibilla* Libica, who, in the image on the pavement of the cathedral at Siena, is accompanied by snakes.

According to the legend of the black madonna of Loreto, Mary had two dwellings at Nazareth: one in a grotto in a rock, now in the Basilica of the Annunciation at Nazareth, the other her everyday dwelling in which she lived after she married Joseph. It is this house of Mary's everyday life that is said to have been brought by angels to Loreto in 1291 when the crusaders were expelled from Palestine.

Considered "the most important Marian church of Europe" from the sixteenth to the nineteenth centuries,[26] Loreto today, like Lourdes in France, is a major destination of pilgrims in pain or desperation.[27] It is also a favorite honeymoon spot, perhaps in memory of the love poetry and Black woman of the Song of Songs. Like other black madonnas, the one of Loreto is a triangular figure fusing mother and child. The papacy has placed this very popular sanctuary under its direct supervision, considering it "the most renowned marian sanctuary in christendom."[28]

The everyday house of Mary, enclosed in the church at Loreto, suggests the *shekhina,* the indwelling of the feminine presence of god of the cabala. Sibyls preceding Jewish prophets are sculpted on the façade of the everyday dwelling of the black madonna at Loreto. The Hellespontic sibyl precedes the prophet Isaiah, the Phrygian sibyl precedes Daniel, the Tiburtine sibyl

A sibyl/prophetess on the façade of the casa *that encloses the black madonna of Loreto. Photograph by Wallace Birnbaum.*

precedes Amos, the Libyan sibyl precedes Jeremiah, the Delphic sibyl precedes Ezekiel, the Samian sibyl precedes Moses, the Persian sibyl precedes Zechariah, the Cuman sibyl precedes David, the Eritrean sibyl precedes Malachi, and the Cumaean sibyl precedes Balaam.[29]

The sibyls of Loreto are identified with the everyday life of Mary and with the world known to Europeans of the thirteenth century: Asia, Greece, Rome, and Africa. On the façade of the *casa* of the black madonna of Loreto, Jeremiah, the prophet who inveighed against the fall from faith, resembles Moses in carrying the scroll of the moral law. Preceding him, however, is the black Libyan sibyl, who carries a scroll of an earlier moral law.[30]

The meaning of the sibyls and Hebrew prophets on the façade of the house of the black madonna of Loreto may have been uncovered by Elisabeth Schussler Fiorenza. Studying the woman figure in the wisdom literature of the Hebrew scriptures, Fiorenza has documented the hypothesis that Sophia was the god of Israel expressed in the language and imagery of the goddess. Sophia's envoy was Jesus, with a message of equality for all outcasts: women, the suffering, the poor.[31]

The litany of the black madonna of Loreto refers to the *Arca foedris,* the ark of the covenant of Hebrew scripture.[32] In her house at Loreto, the triangular black madonna is tightly swaddled in a robe with semicircular bands, binding the adult Jesus to his mother and evoking Fiorenza's theory that his mother sent Jesus to do her work in the world.

In her landmark theological reconstruction of biblical origins, Fiorenza demonstrates that the same basic story informs all four gospels: "a woman anoints Jesus."[33] The earliest interpretations of Jesus' life and death understood him as "Sophia's messenger and later as Sophia herself."[34] Fiorenza's view that Jesus, as the child of Sophia, was in a long succession of prophets who identified god with the poor, the suffering, outcasts, and those who suffer injustice is suggested in the sibyls who precede ten male prophets on the façade of the dwelling place of the black madonna and her child at Loreto.[35]

The "converging parallels" foreseen by Aldo Moro are visible today in Apulia in vernacular rituals of catholicism and communism. The large pilgrimage to the very black madonna l'Incoronata outside Foggia takes place in the last week of April. The same pilgrims converge, on May 1, at nearby Cerignola for a communist celebration.

May day as the international holiday of workers has historically held connotations of a counterculture celebration. In the early modern period, authorities frowned on the May 1 celebrations of the pagan divinity featuring

The black madonna of Loreto, a national shrine. Reproduced by permission.

dancing around trees in the piazza and roistering. In 1519, the first of May at Rome was celebrated as a festival of sweethearts; doors were decorated with fronds and flower garlands to which sonnets were attached. Vernacular, as opposed to papal, beliefs were suggested at Imola in 1908 when, at the festa of *primo maggio,* prizes were given to nonbaptized babies and to women not married in the church. As worker movements grew in the twentieth century, May day was celebrated as a combination of Workers of the World, Unite and Love One Another.[36]

The convergence of religious and political rituals in Apulia has been noted by Italian cultural anthropologists who bring an "unedited" marxist perspective to popular religious beliefs. In *Il simbolo conteso,* anthropologists point out that in the area around Foggia and Cerignola, after each world war of the twentieth century, women with babies, *bandiere rosse* (red flags of international communism), and statues of their madonnas occupied the lands; easter rituals of the area, moreover, feature red christs portrayed by emigrant workers.[37]

According to legend, on the last Saturday of April in 1001 the black madonna called l'Incoronata appeared in an oak tree in a forest near the present sanctuary. She was seen first by a hunter, then by a poor peasant, Strazzacappa, who (along with his oxen) fell to his knees before the vision. A sanctuary was built, and pilgrimages to this black madonna have flourished for a millennium. About eight hundred thousand pilgrims come to the sanctuary of l'Incoronata each year.[38]

In the middle ages, pilgrimages coincided with pastoral rhythms; Abruzzese shepherds left their families and took their flocks to pasture in the meadows around the sanctuary.[39] Today, in addition to the April pilgrimage commemorating the first appearance of the madonna, the month of August is dedicated to returning emigrants forced by poverty to find work in northern Italy or in foreign countries. Pilgrims to the sanctuary of l'Incoronata bring oil for the lamp that has been burning for a thousand years.

A folk procession called *la cavalcata degli angeli* is part of the pilgrimage. It is a ritual with no equivocation about why the madonna is black, as we observed in 1990, when a Black child was chosen to portray the black madonna in the procession. Symbolizing liberation theology in Italy, the sanctuary is named *Santuario della povera gente* (sanctuary of poor people), where they may find a *segno di sicura speranza* (sign of certain hope) in their pilgrimage in the world. The theme of the pilgrimage is carried on banners declaring *siamo un popolo in cammino* (we are a people on the way).

Underlying the occupations of the land in Apulia after the world wars of the twentieth century was an Italian anarcho-communism combining belief in a miracle-working madonna, ideas from Tommaso Campanella's *Città del Sole,* and beliefs from Karl Marx. Equality is assumed, because "we are all her children." The hope for a world without wars, a world of harmony, joy, love, and happiness, is grounded on this equality, looking to a future when there will no longer be servants and lords, poor and rich, exploited and exploiters.[40]

Apulia is a region economically subordinated to Italy's industrialized north, a case of the Gramscian dichotomy between hegemonic and subaltern cultures. In contemporary unedited marxist language, southern Italy is a subaltern culture that, in addition to economic exploitation, has been *una cultura negata* (a culture denied) by hegemonies that include the church hierarchy, rationalist marxists, and intellectuals who look down on the "magic" in peasant religious beliefs. The ethnographer Ernesto De Martino was influenced by the religious beliefs of Apulians to think about the relevance of ancient myths for a new society, and to ponder the meaning of the immense silence of black madonnas.[41]

One of the meanings of the muteness of black madonnas may lie in a theory of anarchism that Edward Abbey describes as "keeping true to the earth," wherein a good society is characterized by the "voluntary association of self-reliant, self-supporting, autonomous communities made up of free and independent families bound by friendship, kinship, and a tradition of mutual aid." Putting aside the pejorative meanings given the term by people in power, for Abbey "anarchism is democracy taken seriously," as it was in "pre-agricultural, pre-industrial times."[42] Anarchy does not mean "no rule," it means "no rulers."[43] One of the meanings of this kind of anarchism refers to what is implicitly emerging in Italy today, women not as leaders over anyone but as inspirers of genuine democracy.

In the 1970s there was hope that the gains of communists in northern Italy would soon be augmented by a great wave of popular religious and political fervor in the south. However, the contemporary struggle for justice in southern Italy must first deal with organized crime and drug trafficking. In 1990, after the April pilgrimage to the madonna l'Incoronata and the May day political rituals, workers in Cerignola organized a large demonstration and general strike on May 6 and 7 against the mafia in all its many incarnations.[44]

Cerignola, located a few kilometers from the sanctuary of l'Incoronata, black madonna of the poor, has been communist since the end of world war II. Red christs in easter rituals of the region signify *Gesù socialista.* Giuseppe

Di Vittorio, communist leader of the *braccianti* (farmworkers), was familiarly called Peppino; in Italian popular beliefs, there is no deference to religious or political figures. A good source for understanding the meaning of Di Vittorio to braccianti of the south was the large mural located in the town square at the site of the old train station. It was here that emigrant workers departed throughout the twentieth century to find work in the north, and here that they returned, often with bitter, humiliating memories. The mural was so potent in meaning that fascists shot at it. When we searched for the mural in 1990 we were told that it had been moved because it had become a target of mafia and fascist depredation. Houses in Cerignola to this day have pictures of the madonna, of Jesus, and of Giuseppe Di Vittorio. The madonna and her envoy? Does "Peppino," generic name for every man, symbolize all her sons?

In 1990 the traditionally communist May day celebration at Cerignola was blessed by catholic priests, who joined communist mayors and labor leaders in celebrating farm and other workers. The bishop of Cerignola–Ascoli Satriano sent a message celebrating a "diocesan day for solidarity with the world of work," aligning the day with world peace, ecological safeguarding of all creation, and the interdependence of humanity.[45]

Earlier in the twentieth century, catholic priests did not bless worker struggles, siding instead with padroni. Farmworkers, pressed into the deepening miseria of inhuman working conditions, malaria, low wages, having to travel many kilometers to work a fourteen-hour day, seasonal work, isolation, large families, and food reduced to bread in salt water, organized socialist circles. Although their agitation for shorter hours was resisted by the landowners, in 1908 Cerignola won the battle for an eight-hour day and became known as *Cerignola rossa,* or red Cerignola.[46]

Early in the twentieth century, Italian workers dedicated May day to the 1886 Haymarket massacre in the United States when corporate and government police killed striking workers in Chicago. May day in southern Italy became a farmworkers' festival, first socialist, then communist, and always with memories of an earlier age of harmony; tractors were decorated with flowers as well as red flags. In the fascist era, May day was prohibited, but people continued to celebrate the religiopolitical festa by abstaining from work and wearing new clothes. After world war II, workers all over Italy arose spontaneously, inspired by socialist and communist hope. On May day, 1947, at Portella della Ginestra, radical trade unionists and peasants were having a picnic celebrating successes in their struggle for full employment and legal land reform when they were killed in machine-gun crossfire.

"Armed by the American Office of Strategic Services, Giuliano's gang did the job."[47]

Long before the liberation theology of the 1960s and later, popular beliefs of southern Italians identified the hope for a better life with black or dark madonnas and the son, *Gesù socialista*. Rooting their hopes in the earth and madonnas who resembled the earth, they enacted the easter passion with red christs and found the promise of the Judeo-christian scriptures and the promise of marxism mutually sustaining.[48]

Stornelli, short pieces against injustice declaimed during feste, are similar all over Italy. In a collection published at Florence in 1987, stornelli adopted vegetables and fruit to convey masked messages against the authorities. One of the stornelli in the Florence collection identifies a peasant woman with the Black woman of the Song of Songs: "I am naturally black and the sun has not darkened me."[49]

Just as the church attempts to whiten black madonnas, papal authorities, on more than one occasion, have attempted to eliminate rituals of red christs.[50] The connotations of the figures are simultaneously heretical and subversive. Red, analysts have pointed out, connotes the blood of Jesus, the color of international communism, the blood of those who live in misery, and the blood of those who fight for justice. The red cape worn by emigrant workers who portray Jesus in easter rituals resembles the franciscan *cappuccino,* melding the identity of the person into a symbol of everyone. The cross recalls the passion of Mary's son, as well as the misery of life for the poor. Bare feet are a sign of humility and poverty.

Almost all red christs are emigrants who have returned to Cerignola to enact the role in good Friday processions; there is a silent dialogue between red christs and the crowd. "Not one red christ has ever belonged to the middle or upper classes."[51] They obviously differ from the christ of the church; in vernacular belief, red christs identify workers with christ and with equality, liberty, and social justice on earth.[52]

May day at Cerignola has always featured *bambini,* young people, and women, who on the first of May change easter black cloaks for red dresses.[53] In this folk festa, whose ground of belief is similar to that of carnevale, there is cross dressing, singing with sexual allusion, and dancing around a maypole. In the folklore that has grown up around May day in southern Italy, Di Vittorio is said to have gone to work when he was seven, and his voice was so powerful he did not need a megaphone. Asked when they became communist, braccianti say that they were "born communist" and so was Di Vittorio.[54]

The folklore of the black madonna l'Incoronata is found in legends of her apparition in an oak tree in 1001 and in contemporary rituals. Stories of the shepherd who fell on his knees before the apparition are supplemented by contemporary rituals enacted in the "cavalcade of angels" organized by women and men of nearby comunità di base. Base communities, which consider marxism compatible with the gospels, decorate special floats for the cavalcade of angels; saint Agatha is a favorite subject.

Sant'Agata, associated with the festival of the black madonna l'Incoronata, may be in continuum with the Middle Eastern goddess Astarte. Often depicted with bare breasts,[55] in christian interpretation Agatha is a virgin martyr who, because she refused to marry the king of Sicily, was condemned to have her breasts cut off; in church iconography she carries her breasts on a plate. In the vernacular satire of the church story, saint Agatha is celebrated at Catania in Sicily with pastries shaped like breasts.

In the *cavalcata* for the black l'Incoronata, women participants sing in an impassioned manner that conveys their special miseria.[56] In their close relationship to black madonnas, women address them very familiarly. In a popular lament, a recent widow keens that the madonna has "betrayed" her by taking her husband.[57] The allusion suggests seduction by the goddess, who conveys sexuality as well as death.

In stories about l'Incoronata and her appearance in 1001 in an oak tree in the forest of Cervaro, she is said to have proclaimed that she was Madre di dio (mother of god) and asked that a church be built on the site, promising joy and blessings to those who came to venerate her. Basilian and Cistercian monasteries came to be associated with the popular pilgrimage to this black madonna. Later, a shelter for pilgrims and travelers and a hospital were added. After the Napoleonic occupation and the establishment of the Kingdom of the Two Sicilies, the sanctuary of l'Incoronata fell upon hard times, with authorities confiscating its funds.[58] After the 1901 celebration of the apparition, the pilgrimage to l'Incoronata increased in popularity, along with the growth of the Italian worker movement of the twentieth century.

Today the complex of buildings is called *cittadella di Maria* (little city of Mary), "the sanctuary of poor people,"[59] where "everyone feels themselves brothers and sisters because we are children of the same mother."[60] Celebration of Mary in the month of May, now widespread in the christian world, is said to have begun with the apparition of l'Incoronata.[61]

Acting out a ritual with ancient notes, pilgrims to the black madonna circle the sanctuary three times before they enter and sing ancient litanies to the accompaniment of bagpipes. Inside, pilgrims, often on their knees,

L'Incoronata dei Poveri, *the black madonna of the poor, outside Foggia. She personifies the liberation theology of Italy. Reproduced by permission.*

ascend *la scala santa,* the holy ladder, in a "human symphony" of prayers and hopes. At the feet of the black madonna is a perpetually burning lamp whose oil is believed to have healing powers. Villages around the sanctuary are renowned for their healers; Padre Pio of nearby S. Giovanni Rotondo, whose miracles are still recounted, drew thousands a few decades ago.

Like other black madonnas, l'Incoronata suggests African, Semitic, Asian, and European origins. She is black as African goddesses and the Black woman of the Song of Songs of the Hebrew scriptures, and Asian in feature. The black madonna l'Incoronata may be a metaphor for multicultural liberation theologies of Italy.

Sicilian historians of nineteenth-century Italy assumed that the island was originally attached to the land mass of Africa, and that the original racial origin of Sicilians was African.[62] The late Professor Matteo Sansone, the archaeologist who directed me to sites of the goddess in Apulia, advised that the prehistoric peoples of the Gargano and of Sicily were Eurasian.

Referring to his archaeological investigations in southern Italy, Professor Sansone advised that the prehistoric woman divinity was called *la dea madre* (mother goddess) and *signora della vita e della morte* (woman divinity of life and death). Her images were often *senza volto e senza nome* (without a face and without a name).[63] In our discussion of black madonnas, he said that church whitening had "ruined" them, a depredation he considered similar to the recent theft of the black madonna of Conversano.

CHAPTER 8

multicultural dimensions of black

madonnas • multicultural liberation

theologies and politics

B LACK MADONNAS of Italy imply multicultural liberation
theologies and politics, a dynamic spiral from the
prehistoric earth mother, the Black woman of the Song of Songs of Hebrew
writings, the subordinate role of women in established religions, the experience of the Jews and Muslims of Italy, the franciscan strain of catholicism,
the Waldensian protestants of Italy, the liberation theology of contemporary
left catholics, Aldo Moro's belief that catholicism and communism are
"converging parallels," and the contemporary base communities of Italy that
extend a hand to liberation movements of the east and the south of the
world.

At the center of this spiral is a black woman the color of the earth, the
goddess denigrated by male-dominant religions who endured in vernacular
traditions, a metaphor for the subaltern similarity of women, the persecuted,
the marginal, outcasts, the poor, and those far from home.

Contemporary scholarly interest in the relationship of black madonnas to
the Black woman of the Song of Songs may be traced to Leonard Moss. An
American soldier of Jewish heritage wandering around southern Italy at the
end of world war II, he came upon the black madonna of Lucera and was
reminded of the Song of Songs:[1]

Yes, I am black! and radiant—
O city women watching me—
As black as Kedar's goathair tents
Or Solomon's fine tapestries.

Will you disrobe me with your stares?
The eyes of many morning suns
Have pierced my skin, and now I shine
Black as the light before the dawn.

And I have faced the angry glare
Of others, even my mother's sons
Who sent me out to watch their vines
While I neglected all my own.[2]

When Moss asked a priest why the madonna of Lucera was black, the cleric closed the subject: "My son, she is black because she is black."[3] Finding his insight about a bond between black madonnas and the Black woman of the Song of Songs confirmed in the inscription at the base of the black madonna of Tindari in Sicily, *Nigra sum sed furnosa* (I am black and beautiful), Moss collected a hundred examples of black madonnas of Europe, and in 1952 he presented a paper to a professional conference in the United States.

Whereupon, "every priest and nun walked out."[4] Afterward, in Moss's university town, a local priest delivered a sermon against "campus atheists" who would "defile the name of the Blessed Virgin."[5] His attention now seriously engaged, Moss became a cultural anthropologist. Continuing his study, he noted that rituals associated with black madonnas resembled rituals associated with the prechristian woman divinity.[6]

The Semitic element in the phenomenon of black madonnas, first noted by Moss, has piqued my interest and that of others. In 1990 a museum guide at Avellino asked, "Have you noticed the similarity between the women Modigliani painted and black and Byzantine madonnas of Italy?" Amedeo Modigliani's twentieth-century paintings of his Jewish mistress are a reminder that the thread from the prehistoric woman divinity to black madonnas may have circled Lilith (the rebellious first wife of Adam), Hagar (the Egyptian slave woman who bore Ishmael and was cast out with him), Miriam, sister of Moses and prophetess, the Black woman of the Song of Songs, and Mary, the Jewish mother of Jesus.

Modigliani's paintings are collected in the museum at Leghorn, a city that Arnaldo Momigliano, Jewish-Italian historian, has located as a major point of the Jewish diaspora in the early common era and a major destination of Jews after their expulsion from Spain in 1492. A center of radical religious and political beliefs, Leghorn is near the black madonna of Montenero. Other Italian cities where there are Jewish communities and black madonnas include Venice, Bologna, Naples, Noto, Padua, Palermo, Siena, Trapani, and Rome.[7]

Marranos are central to this story. Forcibly converted to christianity during the inquisition and expelled from Spain in 1492, Marranos continued to observe christian rituals outwardly while keeping their own faith secretly.[8] This is analogous to Italian women who historically adopted external forms of catholicism while keeping prechristian beliefs.[9]

Phoenicians, or Semites of Canaan, settled on the western shore of Sicily long before the christian age. Asherah, goddess of the Canaanites, was officially suppressed, but her memory was kept alive in the oral tradition and preserved secretly in cabalistic writings not accessible to women. In vernacular Judaism, the memory of the goddess may have melded Asherah (Astarte) with Lilith, the *shekhina,* the Shabbat, Hochmah (goddess of wisdom), and with the woman divinity Matronit.[10]

The memory may have encircled Hagar, the Egyptian slave who conceived a child with Abraham. Phyllis Trible describes Hagar as one of the first females in scripture to experience use, abuse, and rejection.[11] In Canaan, Sarai said to Abram that she was barren and that he should go to her Black slave Hagar to conceive a child. Sarai afflicted Hagar, Abram expelled her, and the "runaway pregnant maid" fled "from the house of bondage to the wilderness." The lord sent a messenger to tell Hagar that she would bear a child. Unlike the case in a later annunciation, the child Ishmael "will be a wild ass of a man, his hand against everyone and everyone's hand against him. And against the face of all his brothers he will dwell."[12] Hagar, mother of an outcast, is herself, for Phyllis Trible, a symbol of the oppressed, an exploited Black woman who mirrors the afflictions of others.[13]

In the prechristian era there was a constant interchange of Jews from the Middle East with Blacks of Africa and an intermingling of the Semitic goddesses of Carthage and the African goddesses of Egypt. After the destruction of the temple in 70 C.E., Jews in diaspora around the Mediterranean founded their oldest European settlement at Rome. Christianity in Italy arose in Trastevere, the Jewish quarter of Rome. In Santa Maria in Trastevere, the earliest christian church of Rome, the madonna is depicted as the Black woman of the Song of Songs. Jews in diaspora came to the Adriatic coast and, after their expulsion from Spain in 1492, to Liguria. The Adriatic and Ligurian coasts of Italy are characterized by evidence of the culture of the goddess, Jewish communities, sanctuaries of black madonnas, and a politics of justice.

Primo Levi, the great Jewish writer of Italy whose works on the holocaust are required reading today for Italian schoolchildren, had a perceptive passage in *If Not Now, When?* Someone said that perhaps Italians saved Jews during world war II because they were "good Christians." Someone else responded, "I'm not sure of it. Even as Christians, the Italians are odd. They go to Mass, but they curse. They ask favors of the Madonna and the saints but they don't seem to believe much in God."[14]

"Italian Jews are as odd as the Catholics," one of Levi's figures noted. Jews of Italy speak Italian dialects and look Italian. There has never been a pogrom in Italy, "not even when the Roman Church told the Christians to despise the Jews and accused them all of being usurers, not even when Mussolini decreed the racial laws, not even when northern Italy was occupied by the Germans; nobody in Italy knows what a pogrom is."[15]

Vernacular Jewish and vernacular christian beliefs may have merged in Italy. Asherah, goddess of Canaan, like certain Graeco-Roman goddesses and christian saints, was believed to promote fertility in women and to ease childbirth.[16] In public shrines on hilltops, or under leafy trees,[17] Asherah was popularly associated with Yahweh, probably as his wife,[18] a divine couple evident in the folklore of Italy.[19] The original meaning of the name Astarte (Ashtoreth), like that of Demeter, was "womb." After the fourteenth century, a figure, Matronit,[20] appears in the Jewish folklore of Italy who considerably resembles la Signora of christian folklore.

Raphael Patai, a scholar of the "Hebrew goddess," has analyzed the significance of the shekhina, particularly in the cabalistic and hasidic traditions, and among Sephardic and Oriental Jews: "The *Shekhina,* the feminine aspect (or 'person') of the Godhead was (and is) a living reality in the belief system of considerable contingents of the Jewish people,"[21] an "independent, feminine divine entity prompted by her compassionate nature to argue with God in defense of man."[22] Observing a similarity between the popular Hebrew shekhina and popular Italian christian madonnas, Patai found that "the deep emotional attachment of the simple, unsophisticated followers of the *Kabbala* to the *Shekhina* was comparable" to the relationship of Italian or Spanish villagers to their madonnas. "In both cases it cannot be denied that one is faced with the veneration of a goddess, and it is impossible to dispute that she means more for the satisfaction of deep-seated religious emotional needs than God Himself."[23]

The dark madonna of santa Maria in Trastevere, who has been identified with the Black woman of the Song of Songs, resides in a church whose neighborhood has always been that of the poor. Saint Francis selected Trastevere as the place for his service to lepers.

At the altar of the church of santa Maria in Trastevere ("the first christian edifice of Rome, certainly the first dedicated to the veneration of the virgin"),[24] there is a motto, *Fons Olei*, referring to a spring of mineral oil that emerged in 38 B.C.E. and where the church was built. Jews of the neighborhood regarded the effusion as a sign of the coming of the messiah, an interpretation taken up by christians, who built the church to Maria in Trastevere in 337–52 C.E.[25] Today the church presides over a fountain in the piazza of santa Maria in Trastevere where people come to organize demonstrations for the homeless and to protest racism and imperialist aggression against third-world peoples. A mosaic on the façade of the church depicts Mary nursing her son, with two women alongside holding lamps. The image suggests the *"ekklesia* [church] of women" analyzed by Elisabeth Schussler Fiorenza.[26]

Marcia Falk has added another dimension to understanding the dark madonna of santa Maria in Trastevere, who is identified with the Black woman of the Song of Songs. A Jewish feminist biblical scholar, for whom the Song "is the only book of love poetry in the Bible,"[27] Falk has found many voices in this poem, which was created between 950 and 200 B.C.E.[28] The Song, according to Falk, is not concerned with religious ritual or with marriage, "but with the various emotions of erotic love."[29] Orally transmitted by the Jews for two millennia, the Song is still chanted on the sabbath of passover. Sephardic Jews, who follow the cabala, chant the Song weekly, just before the sabbath.[30]

"The . . . rich, sensual, emotionally expressive, and often playful language of the Song's female and male voices," states Falk, "seems to evidence a nonsexist, nonhierarchical culture—unique in the Bible."[31] Nature, in the Song, "is neither idealized as good nor subjugated—or demonized—because wild. Instead, it is depicted in the richness of its many manifestations, and always with respect for its power."[32] The mother is a pervasive theme: "The mother's house is the most intimate and protected environment in the Song." There is "no mention of a father—or of the father's home" anywhere in the poem.[33]

The black madonna of Lucera, whose sanctuary is built on a site of the indigenous goddess Mefite, suggests the mingled history of Jews and Muslims in Italy. At Lucera, whose black madonna inspired Leonard Moss, Jews arrived in diaspora in the first centuries of christianity; Muslims come in the eighth century and fortified the ancient Samnite settlement.[34] In 1237 the Holy Roman emperor Frederick II called on the Muslims of Lucera to defeat the Milanese, whereupon the pope excommunicated him for favoring Saracens. Christian Normans, allied with the pope, fought Muslims. Muslims who returned to Lucera had to feign christianity if they chose to remain. Does the black madonna of Lucera connote deep beliefs in the indigenous Samnite goddess Mefite, the Black woman of the Song of Songs of Hebrew scripture, and suppress woman-centered beliefs of Muslims who ruled southern Italy for six hundred and Sicily for four hundred years?

More culturally advanced than the Goths who preceded them, Muslims "spoke a language enriched by poetry." Their geographers, poets, musicians, doctors, mathematicians, astronomers, philosophers, and jurists made the Muslim towns of southern Italy and Sicily centers of arts, agriculture, and commerce.[35] Today, Muslims live in North Africa, the Middle East, and Asia, the arc of the earth where Isis, Astarte, and Cybele were once venerated and whence beliefs in African and Asian goddesses came to southern Italy, the islands, and Rome.

Almost a thousand years ago, Muslims were defeated politically by the Normans, but their presence in Italy has remained in the dialects, in the folk stories about Giufà and his mother, Giustizia (Justice), in the Moorish motifs of the mosaics of Monreale, in the ice cream and sweets Muslims brought to the south, and in the carob trees, date palms, mulberry, and bitter orange and lemon trees they planted. The legacy may also be felt in the sense of justice of Sicilian writers—notably Leonardo Sciascia, who traced his ancestry to Muslim forebears.

Tullio Tentori, Italian anthropologist and close friend of Leonard Moss, has brought a contemporary left-catholic perspective to the subject of black madonnas. Pointing to pervasive evidence of the culture of the prechristian goddess in the Naples area, Tentori analyzed the fervent pilgrimage to the black madonna dell'Arco as popular resistance, grounded on prechristian beliefs, to the catholic church.

Outside Naples at Baia are a temple to Diana and a grove named for the triple goddess, Hecate. The "cave of the Sibyl," a black sibyl, may be found at Cuma. Temples to Isis and Venus have been found at Pompeii,[36] and temples to Hera and Athena at Paestum, south of Naples. The National Archaeology Museum at Naples houses a renowned Aphrodite and a stunning black Diana. In almost pointed fashion, the pilgrimage to the madonna dell'Arco takes place on Monday, the day of the moon goddess, after easter Sunday, the church holiday celebrating the resurrection of Jesus.

Pomigliano dell'Arco is a suburb of Naples, with its tumultuous culture and politics, whose sanctuary to a black madonna is located in a neighborhood where automotive workers of Alfa Sud live. In the 1990s people of this area continue to respect the name "communist," in spite of the downfall of the former soviet bloc, and many have joined the small Rifondazione comunista, dedicated to reconstructing a democratic communist party. Ferdinando Balzamo, communist activist, said that he signed up in the party after the death of Berlinguer; that communism for his generation meant struggles for peace, the referendum for legal abortion, and the battle for rights; and that communism has nothing to do with central and eastern European dictatorships.[37] Women and men workers of this area rejected the proposal in 1990 to drop "communist" from the name of the Partito comunista italiano, insisting that communism means "justice." Vincenzo Barbato, secretary of the Enrico Berlinguer section of Alfa-Lancia of Pomigliano and member of the central committee of the communist party, spoke in 1990 of the continuing significance of communism for Italian workers of the south, and for all workers in the "society of wolves" of postindustrial capitalism.[38]

In ex-voto drawings of the madonna dell'Arco, she is painted black; images whose sale the church supervises are white. The statue I saw inside the sanctuary had a pneumatic gray face that seemed to reflect all the pain and hope pilgrims bring to her, along with overtones of an avenging deity of justice that is dramatically different from the resigned and sorrowful *Pietà* in the vatican.

Multitudes visit the madonna dell'Arco. In 1972, the year Tentori closely analyzed the ritual, two hundred thousand people came; the number has subsequently grown to half a million.[39] At dawn on the Monday after easter, *fujenti* (literally, those who flee) come running from Naples and surrounding villages carrying heavy candles, banners, ex-voto objects, and flowers. Labor unions, sometimes catholic, sometimes not, organize the pilgrim groups.[40] The socioeconomic base of the pilgrimage, for Tentori, is a "destitute and abandoned population readily inclined to invoke magic and the supernatural against the exploitation and domination to which other men subjected them."[41] Both genders and all ages participate in the highly emotional pilgrimage; in 1990 I observed that most of the pilgrims were young men.

"At the door of the church, just before entering, each company regroups," states Tentori, "and, with dancing steps, all move forward and then backward three times." This dance step, which I had earlier observed in easter rituals of the black madonna of Trapani, has been analyzed by musicologists as having sexual overtones. The pattern also reminds me of the down-and-up curves of the spiral of the goddess.

Pilgrims cross the threshold of the sanctuary on their knees. Before the church and the civil authorities prohibited the practice, they kissed the ground as they dragged their bodies to the altar (some still do).[42] In a setting of moans and loud cries, "the *fujenti* seem to be in a trance, to be 'different' from their usual selves." Some kneel, some stand, some run; others fling themselves "abruptly to the ground and the impact of their bodies on the marble floor resounds like a series of slaps."[43] Fainting, convulsive fits, and the sound of ambulances accompany "aggressive and insistent supplications that reflect all the sufferings and frustrations of the poor."[44] In 1972, 25,000 fujenti came on pilgrimage, of whom "about 1,000 required treatment in the first aid station."[45]

Two thousand years ago, on nearby Mount Vesuvius, Roman slaves venerated the woman divinity. The detritus of two millennia of patriarchal culture may be evident in the "violent aggressiveness with strong sexual overtones" that Roberto De Simone, a musicologist, has found in contemporary dancing in the streets after the pilgrimage to the madonna dell'Arco. Men perform most of the dances. Women dance by themselves in others. In a dance that may express male love and fear of the goddess (and ambivalence toward women), a group of men put a woman in the center of a ring and seem "to feign an assault upon her." The sound of tambourines and castanets that accompanies the dancing reminded De Simone of "the music that accompanied the ancient cults of Cybele."[46]

On May day, 1593, the church laid the cornerstone of the present sanctuary of the madonna dell'Arco. Tentori suggests that the church may have adopted the pilgrimage of the madonna dell'Arco as part of the expansion of the marian cult after the Council of Trent (1545–63), embracing the pilgrimage to this popular madonna in the hope of controlling it.[47] Church control has been somewhat short of effective.

Differing from anthropologists who take a patronizing view of peasant belief in magic or who posit passivity as the political implication of catholicism, Tentori describes pilgrims to the madonna dell'Arco as "outcasts, the downtrodden, the exploited," who strain at the "yoke other men inflict upon them," who put their trust in the supernatural in a blend of magic and religion that may be an empowering "act of liberation."[48]

Noting nearby monuments to Cybele and Isis, Tentori argues that the church may have grafted the cult of the madonna "onto a deep-rooted pre-Christian religious tradition that was congenital to the people."[49] A spring ritual, the pilgrimage to the madonna dell'Arco may tap the memory of Attis, son of Cybele, who was called "the good shepherd," who died and was reborn. His mystery, like that of another son, was celebrated in springtime.[50]

Today Dominicans administer the sanctuary of the madonna dell'Arco with alms collected by fujenti and record the miracles she is believed to have performed over the last three hundred years for peasants, fishermen, sailors, and others. In attempting to control the pilgrimage, the church has used persuasion as well as prohibition. In 1972, calling fujenti "beloved brethren" whose "simplicity," "sacrifices," and "enthusiasm" were admirable, the bishop "recommended" that pilgrims not dance and not carry the image of the madonna when soliciting alms. Pilgrims were admonished to behave with dignity, propriety, and discipline lest the popular pilgrimage become "nothing more than an expression of resurgent paganism." Condemning roistering after the pilgrimage, the episcopal missive pronounced: "The family is sacred. God curses anyone who endangers the welfare of the family."[51]

The pilgrimage to the madonna dell'Arco, for Tentori, demonstrates the "antithesis between the state religion and the religion of the people." He finds this antithesis throughout the "unbroken religious history of Italy," including christianity, to which the "Roman state assigned the task of resolving the age-old problem of the religious unification of the empire."[52]

Member of a comunità di base at Rome, Tentori expresses left-catholic dissent in describing the catholic church as a complex theological and financial structure that historically took on the characteristics of a secular state. For him, popular beliefs, in contrast to church doctrine, are "the living religion of man: the Christian religion of the people, imbued with misery and suffering, wavering between faith and magic . . . a liberator of man the slave."[53]

Franciscan christianity, Tentori points out, was originally a folk religion that rendered the secular holy and the sacred profane. Papal and popular religions have coexisted in the history of christianity. "So-called popular forms of religion are the religion of the subordinate class (even though members of the dominant class may participate in them)."[54] Amplifying Annabella Rossi's thesis that pilgrimages to popular madonnas are festivals of the poor,[55] for Tentori, middle- and upper-class "haves" look to god to reassure privileged positions. The poor put their trust in holy figures to liberate themselves from personal misfortune and social exploitation.[56] An "unedited" marxist, Tentori believes that the religious beliefs of the poor were expressed in popular pilgrimages and historically persecuted by state and church.[57]

The somewhat tense relationship between the catholic church and pilgrimages to black madonnas was evident in a 1966 proclamation requiring pilgrims to the madonna dell'Arco to attend church before departing. Women were singled out: "Women are hereby forbidden to take part in the companies or squadrons formed by men. It is fitting that they proceed in separate groups, in a dignified manner, without running and that they be decently dressed. Let them exercise self-control to avoid the ridiculous fainting spells to which their highly emotional natures may incline them."[58]

An ex-voto painting of the madonna dell'Arco depicts catholic priests of the inquisition interrogating and torturing two women as witches, while the black madonna watches.[59] The area around the sanctuary is popularly known as *il paese delle streghe,* the land of witches. A recent study of this area describes the "history of a mentality that lasts longer than historic time," a mentality more concerned with "coherence" than with scientific truth,[60] looking to "a vision of the world that satisfies the soul."[61]

The vision is viewed with some hostility by the catholic church; many popular beliefs do not adhere to official doctrine. The pervasive vernacular belief in the evil eye, *mal'occhio,* implies the reality of the goddess, her negative as well as beneficent characteristics. The evil eye is thought to bring misfortune, which healers in the tradition of the goddess can exorcise. A prayer exorcising the evil eye contains heretical phrases:

Occhio che m'hai occhiato
duie santi m'hanno salvato
Gesù Cristo e la Madonna
Vattene
via via
lu cumanda la Vergine Maria
Nel nome del Padre, del Figliulo, ecc. (per tre volte)[62]

In this popular prayer, two "saints" have saved the person from the consequences of the evil eye: Jesus and the madonna. Mary's "command" exorcises the mal'occhio. There are at least two heresies in this prayer, that of calling Gesù Cristo a saint and that of believing Mary to be more powerful than her son. The heresies are covered by ritual invocation of church doctrine, *"Nel nome del Padre, del Figliulo, ecc. (per tre volte)"* (in the name of the father, the son, etc., for three times). The widespread finger symbol for exorcising the mal'occhio suggests the vulva and legs of the goddess.[63]

Small wonder that bishops of this region constantly searched for heretics. In 1692 a bishops' synod castigated activities of women in the area of the Sannio in the Campagna, the locality of the black madonna dell'Arco, a region where archaeological evidence of the culture of the goddess is pervasive, sanctuaries of black madonnas attract passionate pilgrims, and stories about witches abound. The synod declared, "Be on guard that bad women have made a pact with the devil, that on the night of Saint John the Baptist they go into the meadows to pick a certain green ['*cardo*'] from whose flowers they can find signs of marriage or not, depending on whether the flowers bloom or die."[64] As late as 1940, bishops warned against the popular custom of placing bull's horns (sign of the goddess) over doorways and against popular beliefs in La Dormiente del Sannio, a mountain in the area whose form is popularly believed to be the earth mother sleeping.[65]

In April and May 1990 I went to southern Italy to see for myself and learned, almost physically, the depth of the beliefs associated with the black madonna dell'Arco, the religious and political implications of the "great black slave mother" of Montevergine near Avellino, and the import for liberation theologies and politics of the pilgrimage of the black madonna l'Incoronata near Foggia.

We arrived in the Naples area the day after easter in time to see the end of the pilgrimage to the madonna dell'Arco. The sanctuary, strewn with flowers, ex-voto objects, and candles, looked as if it had been invaded by an army of believers. The wail of ambulances continued into the night as pilgrims went on hurling themselves to the marble pavement of the church.

Contrasting with conventional descriptions of religion in Italy, this was clearly not a matter of old women in black. Pilgrims, mostly young and male, were dressed in white with blue sashes, and it was for young men, for the most part, that the ambulances came. And many came. The number of pilgrims and visitors to this sanctuary has increased in recent years to five hundred thousand annually.[66]

The next day we went to the sanctuary of the madonna of Montevergine, built on a mount above Avellino. Here we encountered one of several black madonnas that have been whitened by the church. Men, women, and children climb the forty-five hundred feet to the sanctuary; until the church prohibited the practice in the middle of the twentieth century, they kissed the earth at each step.

The sanctuary is situated in the massif of Partenio at the eastern limit of the valley of the Irpinia. A popular story recounts that once there were seven madonnas, sisters, of whom the madonna of Montevergine was considered the ugliest. She ran away to the high mountain above Avellino so that the faithful would have to search to find her. When pilgrims reach the madonna, they discover that she is the most beautiful of all. Black before she was whitened by the church, the madonna of Montevergine is popularly known as Mamma schiavona, great slave mother.[67] In memory of the outcast Egyptian black slave mother, Hagar?

Surprised to find a throng of pilgrims in the sanctuary the week *after* easter, I realized that in Italy the days after the church holiday that commemorates the resurrection of the son are a time of popular celebration of black madonnas, culminating in May day rituals. These hark back to prehistoric celebrations of the goddess, and, in the modern era, came to be associated with the international holiday of workers of the world.[68]

Although whitened by the church, the originally black madonna of Montevergine, like Cybele, on whose site her sanctuary was built, is an Asian woman. On her lap she holds Jesus depicted as a miniature adult. The guidebook of the sanctuary describes *"la taumaturga Immagine della Madonna,"* the miracle-working image of the madonna.[69]

Adjoining the sanctuary of the madonna of Montevergine, a permanent vernacular art exhibit depicts nativity scenes of the world, suggesting the great black slave mother's nurture of all her different children. Nativity scenes created by folk artists depict the story of mother and child in Africa, Asia, North and South America, and Europe. Different cultural versions of this ancient story of mother and child are depicted in Native American, African, Eskimo, and Vietnamese nativity scenes. Extending the story backward in time, one setting is a nativity scene in a prechristian Sardinian *nuraghe* (large conical dwellings constructed of rocks). Corroborating Gramsci's view that there are many kinds of catholicism in Italy, one nativity scene depicts Sicilian peasants, while another presents courtiers in an elegant Venetian salon.[70] An arresting aspect of the vernacular art exhibit adjoining the sanctuary of Montevergine is that the Italian sites chosen to portray the story of mother and child are Bologna, Venice, the Irpinia, Naples, Rome, Molise, the Abruzzi, Apulia, and Sicily, all places with sanctuaries of black madonnas.

The Museo Irpino, near Montevergine, has a rich collection of images of the prechristian woman divinity. Near Benevento, renowned in Italian folklore as the site of witch reunions, a wooden sculpture of the formidable goddess Mefite of the indigenous Samnites was found—an image of a goddess with circle eyes, dated the fourth century B.C.E. Images in the museum include Demeter carrying a little pig[71] and Hera, the Greek mother goddess, seated on a throne. Conveying a sense of time that looks backward as well as forward, the "italic" sanctuary in the museum merges the Roman goddess Juno with the indigenous goddess in a figure called Giunone Mefitide. The spiral of time is also suggested in a neolithic image of the prechristian goddess, who is given a christian name, Madonna delle Grazie.[72]

After observing black madonnas of the Campagna, we went to Apulia, where red poppies and wild spring flowers covered hillsides and meadows in a dazzle of color and where the "converging parallels" of communism and catholicism envisioned by Aldo Moro are palpable. In this region bordering the Adriatic, where the culture of the goddess survived longer than it did elsewhere, there are many sanctuaries of black madonnas. Living in a restored *pagliaia,* a peasant dwelling where *contadini* used to live with their farm animals, by day we explored archaeological sites of the goddess and sanctuaries of black madonnas. At night we listened to speeches for upcoming local and regional elections. Communists, christian democrats, socialists, social democrats, and *missini,*[73] in the Aldo Moro square of Mattinata, offered similar programs to foster employment, oppose the mafia, and save the environment.

In the last week of April we joined pilgrims going to the procession of angels of the black madonna l'Incoronata near Foggia and one week later joined them again in May day communist rituals. Mattinata, like many cities of Italy today, has a communist mayor; in 1990 the mayor presided with a catholic priest over the communist May day celebration, implicitly enacting Aldo Moro's version of liberation theology and politics.

Enacted on May day in 1990 at Mattinata was a deepening of marxist theory to include loss of culture. Southern Italians who left Italy early in the twentieth century hoping for a better life in the Americas were commemorated in a ceremony with a mother forged of dark metal watching her children leave. The May day ceremony was sponsored, in part, by emigrants who have returned to their homeland.

From our pagliaia we could see the Adriatic coast, where the history of southern Italy had been enacted—Dauni, Greeks and Romans, and Jews in diaspora. Saint Peter, according to legend, stopped here, followed by Byzantines, Muslims, Normans, and others. Apulia's indigenous goddess culture welcomed other women divinities but resisted invading cultures with a dominant male divinity. Marija Gimbutas has pointed out that peoples of the coastal areas of Apulia, as well as islands of the Mediterranean, kept their goddess cultures a very long time, in Apulia until 1500 B.C.E.

Apulian archaeological sites of the goddess near the black madonna l'Incoronata of Foggia are found at Paglicci, Castelluccio dei Sauri, Passo di Corvo, Grotta Scaloria, and Porto Badisco. The goddess culture of prehistoric Apulia is documented in museum artifacts painted and incised with her signs: whorls, dots, meanders, spirals, and circles.[74] The political implications of the civilization of the goddess are suggested in the reconstruction, in the Museo Civico Foggia, of a neolithic communal village at Passo di Corvo. People lived in circular or elliptical huts in small cooperative villages. Each dwelling was surrounded by a circular ditch to protect domestic animals. The village was circumscribed by a large irrigation circle. Circular houses in circular villages seem to me a creative architectural resolution of the conundrum of keeping individualism within communalism.[75]

Many artifacts with signs of the goddess, particularly the double spiral, are found in the Museo Civico Foggia.[76] One stela of the late bronze age found at Castelluccio dei Sauri is an image of the goddess in which it is unclear whether the circles are eyes or breasts;[77] enlightenment as nurturance? The museum guide showed us uncatalogued holdings, inquired about my research, and offered himself as an instance of a person who considers the goddess, black madonnas, and liberation theology and politics a coherent spiral of beliefs.

At the Museo Nazionale at Manfredonia, we studied artifacts of the Dauni, who crossed the Adriatic and established themselves first in sparse agricultural holdings and then in villages on the tableland of Apulia. Funerary stelae of the Dauni of the seventh and sixth centuries B.C.E. abound with symbols of the goddess: whorls, meanders, spirals, circles, dots, and depictions of women engaged in peaceful activities. Men on Dauni stelae are depicted carrying weapons. Professor Matteo Sansone, an authority on the history and archaeology of the Gargano, advised that the culture of the Dauni was largely peaceable (perhaps because the values of the goddess still prevailed), in comparison with subsequent invading cultures of Greeks, Romans, Longobards, Moors, and Normans, who tried to impose warrior religions.

At the museum in Bari an exhibit on the women of classical Magna Graecia documented the persistence of symbols of the goddess: *fibulae* (safety pins in the shape of a serpent), spiral bracelets, and spiral necklaces.[78] Fifth-century B.C.E. gorgons with tresses of serpents suggest that by this date the values of the goddess were interpreted negatively by a dominant male culture. Yet the ubiquity of busts of Demeter in the fourth and third centuries B.C.E. indicates the continuing valence of the mother goddess. Resistance to invading male cultures in Apulia is visible in many artifacts of women figures holding serpents. Popular resistance to invading male-dominant cultures is evident in the comic, bottle-shaped authority figures people have put up over their doors for more than two thousand years.

Atop a mountain in the Piedmont is the sanctuary of the very black madonna of Oropa. Originally a Waldensian sanctuary for the poor, later it became a place where heretics were persecuted in a region where women were burned as witches.[79] Waldensians, espousing an ideal of poverty and simplicity, were twelfth-century precursors of the protestant reformation. Persecuted because they held that lay men and women held the right to preach, and that one could pray outside of the church, today Waldenses, the major protestant sect in catholic Italy, add another cultural thread to contemporary Italian religious beliefs and politics.[80] Together with the Jews and left catholics of Italy, Waldensian protestants are associated with liberation theologies and politics from the perspective of the poor.[81]

The shelter for the poor at Oropa, according to folklore, was founded by saint Eusebius, who is said to have brought a Lucan wooden statue of the madonna from Jerusalem. Like other black or dark madonnas of Italy, the face of the madonna of Oropa is at once archaic, African, and Asian. "The stylish waving of the hair, the belt around the hips, the draping of the robe and of the cloak are also archaic and oriental in character. . . . The face of the infant Jesus is not that of a child, but that of a little man."[82] Among the miracles associated with this madonna, as recounted by local storytellers, is that, although the statue has been located in a damp place for hundreds of years, there is no sign of deterioration and never a speck of dust on the faces of the mother and child.[83]

The Lucan image of the black madonna is said to have been placed at Oropa by saint Eusebius[84] when the area was "still a seat of superstition and pagan cult" and a favored retreat for hermits.[85] After the fourteenth century, the black madonna of Oropa was called upon to protect the people from drought, floods, and famine.[86] In 1990, Lidia Menapace, Italian feminist theorist of a "good marxism," encouraged my research of black madonnas and told me of a popular song, "Tu sei bruna ma che bella," ascribing the inscription from the Song of Songs, "I am black and beautiful," to a beloved. "Be sure," she said, "to visit the black madonna of Oropa," which she remembers from her childhood in nearby Novara.[87]

In 1991, the mafia was responsible for a particularly bloody assassination at Palmi in Calabria, a few yards from the black madonna della Sacra Lettera e della Varia in the city's duomo. In southern Italy and Sicily, cities share black madonnas, a custom that upsets scholars' categories. In folklore, the madonna of Palmi is black; the madonna of Messina, with whom she is associated, is painted white. In vernacular belief, however, the madonna of Messina is considered black.

According to the popular story, early in the christian era the madonna sent a letter to the people of Messina blessing them. The Messinese adopted her as the patron saint of their city and placed a statue of the Madonnina in the Strait of Scylla and Charybdis to protect people against pestilence, earthquakes, and, in a revealing phrase, "atrocious dominations."[88] A few kilometers away at the tip of the Italian boot, the people of Palmi adopted the madonna of Messina and depicted her as black. During the great plague of 1571, the people of Palmi took in refugees from Messina. Sharing madonnas, as they later were to share work and responsibility in cooperatives,[89] the Messinese, in gratitude to the people of Palmi, gave them a black hair of their madonna, said to have been sent by Mary from Jerusalem.[90]

The lock of hair is placed in a special vessel and presides over the festa of the black madonna of Palmi. In this ritual, two giants (one black, one white), representing the progenitors of the people of Calabria, parade through the streets, and a poor girl with black hair is chosen to represent the black madonna. In a vernacular version of the church doctrine of the assumption of Mary to heaven, men carry a heavy iron construction, the Varia, on which the girl personifying the black madonna ascends. The ritual implies, heretically, that people construct their own salvation.

Contemporary vernacular rituals of Italy, according to a southern Italian historian, express the passage of western civilization in the sixteenth century "from scholasticism into the piazza."[91] When the clergy as actors in religious rituals gave way to artisans of confraternities and people's leagues of mutual aid, popular processions enacted beliefs previously suppressed by the church. In sixteenth-century processions at Messina, people carried giant figures of Saturn, who presided over saturnalias, and his "wife Rhea," "or Cybele,"[92] a popular ritual that merged the Cretan goddess Rhea with the Anatolian goddess Cybele.

In the popular festival at Palmi that celebrates the assumption of the madonna to heaven, the heavy iron Varia is carried by confraternities of porters, mariners, peasants, butchers, iron workers, and others while the crowd moans, cries, and shouts. In the 1920 festival of the assumption, a poem lamenting "another war" addressed *"padre eterno"* in a manner that suggests why popular beliefs and rituals look to dark madonnas connoting

The black madonna of Palmi. Reproduced by permission.

the earth and to human effort, not to a transcendent father. "Forgive us, *patreternu,* you are old and do not see that people are dying of thirst, without homes, miserable, and that Palmi is an abandoned city."[93]

At Seminara, in Calabria, the black madonna is called Maria Santissima dei Poveri, very sainted Mary of the poor, "queen of nations." Popular celebration of this black madonna on August 15 offers a vernacular counterpoint to church celebration of the canonical version of the assumption of the madonna to heaven. Carmela Piccolo, who has migrated from Seminara to the United States, remembers that the festa was the largest in Calabria, with thousands of people coming by train, bus, mules, horses, and on foot. The citizens of

Seminara put food on outdoor tables so that all could eat, and pilgrims danced in a circle to the music of harmonicas and of ancient musical instruments, bagpipes and tambourines.

The folk story about the black madonna of Seminara underlines that she is, indeed, the madonna of the poor. The image was found by a poor person; people sought to transport her to a place where the wealthy could view her, but the image could not be budged. Next they tried to put the image of the black madonna where the bourgeoisie could see her; again, she would not be moved. Finally, they decided to put the black madonna where she could be venerated by the lowliest and the poorest; whereupon she allowed herself to be moved. And that is why she is called the madonna of the poor.

The black madonna of Seminara personifies the liberation theology of Italy; she is invoked to "save the nations . . . comfort the sick . . . heal the suffering." The mutuality of black madonnas and believers is conveyed in a prayer: "we believe in you . . . believe in us."[94] An enigmatic last sentence in the prayer to the madonna of the poor of Seminara invokes "Mother of Salvatore and Mother of God." Peasant mothers name their sons Salvatore (savior), give them the diminutive, affectionate name Turiddu, and leave interpretation of the mother of god to the person praying.

Like other black madonnas of the poor, Maria Santissima dei Poveri di Seminara is venerated by those who have emigrated far from home. "We are very tired and we cannot go on" is the lament of pilgrims to the madonna dei poveri of Seminara; "we are strangers who have come from afar."[95] Carmela and Giovanni Piccolo remember the conviviality and sharing of the feste of the black madonnas of Palmi and Seminara, the dancing, the tables of food, the processions . . . Their daughter, Pina Piccolo, a *sibilla* of Seminara, now of Berkeley, California, has written a poem in the spirit of the black madonna of Seminara:

> The beggar dwarf stole my soul
> so small and dejected
> with his lame little leg
> sprawled on the sidewalk,
> to trip distracted tourists
> and haughty Florentines.
>
> His eyes chose me in the crowd,
> begging for love, not for alms.
> Like a magnet he sensed

The black madonna of the poor of Seminara. Reproduced by permission.

I was poorer than he,
and regaled me with a glance.
Nothing less than my soul
was an adequate exchange.

My body now wanders the earth
hollowed,
the gypsy dwarf keeps my soul on a leash
with a diamond collar, and pets it
on his way to begging for alms.[96]

■   ■   ■

LIBERATION BELIEFS associated with black madonnas characterize many comunità di base in Apulia. In this region, *trulli* (cone-shaped dwellings) resemble those of the goddess culture of the Greek Cyclades; a striking group of trulli may be seen at Alberobello. Apulians call their land of many black madonnas *terra di speranza,* land of hope.[97]

In Apulia, in the days after easter people of base communities go on pilgrimage to black madonnas and then attend May day communist festivals. In 1990, along with struggling against drugs and poverty, they declared a general strike against the mafia. This region of Italy has been historically crossed by many peoples, notably Hannibal, the African general with whom Rome warred and who defeated the Romans in Apulia in 216 B.C.E. Later, the Romans cut the Via Appia across the peninsula, a road to the east that ended at Brindisi, their port to the Middle East. After the Romans came the Byzantines, and then the Lombards from the north, who settled in the Duchy of Benevento near Naples. The Muslims took Bari away from the Byzantines in 840 C.E., but the latter left their religious imprint in the monasticism of Benedictines and Basilians and in caves decorated with Byzantine frescoes, where hermits fasted. The Normans arrived with their masculinist cult of saint Michael, followed by French Angevins, Spanish Aragonese, and Turks. In 1735 Apulia was incorporated into the Bourbon kingdom of Naples and Sicily. In 1860 Garibaldi chased off the Bourbons, and Apulia became part of the new kingdom of Italy.

People in Apulian base communities feel that their geographic position, historic memories, and multicultural values make their region *una mano tesa verso l'Oriente e verso il Sud del mondo,* a hand extended toward the east and the south of the world. Comunità di base of Apulia consider peace movements a sign of the times, renounce all military installations, denounce all forms of violence, protest aggression against the weak, and align themselves in solidarity with global *movimenti di liberazione*. In these liberation movements, perhaps symbolized in black madonnas, there is a preferential choice for the poor, a commitment to a simpler life, and work for a model of economic development focused not on wealth, but on health and life.[98]

CHAPTER 9

multicultural liberation theology

of easter in the streets

E ASTER, in Italian vernacular belief, celebrates not the resurrection of the son, but the son rejoining his mother on Sunday afternoon outside the church. Contemporary easter mysteries at Trapani, Sicily, reflect the multicultural heritage of this island's western shore, where Phoenicians of the Middle East and Africa came, and beliefs enacted in the streets suggest themes of Italian liberation theology.

In the street enactment of the easter story, many women sustain the mother during the events leading to the crucifixion of her son. The difference between the church ritual of the passion of christ and popular beliefs centered on the madonna is played out in popular rituals, one of them an easter Sunday afternoon soccer game. The difference between belief in the white madonna of the church and belief in the black madonna of the workers is sublimated in a ritual exchange of candles.

The ultimate referent of the heresies that hover over easter mysteries on this coast may be found in the paleolithic drawing in the Levanzo cave on the offshore Egadi islands. Susan Caperna Lloyd describes what she saw: "Because she was so large, we almost hadn't seen her. A black form, she loomed among the dancing men and animals. With a small head, she was spade-shaped and pregnant looking, like an inverted triangle."[1] Like subsequent black madonnas.

Easter, the church holiday that marks the resurrection of Jesus,[2] was not a significant holiday for nineteenth-century Sicilian peasants. Today, holy-week mysteries of Trapani draw world travelers, but in Pitré's nineteenth-century description of feste there is no reference to easter. One vignette about easter is recorded by the nineteenth-century Sicilian folklorist Salvatore Salomone-Marino. Discovering peasants on his land cutting branches of an olive tree, he was told that this was an "ancient ritual" for Palm Sunday. Thinking this curious, Salomone-Marino pointed out that *palm* leaves are brought into churches on Palm Sunday to commemorate Jesus entering Jerusalem. The peasants insisted that *olive*, not palm, branches were part of an ancient ritual on Palm Sunday. The story suggests that in popular (perhaps unconscious) belief the mother, whose sacred tree is the olive, preceded the son, who is associated with palms. Olive trees are among the "earliest trees to be cultivated, from wild natives in Asia and the Mediterranean."[3]

Peasants regarded easter not as a celebration of the resurrection of Jesus but as a day for peacemaking, modeled on the ritual of the *giunta* (reunion) of the son with his mother on easter afternoon. In the nineteenth century, peasants sought out estranged relatives or friends and embraced them in the piazza. *Giunta* literally means "joining." In icons of black madonnas, Jesus is fused with his mother. After he separates from her, and after the story of the church is played out during the week before easter, mother and son are reunited on easter afternoon, outside the church.

A tablet accompanying the icon of the black madonna *SS.ma Icona* of Spoleto records the dialogue of reconciliation of mother and son, a dialogue in which the mother is the protagonist:

> What are you asking of me, Mother?
> The salvation of humans.
> They provoke me to wrath.
> Pity them, my son. And mercifully save them.[4]

As they did at christmas and at festivals of the town's patron saint, peasant women at eastertime brought breads to the padrone. Easter bread contains hard-boiled eggs.[5] For Pitré, the egg in peasant culture signified *"la divinità suprema"* (the supreme divinity), the life of the world, the fecundity of the earth, and the productive forces of nature.[6]

▪ ▪ ▪

IN APRIL 1988 I traveled to Trapani to observe the easter mysteries. In earlier times, sacred representations, or mysteries, were enacted at any time of the year, sometimes during lent, sometimes at easter. Under the aegis of the church, early subjects of mysteries were the birth of the child, the triumph of the martyrs, stories of the saints, and increasingly, in the modern era, the easter story of Jesus.

Peasants liked mysteries that enacted the life and death of popular women saints like Rosalia, Cristina, Agata, Barbara, and Lucia, as well as the story of Jesus. In large cities, sacred representations were staged in churches or in a theater; in smaller towns, they were performed in the streets, as they are today. Earlier, priests took roles in the dramas; in the modern age, they were replaced by confraternities, artisan guilds, and other lay groups, who rendered a vernacular interpretation of church doctrine.[7]

Carnival spirit, as Bakhtin points out, infiltrated all rituals in peasant culture. We know, because of synod denunciations, that hilarity often accompanied holy presentations. As lay confraternities increasingly came to organize the spectacles, a subversive spirit, sometimes muffled, sometimes not, emerged. Pitré mentions several holy presentations marked by allusions directed at padroni, allusions that were *"non sempre decenti,"* not always decent.[8]

Ribaldry, by the late nineteenth century, clearly permeated church piety. At Chiaramonte Gulfi, site of a pilgrimage and of rebellious political activity in an area named for the goddess, a popular play about saint Joseph and his virginal wife contained scurrilous poetry that bandied the wager that if the child were born with curly hair it was his.[9] In an outburst during a sacred presentation described by Pitré, women, covered in black silk cloaks that hid their faces except for one eye, started singing, leaping, dancing, inserting themselves among the priests, and declaiming witty poetry, all to the crowd's thunderous acclamations of *"Viva Maria!"*[10]

La divina giustizia, divine justice, the central woman figure of Italian folk stories, was featured in a 1772 easter procession at Carini that enacted the vernacular belief in the prechristian woman divinity and her motherhood of equal human tribes. Instead of the church story of Jesus as the son of god with twelve apostles, the popular easter ritual featured the woman figure Divine Justice leading twelve equal human tribes. In a popular story that accompanied the ritual, la divina giustizia was said to have preceded Adam and Eve.[11]

Mary Magdalene, the first to see the risen Jesus,[12] has become a favorite figure in popular easter processions. She is often "dressed in black like the

Virgin."[13] Vernacular rituals celebrate the woman the church considers "fallen," perhaps remembering the goddess who loved anyone she chose to love. The popularity of Mary Magdalene suggests the resistance of peasant women to the patriarchal elevation of virginity and obedience as the meaning of the madonna, as well as women's unwillingness to accept church separation of their gender into good and bad.

During easter week 1988, I listened to the bishop address a crowd in front of the cathedral of Caltagirone. Presenting church doctrine to an audience that included many emigrant workers come home to see the giunta on easter afternoon, the bishop advised Sicilians who had been forced by unemployment to go elsewhere to find work that the lesson of the blessed virgin was *pazienza,* patience.

The economic and cultural context of vernacular easter rituals in today's Sicily has been analyzed by Justin Vitiello in a study of contemporary fishermen of Trapetto, a village a few miles from Trapani. Fishermen who had to emigrate to earn a living are drawn back to their native places at festival time. With a sense of a long history, a contemporary Sicilian emigrant included popes and Americans in a long list of invaders: "Even the Sicels and Sicanians were invaders. But after them it was all one swarm of locusts. Phoenicians, Greeks, Romans, Goths, Arabs, Normans, French, Aragonese, Castilians, Germans, Popes, every kind of Italian you name them . . . finally, America."[14] A returning emigrant said, "Some of my northern Italian acquaintances" consider Sicily "the beginning of Africa, the Third World of Europe."[15]

Recording the conversations of emigrants, Vitiello has come upon ultimate beliefs. "What I know is this," said a fisherman, "earth, sea, sky. Violate them, you choke on your own filth. Respect them, with some prodding, they yield all we need to live. That's why we need schools, so our children can grow healthy and decent. Good like bread. Like we're made to be."[16] Many people in these parts are unedited marxists and unedited catholics, building sanctuaries for local healers they consider saints.[17]

The madonna in vernacular Sicilian easter rituals appears to be the woman in the apocryphal literature of the bible transmitted in the oral tradition.[18] In the apocryphal Vangelo di Gamaliele, Mary was present the entire way of the Via Dolorosa, not solely at the foot of the cross, as the church version has it. The apocryphal Lamentazione di Maria narrates a story with several women, Giovanna (wife of Cusa), Mary Magdalene, and Salome, embracing and sustaining the madonna during the Via Crucis.[19] This belief has been condemned by the church, but it persists (notably in the pilgrimage of the

Gypsies of Europe to the black Sarah-Kali and her two white half sisters at Stes-Maries-de-la-Mer in France). In popular Italian easter-week rituals, many women, identifying with Mary, accompany her.

Other differences from church doctrine emerge. During easter week at Trapani, there are *two* processions: a crowned, saddened white madonna Addolorata of the church and her official procession, and a beautiful black madonna who resembles Astarte, Aphrodite, and Venus and *her* procession of women and workers. The black madonna, like her white counterpart, has a crown, jewels, and a scepter.

The black madonna carries pine cones connoting regeneration. Black rice, or *riso nero,* is cooked in her honor. The recipe requires *riso originario* (indigenous rice), as well as local milk, cocoa, cinnamon and sugar from elsewhere, and the toasted almonds that are always found in pilgrimages to black madonnas.[20]

Whether the distinctly black madonna or the saddened white madonna whom an American woman observer perceived as black, the centrality of the mother in the easter passion at Trapani is evident. Susan Caperna Lloyd, who has produced a brilliant film depicting the good Friday procession at Trapani, asked local women why the mother was central. She learned that women regard Mary's son as *pazzo* (mad). If he were the son of god, why did he allow himself to be crucified? Furthermore, he was somewhat less than a good son in causing such grief to his mother.[21]

Women are central in the Trapani mysteries. The mother is the first figure, women on foot follow the statue of the madonna, and a black-clad statue of the mother is the last figure of the ritual.[22] Nowhere in the canonical synoptic gospels is there mention of Jesus "separating" from his mother before the events of easter week. In popular easter rituals at Trapani, the first sequence of the passion procession is the son "separating" from his mother before he leaves for the way of the cross. When Maksim Gorky saw easter rituals in southern Italy, he was intensely moved by the figure of the mother: "black and mute, as if enchained by an invincible sadness, the woman in the black mantle looks for something . . . she transports the fantasies of obscure ancient beliefs."[23]

Trapani is not far from Enna, where Sicilians believe the story of Demeter and Persephone took place. In the christian era, Demeter's search for her daughter was replaced by the madonna's search for her son. During the mysteries at Trapani, the statue of the madonna, accompanied by saint John the evangelist, is carried all over town, hunting for her child. Responding to vernacular beliefs, not to church doctrine, the statue of the mother is made to hesitate, agonizingly (sometimes for forty-five minutes), before she enters the church.

Papal displeasure at popular veneration of the madonna was evident in 1700, when the church formally limited the role of the mother in the passion ritual to Mater Dolorosa. Disregarding the edict, Italian mothers and *cantastorie* continued to tell the tale of the mother and child, a story of death, a time of demons, a time of angels vanquishing demons, a mother's search for her child, and rebirth to new life; this is the story that appears to be enacted today in easter rituals in the street at Trapani.

Sicilians respond sardonically to the query, Who is the more significant figure, Jesus or his mother? At San Biagio Platani, Sicily, during holy week of 1988, the community divided into two factions: *i madunnara,* devoted to the madonna, and *i signurara,* devoted to her son. Satirizing the rivalry between church doctrine and popular religious beliefs, the issue was taken to the playing field to resolve, with an easter-day soccer game between the two groups![24]

In the giunta, or reuniting, of mother and son on easter Sunday afternoon, townsmen carry two large figures of the madonna and Jesus to the town piazza. At the dramatic moment when she meets her son, the men carrying the statue of the madonna have her drop her black cloak, revealing a diaphanous blue peignoir. A local woman observing me watch the giunta at Caltagirone said that the ritual was a manifestation of religious belief crossed by *la fantasia meridionale*. In southern fantasy encircling the reuniting, there are unmistakable sexual overtones in the mother's love for her son and in his love for her ever since. As played in the street in front of the cathedral, the role of the church is irrelevant in the encounter of Jesus and his mother. The puppet san Pietro, somewhat of a buffoon, is made to dash hither and thither (to gales of laughter from the crowd) looking for some role for the church in this heavily valenced encounter of mother and son.[25]

Arches, or semicircles, of bread decorated with vegetables and flowers at S. Biagio Platani may signify the prechristian *albero della vita,* tree of life, that became a symbol of the goddess. Her many names have been succeeded by the many names of the madonna. She eludes analysis. During lent at San Cataldo, priests celebrate l'Immacolata, burghers venerate the Madonna delle Mercede, artisans carve figures of the Madonna del Rosario, landowners look to their Madonna delle Grazie, fruit growers kneel before *la Pietà,* and workers pray to la Madonna del Carmel.[26]

➤ In her black manifestation, the madonna taps very deep emotions. The sirocco comes up from the African desert on this Phoenician/Canaanite coast of Sicily. The hot African wind was blowing during easter week of 1988 as I watched the rocking, nurturing movement, *l'annacata,* of workers carrying their black madonna. This motion, which resembles that of a parent rocking a child, has three steps forward, three steps backward, and then forward again, evoking the spiral of the goddess. Deeply moved by the dirge, in empathy with workers carrying the heavy statue with a rhythmic, rocking movement, and perhaps overwhelmed by an ancient memory, people all along the route of the procession were in tears.

Afterward, the black madonna remains all night with other women in a makeshift tent outside the church. There she waits for the agony of her son's crucifixion and her reunion with him.[27] Of the people, not of the church, these religious beliefs seem marked by *la presenza,* described by Ernesto De Martino as oneness with a personified universe. This oneness does not lead to transcendental mysticism, but to identification with the humanity of the madonna and her child.

Sicilians seem to be conscious of the prechristian notes in easter rituals on this coast where the indigenous goddess Ibla was loved and where Phoenicians brought their goddess Astarte. They are perhaps aware that the figures in the easter processions are not the ones actually being venerated: the frontispiece of the 1988 pamphlet that described the easter passion at Marsala featured not Jesus but the "lad of Mozia,"[28] a sculpture of a young man found on the island off Marsala where an ancient Phoenician/Canaanite city was located.[29] "Like the Canaanites, of whom they formed a branch, the Phoenicians connected their religion with the great powers and processes of nature."[30]

Heresy dances in and out of easter rituals on this Canaanite shore. In a Trapani newspaper article at eastertime 1988, Jesus was portrayed as a contemporary young radical, whom a woman described, not as the christ and son of god, but as *"un bravo ragazzo,"* a fine young man. Young radicals at Trapani in the last few years have taken the lead in openly defying corrupt governments in league with the mafia, founding the journal *Il pungolo* ten years ago to present their courageous denunciations.[31]

The pagan past feels vividly present in southern Italian easter processions. At Trapani the sea has brought Phoenician, African, Greek, and Roman goddesses to join the primordial Sicilian female divinity Ibla. Easter mysteries are enacted a few minutes away from the mount of Erice, site of the goddess Astarte, who became Aphrodite, who became Venus, and to whom sailors from time immemorial climbed with offerings of wine. Bronze statuettes of Isis and Horus, Hebrew inscriptions, a sculpture of Aphrodite, and a painting of Mary Magdalene may be seen in the Municipal Museum of Erice. A few kilometers away at Enna, women long ago danced in Eleusinian rites; at nearby Agrigento and Gela, followers of Hera, who became Juno, left hundreds of statuettes of the woman divinity.

The story of the events of the week Jesus was killed is enacted at Trapani within view of a primitive ritual for the killing of food—*la mattanza,* off the Egadi islands, where Trapanese fishermen have killed tuna for centuries. At dawn, they say a prayer that reveals the syncretism of popular beliefs: "Queen and mother of God of Trapani, Queen and mother of God of the rosary . . . Queen and Santa Teresa, Queen the Madonna of Fatima."[32] The prayer includes "Patrinostru e San Giuseppe" (our father and saint Joseph) and *"i nostri morti"* (our dead).[33]

The prayer places objects of faith locally ("Queen and mother of God of Trapani"), defers to church institutions ("Queen and mother of God of the rosary"), incorporates Muslim elements ("Madonna of Fatima") and Spanish-Jewish *converso* figures ("Queen and Santa Teresa"), and conflates the ultimate father with the earthly father ("Patrinostru e San Giuseppe") and saints with *"i nostri morti"* (our dead).

The veneration of the dead is a living custom in western Sicily, as elsewhere in Italy. On the *festa dei morti,* November 2, dead relatives are said to visit, bringing sweets and dried fruit. Sweets are sometimes shaped as *ossa di morti* (bones of the dead) or *pani di morti* (breads of the dead); today, they are given to orphaned children.[34]

In the work of preparing the tuna nets, the fishermen of Trapani chant *"Aimolo lu santu Sarvaturi"*[35] (Let's help the saint savior), words that are heretical in calling Jesus a saint, not the son of god. Another work chant invokes Maria, san Cristofaru, Maddalena, and Gesù, equally, in a sequence in which the mother is first, a person removed from sainthood is next, the fallen woman of the bible follows, and Jesus is last.[36] When the fish are caught and the sea is bloodied, fishermen sing songs whose content is *"erotico-scherzoso,"* erotic and witty.[37]

In the quattrocento an effusion of faith created churches, monasteries, convents, and confraternities of lay brothers on this Sicilian shore. Some confraternities became artisan syndicates that sponsored a popular form of catholicism that Giovanni Cammareri describes as "competitive with the church."[38] Heretical religious beliefs are accompanied by radical political stances. Worker unions, or artisan guilds, create the sculptures of holy figures of the good Friday procession at Trapani. Many of the artisan groups that organize the easter mysteries are guild/cooperatives; on this island, cooperatives have been the economic ground of socialist hopes since the 1890s.

The 1988 sculptures of the good Friday procession at Trapani were paid for and constructed by individual artists and by artisan guilds of jewelers, fishermen, greengrocers, metalworkers, sailors, fruitsellers, barbers and hair-dressers, fish vendors, masons, stonecutters, bakers, shoemakers, butchers, clothiers and textile workers, joiners, carpenters, cartwrights, rope makers, painters and decorators, tailors and carpetmakers, saltworkers, pasta makers, waiters, drivers, hotel keepers, candy makers, and tavern keepers[39]—the entire economic and social fabric of Trapanese society.

Musical instruments played during easter rituals at Trapani ring with the histories of many peoples. *Scacciapensieri,* the name of the mouth harp, of Jewish and Arab origin, refers to the ancient belief that music disperses worries; the *tamarreddu,* or drum, of Graeco-Roman dionysian and bacchic rites, celebrates abundance and sexuality. There are hymns of love of the earth, toasts to the sea, work chants, and songs of the sorrow and joy of love. An ancient *canto* of *fimminazzi* celebrates women who work marble; another is a lament of women waiting for husbands and sons to return from the sea. An ancient pitcher rings with different tones depending on how much wine has been drunk.

The scenarios of religious rituals of southern Italy, Cammareri has pointed out, are written by no one and interpreted by everyone. On the deep, ambivalent level of popular religious beliefs noted by Bakhtin, easter rituals of southern Italy are cadenced to funeral sadness and lifted by transformative carnival laughter. Balloons for the children soar above somber enactments of the stations of the cross. Carnival overturning of church doctrine is evident during holy week, when chaste matrons dress as Magdalenes and catholic men play Jews.

This is a vernacular catholicism dense with history. Celebration of the spring equinox reaches back to the beginning of time. The ritual of the last supper enacts the Jewish *pesach,* passover. Vernacular rites are woven with threads of diverse cultures and different peoples: Phoenicians/Canaanites, Jews in diaspora, Greeks, Romans, medieval Jews, Saracens, Provençal troubadours, and Norman crusaders. After the twelfth century, threads of the patron saint of Italy, Francis, are apparent in the brotherhood of friars of the franciscan order of Santa Maria di Gesù, who today help organize popular easter rituals. The heritage of Spain, which ruled southern Italy and Sicily in the early modern era, edges the cultural tapestry with baroque embroidery.

The church has tried to control popular easter rituals with heavy-handed measures like abolishing the procession of the three Marys. Today, the church relies on indirection and co-optation, trying to pour water on the conflagration of faith, flowers, and candles that turns the churches and streets of southern Italy, and of other Latin countries, into theaters of madonnas, saints, Jesus, centurions, and angels. The folk performance is directed by the sound of *ciaccole,* clackers that cut the air with the sharp and eerie sound that determines the rhythm of easter processions in Mediterranean countries.

Competition at Trapani between the black madonna of the syndicate of porters and the madonna of the church (Madre della pietà del Popolo) is respectful. The rivalry of artisan groups devoted to the black madonna and lay representatives of the madonna of the church is sublimated in a ceremonial exchange of candles.[40] Competition between beliefs in Mary or Jesus may be played out in a soccer match, as indicated above, but the characteristic expression is conveyed in the exclamation *"Santamariagesù!"* In this outcry, which identifies southern Italians when they go north, the mother precedes her son, who is familiarly addressed as Gesù, not by his church name of Gesù Cristo, the messiah or the son of god. The popular expression binds the son to the mother.

Implicit religious beliefs of the easter mystery at Trapani seem similar to this exclamation. Mary and Jesus are bound, as in the fused figure of a black madonna and child, before the mysteries begin. The first sequence of the holy-week procession has the son "separating" from his mother. After the son has done his mother's errand in the world and the story of Jesus is played out, the two are joined again in the giunta on easter Sunday afternoon, outside the church.

The first sculpture in the holy-week procession of 1988 was of three figures, but not the father, son, and holy ghost of church doctrine. In this enacted vernacular trinity, Jesus is placed between his mother and saint John the evangelist. And Jesus *"è leggermente più basso degli altri,"*[41] is slightly lower than his mother and John. If sculptural placement, in this passion ritual, has theological implication, the people's understanding replaces the church trinity with one of mother, child, and the meaning of the gospel of saint John the evangelist, to whom Jesus entrusted his mother and who, in vernacular belief, is merged with saint John the baptist.[42]

The significance of Mary and other women in the first centuries of the church has been analyzed by feminist theologians, notably Elisabeth Schussler Fiorenza and Elaine Pagels, who have carefully studied the canonical and noncanonical gospels.[43] Popular liberation theology enacted in the street at eastertime in Sicily has many similarities to feminist liberation theology.

In Fiorenza's definitive interpretation of the early gospels from a feminist perspective, the Johannine community was an alternative one to the church represented by Peter; the hierarchy of pope and apostles is countered by Johannine equality in the spirit and a replacement of the misogyny of church doctrine. In John's gospel, there is an analogy between women's experience in giving birth and the experience of Jesus on the cross: "the Johannine Jesus likens the 'hour' of his exaltation on the cross and the time of the disciples' bereavement to the experience a pregnant woman has before and after giving birth." In Fiorenza's interpretation, "just as the woman experiences anxiety and sorrow in anticipation of the child's birth, so the disciples are sorrowful and afraid because of Jesus' departure. But just as the woman is glad and full of joy when the child is born, so the disciples will have peace and joy after their new life and future is revealed in Jesus' resurrection (16:20–22)."[44]

In contrast to the official, Petrine tradition, the Johannine community included women and men. The fourth gospel begins and ends its account of the public ministry of Jesus with a story about Mary, the mother of Jesus, and Mary of Bethany.[45] Four women stand under the cross. "Mary of Magdala is not only the first to witness the empty tomb but also the first to receive an appearance of the resurrected Lord."[46] Not only the mother of Jesus but his mother's sister follows the cross. The last woman in John's gospel is Mary Magdalene, whom Fiorenza considers the "primary apostolic witness to the resurrection."[47] The gospels of John and Mark suggest an alternative christian community, one in which women have apostolic and ministerial leadership.[48]

Popular enactment of the easter passion that I observed at Trapani in 1988 seemed very close to themes of Fiorenza's interpretation. Women began and ended the ritual; the mother and John the evangelist accompanied Jesus; the mother, Mary Magdalene, and John were at the foot of the cross, and they transported him to the tomb; and the mother, draped in black and followed by other women in black, closed the easter passion.[49]

In Revelation, John proclaimed a great portent, "a woman clothed with the sun, with the moon under her feet, and on her head a crown of twelve stars; she was with child and she cried out in her pangs of birth, in anguish for delivery."[50] For D. H. Lawrence, this woman was the prechristian goddess.[51]

Traditionally, organizers of easter rituals in Italy have been men. When contemporary women design the rites, the religious and political implications are startling. In 1988 at Pietraperzia, Sicilian women enacted their own interpretation of the easter story. Near the very place (Lago di Pergusa, in the navel of Sicily) where the god of the underworld was said to have abducted Persephone, leading her mother, Demeter, to darken the earth with her grief until she found her daughter and caused the flowers to bloom again, contemporary women gave feminist meaning to easter rituals.

In the good Friday procession at Pietraperzia, women carried a statue of Mary, and a red ribbon measured the length of the dead body of her son. After his death on the cross at dusk on good Friday, women brought a tree of life into the piazza, a maypole. Different linen streamers edged with lace, handmade, and carried by women were fastened onto the prechristian tree of life that signifies the goddess. The maypole supported a small cross above a globe of many different colors.[52]

Women's easter rituals at Pietraperzia in 1988 acted out the contemporary Italian feminist belief that differences are pivots of social transformation.[53] Women carrying the statue of Mary on good Friday personified the cultural message of contemporary Italian feminists, "women are the carriers of the future,"[54] and conveyed their political message—*"Dalle donne, la forza delle donne,"*[55] from women, the strength of women.

CHAPTER 10

heresies, sibyls, fables, Lilith,

and witches ▪ *"un mondo senza padroni*

e senza guerre," a world without

bosses and without wars

HERESIES of the twelfth and thirteenth centuries, sibylline values of "all our grandmothers," meaning hidden in fables, the death of many condemned to the stake as witches, and the continuing story of Lilith may be regarded as precursors of contemporary Italian feminists and of liberation theology embodied in black madonnas.

In the trinity of the catholic church (father, son, and holy spirit) a flame, or a dove, symbolizes the holy spirit. In the twelfth and thirteenth centuries, when a wave of fervor for the madonna swept over Europe, two heresies arose that referred to the holy spirit. Joachim of Fiore proclaimed the coming age of the *spirito santo*. Guglielma and her followers said that the *spirito santo* was a woman.

In the eschatological unease and hope at the end of the twelfth century, Joachim of Fiore, an abbot from Calabria, reread the scriptures and envisioned a new age of spirituality. Born about 1130, he went (as a mystic, not a crusader) to the holy land.[1] On his return, he entered the Cistercian monastery of santa Maria di Corazzo, studied the gospels, and, in the pine forests of the high Sila, founded a new monastic order dedicated to the spirito santo and to saint John the evangelist. The deep memory of Joachim's Ordine Florense, the order of flowers, together with the preaching of saint

Francis of Assisi, may have inspired the flower children of San Francisco in the 1960s.

Setting himself against the view that the Hebrew scriptures were antithetical to the new testament, Joachim presented an allegorical, moral, contemplative, and mystical interpretation of history as a chronological dynamic of three ages:[2] the age of the father, the age of the son, and the age of the holy spirit. The year 1260, according to his calculations, would mark the end of the age of the son and the beginning of the age of the holy spirit. Finding the pattern of three everywhere (winter, spring, and summer; grass, stalks, and harvested grain; water, wine, and oil), Joachim said that the age of the holy spirit would usher in a new society and a new era of liberty and peace.[3] In 1215, the catholic church condemned his teachings as heresy.[4]

For a contemporary interpreter, Antonio Crocco, it is natural that the Calabrian abbot attribute the spiritual maternity of the third stage to the mother of the physical christ. The interpreter's explanation skirts heresy and lapses into equivocation: *"È quindi naturale che sia attribuita alla Vergine, madre del Cristo fisico, la spirituale maternità del terzo stato, che dovrà essere l'immagine perfetta del 'cristo mistico.' "*[5] Note the ambiguity: "It is therefore natural that the spiritual maternity of the third state be attributed to the virgin, mother of the physical christ, the mother who will be the perfect image of the mystic christ."

Although condemned as heresy, Joachim's theory is faithful to church doctrine in holding that in Jesus there is neither male nor female, a conflation of genders that Italian feminists consider a major source of the obfuscation that undergirds the oppression of women. It is precisely this area of the historical *difference* of women from men that Italian feminists consider significant for a new society of equality with difference, liberty, and justice.

■   ■   ■

STUDENTS of Dante have considered Beatrice in the *Commèdia* as a symbol of Joachim's vision of the *"Ecclesia spiritualis."*[6] Saint Francis, in the thirteenth century, also preached a new spirituality; Franciscan Spirituals, indebted to Joachim, looked to the renewal of the church. For the papacy, Joachim was a heretic because he seemed to be replacing the christocentric theology of the early church fathers with a mystical conception of the trinity.[7]

Joachim preached in a region that had earlier been aligned with the Byzantine church, centered at Constantinople. Invasions by Lombards, Muslims, and Normans, and the reassertion of Roman papal sovereignty, dealt blows to the Basilian monasteries of Calabria. Normans supported Benedictine monasteries; reformers looked to rejuvenate the Cistercian order. Joachim perfected his message in a monastery originally Benedictine, then Cistercian, in a community dedicated to santa Maria.

In his mountain community in the Sila, there were peasant families, shepherds and goatherds, mulekeepers, shoemakers, ironworkers, two barrelmakers, three fishermen, two tailors, one carpenter, a barber, a tavern keeper, a butcher, a hermit, and women who did the caring, cooking, and teaching. This peasant farm community with a few artisans was humble and unschooled,[8] but there was fire underneath its seeming docility: people of this area had little or no faith in religious and political rulers, and Joachim found a receptive audience for his teachings.[9]

Contemporary scholars place Joachim in a continuum with the Hebrew prophets.[10] His vision is considered close to the Revelation of saint John the evangelist[11] and his teaching close to that of the medieval cabala.[12] Like Karl Marx and Antonio Gramsci, Joachim taught an attitude of pessimism about the present and optimism for the future. His relevance for contemporary Italians, and others, lies in a radical communal vision incorporating monastic, ecclesiastic, and lay themes in a theory both traditional and radical: every historical event has a memory and a future.

Joachim's vision of the future city resembles that of Marx: everyone will have equal access to the necessities of life, yet differences according to varying gifts will be recognized. In the abbot's view, however, a good society was to be modeled on a reformed monastery whose ultimate purpose is not production but salvation: the higher a person's status, the more ascetic his or her way of life should be.[13] For lay people as well as the clergy, economic security will provide the foundation for a contemplative life. Joachim's vision of a good society resembles the later one of Mao Tse-tung in assigning work equally to clerics (intellectuals) and lay people and to women and men. Differing from later utopias, Joachim's communal society assured areas of individual privacy.

There was a flaw, however. In Joachim's utopian community, *"alle donne non è concessa assolutamente nessuna possibilità di raggiungere il vertice della gerarchia,"* women could not reach upper spiritual or political levels of the community. He may have been a heretic, but the abbot adhered to traditional doctrine of the catholic church in allocating to women the work of keeping the home, rearing the children, and furnishing clothing to the monks.[14] There were other equivocations. Joachim alluded to the female personification of the holy spirit, but he did not say so outright. He referred to the crow (a sign of the goddess) as a divine symbol, but he said that the crow symbolized christ.[15]

Joachim of Fiore has endured in the vernacular beliefs of subaltern classes of Calabria as a prophet of peace, love, and humanity.[16] In what people of this region describe as "an old and a new socialism," the values of thrift, work, "respect for others and for nature, and a sense of the sacred" are considered the ground of equality and liberty.[17] A few years ago when we visited san Giovanni in Fiore, the local secretary of the communist party was eager to show us where Joachim had preached.

Calabria, in recent years considered the poorest region of Italy, has been suffocated by the *n'drangheta,* the local version of the mafia, and militarized by NATO installations. The region has at least three significant black madonnas—the Madonna di Capo Colonna, described below, and the black madonnas of Seminara and Palmi, described in the last chapter. Today Calabria has become a region of spontaneous uprisings against the n'drangheta, against basing F-16 aircraft at Crotone, and against the nuclear installation at Gioia Tauro. To be a contemporary communist in Calabria is to be in the vanguard of the movement against the mafia and to be intent on bringing an alternative society into being.

In southern Italy, the energy for democratic communism seems to be coming from women, indigenous intellectuals, and the young. The Partito democratico della sinistra works with socialists, the Democrazia proletaria, and *Verdi* (greens) to make Calabria a denuclearized zone, opening their lists to independents, priests, and to relatives of people assassinated by the mafia.[18]

Crotone, which has a sanctuary to the black madonna di Capo Colonna, is a political "red zone" of Calabria located a few kilometers from the town of San Giovanni in Fiore. The sanctuary is built on a temple to Hera Lucina, the Greek divinity who was the consort of Zeus and became the Roman goddess of light. Hera, a name whose root may have been "He Era" (the earth), was sometimes called "Lady" or "la Signora." She appears to be a Greek form of "the Great Goddess of early Aegean civilization" who preceded the pantheon of Greek gods and goddesses.[19]

Although she was mother of the gods, Hellenic writers tried to make Hera subordinate to Zeus; she was older than he, however, and legends recount that she had married him against her will. Europe may be named for Hera.[20] Romans called her Juno Lucina (Mother of Light), who "bestowed the gifts of light, enlightenment, and eyesight" and opened the eyes of newborn children.[21] Lucina, the Roman goddess, became santa Lucia, virgin martyr of the christian era, who, as discussed earlier, was remembered in popular culture with prechristian beliefs.

Also at Crotone, feminist scholars looking for women who have been left out of the history of philosophy have found women Pythagoreans. Who taught whom is unclear; in the classical literature it was said that Pythagoras of Samos derived the "greater part of his ethical doctrines from Themistoclea, the priestess at Delphi."[22] Early Pythagorean philosophers included members of his family and their successors, who headed Pythagorean societies in southern Italy from the fourth to the second centuries B.C.E.[23] Theano was a pupil of Pythagoras who later became his wife. The concept of *harmonia,* recalling the goddess, was central to women Pythagorean philosophers, who applied the concept to the family and to the state.[24]

Seeing the universe as orderly and harmonious, Pythagorean philosophers considered evil or immoral actions contrary to law because they contribute to discord. Women Pythagoreans, holding that the natures of men and women are different,[25] believed social justice was possible because women brought principles of justice and harmony into the household.[26] According to Aesara of Lucania, since the home is the microcosm of the state, women are ultimately responsible for harmony, law, and justice in the state.[27] There are echoes of these beliefs in nineteenth- and twentieth-century Anglo-American feminist thinking, as well as in the Italian proverb "It is the woman who creates the home."

However impressive their views of justice and harmony, women Pythagorean philosophers accepted a double standard for marital fidelity. Men's adultery was overlooked; women's adultery was considered unworthy of women concerned for harmonious households. Although important in the history of philosophy, women Pythagorean philosophers mark the decline in women's status in the Greek and Roman eras. Phintys of Sparta, in "On the Moderation of Women," describes a woman trained in moderation as characterized by piety and reverence and by "decency" with respect to her body. Significantly, the woman trained in "moderation . . . piety . . . reverence" did *not* indulge in "mystery rites and celebrations of the festival of Cybele."[28]

More than a thousand years later, the great yearning in the age of Joachim and of Guglielma tended to make men of the catholic hierarchy anxious. Joachim's teachings of a coming age of the spirito santo were condemned in 1215. Shortly thereafter Guglielma and her women followers said it straight out: the holy spirit is a woman, and women will lead the renewal of society.

The response of the church, in 1300, was to put Guglielma's corpse, and the live bodies of her followers, to the stake.

Her story has recently been revisited by an Italian feminist scholar, Luisa Muraro,[29] who describes it as a feminist heresy, a story of women's unwillingness to be subordinated to the interests of male-dominated institutions. In the thirteenth century, saint Thomas Aquinas said that women were excluded from the priesthood because they did not have the capacity to know the holy.[30] Today, the vicar of christ at Rome states that women cannot become priests because they did not number among the first disciples of Jesus. Feminists ask, Mary Magdalene?

A daughter of queen Constance of Hungary, Guglielma found herself in Milan, a young woman in a wealthy city open to Waldensian, Catharist, and Albigensian beliefs. She was a healer, but that by itself did not adequately account for the feeling Guglielma aroused in her followers, one that they associated with Jesus christ and the holy spirit.[31] The doctor who attended Guglielma before she died, and her followers, were convinced that the holy spirit *"era presente e incarnato in lei,"*[32] was present and incarnate in her. Some who "had been inflamed by the prophecies of Joachim of Fiore" believed that she was an incarnation of the holy spirit and became early followers.[33]

Guglielma said that her body and christ's body were the same body, that of the holy spirit.[34] She left the distinct impression that she had proclaimed two heresies: the physical consubstantiality of christ and Guglielma in the spirito santo, and the critical importance of women for the salvation of humanity.[35] A fresco in her cell, still visible, depicts her with a red face. In catholic liturgy, the color red (the color of life, heat, and renewal) is associated with the holy spirit.[36]

In the manner that peasants disguised heresies by invoking church figures, Guglielma's followers honored her under the cover of venerating santa Margherita and santa Caterina. Stories about saint Margaret and saint Catherine contained significant symbols. For the church, santa Margherita was a christian martyr of the third century who was devoured by a dragon (symbol of the goddess) yet had emerged alive, a story regarded by the church as an allegory of salvation. Women, remembering the goddess, call on saint Margaret when they are about to give birth.[37] Santa Caterina d'Alessandria, the christian cover for Ipazia (Hypatia), who was put to death by christians for neoplatonist ideas, is considered the protectress of philosophers.[38]

Among Guglielma's followers was Maifreda, a nun in the order of the Umiliati, who became the leader of those who believed that she incarnated the spirito santo.[39] Maifreda resembles other women of this period who, although barred from the priesthood, were heads of monasteries, sometimes exercising power equivalent to that of bishops. One of these women was the *badessa* of the Cistercian monastery of Conversano in Apulia. This monastery, with a strong woman abbot, contained an image of a black madonna.[40]

In Muraro's interpretation of the Guglielmite heresy, she carefully analyzes the adherents' belief that Guglielma incarnated the spirito santo. The violent reaction of the catholic church to this heresy may have been related to a belief of one of Maifreda's disciples: Guglielma had "grace, virtue, and authority" superior to that of Peter, who, according to the canon, symbolizes the church.[41]

After the inquisition trial, burning of the women in 1300, and suppression of Guglielma's beliefs, stories were told. One, dated 1503, was about a woman heretic named Guglielmina who lived with a man and presided over a subterranean *sinagoga* where women gathered to practice heretical beliefs, followed by a sexual orgy.[42] This story, scapegoating Jews for heresy and associating it with sexual license, was not, according to Muraro, created by the people, but consciously constructed by religious authorities in their campaign against heretics.[43] In the next few centuries, this effort became a great witch-hunt by catholic inquisitors and protestant reformers, who murdered Jews, lepers, and peasant women healers, seers, and dissenters.[44]

At the inquisition trial, her followers said that Guglielma was the spirito santo, the divine substance was in her, and, because of Guglielma, Jews, Muslims, and pagans would be saved.[45] The contemporary feminist relevance of Guglielma's beliefs inheres in the emphasis on women's difference from men. Stressing women's alterity, Guglielmites conveyed the belief, similar to the later teaching of saint Teresa of Avila, that women had a direct and original rapport with the deity.

Heretical aspects of Guglielma's teaching included the assertion that the holy spirit of the trinity was a woman and that, because of this, salvation extended to nonchristians. For Muraro, the most heretical implication of Guglielma's teaching is that she implied "a plural God, not hierarchical . . . sensibly present in everything that exists: visible in the body of woman, body of the holy spirit."[46] The Guglielmite heresy may be a remembrance of the equality characteristic of the culture of the goddess and a vision of the future when the earth and all life again become sacred.

As a feminist heresy, Guglielma's teachings differed from church doctrine, wherein Jesus represents both men and women. For her followers, Guglielma's divinity did not derive from assimilation to christ. The point, rather, was consubstantiation: *"Guglielma e Gesù / Cristo e Gesù / Cristo e Guglielma"*[47]— Guglielma and Jesus / Christ and Jesus / Christ and Guglielma.

The church burned Guglielma. One of her followers was named Sibilla, the Latin form of the name of Cybele, Anatolian mother goddess venerated in the Roman empire. Related to Ishtar of Mesopotamia and to Inanna, the Semitic goddess of Sumer, Cybele at Rome was called Magna Mater, "mother of deities." She rode astride a lion while her priestesses rode in a chariot drawn by lions. On her throne, with a cymbal in her hand, she was flanked by lions. Cybele's son and lover was Attis, a shepherd who played the flute and died beneath an evergreen tree. She wrapped his body, buried it beneath the tree, and mourned his death every spring.

Sibyls, as Cybele's priestesses, used bee honey in sacred rituals; as prophetesses, they decreed that the black sacred stone associated with her be brought to Rome after the war with Carthage. "On the fourth day of April, two hundred and four years before the time of Christ," Cybele's black stone was placed in the Temple of Victory, on the ancient Palatine of Rome.[48] Whereupon, after three days, her son arose from the dead, exciting great shouts that, as Attis had been saved, "so shall we in turn be saved."[49] The Roman emperor Claudius I, fifty years after the birth of Jesus, also joined rituals to mourn Cybele's dead son (whose image hung upon a tree) and paid homage to the great mother of deities.[50]

Today, one can view ten sibyls, created by several artists in 1482–83, on the pavement of the cathedral of Siena. The Delphic sibyl taught the precept "Know yourself"; this was changed by christian interpreters to "Know your God himself, who is the Son of God." The Tiburtine, Erythraean, and Cumaean sibyls were said by christian exegetes to have prophesied the birth of Jesus. The black sibyl of Cumae holds books of learning and the golden bough that she offered Charon to take Aeneas across the river Styx. The Persian sibyl is said to have foretold Jesus' miracle of the loaves and fishes. The Samian, Hellespontic, and Libyan sibyls were said by christian exegetes to have predicted events in the passion story of Jesus.[51] The Cimmerian sibyl is said to have foretold the resurrection.

The Phrygian sibyl holds a book open to a page that reads, "I alone am God, there is no other God," with a table of doomsday prophecies.[52] The black Libyan sibyl holds a book open to these words: "Receiving blows, he shall be silent, he shall offer his innocent back to the scourge . . . he, wretched and ignominious, will offer the wretched hope."[53]

Sibyls are connected to Gypsies by Paolo Toschi: both were believed to be able to foretell the future. In christian interpretation, Gypsies were con-

The Sibylla Lybica, *on the floor of the duomo of Siena. Reproduced by permission of the* Opera della Metropolitana di Siena.

demned to wander for this sin of pride. Sibyls, because they believed they were bearers of the word, were condemned to stay in the subterranean world of grottoes (e.g., la Sibilla di Norcia). Gypsies, according to contemporary scholars, were originally from Egypt and are identified with the dark Eritrean sibyl.[54] For Peter Dronke, a christian Cambridge medievalist, the meaning of the sibylline pavement at Siena is that "out of every region of the known world, ten pagan women, of inspired wisdom, bring their prophetic intuitions of Christian history, from the birth of Christ to the judgment."[55]

What little information we have about sibyls that is not distorted by the church comes from an early fourth-century work by the African church father Lactantius, who cites Varro, a first-century B.C.E. Roman, and a collection of sibylline oracles written in Greek. Christians, Jews, and Muslims have cited sibylline prophecies to support their doctrines.[56] In the christian middle ages, sibyls were associated with Hermes Trismegistos, the Greek name of the Egyptian god Thoth, the deity responsible for alchemy, astrology, and magic. Official culture in the middle ages and the renaissance regarded the sibyl as *una bellisima incantatrice* (a beautiful enchantress) depicted as a malevolent serpent, whose aim was to distract men from the correct path.[57]

■   ■   ■

JOYCE LUSSU, a world war II partisan and feminist, has written a study of the Apennine sibyl, for whom *i monti Sibillini* in the Marche are named. Near the sanctuary of the black madonna of Loreto, whose façade of Mary's everyday dwelling inside the church depicts ten sibyls standing before ten male Jewish prophets, Lussu explored her native region. Coming upon an abandoned town in the mountains, she found traces of an ancient sibylline civilization at Cerreto. "Sibylline," for Lussu, connotes the values of the goddess as they persisted in peasant culture. Romans, invading Germans, and christian bishops tried to destroy this culture, she says; later, its women were persecuted as witches.

"Una sibilla?" What does it mean, Lussu asked an old woman she found in the ancient town. Her own mother, said the crone, had been a sibyl in Cerreto thirty centuries ago. "The sibyls who lived before us are all our mothers. Their memory becomes ours, in a continual cycle . . . of past and future."[58] Sibyls, in Lussu's view, are all our mothers and all our daughters who keep the memory of the prehistoric peaceful civilization and envision a future of communitarian democracy wherein people share ethical and social responsibilities in a society in close rapport with nature. Sibyls point to the

submerged culture of women, the *cultura sommersa* of women storytellers who remember and envision, in her words, a world "without bosses and without wars."

Long ago in the town center of Cerreto, the old woman told Lussu, there had been a round rock table encircled by oaken seats and shaded by oak and maple trees. When the wind blew, the leaves of the trees "seemed to be hands." The round table and seats in the town center symbolized a communal democracy with widely shared moral and social responsibilities, rapport with nature, and peaceful exchange with neighboring communities. In contrast to the war and slavery of subsequent male-dominant cultures, in sibylline civilization women held moral power. This was not power over others. In Cerreto's communal democracy, people determined their own destinies with freely selected division of labor and equal distribution of goods. Women, versed in agriculture and artisanry, knew how to use natural products, how to heal with herbs, and how to defend against wild animals and "detribalized" human adventurers.

Sibylline civilizations, for Lussu (and in consonance with archaeological evidence of the neolithic civilization of the goddess), were located all around the Mediterranean, connected by networks that extended into the interior of Europe, Africa, and Asia Minor. In the neolithic age, when artisans turned to the manufacture of weapons, communal democracy was destroyed, but sibylline values were subsequently transmitted by women, notably by healers and witches.

Joyce Lussu had not read the works of Marija Gimbutas when she wrote "La sibilla appenninica." The Italian feminist and the Lithuanian-American archaeologist agree that the values of the culture of Old Europe were characterized by good sense, rejection of abstract codes of morality, and nurturance of all life.

■   ■   ■

STORIES, or fables, were the theme of a conference held in 1989 by women socialists and communists at Bari, where a jeweled black madonna resides in the duomo.[59] Old Bari resembles a Middle Eastern city with winding streets; new Bari has become a major commercial hub of southern Italy. Important for paleolithic and neolithic findings, and as a port to the east and to Africa, Bari has a Museo Archeologico, a Museo Etnografico Africa-Mozambico, and the cathedral of san Niccola.

The spirit of saint Nicholas may have hovered over the conference on fables, because his story reveals how the church replaced veneration of the goddess Diana with a male church figure. Nicholas was born at Myra in the eastern Mediterranean area, not far from Ephesus, site of a major temple to Artemis/Diana, the "triple Goddess" who was believed to be a lunar virgin, mother of all creatures, and huntress/destroyer.

Calling the goddess by her Greek name, Pausanias says that "all cities worship Artemis of Ephesus, and individuals hold Her in honour above all other deities. This is due to the renown of the Amazons, those who first consecrated the land of Ephesus, those who dedicated the first image of the Goddess, long before Ionian Greeks arrived."[60] The Romans considered Diana protectress of childbirth, nursing, and healing.

The statue of Diana of Ephesus in the Farnese collection of the Museo Nazionale at Naples is eighty-one inches tall, of alabaster and bronze, with striking black hands and face. At Ephesus, she was known as mother of animals, the "many breasted Artemis." In the fifth century, she was regarded by Gauls "as their supreme deity." Today, she is recalled in the statue of Diana at Tivoli, outside Rome; her many breasts nurture all living creatures.[61]

In 431 C.E. the church expropriated the shrine of Artemis/Diana at Ephesus and rededicated it to the madonna. Diana was absorbed into christianity as saint Anne, mother of Mary and grandmother of Jesus. Her haunting face may be seen in some Italian paintings of the holy family, and her values are suggested in the significant role of grandmothers in Italian folklore. Gnostic christians identified their wisdom goddess Sophia with Diana. When Diana's temple was pulled down, pillars were taken to Constantinople for the church of Hagia Sophia. Later, the inquisition was to call Diana queen of the witches.[62]

Nicholas, known in American culture as Santa Claus, was bishop of Myra in the fourth century of the common era. He destroyed the temple of Artemis with his bare hands and was beatified as a saint by the church. Diana, triple goddess of birth, life, and death, was replaced by Nicholas, whose legend has it that he saved three young women from a life of prostitution by giving them three bags of coins for their dowries. Replacing Diana as protector of childbirth, Nicholas became the patron saint of children. The christian successor of Poseidon, protector of the sea, Nicholas shares this role with saint Mary of the Sea. Very beloved in southern Italy and in the Greek branch of christianity (perhaps because of an unconscious association with Diana), a twentieth-century census indicates that his popularity in these areas is second only to that of the madonna: she has 752 dedications, Nicholas has 359.[63]

Considering popular fables an expression of the collective unconscious, Arcidonna di Bari (made up of communist, socialist, and other women) convened a 1989 conference at Bari of women scholars who had been exploring *la cultura sommersa,* or the submerged culture and lost languages of women. The purpose of the conference was to consider the meaning of fables in contemporary feminist discourse on sexual difference *("pensiero della differenza sessuale"),*[64] exploring what women mean when they say *"libertà"* and *"felicità"* (liberty and happiness) and considering the relevance of fables to the task of inventing the future.

For Laura Marchetti, fables have been variously interpreted as stories that refer to *"una fede antica e popolare"* (an ancient popular faith), a remembrance as in a dream, the collective unconscious, or the elementary thought of humanity. The fable, as an anonymous and collective story whose origins are ancient and that is handed down orally, always has the same structural function: a misfortune followed by a journey, a challenge that culminates in a happy ending. A myth holds a social and religious (in the sense of "religio," or binding together) secret. The fable, differing from ritual or myth, has a quality of the sacred, and, since they are not "true," a quality of play, attributes characteristic of Italian vernacular beliefs.

Fables are democratic, but not in the constitutional sense wherein definitive rules enable power to decide once and for all who can talk and who cannot, what is sense and what is nonsense. In fables, everyone talks, everyone is believed, every word is recognized as a word of truth. In fables, there is no insanity and therefore no marginality. The conference statement on fables offered a description of postmodernism: "Every voice has a right, every subject can put her or himself at the periphery or at the center, every knowledge has its possibility."[65]

Remembering the age when nature was sacred and alive, and envisioning a postmodern future where everything is open, everyone and everything talks, participants in the conference pointed out that in fables everyone and everything is a subject: witches and workers, queens and dwarfs, princesses and frogs. In fables, animals talk, and so do mountains, trees, and stars in a universe of golden geese, prodigious people, winged chariots, and magical helpers.

Concerned to retrieve the vernacular wisdom lost in the modern age, Italian feminists are thinking about the stories they heard as children.[66] Lidia Menapace remembered that stories her emancipated mother told the children transmitted patriarchal values. On the other hand, stories her grandmother recounted stayed close to the earth: when her *nonna* told the story of Cinderella, she would remind the children that ashes are good for doing the laundry. In stories, Menapace's nonna taught that life is bonded with death, that all of us are finite, that the point is not to win, but to transform. Feminists need stories that will transform relations between women and men, transform meaning, and convey possibilities: anyone can take a pumpkin and turn it into a carriage—anyone can take a familiar object and, looking at it differently, turn it into a journey of discovery.[67]

For Laura Marchetti, the meaning of fables may be men trying to understand the goddess in order to conquer her. Women figures in fables vary from the good mother (generating nature) to the witch/dragon (bad in masculinist thinking) to the princess (nature subjugated and reworked by men). For contemporary Italian feminists, the submerged moral and political meaning of all fables is *"uguaglianza . . . unità . . . pace . . . amore,"* equality, unity, peace, and love.[68]

Roberto Sicuteri's Jungian analysis of the archetype of Lilith may be regarded as a contemporary fable of how this figure became transmuted in the Graeco-Roman and Judeo-christian ages into *la luna nera* (the black moon) and then into a witch.

The epigraph of the contemporary feminist magazine *Lilith* states, "After the Holy One created the first human being, Adam, he created a woman also from the earth, and called her 'Lilith.' "[69] Beautiful as a dream, Lilith appeared to Adam in the garden of Eden in the shadow of a carob tree. They loved one another. The force of their passion is felt in the Song of Songs:

> How beautiful you are my friend
> how beautiful!
> Your eyes are like doves
> How beautiful you are. . . .
> Our bed is the grass
> the walls of our house the cedars
> our roof the cypresses.[70]

Love shatters when, in the first violence done to women, Adam insists that Lilith be subordinate to him in body and spirit. She insists on equality with Adam: "We are equal because we both came from the earth."[71] She would not be *sotto di lui* (underneath him) physically and spiritually, and she fled. Adam felt abandoned. Patriarchs of the Hebrew and christian scriptures said she went to the devil and coupled with him. And from that time to the present, there has not been peace between women and men.[72]

In Sicuteri's interpretation, Lilith, in the heated imagination of the authorities of the dominant culture, became a malign figure who evolved into the witch. She became the moon goddess Ishtar of the Middle East and the Egyptian moon goddess Isis. The sun god tried to subject her to masculine power. The moon, as projection of the collective unconscious yearning for the great mother, symbolizes fertility when it is rising and abundance when it is full. As the moon declines, the dark of the moon (the fearful side of the goddess) reigns.

Trying to bring order to the many moon goddesses, Roberto Sicuteri lists Ishtar, venerated in Babylon from 3000 B.C.E.; Astarte, adored by Jews, Phoenicians, and Canaanites from 1478 B.C.E.; Isis, of Africa, venerated from 1700 B.C.E.; and Cybele, merging with Demeter and Ceres, who became the great mother goddess of the Graeco-Roman world in the last century before Jesus.[73]

An ancient statuette depicts Isis with a black half moon on her head.[74] This symbol became identified with Hecate, the Greek version of the triple goddess who ruled heaven, earth, and the underworld. Later, she was called queen of the witches, and, in peasant folklore, *la Signora*.[75] Manifestations of Hecate as witch *(maga, strega, demone, megara)* were feared because prophetesses, witches, and healers connote, for men, sickness and death.[76] Circe, whom I discussed in connection with the festa of snakes, is a significant Greek dark moon goddess, a black Demeter who became the prototype of the medieval witch.

After the thirteenth century, the specter of witches, symbolized by Lilith, may have been created by men of the high culture driven mad by church injunctions to suppress their bodily instincts. Stories about witches and their nocturnal meetings swept over northern European culture (and colonial America), stories that Sicuteri believes were fabricated in the sexual fantasies of male celibates.

Probably, states Sicuteri, a witches' sabbath was a reunion of heretics persecuted by the church. Popular fantasy, autosuggestion, and collective psychosis, not to speak of manipulation and mystification by ecclesiastical authorities, transformed peasant customs into a charnel house.[77] Torquemada of the Spanish inquisition sent ten thousand witches to the stake within two decades and hanged one hundred thousand in a massacre that may have been the grossest in Europe before the Holocaust.[78] The two massacres shared a dynamic wherein a majority kills a minority. In the case of the witch craze, an unholy fear seized men, maddened by women they could not understand.

In the Jungian theory of animus/anima, the personal unconscious of every woman has a masculine element, that of every man, a feminine. The enterprise before us is to repair the rupture that happened at the beginning of time. For Italian feminists, the rupture cannot be sewn together until men recognize that women have historically been different, as different as the black madonna is from her white counterpart.[79] Lilith, although degraded by the high culture for her independence and strength, remains "possessed of an undeniable power" for contemporary feminists. "Free, strong, and alive, Lilith represents the ability to choose between oppression and freedom."[80]

In Liguria, paleolithic images of the goddess (the Venere di Chiozza, near Scandiano, and the Venere di Savignano)[81] are near the black madonna of Montenero. In this region in 1990, the Centro Donna of Arcola and peace centers of Liguria published *La Gana,* a study of the peaceful and harmonious women's culture that the authorities tried to suppress when they burned witches.

Two hundred years separate us from the last witch burnings, states Carla Sanguinetti in the introduction. The suppression of information on the culture of witches has been virtually total. Not until 1976 was an account published in Italy of a witch trial from the perspective of a woman scholar, Luisa Muraro's *La Signora del Gioco.*[82] Not until 1989 was a scholarly study published in Italy of the connection of witch rituals to prechristian beliefs, Carlo Ginzburg's *Storia notturna.*[83]

In *La Gana,* Nives Fedrigotti, a woman historian who has studied the sources for twenty years, has reconstructed a witch trial. The proceedings reveal a profound, complex, and peaceful culture characterized by an "intense rapport with nature, with the dead, and with the vital cycle of the universe."[84] On the cover of *La Gana* is an image of the goddess.

The persecution of witches in the period 1300–1700 is relevant today, Sanguinetti says, because scapegoats, then and now, are needed by those who control the state to wash away with blood the disequilibrium caused by rebellion from below. The first massacres of modern European history occurred at the time of widespread peasant rebellions. *"La caccia alle streghe, a tutte le streghe, eretici, ebrei, donne . . ."*[85] Scapegoats included "witches, heretics, Jews, women . . ." In Italy, san Bernardino da Siena called for the extermination of witches as a purifying sacrifice to god.[86] In "hunting down scapegoats," recounts Sanguinetti, "protestants were as cruel and merciless as catholics."[87]

In witch-hunts between 1300 and 1700, accused women and rebellious peasants were both violently suppressed. Peasants arose in France, Germany, England, Spain, the Tirol, Bohemia, and Yugoslavia. "The nation states were

formed, and their codification of legal violence, from torture to extermination, was created on the ashes of witches and on the extermination of
peasants."[88]

The play *La Gana* is based on a witch court trial in the Val Poschiavana in
Switzerland,[89] near the present Italian border and not far from the sanctuary
of the black madonna of Einsiedeln. The prosecution took place after the
defeat of peasants in 1525 and before the opening of the Council of Trent in
1545. Women who transmitted the values of the goddess, and rebellious
peasants of both sexes, were considered dangerous, since they challenged
patriarchal authority.[90]

The Council of Trent condemned popular medicine as "superstition," and
subsequently an ascendant male medical profession pushed women healers
aside. But peasant women of Italy, and elsewhere, continued to teach (usually
under the cover of names of catholic saints) the values of the ancient peaceful
and harmonious civilization. Peasant women, before and after the witch-
hunt, presided over the cycle of life as healers, midwives, obstetricians,
herbalists, chiropractors, veterinarians, botanists, and hygienists.[91] Women
were responsible for birth and abortion (one of the accusations constantly
directed against witches was that they had practiced abortion), contracep-
tion, cure of sterility, love and marriage, medicines, death, euthanasia, and
the care of the dead.

One woman who performed all of these activities was Gana, named for
Aquana, a prechristian divinity of water and the earth who figures in folk
stories of the Val Poschiavana. As the botanist of her community, Gana
gathered herbs, mushrooms, and flowers. She knew how to work flax, hemp,
and linen; to card wool, dye, weave, and embroider; to dry plants and distill
liquors and perfumes; and to model with clay. Most of all, Gana liked to
make paper; it was forbidden for unauthorized people to make paper, but
she did so.

Women of the ancient civilization of Le Naquane were Gana's antecedents.
Her grandmother Benvegnuda, called Dottorella, had been an herbalist,
botanist, healer, midwife, and astrologer. A rebel who had never married,
Benvegnuda agreed with the Taborites, evangelical opponents of the established church, who spoke of an equal community of wealth. "The earth is a
loan to humans," said Benvegnuda, "to cultivate and enjoy its fruits, like the
air, the water, and sunlight, things that nobody can catch and possess."[92]

Benvegnuda participated with rebelling peasants in assaults on castles in
the Val di Sole. Banners declared that they were hungry for justice and called
upon a divinity of the poor.[93] The authorities banished Benvegnuda. In

Bohemia, she found the infant Gana in a cart that had been torched during a peasant uprising. She cared for her, calling her Fortuna, after the Roman goddess of abundance. Benvegnuda was seventy years old when she was burned as a witch.

La Gana, her only survivor, was then thirteen years old. Called "granddaughter of the witch," Gana grew into an intrepid woman who fearlessly crossed forests by night, walked for hours in search of medicinal herbs, healed the sick, cared for the dead, and treated men as equals. The persecutors came. "I am a healer, a midwife, a botanist, I gather and prepare herbs for medicines, help the sick, take care of children, women, animals, and all who cannot pay a doctor."[94]

She was burned as a witch.

CHAPTER 11

black madonnas and remembering

the future • contemporary cultural

and political transformation of Italy

Every profound new movement makes a great
swing also backwards to some older, half-
forgotten way of consciousness.
                                    —D. H. Lawrence

VERNACULAR BELIEFS in justice and equality with difference, embodied in black madonnas, are visible in the contemporary nonviolent cultural and political transformation of Italy. The theme of stories wherein the mother sends her child to do her errand in the world may be considered a metaphor for the contemporary women's and students' movements of Italy. Italian men are acute interpreters, and significant movers, in the momentous shift today to a nonpatriarchal and nonviolent new egalitarian society celebrating life.

In the rapid spiral in Italy to the third millennium, the past is remembered in the spin toward the future, a whirl of past and future that the contemporary Italian left likens to a skid on an iceberg, to a labyrinth showing flashes of the vital black depths of vernacular cultures submerged below. Postmodern, the wide democratic left of Italy believes that the labyrinthine journey to the future will be traversed with "unedited" thinking.[1]

At the bottom of the spiral may be the death gasp of patriarchal politics and religion: a chief magistrate who fires judges investigating governmental crimes,[2] mafia assassinations,[3] Lombard racism against dark immigrants, and a pope who excludes women from the priesthood while calling sexism a sin.

At the top of the spiral are young Italians nurtured by sibylline values of peasant grandmothers, along with beliefs in justice, equality with difference, opposition to violence, and *autogestione* (self-management) that they have learned from feminist mothers.[4] Young Italians have also been taught by new-left fathers, who have seceded from patriarchy into nonviolence and green movements.[5]

In a move with implications for global postcolonialism, students at the University of Palermo late in 1989 declared, *"La pantera siamo noi"* (We are the panther), and commenced a movement to change the universities and to transform Italy. Women, who now outnumber men in Italian universities and high schools, set up their own commissions. Dynamic with contradictions, students of *novanta* (the nineties) chose for their symbol a feline, perhaps in memory of the felines who accompanied the ancient African and Asian goddesses Isis and Cybele, while they use fax machines to communicate with companions throughout Italy, writing "fax fables" and publishing instant books.

La pantera siamo noi, a collection of documents, lists all university faculties occupied as of February 1990. Religious sites, as Peter Brown has pointed out, may have long and continuing influence.[6] At Palermo, where the uprising began, and which is near sanctuaries of the black madonnas of Milicia, Tindari, and Trapani, *"tutto"* (all) faculties were occupied; at Salerno, near the many black madonnas of the Campagna, faculties of law, economics and commerce, and letters and law; at Venice, whose black madonna came from Bari, architecture, and languages and literatures; at Perugia, letters, philosophy, and law; at Genoa, humanities; at Florence, whose icon of a black madonna resides at the Ponte Vecchio, letters, physics, law, agriculture, architecture, economics, and commerce; at Bari, near the ancient black la Sipontina, home of a Lucan black madonna, and close to the pilgrimage site of l'Incoronata, the black madonna of the poor, letters, law, languages, and geology; and at Camerino, near the *casa* of the black madonna of Loreto, the entire university.

At Naples, home of a black Diana, a *madonna bruna,* and near the black madonna dell'Arco and the black slave mother of Montevergine, students occupied faculties of political science, sociology, science, mathematics, physics, law, letters, philosophy, architecture, the naval institute, economics, sociology, and geology; at Padua, city of a dark santa Maria of the serfs, psychology, letters, philosophy, political science, chemistry, and pharmacy; at Pisa, near the sanctuary of the black madonna of Montenero, chemistry, pharmacy, letters, languages, medicine, veterinary science, political science, communications, and medicine; at Turin, political science and the libraries;

at Reggio Calabria, near the black madonna of Palmi and the black madonna of the poor of Seminara, the entire university; and at Cagliari, home of a black madonna, letters, law, and languages.

At Bologna, site of the Lucan black madonna della Guardia, the faculties of letters, political science, economics, law, and agriculture; at Siena, home of another santa Maria dei Servi and of images of sibyls on the floor of the duomo, science, economics, law, political science, and letters; at Catania, close by the black madonna of Chiaramonte Gulfi on the slopes of the Iblaean mountains, letters, philosophy, languages, political science, and economics and commerce; at Macerata, philosophy; at Parma, the library; at Chieti, letters and philosophy; at Pavia, political science; at Milan, the great hall; at Cassino, law; at Trieste, *"stato di agitazione dell'ateneo"* (state of agitation in the university); and at Cozenza, near icons of the black madonna of Crotone and black madonnas of Palmi and Seminara, *"tutto l'atene compreso il rettorato"* (the whole school, including the rectory). At Rome, with black madonnas in churches of S. Maria Maggiore, S. Maria Nova, S. Maria in Ara Coeli, S. Maria in Trastevere, S. Maria in Cosmedin, and S. Maria del Popolo, there were chaos, organization, agitation, and debates on the difference between formal and real democracy.

The *bocca della verità* (mouth of truth), an image often depicted on student pamphlets, is located in the portico of the church of santa Maria del Cosmedin in Rome. The mouth of truth was found in a temple to Ceres, Roman grain goddess, on whose site the church was built; today, it also houses a black madonna. The mouth of truth is round, with scrota and horns and two heads of wolves in profile on the sides; the popular belief is that it will bite the hand of liars.[7] In this temple of Ceres (who was called the "lawgiver"), four centuries before Jesus, grain was distributed to the poor. Priestesses of Ceres were considered the founders of the Roman legal system.[8]

Concerned about justice and the poor, students of novanta adopt symbolic strikes that do not destroy civil life, often occupying departments after closing hours and keeping libraries open for study. Intent on nonviolent resistance to what they regard as the unjust Ruberti law (which would, in effect, turn university research over to making a profit) as a symptom of the corruption of the prevailing system, students of novanta pass out leaflets, *"La pantera chiama,"* and declaim poetry:

Noi siamo pazzi
pazzi di vivere
pazzi di parlare

avidi di ogni cosa
nello stesso momento,
noi che bruciamo,
bruciamo come fantastiche candele.[9]

Perhaps remembering peasant grandfathers in carnevale and peasant grandmothers burned as witches, students of novanta declare themselves to be mad—mad to live, mad to speak, avid for everything: "we are burning, burning like fantastic candles." Ribald like their peasant *nonni,* they refer to an authority figure as *"una stronzata"* (a piece of excrement). Like carnival celebrants, students combine ribaldry with political pungence, satirizing all holders of power.

Identifying with the felines who walked alongside Isis and Cybele,[10] students describe *la pantera nera* with nouns and adjectives of both sexes: *"un*

Bocca della verità, *the mouth of truth, of the contemporary Italian student and human resistance movement. In the church of santa Maria del Cosmedin, Rome, the site of the goddess Cerere. Photograph by Wallace Birnbaum.*

felino," who is *"Bella, Agile, Furba, Coraggiosa, Elegante,"* a beautiful, agile, shrewd, courageous, elegant feline, who "likes to eat" Italy's industrial, communications, and political "barons." Borrowing rhythms from Marx, they say, "A wild element is breaking out in the cities to disturb the tranquil sleep of the many." Reaching far into the past, a manifesto declared an "uncontainable desire for liberty."

Refuting the racism of the Lombard League against African emigrants, as well as migrants from southern Italy, the students say of the panther, "She is black because she was constricted to emigrate clandestinely from Africa," black because she is enraged that "she cannot run free," and black in fury at the proposal to determine university research by commercial funding,[11] thereby inviting the mafia, as well as industrial and communications "barons," to govern higher education. Intuition racing ahead of their knowledge, they had not yet learned that black, in the vernacular lore of the cabala, is also the color of justice.

Students of *novanta*, said one of them, Stefania, want "a free and democratic university, a critical and wise culture, a society without manipulative managers, corrupters, exploiters,"[12] a genuinely democratic university open to everybody, and a university dedicated to authentic culture and in solidarity with the suppressed of the world. At Rome, the square of Minerva, Roman goddess of wisdom, was named Piazza Tien An Men.[13]

Daughters of feminists, women students have taken "a space and a time that is ours." In their own groups they declare the management of their own bodies and set themselves against "the violence that permeates the everyday life of every woman."[14] Concerned that the Ruberti law will skew biological research toward profit instead of human well-being, they oppose all knowledge that claims to be *"falsamente neutro"* (falsely neutral) and demand the redesign of all academic disciplines from the perspective of women's historical difference.[15]

Simultaneously sensitive to beauty (*"Che bello è davvero il novanta!"*—How truly beautiful the nineties are!)[16] and furious at the prospect of *"tatcherismo all'italiana"* (Thatcherism Italian style), students fear that the country's mixed economy will be replaced by unchecked capitalism. At present, the economy is a highly successful *capitalismo assistenziale,* or capitalism with state-owned enterprises and extensive social services (e.g., free nursery schools, free medical insurance, equal family rights, equal pay for equal work, legal abortion, free education, pensions, etc.). Italy's large corporations are balanced by a significant sector of family-operated businesses (whose shadow is the large, uncounted number of families in cottage industry) and by many cooperatives: about one-third of the economy is democratized into coopera-tives.[17] The political economy of Italy also has activist regional and local governments. Students of novanta are less interested in the final contours of an ideal economy than in preventing unchecked and unbalanced capitalism from concentrating more power in the hands of Italy's industrial and communications "barons," with consequent "competitiveness, profit, an-guish, neo-racism toward the weakest."[18]

Students of novanta want research into "a new democracy without leaders," a democracy that does not institutionalize inequality ("as do existing parliamentary democracies"), a democracy without the demagogy of open assemblies.[19] Describing themselves as "antifascist, democratic, and nonviolent,"[20] many dislike political parties, align themselves with the ecology and nonviolence movements, and prefer to consider their movement "cultural," hoping to reach "the collective unconscious of millions of persons who do not recognize themselves in this democracy."[21]

With the wisdom of recent history, students of novanta respect, but differentiate themselves from, the generation of 1968, saying that "people make revolutions and revolutions are not made by one generation, nor by one sector of society, nor, even worse, by one sect." Heirs of Gramsci,[22] and influenced by Jung, contemporary Italian students consider revolutions genuine (in a phrase they like) when they reach the "collective unconscious of millions of people."[23]

Implicit in student proposals for new seminars is the feminist value of equality with difference and new-left beliefs in unedited marxism and authentic democracy. Students propose recognition of "sexual difference in categories of study in the social sciences," study the difference between "formal and real democracy," and want to reread the first chapter of *Capital* by Marx. Unedited marxists, students propose to investigate "the ethnic question in Italy and racism." Satirizing themselves, the last cartoon of the first edition of *La pantera siamo noi* depicts homeless people at the door of the university asking, Have you finished with your inanities? We need to sleep on the study tables.[24]

Supported by the feminist and nonviolence movements, *La pantera* is applauded in the journal *Avvenimenti,* newsmagazine of "other" Italians of the democratic left. The journal of Italy's ecology movement, *Arancia blu* (the earth as a blue orange), describes students of novanta as defending "the ecology of the imagination,"[25] noting that students in resistance, like activists in the nonviolence and ecology movements, want to "live in harmony with the earth."[26]

"There is nothing more dangerous," proclaims a student graffito, "than an idea when it is the only one we have."[27] With overtones of the belief that the earth, embodied as a woman, has deep waters that periodically spring to the surface, young Italians poetically describe themselves as seeds.

Eravamo tanti semi
buttati sulla terra secca del confine
non ci hanno dato acqua
per far crescere le nostre idee
ma noi l'abbiamo presa dal profondo della terra
ed è nata una foresta
che anche da lontano puoi vederla
e crescerà vedrai
che crescerà.[28]

We are seeds thrown on dry earth, this poem of architecture students at the University of Palermo declares, seeds left unwatered. But "we have found water in the depths of the earth," and a forest has been born that can be seen from afar. "And you will see that it will grow. That it will grow."

In aiming to reach the "collective unconscious" of Italians, students have taken up the enterprise of their mothers, who, since 1968, have been recovering women's history and culture while weaving a network of political strength.[29] In deepening rage after the 1986 disaster at the Chernobyl nuclear plant, women demonstrated against personal and environmental rape, violence, and masculinist idiocy:

Rape, rape
against nature
is another result of your culture. . . .
If the body detaches itself from the mind
it goes completely insane. . . .
Sexual violence
nuclear violence
the same male logic.[30]

"Total destruction is written into the history of man, which yet is made of wars and destruction," declared a broadsheet of the group Vivere Lesbica, attributing rape, nuclear violence, and war to "man's dominance over nature and over that mother who generated him, and who has been identified with nature."[31]

Other young people, calling themselves *gente di cuore,* people of the heart, created a satirical supplement inside the communist newspaper, *L'unità,* and then seceded to found the independent newspaper *Cuore* to satirize the "reactionary left," as well as the established christian-democratic politics of Francesco Cossiga and the socialist politics of Bettino Craxi. At the national festa of *Cuore* in July 1991, questionnaires inquired into the values for which young Italians consider life worth living. Top responses were children, love, and fantasy; other values included working for clean politics, bathing in the sea at dawn, friendship, the end of the christian democrats, the end of party politics, and democracy.[32] Young people "of the heart" consider themselves communist, as they do "anyone who is not enthusiastic about living in Italy under the present christian-democratic regime."[33]

A cultural history of Italy may be found in the plays, novels, poems, and essays of Dacia Maraini. In the 1970s, a record album of feminist songs that she helped to produce was entitled *Siamo in tante* (We are many). On the cover was a photograph of a sculpture of Cybele hewn into a cliff.[34] Recently, Maraini reminded me that santa Rosalia, patron saint of Palermo, who is popularly associated with the black madonna of Milicia, is often depicted as black.

In addition to recovering prechristian myths,[35] Maraini has written the stories of marginal women who, like black madonnas, sibyls, and witches, carried the memory of the goddess into the historic age; these are stories of popular saints, nonconforming nuns, lesbians, the mentally ill, and peasant midwives, mourners, and godmothers—women who saw to birth, death, life crises, and the children. Along with remembering the many ways women have resisted subordination to the patriarchy of church, society, and state, Maraini founded *La Maddalena,* an experimental feminist theater, whose presentations in the 1970s were close in spirit to peasant carnevale and like carnevale in street theater that enacted women's protests against violence and aimed for personal and social transformation.[36]

In 1990 Maraini won the Premio Campiello for *La lunga vita di Marianna Ucria: Romanzo,* a parable of the hidden family history of Italian women historically constrained to silence by sexual violation and the violence of being forced into marriages to enhance the finances of *la famiglia.*[37] Marianna Ucria, a woman of the Palermitan nobility of the first half of the eighteenth century, was destined to marry to enhance her family's wealth and status; her only other option was to be enclosed in a convent. One difference separated Marianna from other women: she was a deaf-mute, a silence that followed the trauma of childhood sexual violation by an uncle.

Coerced by her family to marry the uncle who had raped her, Marianna is sustained by a chorus of resisting women: disobedient daughters playing with wild children who tell stories about werewolves, sardonic *nonne* (grandmothers) who describe hell as Palermo without pastry shops, independent midwives, servant women, and a daughter who became an insubordinate nun. Resisting women are in counterpoint to the barbarity of catholicism at the time of the inquisition: an invitation to the public burning of a heretic included a note offering "refreshments afterward" in the convent.

The cruelty of earlier papal catholicism has evolved today to a papal "letter of love" that rejects priesthood for women and defines their difference as acceptance of the role of the white madonna of the church: obedient virgin-mother-wife.[38]

Contemporary feminists who consider themselves catholic may have worked out a way of being catholic similar to that of peasants who historically covered pagan beliefs by following church liturgy and by invoking christian saints. Indebted to santa Teresa (almost a patron saint of Italian feminists), who insisted on "mental prayer," women may remain externally catholic for protective purposes, while keeping their own different beliefs silent.[39]

Some Italian feminist catholics are no longer willing to be silent. Pia Bruzzichelli, earlier associated with the *cittadella cristiana* at Assisi, then with the feminist journal *Noidonne,* said in the late 1980s that "God is not masculine, the celibacy of priests is not sustainable theologically." To be forced to be a mother is morally reprehensible. Liberation theology that refers to the poor, but not to women, is not credible.[40]

In the growing dissent within contemporary catholicism, voices of both genders may be heard. Catholic theologians published a volume dedicated to pope John XXIII entitled "The betrayal of Vatican Council II." Hans Küng called for a catholic ecclesiastic community, not a vatican bureaucracy— "not a pope above the church and the world, in the place of God, but a pope in the church as member (and not head) of the people of God."[41] The young catholic left, predominantly male, meets to discuss the culture of violence, how to leave behind a world system of war and dominion, and how to construct a world of peace.[42]

The women's collective of *Com nuovi tempi,* the journal of base communities in Italy, evaluated *Mulieris dignitatem* and found the encyclical of pope John Paul II on the dignity of women distant from the tone of the encyclical of pope John XXIII of the early 1960s, *Pacem in Terris,* that encouraged the independence of women and other colonized peoples.[43] The reigning pope's encyclical incited women to put a response in *Com nuovi tempi,* an essay bordered with drawings of witch hangings and burnings. Mira Furlani, and women of the comunità di base of Isolotto (Florence), noted that if there has been progress in the church from the time the inquisition burned women as witches to the "letter of love" of the present pope, the progress is dubious.[44]

The transformation of Italian women's identity over the last three generations has been analyzed by Franca Bimbi.[45] A sociologist at the University of Padua, she describes the cultural change in women's identity since world war II as a transformation comparable to the vast population shift after 1945, when peoples of the south migrated to northern Italy. The two phenomena may be connected. The patriarchate, according to Bimbi's studies, has become "a privilege without legitimation."[46] Male identity has become less clear than women's sense of self, although what women mean by their "difference" is unclear.[47] Unclear, but apparently successful as a strategy for delegitimating hierarchy.[48]

Delegitimation of hierarchy spins with what patriarchal attitudes remain in the spiral of contemporary Italian history. "Despite the demise of the patriarchal model of the male, objective imbalances continue to exist in the division of labour."[49] If delegitimation of patriarchy is the up side, the down side of the spiral is continuing violence toward women. An advanced bill on violence against women and children has been stalled in the Italian parliament for a decade by the unwillingness of some men to give up patriarchal privilege.[50]

What some men of the political center and right are unwilling to give up (the entire democratic left supports the bill) may be taken away from them by the dynamic of the Italian economy, a unique capitalism whose dominant form is the family firm. The patriarchal ideas of founders of firms have been transformed since the 1970s by the feminist movement, particularly by the family-rights act of 1975, which ensures equal economic rights within the family. Mothers made more secure by the law have reclaimed ancient prepatriarchal beliefs, seeing to it that *everyone* in the family, including daughters, is given an equal part of the patrimony, thereby subverting the patriarchal custom of males inheriting it and reinvesting in the firm. Since the 1970s, Italian daughters have been more willing to take their fathers and brothers to court to secure their equal share. This is an instance of a very advanced country whose economy has been influenced by values that hark back to the culture of the goddess and black madonnas: the mother's equal nurturance of all her children.[51]

In the middle of Italy's contemporary cultural spiral, a *controcanto femminile*, a countersong of women, is audible, according to Ida Dominijanni, in cadences insisting on women's historical difference. The refrain is women's liberty, which "does not require concessions from others but is an expression of women autonomously thinking, representing themselves, staying in this world."

Liberty is not, according to Italian women (who have a large number of rights in the constitution and legal code),[52] primarily a matter of "rights." Before the regimes of the former soviet bloc collapsed, Italian women had pointed out that abstract proclamations of equality can cover actual inequality. The central and eastern European models of communism are not relevant for Italian women, but neither is the "panacea of western democracy," Dominijanni says, because its rules have perpetuated an "actual inequality" of little or no representation for women.[53]

Women's difference has been the major theme of Italian feminist discussion over the last fifteen years.[54] The French philosopher Luce Irigaray has received a wide positive reception in Italy, perhaps because her analysis of women's historic ethical, social, and religious difference offers a pregnant possibility. If women recover themselves as subjects, women and men can live differently than they have under "men's religions of sacrifice and aggression" in hierarchical societies constructed and governed by men.[55]

The task is to remember, and to create a society with different values.[56] For Irigaray, the patriarchate is founded on rape and violence. To reestablish elementary social justice and save the earth from masculinist values of violence, power, and money, it is necessary to restore the ancient relationship between mother and daughter and to work for a peaceful revolution.[57] A recent analysis suggests that the "conceptual alliance of Irigaray with the Italian women is going to be one of the most exciting sites of theoretical production of this end of the century."[58]

Indebted to Irigaray, and to Simone Weil, in 1987 the Libreria delle Donne of Milan analyzed the impressive number of rights that Italian women have regained since 1968 and published *Non credere di avere dei diritti* (Do not believe that you really have rights).[59] With the Diotima group, they posed the question: How can women become a subject (instead of an object) when symbolic, linguistic, and conceptual modes that envelop her are "not of her own making"?[60]

In 1987 a group of communist women traveled around Italy with *La carta delle donne,* urging women to put their "difference" into politics with the slogan *"dalle donne la forza delle donne"* (from women, the strength of women).[61] A national discussion ensued on the question: What difference would women's difference make for a new society?

Lidia Menapace, stateswoman of feminism and the new left,[62] wrote an analysis of the "political economy of sexual difference." In response to the contemporary "crisis of marxism" (to which, she acknowledged, feminism has contributed), Menapace offered a "multipolar dialectic." The first contradiction in this dialectic is the feminist belief in "quality of life," a value shared by a large swath of Italians—environmentalists, pacifists, and left catholics—who consider it prior to economic development. In Menapace's feminist view of "a good marxist society," no one can speak for women. The political corollary, for everyone, is direct, not indirect, democracy, a radical democracy wherein each person speaks for herself or himself. Menapace's is a women's interpretation of a good society that evokes the radical democracy of fables, wherein every being on earth has an equal voice.

With Menapace, women at the Centro Virginia Woolf at Rome explored the values they want in a new society: free expression, quality of life, contemplation, times of silence, and sentiments. To overcome the historic gender duality between thinking and practical work requires radical political reform of working hours and redistribution of labor. A woman's workplace (in the home, the factory, the community, the culture, or politics) is to be chosen by each woman, herself. Italian feminist suspicion of Lenin's premise that women need to work outside the home to be liberated has been ventilated in two decades of feminist discussion; Menapace reaffirmed the point by warning of the danger of co-optation when women's equality and emancipation are defined with male subjectivity.

A new communal socialist society may be created, from Menapace's perspective, by exploring the "freely given" quality of women's work. Because it is freely given, it cannot be exchanged, its value is wholly subjective, and it is ribboned with pleasure, caprice, and contemplation. If the principle of the father expresses quantity, uniformity, and that which is countable (the market, the normal, the party), the mother expresses "difference, the body, the freely given, care . . . diversity."[63]

In her argument for a "multipolar dialectic in a multiverse," Menapace said that she would rely on Dante's belief that the truth of a vision is evident if it produces pleasure.[64] Differences imply multiplicity as the root of beauty: Why are there thousands of herbs, hundreds of flowers, and myriads of aromas? "Why is the slow shadow of the night never the same, not even from the same window, on the same date and same hour of the year?"[65] For this feminist and new-left theorist, "a good marxism" is grounded in the belief that the world is beautiful because it is always different.

Class is important, but it explains neither gender oppression nor the man/woman contradiction. A "feminist marxism," said Menapace, is grounded in a model of multiplicity implying "a democracy constantly in dialectical motion . . . a science that declares its limits" and in a diversity of values wherein "no value can be absolute for everyone."[66]

"If god is masculine" diversity is impossible, said Menapace, and women "die in a profound sense." Women are, in fact, "dead to history and it is incredible that to reconstruct the historical presence of women, we have to resort to oral history or to the evidence of archaeology." The omission of women from history, as well as the patriarchal exclusion of them from religious institutions, may be regarded as "genocide," or the cultural extirpation of a people. The pope's 1986 encyclical on the holy spirit, decreeing that all components of the trinity are male, said Menapace, is an "absolute masculinism."[67]

For Menapace, whose religious roots are in left catholicism and whose political beliefs derive from the new left, the masculinist values of the 1970s and 1980s have produced violence, inequality, savage competitiveness, social indifference, militarization of the world economy, misery, and war.[68] A society founded on the model of the father lacks the dimension of difference and therefore cannot offer the possibility of real democracy. Women are grounded in what has hitherto been hidden: desires, sex, death, sickness, birth. The goal is a new communal socialist society. Today's tasks are to keep the market from invading all spaces of life, to realize that it may take longer than a generation to demolish patriarchy, and to institutionalize women's historic difference in all parts of society.[69]

The U.S. bombardment of the people of Iraq disrupted this fervent Italian discussion of a good society in January 1991. The shock was followed by huge antiwar demonstrations all over the country.[70] An additional blow, after Italians realized that tens of thousands were being killed, was that the parliament, in voting to send a token military force to the Persian Gulf, had trampled on the Italian constitution, which prohibits war except in defense of the homeland. Outside Catania, students demonstrated at the NATO base at Sigonella. At Ragusa, students engaging in antiwar street theater were beaten. At Naples, students organized with *cobas* (nonunion workers) and with the unemployed to occupy government offices. At Rome, Milan, Padua, and elsewhere, students protesting the war were clubbed and arrested.[71]

In 1992 the student resistance, from Palermo to Trapani, Gela to Naples, Rome to Milan, concentrated on confronting the violence of the mafia,[72] engaging in demonstrations against racism, and waiting.[73] In this struggle, they are inspired by the courageous actions of mothers and wives who become vulnerable to violent death themselves for exposing mafia murderers: "Do you know why they killed La Torre? He was getting close to unearthing the complicity between the State and its tycoons, the mafia and the U.S. military, to traffic in drugs and arms, laundering the money to finance right-wing regimes and terrorism, and consolidating NATO policies."[74]

Contemporary student opposition to violence is part of a very large movement against violence in Italy that crosses gender, generational, political, and religious boundaries. The ultimate origins of the pervasive Italian opposition to war may be related to the memory of the peaceful civilization of the goddess and to the experience of women throughout history who have protested the slaughter and rape of war.[75]

The contemporary nonviolence movement of Italy was founded three decades ago by Aldo Capitini. Rejecting postwar U.S. protestant neorealist justifications for the armaments race and the cold war,[76] he insisted that good ends require good means. The end is liberty: any individual, group, or society that sustains itself, not in liberty but in war and preparations for war, "is directed toward death."[77] In Capitini's theology of a near, not a hidden, god, ethical first principles are do not kill and do not lie. He considers nonviolence the moral center of religion and of a good society and an imperative in a century that has escalated violence to the point of being able to extinguish life and earth.

Movimento nonviolento advocates a variety of creative strategies for conscientious objection to war and to unjust laws connected with war.[78] Italian respect for nonviolence is evident in the January 1992 law that defines conscientious objection to military service as a "right" and that establishes a cabinet post responsible for civilian service as an alternative to the military and for planning nonviolent civil defense.[79]

For the last two decades, Italy's cities have been declaring themselves nonnuclear. In 1992 the movement broadened: Concordia Sagittaria, in the Veneto, declared itself a "nonviolent city." This historic move was the work of a coalition of Verdi (greens), members of the new Partito democratico della sinistra (Pds), and people of catholic peace groups. Concordia Sagittaria bases its declaration of nonviolence on article 11 of the Italian constitution, which prohibits war except in defense of the homeland. As a nonviolent city, Concordia prohibits the manufacture or sale of armaments, offers young people information on conscientious objection to the draft, places books on nonviolence in schools and libraries, organizes debates on racism, and celebrates national holidays with the theme of rejecting war as a means of resolving conflicts.[80]

Sometimes, contemporary Italian tactics of nonviolent resistance take on the ribaldry of carnival. Trade-union workers of Gorizia have suggested an innovative method for nonviolent rejection of a television speech by the chief of state: everyone is urged to go to the bathroom and to flush the toilet.[81]

In March 1991, the conference of Movimento nonviolento at Turin (encompassing the democratic left, catholics, greens, and liberals) reaffirmed opposition to war and to preparations for it and declared "nonviolence as the essential condition for the regeneration of the human condition."[82] With nonviolence precepts of not killing and not lying, Italians opposed the war in the Persian Gulf and sought out the truth about it.

For the truth they looked to Latin Americans, with whom Italians share liberation beliefs. José Ramos Regidor's article in *Azione nonviolenta* placed the gulf war in the historical context of five hundred years of conquest, invasion, and colonialism of the south of the earth, a long war that has profited the north of the world and various puppet elites of the south, killed millions, destroyed the self-determination of peoples, and violated nature.

Racism and cultural arrogance, Regidor believes, are the root causes of this long war in which Native Americans, African Americans, peasants, immigrants, and other marginalized peoples are considered "inferior." Arrogance, and the continuing despoliation of nature, stems from not recognizing the value of different cultures and different religions. Inability to see the "difference" of other peoples was a root cause of the killing in the Persian Gulf.

The debt of the south to the north of the world, for Regidor, was incurred through the purchase of military weapons needed by authoritarian elites to keep their own peoples down, a process that brings an influx of capital to the north. A debt is owed, Regidor says, but it is a historical debt of multiple dimensions. Countries of the north owe the peoples of Asia, Africa, and Latin America for five hundred years of colonialism and neocolonialism that have secured the interests of the north by imposing military governments whose policies have been forced labor, rapine, and expropriation of natural resources. The debt mounts to ethnocide at the cultural and religious levels and to incalculable destruction of nature.

Peace, for Regidor, means peace between men and women, peace between peoples, and peace between people and nature. "We need to dismantle the dominant culture of war and to construct a new culture of peace" grounded on a respect for all the earth's diverse peoples. Genuine peace means abandoning violence, the principle of possession, and the belief in unlimited material growth. The new world will be constructed with a new way of thinking inspired by principles of nonviolence: quality of life, limits, respect for women and men, respect for the diversity of peoples, and "respect for nature."[83]

Changing attitudes toward nature, in Regidor's view, is the most important factor for attaining global peace. Nature is not an object of inexhaustible resources to exploit in the ideology of unlimited growth. Changing attitudes toward nature requires a deep commitment to ecological justice, a change in the way we live, and a change from "dominant masculinist ways of thinking and values." A radical change in our rapport with nature means recognizing "her" value, "her" language, "her" potentialities.[84]

A debate on *"una nuova filosofia della natura"* was conducted in three major Italian newspapers of the left in 1990,[85] centered on considering the earth a "living organism."[86] The debate circled two perspectives: one, adhering to traditional science, holds that what has happened in the past will happen in the future; the other, convinced that things might have gone differently in the past, believes that anything is possible and that humans can direct society and history toward one of several possible futures. Someone pointed out that considering the earth a living organism was an ancient belief. Someone else said that "a change of paradigm" is necessary, one that will reconcile *"la saggezza popolare e la scienza"* (popular wisdom and science),[87] a reconciliation that Gramsci, several decades ago, said was necessary for genuine social transformation.

▪   ▪   ▪

THE CULTURAL REVOLUTION in today's Italy has been set in spiral by the women's movement and by the related nonviolence and ecology movements inspired by women but led, for the most part, by men. In the controcanto of the women's movement, heretical themes of a Jewish woman prophet may be heard. Simone Weil,[88] who embodied the heretical meaning of vernacular Judaism and christianity, was carried by her passion to deny the divine mission of Israel, as well as the divine claims of the christian church. She sought rootedness elsewhere: "We owe a cornfield respect, not because of itself, but because it is food for mankind."[89]

Weil admired the ancient Greeks, but she was appalled by the male violence of the *Iliad,* as she was by the mass murders of the twentieth century. Instigators of violence, in her view, "have encouraged the belief in blind, mechanical force as sovereign in the universe." If we look at the world with a keen sense, "we shall see that these blind forces are limited, made to balance one against the other, brought to form a united whole by something which we do not understand, but which we call beauty."[90]

Giving spiritual context to rights, obligations, and work, Simone Weil considered *liberty* indispensable food for the human soul: liberty consists in the real ability to choose in a community to whose simple rules one consents. *Equality* is also a "vital need of the human soul." Every person is due equal respect and consideration. Differences among human beings do not imply difference in degree of respect, nor do differences negate the equal need of everyone for a house, a little piece of land, and the tools of her or his trade.[91]

Prescient about the dangers of mass society, Weil felt that "a human being has roots by virtue of . . . real, active and natural participation in the life of a community," a participation that "preserves in living shape certain particular treasures of the past and certain particular expectations for the future."[92] Weil refers to a "very ancient civilization" in which physical work was honored as a religious activity and considered sacred. "The Mysteries— a religion which embraced the whole of pre-Roman antiquity—were entirely founded upon symbolical expressions concerning the salvation of the soul, drawn from agriculture."[93] Deepening the marxist concept of unalienated labor, Weil considered work the "spiritual core" of life.[94] In witness to those killed in world war II, and in witness to a western civilization she believed terminally ill, Simone Weil refused food while in a tuberculosis sanatorium and died in 1943.

A sign of the width and depth of the contemporary cultural revolution in Italy is literature written by men that delegitimates patriarchal symbols and suggests heretical old and new vernacular beliefs. Born in the area of the black madonna of Chiaramonte Gulfi, Gesualdo Bufalino wrote *The Plague Sower* in 1988. In this novel set in postwar Palermo, the trinity has become a doctor who rages in anguished unbelief, a priest whose despair is almost bottomless, and Marta, a Jew who survived the holocaust and now lies dying in a tuberculosis sanatorium. The doctor, watching his patients die painfully, shouts, "He exists: there can be no guilt without a guilty party." God was "a blunderer . . . quacksalver . . . bungling sorcerer's apprentice," Jesus "just an alibi, a man of straw." God was not "a house of peace," but "a heavenly hound who follows us and forces us and loves us."

Marta embodies the central enigma of Bufalino's tale. Against the mythic blue of Sicilian seas, she seemed the pagan "Siren, birdwoman, fishwoman, mermaid hidden under the rock." She was a Jewish woman. When Marta died, "the sluice gates of God's flood truly rumbled, sang in those soiled sheets, and there was no dove from which salvation might come." In Bufalino's implicit theology, a pagan/Jewish woman (Lilith? Simone Weil?) dies in a world of sanatorium inmates incapable of belief who wait to die. Yet "the emotion with which we learned of others' deaths, as if they were our own, was itself love."[95]

A shepherd-poet who lives near ruins of Etruscan civilization, Ennio De Santis, describes "planet earth" as holding "Brother Sun" and "Sister Moon" in tight embrace, inviting both to "come down to brighten her who is darkening,"[96] an image that brings to mind Isis holding the sun and the moon. In painting and poetry, De Santis sends a message to "recall us to the rescue of nature, that vital sap of humanity, an appeal to the people of earth who are descending downward step by step . . . to extinguish themselves in a future darkness." The contemporary shepherd-poet invokes "the most ancient spirit of the earth, the 'Nature Spirit' that has permitted man the beginning, the alternating seasons of the world, the dignity to live humanely."[97]

Other male writers of contemporary Italy who tap submerged themes are often from the south. Their stories resemble fables with themes of leaving home, enduring adversity, and surmounting challenges. An overwhelming nostalgia for a land lost, and a need for rootedness before thinking about the future, are shared themes of these writers. Nino Piccione, author of *Isola* (island), expresses the intense longing of the Sicilian who has migrated north, who considers *sicilianità* a lost paradise of the childhood of the spirit.[98] Giuseppe Bonaviri regards Mineo, Sicily, his birthplace on the edge of the Iblaean mountains (named for the goddess), as a medley of science, magic, reality, and fable, and Sicilians as inheritors of a legendary ancient civilization still unfolding. His *Il viaggio* is a journey looking to the past, moving toward the future, in a process of becoming.[99] Saverio Stati, of Calabria, portrays the wild side of saints who transmit the values of the goddess in *Selvaggio di S. Venere*. Looking at the dark side of contemporary Italy, he attributes the success of the mafia to its ability to give the illusion of dispensing justice. Until dialects and the "vernacular culture" are recovered without sentimentality, say other contemporary writers, nothing will change.[100]

Recovering the vernacular culture has become the task of Giuseppe Jovine, of Molise, who gathers fables and stories of the region around *la madonna bruna* of Matera.[101] An eerie town, Matera's houses are built into a porous

Venere/Aphrodite in an Italian garden. Photograph by Wallace Birnbaum.

cliff, one house supporting the other, and connected by a labyrinth of paths. The dwellings resemble those of Turkey, Syria, Greece, and Egypt.[102] Near Matera is a paleolithic site of the goddess at Pisticci; in the Museo Nazionale Ridola are neolithic artifacts of the culture of the goddess. The madonna bruna in the duomo at Matera continues to be important to her followers, even after they have emigrated to America.[103]

Vernacular literature, ignored or deprecated by the hegemonic culture, must be recovered, Jovine says, because it expresses important values of submerged cultures: for example, *"comunismo co' la libertà."*[104] In addition to the hope of communism with liberty, vernacular culture, for Jovine, preserves a sense of wonder at birth, death, and regeneration, a natural predisposition to help one another, sensuality, a rapport with the dead, a sense of the spiral of history that remembers the past and envisions the future, and the hope of realizing the millenarian peasant belief in a world renewed and made peaceful—a belief Jovine sees enacted during festivals, when the "complex, unexplainable dynamic of life" explodes from the unconscious.[105]

Within this cultural ferment, and against the backdrop of war in the Persian Gulf, the Partito democratico della sinistra (Pds) was formed in January of 1991. At Bologna, home of the Lucan black madonna della Guardia, Achille Occhetto proposed to drop the name "communist," while aligning the meaning of communism with popular beliefs in justice and in equality with difference.[106]

"Ricca e rossa" (rich and red), Bologna was built on an Etruscan site of the sixth century B.C.E. Artifacts demonstrate a civilization whose values of equality, harmony between men and women, and respect for sensuality moved D. H. Lawrence in the twentieth century to meditate on the joy in living of this prechristian civilization that contrasted so dramatically with formalized protestant christianity.[107] The goddess is glimpsed in this region enigmatically at Savignano (between Modena and Bologna) in the paleolithic image of a pregnant woman whose head is shaped in the form of a phallus.[108] The image confirms Irigaray's insight that women's sexuality is at least double, perhaps plural.[109]

In the twentieth century, Tuscany was a center of partisan resistance to nazis and fascists. After the war, cities like Bologna, Modena, and Reggio Emilia elected communist governments for the next five decades—Italian socialist republics with democratic rules, political love of liberty, and everyday love of good art and good food: communism with a human face.[110]

Before the *svolta* (change) of 1990–91, the Italian communist party, transformed by a strong women's movement, already differed from other communist parties of the world in considering religious beliefs prior to political beliefs.[111] Yet Italian communists aim for a pluralist *lay* culture in which the rights of the marginal and the different (e.g., homosexuals) are respected. Suggesting his own left-catholic origins, Partito comunista italiano (Pci) secretary Achille Occhetto placed Livia Turco, a young catholic communist feminist, on the central committee of the party. For Turco, a student of postmodernist philosophy, communism is "a project of transformation that passes through different cultures and different subjects."[112]

Differentiating Italian communism from central and eastern European forms, and rejecting the post-1989 disillusioned embrace of capitalism, contemporary Italian communists want a "red and green" party combining social justice with saving the earth.[113] Theorists of the Pds who aim for the "democracy of socialism" hope that the market and accumulation of capital can be put to socialist ends.[114]

What does socialism mean in Italy today? In this country that may be a cultural and political laboratory for the third millennium, 81 percent of Italians consider socialism to mean "a just society." The popular revolutionary triad is no longer liberty, equality, and fraternity, but "liberty, equality, and justice."[115] The model for which Italians feel the most affinity is the social-democratic party of Germany (84%), followed by the Swedish democratic-socialist model (73%).[116]

Italians do not consider their views of socialism analogous to what Mikhail Gorbachev called *perestroika*. Nor are those views analogous to Chinese communism; indeed, it was after the brutal communist suppression of young Chinese dissidents in 1989 that the issue of changing the name of the Italian party became urgent. As to the United States, Italians in the past linked their fondness for Americans with the critical view that the U.S. is "the mirror of all the contradictions of the western world."[117] After the Persian Gulf war, with its massive killing of children and burial of soldiers alive, Italian popular attitudes toward U.S. military policies have become more volatile.

Looking into their own experience, and respecting theorists of the third world, Italians are transforming the terms "religious" and "secular." For Giancarlo Zizola, the first "religious" task is to desacralize politics, which blasphemously invokes religion for purposes of war, and to desacralize war, which has inherited a displaced religious sense in an age that has lost belief.[118] Contemporary Italian secularism, with its nurture of differences, may hark back to the ancient belief that the earth and all its creatures are sacred, all of them. A signal characteristic of the Pds is that it aims to preserve all the differences of the many sectors of the Italian left, so that Livia Turco can call herself a feminist, a catholic, and a communist, and so that Fabio Mussi can state, "I am a communist but I also define myself a socialist, a democrat, and an environmentalist."[119]

Differences may be stressed in Italy because, on the deepest level, there may be shared beliefs. Occhetto's proposal to drop the name "communist" was followed by intense discussion. Both "no" and "yes" groups wanted radical politics from the base, a willingness to challenge, and identification with the weak and the oppresssed of the world.[120]

The historic difference of the new Partito democratico della sinistra may inhere in the central role of women. In the Pds, Giglia Tedesco explains, women are exercising power that "has never been exercised by a political party in the world . . . [it is] a revolution."[121] In an April 1991 interview in *Confronti,* a journal addressed to the "faith, politics, everyday life" of independent catholics, protestants, Jews, feminists, and others in Italy, Livia

Turco discussed "the culture and politics of difference in the Pds." Women are involved with the Italian communist party, she said, because "they have modified it,"[122] overcoming premises of centralized government and economic development that were associated with existing communist regimes.

Turco, an initiator of the *Carta Itinerante,* which proposed to place women's difference into politics, and an advocate of the proposal of communist women to legislate work times close to human rhythms,[123] discussed immediate influences on contemporary feminist communists. She acknowledged the women theorists of difference of the Libreria delle Donne of Milan and of the Centro Virginia Woolf of Rome, whose interpretation of the writings of Luce Irigaray, said Turco, have produced an "autonomous" body of ideas about democracy and the transformation of society that have influenced the communist party. In her discussion of the "democracy of socialism," Turco observed that women work for the fruition of a "culture of democracy," with individual rights and equality of peoples, a democracy of "everyday life." The dynamic of "transformation," for Turco, means that men and women should value "life and the seasons of life."[124]

In the emerging body of Italian thinking concerned with transformation, an initial premise is "consciousness of limits" in envisioning and working for a polity and a culture "measured to the differences of the two sexes." The svolta (change of the Pci to the Pds), said Turco, was more acceptable to her as a feminist than as a communist, because women of the Pds were the founding principals of the new political grouping: "Women are no longer guests inside a political group" constructed on the base of industrial workers and a political culture that glossed over differences.

No longer a matter of demanding women's space, the agenda for feminist communists is to "start with women's culture" and with a consciousness "of our own partiality" to generate ideas and actions for the new democratic party of the left.[125] Differences between men and women are expressed, not in destructive conflict, but in the realization that the historical experience of the genders has been "different yet interdependent."[126] The political autonomy of women, the value of gender difference, and "individualization" are bricks to build a society to the measure of the genders, in which women and men are both responsible for social transformation.[127]

At the *festa delle donne* of the Pds at Rimini in June 1991, the paradox of the concept of differences was inherent in the theme—*"Libere, insieme"* (free, together). Open to all differences and stressing "liberty in the world, in everyday life, in politics, in culture, in the sentiments," women of the Pds share a belief in a newly conceived socialism, a commitment to alternative politics and institutions, and the will to construct a program for an alternative government. Festa coordinators arranged for special entertainment for the children, fund-raising for *"Sorella Palestina"* (sister Palestine), and a dance in the piazza.[128]

Celebratory, yet serious, the atmosphere of transformation in Italy is streaked with an acute awareness of the importance of the rule of law. In part this is a reaction to the uncovering of government attempts in recent decades to circumvent democratic processes.[129] On the cover of the copy of the 1947 constitution of Italy (called the most democratic constitution in the world) distributed to subscribers to *Avvenimenti,* a painting by Renato Guttuso, the Sicilian poet and painter laureate of the Italian communist party, depicts a woman who resembles the goddess Diana, running.[130]

Nonviolence is the recurring thread in the tapestry of transformation woven by the values of Italian feminists and of the largely male membership of Movimento nonviolento, whose headquarters are at Perugia and whose chapters are proliferating in all parts of the country. In the Iblaean region of Sicily, Movimento nonviolento encourages natural agriculture, the use of alternative energy, research into appropriate technology, and nonviolent resistance to military installations and to war.[131] A nonviolence conference at Verona in October 1991 had the theme "Development? Enough!" and renounced "the war of the north against the south of the earth."[132]

Culture and politics are intertwined in the contemporary transformation of Italy. A recent UNESCO survey suggested that one-half of the world's cultural heritage has come from Italy. This seems improbable until one remembers Etruscan sculpture, Roman architecture, Byzantine mosaics, the Renaissance masters Leonardo, Michelangelo, Raphael, Bernini, Canaletto, and Tiepolo, and twentieth-century artists like Modigliani and De Chirico. One sign of the contemporary cultural revolution in Italy is the emergence of women artists in touch with conscious or unconscious ancient memories.

The sculpture of Alba Gonzales is grounded in the goddess culture of the Etruscans and earth-mother goddesses of the ancient Middle East.[133] Adapting the Etruscan couple in the Villa Giulia Museum to an age of high technology, she used black African marble and red granite to sculpt two figures who "form a harmony . . . in the magical aura of loving complicity . . . a hymn to love that overcomes death and time."[134] For her sculptures of goddesses of the ancient Semites of Babylonia, Gonzales uses black and red travertine marble.[135]

Anna Belardinelli, whose art is sponsored by the center for equality of the region of Umbria (a women's center of christian democrats and communists),[136] used to paint "fantasies, dreams, women, the eye, the profile, of one who thought she/he was a spectator, multiplying antinomies, inside/outside, obverse/reverse, limited/unlimited, spectator/actor, life/death, male/female, self/non-self."[137]

Thinking about the meaning of black madonnas, Belardinelli sent me a pen-and-ink interpretation of the madonna del parto, the very popular madonna of childbirth; she depicted her with shells and cockleshells on her head and shoulders, an earth mother.

Pregnant, the earth-mother madonna has a clock in the front folds of her gown, timing the birth pains of a new civilization—in Italy, and the world. Sharing the same planet, the radically democratic socialisms of the new civilization, it seems to me, will be as different as children of the same mother.

notes

1. Vernacular liberation beliefs of Latin Americans, in contrast to liberation theology written by male clerics, may be found in stories about dark madonnas, particularly the Virgin of Guadalupe in Mexico, patron saint of Latin America. In popular stories and songs, this dark madonna is called *madre tierra*. Popular liberation beliefs of Latin America, as well as of Italy, suggest not only the difference of vernacular beliefs from church doctrine but also the difference of such beliefs from the son-centered liberation theologies of male clerics. In Latin-American folk stories about the madonna of Guadalupe, the main characters are an Indian, the dark madonna, and the bishop who lives in a palace constructed with stones taken from an Aztec pyramid. Latin-American women know the centrality of the black madonna: see, for example, the dedication of Gloria Anzaldúa's *Making Face, Making Soul: Haciendo Caras: Creative and Critical Perspectives of Women of Color* (San Francisco: Aunt Lute Foundation, 1990); see also Gloria Anzaldúa, *Borderlands: La Frontera: The New Mestiza* (San Francisco: Spinsters/Aunt Lute, 1987).

Although he has been censured by the vatican, the major liberation theologian Leonardo Boff does not, in my view, articulate vernacular liberation beliefs; in Italy such beliefs are centered on black or dark images of Mary, other saints, and the people who identify with them. Boff acknowledges the appeal of the madonna but retains, perhaps for obvious reasons, the church trinity of father, son, and holy ghost. The liberation theology of Gustavo Gutiérrez is also centered on the son; see, for example, *The Power of the Poor in History,* trans. Robert R. Barr (Maryknoll, N.Y.: Orbis Books, 1983). See also the following books by Leonardo Boff: *Liberating Grace,* trans. John Drury (Maryknoll, N.Y.: Orbis Books, 1981); *Teologia della cattività e della liberazione* (Brescia: Editrice Queriniana, 1976); and *Quando la teologia ascolta il povero* (Assisi: Cittadella Editrice, 1984). See, as well, Virgil Elizondo, *The Future Is Mestizo: Life Where Cultures Meet* (New York: Crossroad, 1992). The best analysis in this genre is that of two South American women theologians, Ivone Gebara and M. Clara Bingemer, in *Maria Madre di Dio e madre dei poveri* (Assisi: Cittadella Editrice, 1987).

2. An excellent realistic appraisal of the political contradictions of contemporary Italy is found in the *Economist,* "A Survey of Italy: Awaiting an Alternative," May 26, 1990. See Mario Perniola, "Post-Political Styles," *Differentia* 1 (Autumn 1986), for Italy as a contemporary laboratory. For a long view of the meaning of Italy's spring elections of 1992, see Sergio Turone, "Mai voto in Italia fu migliore di questo," *Avvenimenti,* April 22, 1992, which points out the historic significance of the sharp decline of the christian democrats (Dc) in the 1992 elections, the rejection of the equivocations of the socialist party (Psi), and the emergence of a strong pluralist left, shorn of connections with stalinist communism, which now holds 25 percent of parliament. The importance of this election as a pointer to a new civilization in Italy is suggested in that the democratic pluralist left now has a majority of votes to support the law against sexual violence. Other indicators of the emergence of a genuinely democratic civilization are the overwhelming majority of parliamentarians who oppose "presidential democracy" and the historic number of legislators who support the right of conscientious objection to war ("Dopo le elezioni/gli scenari: Vicini e lontani," *Avvenimenti,* April 22, 1992).

3. Quoted in Rosi Braidotti, *Patterns of Dissonance: A Study of Women in Contemporary Philosophy,* trans. Elizabeth Guild (New York: Routledge, 1991), p. 7.

4. See Gunther Zuntz, *Persephone: Three Essays on Religion and Thought in Magna Graecia,* 2d ed. (Oxford: Clarendon Press, 1971).

5. See gazetteer in Ean Begg, *The Cult of the Black Virgin* (London: Arkana, 1985).

6. See Pauline Marie Rosenau, *Post-Modernism and the Social Sciences: Insights, Inroads, and Intrusions* (Princeton, N.J.: Princeton University Press, 1992), a study helpful in pointing out affirmative, as well as skeptical, interpretations of postmodernism. For Italy as a laboratory for the third millennium, see the journal *A sinistra: Laboratorio per l'alternativa sociale e politica.*

7. Samir Amin, *Eurocentrism,* trans. Russell Moore (New York: Monthly Review Press, 1989).

8. In the twentieth century, Ignazio Silone articulated the Italian peasant thirst for justice, and the inadequacy of the church before this challenge. In his last writings, Silone put his beliefs in the voice of a conscientious nun, Severina, who would not place obedience to the church before justice; in her words, "the church has substituted the cult of quietism for the thirst for justice." See Ignazio Silone, *Severina,* edited with text by Darina Silone (Milan: Arnoldo Mondadori, 1981), p. 57; see also *Fontamara* (Milan: Arnoldo Mondadori, 1949) and *L'avventura d'un povero cristiano* (Milan: Arnoldo Mondadori, 1968). Silone's characters voice popular beliefs in justice, rejecting deformed institutional

versions of the concept in the teaching of christian churches and in the practice of the soviet version of communism.

9. See Lucia Chiavola Birnbaum, *Liberazione della donna—Feminism in Italy* (Middletown, Conn.: Wesleyan University Press, 1986).

10. See "Lo statuto del PDS: Istruzioni per l'uso," *Avvenimenti,* February 20, 1991. In the table of organization of the new party (p. 87), women's difference is institutionalized in Centri Iniziative di Donne. These are composed of women (inscribed or not in the Pds) at all levels of the party structure, in separate women's congresses, and in separate regional and local organizations. For a description of the congress at Bologna, see Luigi Pintor, "Pci, le cose sono due," *Il manifesto,* March 11, 1990.

11. "Lo statuto del PDS."

12. See Filippo Gentiloni, "Il ritorno del'etica," *Il manifesto,* March 4, 1990.

13. For stories of madonnas in trees, see Tullio Seppilli, "Le Madonne arboree: Note introduttive," in *Le grandi madri,* ed. Tilde Giani Gallino (Milan: Feltrinelli Editore, 1989).

14. See chapter 11, this work.

15. See Birnbaum, *Liberazione della donna,* chapter 17.

16. "Lo 'zoccolo duro' non abita più qui," *La repubblica,* January 31, 1991.

17. See "Divided Italy: Fear of New Europe," *San Francisco Chronicle,* February 6, 1991.

18. See Marija Gimbutas, *The Language of the Goddess* (San Francisco: Harper & Row, 1989), and *The Civilization of the Goddess: The World of Old Europe,* ed. Joan Marler (San Francisco: HarperSanFrancisco, 1991). A 1988 Italian conference on the "great mothers" held at Turin posed the question, Does a popular pagan religion exist alongside the official christian one? Neither the possibility of a continuum from the goddess to black madonnas nor the radical political implications of vernacular beliefs associated with black madonnas were discussed. See Gallino, *Le grandi madri,* and Lucia Chiavola Birnbaum, "Black and Other Madonnas," *La bella figura: The Literary Journal Devoted to Italian American Women,* no. 3 (Fall 1988): 21–31.

19. See Gimbutas, *Language;* see also Enzo Bernardini, *L'Italia preistorica* (Rome: Newton Compton Editori, 1983), pp. 226–28.

20. Differing from prehistoric Maltese temples shaped to the body of the prechristian woman divinity, the floor plan of medieval christian churches reproduced the cross.

21. See discussion of Maltese temples in Elinor W. Gadon, *The Once and Future Goddess: A Symbol for Our Time* (San Francisco: Harper & Row, 1989), an excellent synthesis of research and scholarship about the goddess.

22. Gadon, *Once and Future Goddess,* p. 62. See Bernardini, *L'Italia preistorica,* p. 295, for "la Venere di Macomer," image of the goddess in Sardinia in the neolithic age.

23. See Bernardini, *L'Italia preistorica,* pp. 355, 367.

24. In Italian vernacular culture, characteristics of the prechristian goddess often merge with characteristics, or activities, of women (sometimes men) saints, and the past is enveloped in the present in a spiral perception of time; e.g., statues of the prechristian goddess are popularly called *santoni* (great saints).

25. Italy, like Japan, is a rapidly growing economy with old and new forms like

family firms, whose course has been influenced, in Italy, by the women's movement, particularly the 1975 law assuring equal family rights of women and men. See chapter 11, this work.

26. For a discussion of postmodernism as it appears to Italian theorists, see Giovanni Mari et al., eds. *Moderno postmoderno: Soggetto, tempo sapere nella società attuale* (Milan: Feltrinelli, 1987). The political implications of postmodernism vary in different cultures. In the United States, its first impact appears to be the fragmentation of a radical perspective; see Michael Albert et al., *Liberating Theory* (Boston: South End Press, 1986). In the different cultural context of Italy, the political implications of postmodernism point to radically democratic, and different, socialisms (see chapter 11, this work). For a British evaluation of Italy's paradoxes, see Tim Mason, "Italy and Modernization: A Montage," *History Workshop Journal* (Spring 1988): 127–47, particularly p. 133.

27. See Birnbaum, *Liberazione della donna*, pp. 207–11, passim. See also *Cristiani di base oggi: Atti del VI Convegno Nazionale delle Comunità Cristiane di Base, Roma, 30/31 ottobre e 1 novembre 1982* (Naples: Segreteria tecnica nazionale delle CdB, 1983), and Comunità di base, *La chiesa cresce dal basso* (Turin: Cooperativa Tempi di Fraternità, 1978).

28. Birnbaum, *Liberazione della donna*.

29. Ibid.

30. Adrienne Rich, *Of Woman Born* (New York: W. W. Norton, 1976), p. 79.

31. The militant Black movement was suppressed in the 1960s and 1970s, but has come to life again in the 1990s. See "The Struggle Continues," *Black Panther: Black Community News Service* 1, no. 1 (Spring 1991).

32. I am indebted to Laura Stortoni for helping me to understand the previously pejorative term *terroni*.

33. This is particularly important for a study of southern Italians and Sicilians, who have developed gestures into a separate language known to themselves but not to *forestieri* (strangers). See Giuseppe Pitré, *I gesti dei siciliani: Piccola biblioteca delle tradizioni popolari siciliane*, ed. Antonino Buttitta (1871; repr. Marsala, 1983). See also Luigi M. Lombardi Satriani, *Il silenzio, la memoria e lo sguardo* (Palermo: Sellerio Editore, 1979).

34. See Rosenau, *Post-Modernism and the Social Sciences*.

35. See the discussion in Braidotti, *Patterns of Dissonance*, p. 271.

36. See chapter 11, this work.

37. See George Santayana, *Scepticism and Animal Faith: An Introduction to a System of Philosophy*, in *The Philosophy of Santayana*, ed. Irwin Edman (New York: Modern Library, 1942). See also Lucia Chiavola Birnbaum, "Enlightened Behaviorists and American Democracy" (1992).

38. Alessandro Falassi, a cultural anthropologist from Siena, reminds me that the number of black madonnas in the world may be uncountable because the original blackness has been covered over; e.g., the Jeman-ja cult in Balia, Brazil—"She is now a fair blonde mermaid but she was black" (communication to author, April 2, 1992).

39. See Merlin Stone, *Ancient Mirrors of Womanhood: A Treasury of Goddess and Heroine Lore from around the World* (Boston: Beacon Press, 1979). For Kuan Yin, see p. 28; for Ashtoreth, see p. 113; for Cybele, see p. 198; and for Isis, see p. 280. See also Charlene

Spretnak, *Lost Goddesses of Early Greece: A Collection of Pre-Hellenic Mythology* (Berkeley, Calif.: Moon Books, 1978).

40. For Falk, see the discussion of the Song of Songs in chapter 7, this work.

41. Mary Daly, *Pure Lust: Elemental Feminist Philosophy* (Boston: Beacon Press, 1984); see pp. 116–17: "Nag-Gnostic Searchers can see in these images glimmerings of our Archaic Elemental heritage. These stir deep Memory, enabling Hags to ride the Metaphors of the Black Madonnas to spheres of imagination that transcend insipid caucasian cookie-cutter depictions of the Arch-Image. Having glimpsed the Arch-Image as black earth, we are prepared to see her associations with the other elements."

42. Ibid., p. 25. See also Mary Daly, *Gyn/Ecology: The Metaethics of Radical Feminism,* with a new intergalactic introduction by the author (Boston: Beacon Press, 1990).

43. See Egon Sendler, *The Icon: Image of the Invisible,* trans. Fr. Steven Bigham (Redondo Beach, Calif.: Oakwood Publications, 1988). I thank Emily W. White for this reference.

44. See Nelle Morton, "The Goddess as Metaphoric Image," in *The Journey Is Home* (Boston: Beacon Press, 1985), pp. 147–75.

45. Ibid. She explains that while she likes the goddess as a metaphor, she is "not interested in a Goddess as an object of worship" (p. 150).

46. Judith Plaskow, "Jewish Anti-Paganism," *Tikkun,* March–April 1991.

47. Ibid.

48. Ibid.

49. See Begg, *Cult of the Black Virgin.*

50. Anzaldúa, *Borderlands: La Frontera,* pp. 29–30.

51. Quoted in China Galland, *Longing for Darkness: Tara and the Black Madonna, a Ten-Year Journey* (New York: Viking/Penguin, 1990), pp. 50–53.

52. The bibliography for this development is found throughout the book, but important landmarks, for me, include: Gimbutas, *The Language of the Goddess;* Elaine Pagels, *The Gnostic Gospels* (New York: Random House, 1979), and *Adam, Eve, and the Serpent* (New York: Random House, 1988); Elisabeth Schussler Fiorenza, *In Memory of Her: A Feminist Theological Reconstruction of Christian Origins* (New York: Crossroad, 1983); and Marcia Falk, *Love Lyrics from the Bible: "The Song of Songs," a New Translation and Interpretation* (San Francisco: HarperSanFrancisco, 1990). See also Karen L. King, ed., *Images of the Feminine in Gnosticism* (Philadelphia: Fortress Press, 1988), particularly Elaine Pagels, "Adam and Eve and the Serpent in Genesis 1–3," pp. 412ff. Other signposts have been Robert Graves, *The White Goddess: A Historical Grammar of Poetic Myth,* amended and enlarged ed. (New York: Farrar, Straus and Giroux, 1966), and Riane Eisler's exceptionally fine synthesis of feminist theory, *The Chalice and the Blade: Our History, Our Future* (San Francisco: Harper & Row, 1987). Indispensable to any study of popular culture is Barbara G. Walker, *The Woman's Encyclopedia of Myths and Secrets* (San Francisco: Harper & Row, 1983).

A glimpse of the riches of women's historiography is offered in Frances Richardson Keller, ed., *Views of Women's Lives in Western Tradition: Frontiers of the Past and the Future* (Lewiston, N.Y.: Edwin Mellen Press, 1990); see, in particular, Elizabeth Judd, "The

Myths of the Golden Age and the Fall: From Matriarchy to Patriarchy." Judd points out that myths of the golden age were not confined to Sumerian, Hebrew, Persian, and Greek sources—they are "also found in Africa, South America, and other areas in the modern period" (p. 15); "Golden age myths emphasize . . . an absence of social stratification, of warfare, and of gender distinctions and rape" (p. 24); and after the end of the golden age, there was a "loss of the earlier egalitarianism and the introduction of a class system and slavery" (p. 35).

Mary Elizabeth Perry, in "The Black Madonna of Montserrat" in the Keller volume, suggests (pp. 110ff.) that the religious symbol of a black madonna "can empower women and men who are seeking to transform society now" (p. 111). The importance of myth in reclaiming a viable past and creating the future is emphasized by Perry, who, contemplating the black madonna of Montserrat, considers "its blending of Eastern Byzantine and Western Iberian influences" a significant case of differences. "In the Spain that produced the Virgin of Montserrat, Jews, Muslims and Christians once lived together and produced an art, architecture and literature unique because of this special blending" (p. 123).

53. Carl G. Jung and Karl Kerényi, *Essays on a Science of Mythology: The Myth of the Divine Child and the Mysteries of Eleusis.* Bollingen Series 20 (Princeton, N.J.: Princeton University Press, 1963), p. 75.

54. Ibid., p. 76.

55. I am indebted to Jean Rosenthal Harris for taking me to see this figure.

56. I Giullari di Piazza, traditional Italian folk music and theater, *Il viaggio della Madonna Nera: The Voyage of the Black Madonna,* a musical and theatrical pageant written by Alessandra Belloni and Dario Bollini, with music by John La Barbera, featuring masks, giant puppets, and frescoes by Antonio Romano.

57. Dominique Mazeaud exhibit, Warsaw, 1991.

58. See chapter 11, this work.

59. See chapters 10 and 11, this work.

60. Ibid.

61. In the spin of contemporary world history, this Italian-American woman was reminded of the root meaning of *ricordare* by Corey Fischer in the premiere of *Sometimes We Need a Story More than Food,* a Traveling Jewish Theatre presentation at the Julia Morgan Theater in Berkeley, California, October 12, 1991.

62. Giorgio Galli, *Occidente misterioso* (Milan: Rizzoli, 1987), introduction.

▪ CHAPTER 2

1. Giuseppe Pitré, *Spettacoli e feste popolari siciliane: Biblioteca delle tradizioni popolari siciliane,* ed. Aurelio Rigoli, preface by Alessandro Falassi (Palermo, 1870–1913; repr. Palermo: Il Vespro, 1978). Contemporary Italian interest in folklore is suggested in the recent republication of all of Pitré's volumes (Palermo: Il Vespro, 1978). See also Salvatore Salomone-Marino, *Costumi ed usanze dei contadini di Sicilia* (Palermo: Remo Sandron, 1879). The range of the Pitré collection is suggested in the titles of the individual volumes, which I cite in the bibliography. See the preface by Alessandro

Falassi, who discussed the chthonic ground of Italian beliefs with me in February 1992 in San Francisco.

2. Giovanni Verga, *The She-Wolf and Other Stories,* 2d ed., ed. and trans. Giovanni Cecchetti (Berkeley and Los Angeles: University of California Press, 1978), p. 9.

3. Verga's classic is *I malavoglia* (Trier, 1881; repr. Verona: Edizioni Scholastiche Mondadori 1968). See Giovanni Verga, *Tutte le novelle* (Milan: Arnoldo Mondadori Editore, 1942). Verga's contemporary Luigi Capuana wrote tales about mothers who remind one of la Giustizia (see chapter 3, this work). In the aftermath of the socialist uprisings of the 1890s, Capuana took a didactic, socially conservative tone in his stories for children. See Luigi Capuana, *Versi giovanili* (repr. Palermo: Vito Cavallotto Editore, 1978).

4. See Birnbaum, *Liberazione della donna.*

5. See Pitrè, *Spettacoli,* and chapter 20, "The Lesson of Pitré," in Giuseppe Cocchiara, *The History of Folklore in Europe,* trans. John N. McDaniel (Philadelphia: Institute for the Study of Human Issues, 1952): "Folk traditions are the result of the past but . . . they live because the present, in renewing them, has taken them as its own" (p. 371).

6. See also *Piccola biblioteca delle tradizioni popolari siciliane,* ed. Antonino Buttitta (Palermo: Coopesa, n.d.).

7. Quoted in Robert N. Bellah and Philip E. Hammond, "The Five Religions of Modern Italy," in *Varieties of Civil Religion* (San Francisco: Harper & Row, 1980), pp. 88ff., p. 91. See Carlo Levi, *Cristo si è fermato a Eboli* (Turin: Einaudi, 1945), pp. 103–5, and *Le parole sono pietre: Tre giornate in Sicilia* (Turin: Einaudi, 1945). Levi used the term "magic" in a manner that is close to the usage of contemporary students of the goddess; see Starhawk, *Truth or Dare: Encounters with Power, Authority, and Mystery* (San Francisco: Harper & Row, 1987). Starhawk regards magic as "the art of liberation, the act that releases the mysteries. . . . The mysteries are what is wild in us, what cannot be quantified or contained . . . also what is most common to us all: blood, breath, heartbeat, the sprouting of seed, the waxing and waning of the moon, the turning of the earth around the sun, birth, growth, death, and renewal" (p. 6).

8. Quoted in Bellah and Hammond, "Five Religions of Modern Italy," p. 91. For a contemporary church view of the madonna that is aware of the unease of women in the patriarchal church, see Salvatore Spera, *Maria, storia e simbolo: Atti della VII primavera di Santa Chiara 1988* (Rome: Edizioni Vivere, 1989). For the perspective of an Italian woman anthropologist, see Ida Magli, "Le funzioni culturali della donna," in *La donna, un problema aperto: Guida alla ricerca antropologica* (Florence: Vallecchi Editore, 1974).

9. Bellah and Hammond, "Five Religions of Modern Italy," p. 106.

10. Ibid., p. 124.

11. The "ground bass" described by Bellah can be recognized by any visitor to Sicily. I thank Gian Banchero for reminding me that Palermo has a radio station that plays a repetitive bass melody all day and all night—an instance not only of the "ground bass" of Italian vernacular beliefs but of the repetitiveness of Sicilian culture, which periodically reaches a crescendo and then breaks into a spiral.

12. Bellah and Hammond, "Five Religions of Modern Italy," p. 92.

13. Ibid.

14. Ibid.

15. Ibid., p. 93.

16. See Pamela Berger, *The Grain Goddess Obscured: Transformation of the Grain Protectress from Goddess to Saint* (Boston: Beacon Press, 1985).

17. See Alessandro Falassi, Preface, in Pitrè, *Spettacoli.*

18. This is not meant to exclude other peasant regions of Italy. See, for example, Roland Sarti, *Long Live the Strong: A History of Rural Society in the Apennine Mountains* (Amherst: University of Massachusetts Press, 1985). This study of peaceful people in mountain villages of northern and central Italy overturns the stereotypes of most social-science studies of peasants.

19. See Dante Germino, *Antonio Gramsci, Architect of a New Politics* (Baton Rouge: Louisiana State University Press, 1990). A significant contemporary analysis of Gramsci is that of Renate Holub, *Antonio Gramsci: Beyond Marxism and Postmodernism* (London: Routledge, 1992).

20. See Bellah and Hammond, "Five Religions of Modern Italy"; and Vincenzo Bò, *La religiosità popolare: Studi, ricognizione storica, orientamenti pastorali, documenti,* essay by Clemente Riva (Assisi: Cittadella Editrice, 1979), pp. 34, 37.

21. See Frank Rosengarten, "Gramsci's Arrest," *Italian Culture* 7 (1986–89), for this important statement of Antonio Gramsci in *Quaderni del carcere,* ed. Valentino Gerratana (Turin: Einaudi, 1975), vol. 3, pp. 1762–63.

22. See Pietro Rossi, ed., *Gramsci e la cultura contemporanea: Atti del convegno internazionale di study gramsciani tenuto a Cagliari il 23–27 aprile 1967* (Rome: Editori Riuniti, 1969).

23. Antonio Gramsci, *Il Risorgimento,* new, rev. ed. (Turin: Editori Riuniti, 1975), p. 211. See also the following works by Gramsci: *Passato e presente* (Turin: Editori Riuniti, 1975), *Elementi di politica* (Rome: Editori Riuniti, 1964), and *La questione meridionale,* ed. Franco De Felice and Valentino Parlato (Rome: Editori Riuniti, 1962).

24. Rosengarten, "Gramsci's Arrest."

25. See Luigi M. Lombardi Satriani, "Gramsci e il folclore: Dal pittoresco alla contestazione," in Pietro Rossi, ed., *Gramsci e la cultura contemporanea,* pp. 329–38.

26. For the development of contemporary Italian cultural anthropology, see *Appunti per la storia dell'antropologia culturale: Materiali antropologici,* series edited by Tullio Tentori (Rome: Editrice Ianua, n.d.). See also Ida Magli, *La femmina dell'uomo* (Bari: Laterza, 1985).

27. See Placido Cherchi and Maria Cherchi, *Ernesto De Martino: Dalla crisi della presenza alla comunità umana* (Naples: Liguori Editore, 1987).

28. See Ernesto De Martino, *La fine del mondo: Contributo all'analisi delle apocalissi culturali,* ed. Clara Gallini (Turin: Einaudi, 1977); see also Ernesto De Martino, ed., *Magia e civiltà: Un'antologia critica fondamentale per lo studio del concetto di magia nella civiltà occidentale,* texts and commentary by Garin, Paolo Rossi, Frazer, Durkheim, Lévy-Bruhl, Cassirer, Freud, Jung, Piaget, Eliade, Volmat, Malinowski, Lévi-Strauss, Jensen, and De Martino (Milan: Garzanti Editore, 1962).

29. De Martino, *La fine del mondo*, p. 8.

30. See Luisa Passerini, *Storia e soggettività: Le fonti orali, la memoria* (Perugia: La Nuova Italia Editrice, 1988).

31. See Lawrence DiStasi, *Mal'occhio: The Underside of Vision* (Berkeley, Calif.: North Point Press, 1981).

32. See chapter 11, this work.

33. Ernesto De Martino, *Sud e magia* (Milan: Feltrinelli, 1959), p. 184.

34. Ibid.

35. Ernesto De Martino, *Il mondo magico: Prolegomeni a una storia del magismo*, 4th ed. (Turin: Paolo Boringhieri, 1986), pp. x–xxxvii.

36. In addition to the titles already cited, De Martino's works include *Naturalismo e storicismo nell'etnologia* (Bari: Laterza, 1941); *Morte e pianto rituale nel mondo antico: Dal lamento pagano al pianto di Maria* (Turin: Einaudi, 1958); and *La terra del rimorso: Contributo a una storia religiosa del Sud* (Milan: Il Saggiatore, 1961). In the last book, De Martino defines ethnology as having a scientific sense only if grounded on a radical and precise choice: to put in question the politics, society, and religious system in which we are born and reared (p. 137). See also Giuseppe Cocchiara, *Preistoria e folklore* (Palermo: Sellerio Editore, 1978).

See also C. Barbati, G. Mingozzi, and A. Rossi, *Profondo sud: Viaggio nei luoghi di Ernesto De Martino a vent'anni da "Sud e magia"* (Milan: Feltrinelli, 1978).

37. Gianni Vattimo, *La fine della modernità: Nichilismo ed ermeneutica nella cultura post-moderna* (Milan: Garzanti, 1985).

38. Francesco Guardiani, "Neo-barocco e post-moderno" (paper presented at the session Mythology and Literature of the ninth annual conference of the American Association for Italian Studies, University of Lowell, Lowell, Mass., April 13–16, 1989). See also Renate Holub, "Strong Ethics and Weak Thought: Feminism and Postmodernism in Italy," *Annali d'Italianistica* 9 (1991): 124–43.

39. For Pasolini, see Birnbaum, *Liberazione della donna*, pp. 180–81.

40. See Arnaldo Nesti, *"Gesù socialista," una tradizione popolare italiana, 1880–1920* (Turin: Editrice Claudiana, 1974), and *Utopia e società: Per una sociologia dell'utopia* (Rome: Ianua, n.d.). See also Roberto Cipriani, Giovanni Rinaldi, and Paola Sobrero, *Il simbolo conteso: Simbolismo politico e religioso nelle culture di base meridionali*. Preface by Alfonso Maria Di Nola (Rome: Editrice Ianua, 1979).

41. See figure 5 in Gimbutas, *Language*.

42. See Martin Bernal, *Black Athena: The Afroasiatic Roots of Classical Civilization*, vol. 1, *The Fabrication of Ancient Greece, 1785–1985* (New Brunswick, N.J.: Rutgers University Press, 1987), pp. 2, 9. See also Robert Graves, *The Greek Myths*, 2 vols. (New York: Penguin Books, 1955).

43. De Martino, *Sud e magia*, p. 184.

44. Gimbutas, *Language*, p. xiii; see also Gimbutas, *Civilization*. Gimbutas has been inspired by the folklore of her native Lithuania, a country particularly rich in evidence of the culture of the goddess because it was not christianized until the fourteenth and fifteenth centuries. Gimbutas disagrees with the position of Erich Neumann in *The Great*

Mother: An Analysis of the Archetype, trans. Ralph Manheim (Princeton, N.J.: Princeton University Press, 1955), the classical Jungian analysis of the archetype of the great mother. She finds no evidence of father artifacts in the paleolithic and neolithic eras: the pattern is that of the mother and her brother. Neumann's analysis of the great mother, from the paleolithic era to the sculptures of Henry Moore and Jacob Epstein, remains valuable, not least for the graphic evidence he presents of the culture of the goddess. Gimbutas states that we do not know when the goddess religion began but that in the lower paleolithic age there are figurines with the pubic triangle. The culture of the goddess celebrated the fertility of the earth, of human beings, and of animals, and symbols mixed all three (e.g., bull's head as human uterus). Regeneration is suggested in many symbols: eyes, labyrinth, hedgehog, double triangles, double axe as butterfly, crescents, and horns. Gimbutas dates the change from a matristic to a patriarchal civilization to the invasion of the Kurgans from the steppes of Asia at the end of the fifth millennium B.C.E.; they arrived first in central Europe, not reaching the Mediterranean until the third millennium B.C.E. Every European culture, according to Gimbutas, is a hybrid of the goddess culture and Indo-European culture. There are many forms of the goddess, but for Gimbutas and others she is most authentically conceived as a universal phenomenon of one great goddess. Gimbutas documents and analyzes the goddess culture of Europe, but she points out that other forms of the culture of the goddess can be found in Africa, the Middle East, Asia, and the Americas. I have personally observed signs of the culture of the goddess not only in Europe but also in Mexico, Australia, and Hawaii. Although she finds no father artifacts in the paleolithic and neolithic eras, Gimbutas considers men to have been important in goddess cultures; here she agrees with Riane Eisler's concept of partnership: gylany (expressed in *The Chalice and the Blade*). Gimbutas's main point is that civilization did not begin with warriors and forts, but with women and peace and the sacredness of all life. (See also the film by Marija Gimbutas, *World of the Goddess.*)

The Neumann volume remains valuable as the work of a male scholar who has collected extensive evidence of the culture of the goddess. See, for example, the following plates: Sleeping Woman, clay, Malta, neolithic; The Goddess, clay, Thrace, neolithic; Diana of Ephesus, alabaster and bronze, Rome, 11th century C.E.; Isis with Horus, copper, Egypt, c. 2040–1700 B.C.E.; Isis-Hathor Suckling Horus, bronze, Egypt, 8th–6th century B.C.E.; Goddess with Young God, bronze, Sardinia, prehistoric; Goddess with Dead Young God, bronze, Sardinia, prehistoric; Atargatis, or Dea Syria, bronze, Rome (with snake); Ceres, terra-cotta relief, Hellenic; Ceremony in Honor of Ceres, fresco, Pompeii (with snakes); Veneration of the Tree Goddess, limestone stela, Egypt, Eighteenth Dynasty; Artemis, stone, Italy, 500 B.C.E.; Cybele in a Lion-Drawn Procession Car, bronze, Rome, 11th century C.E.; Fortuna, Italian manuscript, medieval; Diana Lucifera, stone, Roman; Ceres, fresco, Pompeii; Sophia-Sapientia, Italian manuscript, medieval; *The Madonna of Mercy,* painting by Giovanni di Paolo, Siena, 1437; the Spring of Life, stone relief, Venice, ninth–tenth century C.E.; and the painting of St. Anne, the Virgin, and the Child by Masaccio, Florentine school, 15th century C.E.

45. Gimbutas, in presentation of *Civilization* at St. John Presbyterian Church, Berkeley, Calif., January 27, 1992.

46. See review of *The Language of the Goddess* by Ruby Rohrlich, "Prehistoric Puzzles," *Women's Review of Books,* June 1990. Rohrlich states that Gimbutas is at her best in interpreting the neolithic period, whose art shows "beyond a doubt that its creators worshipped goddesses." She challenges Gimbutas's discussion of the paleolithic era because the "social context" is omitted.

47. Gimbutas, *Language,* p. xiv. See Peter Steinfels, "Idyllic Theory of Goddesses Creates Storm: Was a Peaceful Matriarchal World Shattered by Patriarchal Invaders?" *New York Times,* February 13, 1990. Steinfels acknowledges that Gimbutas is the author of twenty books, has directed five excavations, reads more than twenty languages, and that there is growing acceptance of her theories among scholars who cross disciplines. Experts fault Gimbutas for her acknowledgment of indebtedness to Jakob Bachofen (a nineteenth-century theorist who, before the 1990s, had been discredited for emphasizing the centrality of the mother in prehistoric civilization), for stepping over the boundaries of several disciplines, and for speculating on the basis of a massive accumulation of evidence.

48. Marija Gimbutas, *The Goddesses and Gods of Old Europe, 6500–3500 B.C.: Myths and Cult Images,* new and updated ed. (Berkeley and Los Angeles: University of California Press, 1982).

49. See map 2, Gimbutas, *Language.*

50. See map 7, Gimbutas, *Language.*

51. Gimbutas, *Language,* xvii.

52. Ibid.

53. Ibid.

54. See Galland, *Longing for Darkness.*

55. Gimbutas, *Language,* p. 15.

56. Related to me by Professor Matteo Sansone, Mattinata, Italy, April 1990.

57. See Ramón A. Gutiérrez, *When Jesus Came, the Corn Mothers Went Away: Marriage, Sexuality, and Power in New Mexico, 1500–1846* (Stanford, Calif.: Stanford University Press, 1991).

58. See chapters 3 and 4, this work.

59. Gimbutas, *Language,* p. 159.

60. See ibid., p. 319.

61. Ibid.

62. Ibid., p. 316.

63. Ibid., p. 144.

64. See Begg, *Cult of the Black Virgin,* p. 5.

65. Gimbutas, *Language,* p. 231.

66. See Birnbaum, *Liberazione della donna,* p. 121.

67. Alfonso Di Nola, *Gesù segreto: Ascesi e rivoluzione sessuale nel cristianesimo nascente* (Rome: Newton Compton Editori, 1989).

68. See Alfonso Di Nola, *Gli aspetti magico-religiosi di una cultura subalterna italiana* (Turin: Boringhieri, 1976), and *L'arco di Rovo: Impotenza e aggressività in due rituali del sud*

(Turin: Boringhieri, 1983); see also Bò, *La religiosità popolare,* pp. 17, 19. Gershom Scholem, *Kabbalah* (New York: Dorset Press, 1974), is a good edition of cabalistic writings.

69. See Carlo Ginzburg, Introduction, *Quaderni storici* 41 (1979), p. 393. See also Riccardo Di Segni, *Il vangelo del ghetto: Le storie di Gesù, leggende e documenti della tradizione medievale ebraica* (Rome: Newton Compton Editori, 1985).

70. Carlo Ginzburg, *The Cheese and the Worms: The Cosmos of a Sixteenth-Century Miller,* trans. John and Anne Tedeschi (Baltimore, Md.: Johns Hopkins University Press, 1980).

71. Carlo Ginzburg, *The Night Battles: Witchcraft and Agrarian Cults in the Sixteenth and Seventeenth Centuries,* trans. John and Anne Tedeschi (Baltimore, Md.: Johns Hopkins University Press, 1966); originally published as *I Benandanti: Stregoneria e culti agrari tra cinquecento e seicento* (Turin: Einaudi, 1966).

72. Ginzburg, *The Cheese and the Worms,* p. 4.

73. Ibid., p. 6.

74. Ibid., p. 21.

75. Ibid.; p. 112.

76. Ibid.

77. Ginzburg, *The Night Battles,* p. xviii. He points out that the cult of Diana around Modena was not an adoration of the devil but a celebration of the female divinity, Diana (p. 28).

78. Carlo Ginzburg, *Storia notturna: Una decifrazione del sabba* (Turin: Einaudi, 1989), trans. Raymond Rosenthal as *Ecstasies: Deciphering the Witches' Sabbath* (New York: Pantheon Books, 1991). See also Margaret A. Murray, *The God of the Witches* (London: Oxford University Press, 1931).

79. See interview with Carlo Ginzburg, "Carlo dei lupi," *Il manifesto,* April 1989.

80. Ginzburg, *Storia notturna,* p. xix. He states that there appears to be a belief in going and returning from the beyond ("andare all'aldilà, tornare dall'aldilà" [p. 288]), that humans participate in the land of the living and in that of the dead (in the sphere of the visible and in that of the invisible), and that this belief is a "distinguishing trait of the human species." What he has tried to study in *Storia notturna,* Ginzburg says, is "not one story among many, but the matrix of all possible stories" ("Ciò che si è cercato di analizzare qui non è un racconto tra i tanti ma la matrice di tutti i racconti possibili" [p. 289]). See also Carlo Ginzburg, "Stregoneria e pietà popolare," in *Miti emblemi Spie: Morfologia e storia* (Turin: Giulio Einaudi Editore, 1986), and "Following the Goddess," in *Ecstasies,* pp. 89ff.

81. See Giuseppe Cocchiara, *Storia del folklore in Italia* (Palermo: Sellerio Editore, 1981).

82. Ibid. See also Natalie Zemon Davis, *Society and Culture in Early Modern France* (Stanford, Calif.: Stanford University Press, 1975), 189–206; Mikhail Bakhtin, *Rabelais and His World,* trans. Hélène Iswolsky (Bloomington: Indiana University Press, 1984); E. Le Roy Ladurie, *Les paysans de Languedoc,* 2 vols. (Paris: S.E.V.P.E.N., 1966); and E. J. Hobsbawm, *Primitive Rebels: Studies in Archaic Forms of Social Movements in the Nineteenth and Twentieth Centuries* (New York: W. W. Norton, 1959).

83. Ginzburg, *Ecstasies,* p. 11.

84. Ibid., p. 13.

85. Ibid., p. 100.

86. Ibid., p. 122.

87. See chapter 6, this work.

88. Vittorio Lanternari, "Religione popolare: Prospettiva storico-antropologica," in *Folklore e dinamica culturale: Crisi e ricerca d'identità* (Naples: Liguori Editori, 1976), pp. 85–130.

89. See Gustavo Guizzardi et al., *Chiesa e religione del popolo: Analisi di un'egemonia* (Turin: Claudiana, 1981). See also Carlo Prandi, *Religione e classi subalterne* (Rome: Coines Edizioni, 1977).

90. Guizzardi et al., *Chiesa e religione del popolo.*

91. Lidia Menapace et al., *Le scomode figlie d'Eva: Le comunità cristiane di base si interrogano sui percorsi di ricerca delle donne* (Rome: Edizione Cooperativa Com Nuovi Tempi, 1989).

92. Antonio Carbonaro and Arnaldo Nesti, *La diversità culturale* (Rimini and Florence: Guaraldi Editore, 1975), p. 45.

93. Ibid., p. 54.

94. Ibid., p. 59.

95. Ibid., p. 63.

96. See Carbonaro and Nesti, *La diversità culturale,* preface. The recovery of denied cultures in Italy has stimulated interest in preserving dialects. See G. Gulino and E. Scuderi, eds., *Questioni del dialetto: Atti del convegno di studi sul dialetto siciliano,* Pachino, May 29–31, 1981 (Catania: Aldo Marino Editore, 1981). For the personal meaning of catholicism to Italians, see Arnaldo Nesti, *Una cultura del privato: Morfologia significato della stampa devozionale italiana* (Turin: Claudiana, 1980).

97. Carbonaro and Nesti, *La diversità culturale,* pp. 87–88.

98. Ibid., p. 99.

99. See chapter 11, this work.

100. The pathfinder in the recovery of peasant women's culture is Natalie Zemon Davis in *Society and Culture.* The historiography is growing rapidly; see Piera Carroli, "Major Themes of the Lullabies of Emilia-Romagna and Toscana" (paper presented at the conference Women in Italian Culture, La Trobe University, Melbourne, Australia, June 30–July 2, 1989).

101. Antonino Cusumano, *Pani e dolci della valle del belice* (Marsala: Nando Russo Editore, 1981).

102. Antonino Uccello's *La casa-museo di Palazzolo Acreide* is invaluable for understanding the grounding in material culture of vernacular beliefs studied in chapters 3 and 4 of this work. The Museo del Folclore at Rome was founded by Tullio Tentori, an anthropologist who considers popular beliefs pivotal to the creation of a new society. See also Museo di storia e cultura contadina genovese e ligure, Catalogo (Genoa: Consorzio Agricolo Intercomunale, 1984).

103. See the journal *Confronti: Mensile di fede, politica, vita quotidiana.*

104. Satriani, *Il silenzio.*

105. See Gianfranco Fagiuoli, *Le apparizioni della madonna di Medjugorje,* Grandi Opere Peruzzo, Supplemento (Milan: Ferruccio Spena, 1985); the appendix, "Tutti i santuari italiani della madonna," lists more than one thousand sanctuaries dedicated to Mary in Italy. See also Nesti, *Una cultura del privato,* and John J. Delaney, ed., *A Woman Clothed with the Sun: Eight Great Appearances of Our Lady* (New York: Doubleday, 1960).

106. Galli, *Occidente misterioso,* introduction.

107. Ibid., p. 73.

108. Ibid., pp. 73–74.

109. Ibid., p. 90.

110. Ibid., p. 102.

111. Pagels, *Adam, Eve, and the Serpent;* see also Pagels, *The Gnostic Gospels.*

112. See Fiorenza, *In Memory of Her.*

113. Pagels, *The Gnostic Gospels,* p. 101; Galli, *Occidente misterioso,* pp. 114–15.

114. Galli, *Occidente misterioso,* pp. 120–21.

115. See Robert M. Grant, *Gnosticismo e cristianesimo primitivo* (Bologna, 1976), p. 8, and Pagels, "Adam and Eve."

116. See Walker, *The Woman's Encyclopedia,* p. 457.

117. See chapter 7, this work.

118. Bernal, *Black Athena,* vol. 1. See also Michael Grant, *The Rise of the Greeks* (New York: Charles Scribner's Sons, 1987); Claudio De Palma, *La Magna Grecia: Storia e civiltà dell'Italia meridionale dalle origini alla conquista romana* (Rome: Newton Compton Editori, 1985); Michael Grant, *The World of Rome* (New York: Praeger, 1969); Gerhard Herm, *I bizantini* (Milan: Garzanti Editore, 1985); and Alexander Schemann, *Historical Road of Eastern Orthodoxy* (Crestwood, N.Y.: St. Vladimir's Seminary Press, 1977).

119. See chapter 6, this work.

120. Bernal, *Black Athena,* vol. 1, p. 1.

121. Ibid., p. 17.

122. Ibid., p. 27. See also Jack Finegan, *Myth and Mystery: An Introduction to the Pagan Religions of the Biblical World* (Grand Rapids, Mich.: Baker Book House, 1989).

123. Bernal, *Black Athena,* vol. 1, p. 27.

124. Ibid., p. 29. See also Martin Bernal, *Black Athena: The Afroasiatic Roots of Classical Civilization,* vol. 2, *The Archeological and Documentary Evidence* (New Brunswick, N.J.: Rutgers University Press, 1991).

125. My visit in 1975 to the impressive collection of artifacts of the culture of the goddess at Megara Hyblaea was probably a critical experience in overcoming my earlier skepticism.

126. For Magna Graecia, see Gino Gullace, *Back to the Roots: A View of Magna Graecia* (Rome: International Association Magna Grecia, 1987).

127. See chapters 6 and 11, this work.

128. Georges Gharib, *Le icone Mariane: Storia e culto* (Rome: Città Editrice, 1987), pp. 236–37.

129. Anneli S. Rufus and Kristan Lawson, "Italy," in *Goddess Sites: Europe* (San Francisco: HarperSanFrancisco, 1991), pp. 236–37.

130. Ibid.

131. Gharib, *Le icone Mariane,* p. 19.

132. Ibid., p. 34.

133. Ibid., p. 50.

134. Ibid., pp. 47–48.

135. Begg, *Cult of the Black Virgin,* pp. 3, 6, 28. The many black madonnas of France were tracked by Marie Durand-Lefebvre in 1937, Emile Saillens in 1945, and Jacques Huynen in 1972. Before protestants destroyed them, there were 190 images in France, mostly in the south, in the Auvergne, Pyrenees, Rhône, Provence, and Savoy. For the black madonnas of Spain and of Einsiedeln, Switzerland, see Barbara Groth-Marnat, *A Pilgrimage to the Black Madonnas* (Santa Barbara, Calif.: Red Rose Publications, 1990), and Fred Gustafson, *The Black Madonna* (Boston: Sigo Press, 1990).

136. Begg, *Cult of the Black Virgin,* p. 3.

137. See discussion of the Pci in Birnbaum, *Liberazione della donna;* see also Chiara Valentini, *Il nome e la cosa: Viaggio nel Pci che cambia* (Milan: Feltrinelli Editore, 1990).

■   CHAPTER 3

1. Salomone-Marino, *Costumi ed usanze,* pp. 210–15. See Spretnak, *Lost Goddesses of Early Greece.*

2. Stone, *Ancient Mirrors of Womanhood,* p. 191.

3. Ibid.

4. See chapter 1, this work.

5. Quoted in Walker, *The Woman's Encyclopedia,* p. 198.

6. Ibid., pp. 21–22; see also "The Greek Mysteries of the Grain Mother and Daughter, and Related Mysteries," in *The Ancient Mysteries: A Sourcebook,* ed. Marvin W. Meyer (San Francisco: Harper & Row, 1987), pp. 21–22.

7. Carl G. Jung, "The Psychological Aspects of the Kore," in Carl G. Jung and Karl Kerényi, *Essays on a Science of Mythology: The Myths of the Divine Child and the Mysteries of Eleusis,* Bollingen Series 20 (Princeton, N.J.: Princeton University Press, 1963), p. 162.

8. Ibid.

9. Stone, *Ancient Mirrors of Womanhood,* pp. 370–71; see also Karl Kerényi, "The Kore in Eleusis," in Jung and Kerényi, *Essays on a Science.*

10. Santi Correnti, *Leggende di Sicilia* (Milan: Longanesi & Co., 1975), chapter 3, "La cristianizzazione delle leggende pagane," pp. 59ff.

11. Berger, *The Grain Goddess Obscured,* p. 2.

12. Ibid., p. 27.

13. See "The Anatolian Mysteries of the Great Mother and Her Lover, and the Syrian Goddess," in *The Ancient Mysteries,* ed. Meyer.

14. Will Roscoe, "Other Genders: Problems and Possibilities for Feminist Theory" (paper presented at the Scholars' Seminar, Institute for Research on Women and Gender, Stanford University, Stanford, California, February 19, 1992).

15. Walker, *The Woman's Encyclopedia,* pp. 453–56.

16. Berger, *The Grain Goddess Obscured,* p. 53.

17. Salvatore Quasimodo, "Vento a Tindari," in Carmelo Conti, *Il vento a corde dagli Iblei: Autori del novecento* (Ragusa and Catania: Edizioni Greco, 1987).

18. Communication to author, April 27, 1992.

19. I am indebted to Dr. Norman Birnbaum for sending me this information.

20. Henry Adams, *Mont Saint Michel and Chartres* (1904; repr. New York: Viking/ Penguin, 1986), p. 10.

21. Begg, *Cult of the Black Virgin,* may be consulted for black madonnas of southern France; Groth-Marnat, *Pilgrimage to the Black Madonnas,* is good for Spanish madonnas. For the black madonna of Einsiedeln, Switzerland, see Gustafson, *The Black Madonna.* See also Galland, *Longing for Darkness.*

22. *Santuario della Madonna di Milicia* (undated pamphlet). See also Brancato-Scammaca, *La terra feudale della Milicia nella storia della Sicilia* (undated pamphlet).

23. Quoted in Fernanda Eberstadt, "Annals of Place: The Palace and the City," *New Yorker,* December 23, 1991. I thank Ralph Ballinger for bringing this article, an excellent historical evocation of Palermo, to my attention.

24. Ibid., pp. 63–64.

25. See Mary Taylor Simeti, *On Persephone's Island* (New York: Alfred A. Knopf, 1986), and *Pomp and Sustenance: Twenty-Five Centuries of Sicilian Food* (New York: Alfred A. Knopf, 1989).

26. For Italian feast days and celebratory food, see Helen Barolini, *Festa: Recipes and Recollections of Italian Holidays* (New York: Harcourt Brace Jovanovich, 1988); see also Carol Field, *Celebrating Italy: The Tastes and Traditions of Italy Revealed through Its Feasts, Festivals, and Sumptuous Foods* (New York: William Morrow, 1990).

27. Walker, *The Woman's Encyclopedia,* pp. 554–55.

28. See Birnbaum, *Liberazione della donna.*

29. Serafino Amabile Guastella, *Le parità morali* (Ragusa, 1884; repr. San Casciano: Cappelli Editore, 1968), pp. 25–28.

30. Ibid., p. 29.

31. Ibid., p. 30.

32. Ibid.

33. Ibid., pp. 31–32.

34. Ibid.

35. E. J. Hobsbawm, *Primitive Rebels,* p. 96.

36. Ibid., p. 91.

37. See Birnbaum, *Liberazione della donna.*

38. Linda Barwick, "Women as Performers and Agents of Change in the Italian Ballad Tradition" (paper presented at the conference Women in Italian Culture, La Trobe University, Melbourne, Australia, June 30–July 2, 1989); see also Barwick, "Critical Perspectives on Oral Song in Performance: The Case of Donna Lombarda" (Ph.D. dissertation, Flinders University of South Australia, 1985).

39. Carroli, "Major Themes."

40. Ibid.

41. Claudia Angeletti, *Briganti e Madonne* (Florence: Libreria Editrice, 1982).

42. Ibid., "Storia di un falso oste."

43. Ibid., "Storia di un patto col diavolo."

44. See chapter 2, this work.

45. Angeletti, *Briganti e Madonne,* "Storia di un patto col diavolo."

46. Ibid., "Storia di un falso frate."

47. For example, the mother in the Luchino Visconti film *Rocco and His Brothers.*

48. See Giuseppe Pitrè, *Medici, chirurgi, barbieri e speziali antichi in Sicilia, secoli XIII–XVIII: Curiosità storiche e altri scritti,* ed. Giovanni Gentile (1876; repr. Rome: Casa Editrice del Libro, 1942); see also Elsa Guggino, *La magia in Sicilia* (Palermo: Sellerio Editore, 1978).

49. Guastella, *Le parità morali,* pp. 45–59.

50. Marinella Fiume, *Vita di Orazia, contadina e guaritrice* (Palermo: La Luna Edizione, 1988), p. 10.

51. Ibid., p. 12.

52. Ibid., p. 15.

53. Ibid., p. 20.

54. Salomone-Marino, *Costumi ed usanze,* pp. 210–15.

55. Fiume, *Vita di Orazia,* p. 16.

56. Salvatore Salamone-Marino, *Le reputatrici in Sicilia nell'età di mezzo e moderna* (1879; repr. Palermo: Il Vespro, 1979).

57. Ibid., p. 17.

58. Ibid., p. 21.

59. Ibid., p. 23.

60. Ibid., p. 26.

61. Ibid., pp. 37–38.

62. Ibid., p. 40.

63. Ibid., p. 41.

64. Ibid., pp. 43–44.

65. See Peter Brown, *The Cult of the Saints: Its Rise and Function in Latin Christianity* (Chicago: University of Chicago Press, 1981).

66. See Raffaele Castelli, *Credenze e usi popolari siciliani* (Palermo: Il Vespro, 1980).

67. Salomone-Marino, *Le reputatrici,* pp. 63–64.

68. Ibid., "Miracoli della madonna di Boccadirio."

69. A similar celebration of snakes is found at Pretono (Chieti).

70. Gimbutas, *Language,* p. 121.

71. Alyson Stasak, "The Spiral: The Symbol of the Goddess" (paper presented to class in feminist cultural history, California College of Arts and Crafts, Oakland, December 2, 1991).

72. Gimbutas, *Language,* pp. 136–41.

73. Ibid., p. 317.

74. Buffie Johnson, *Lady of the Beasts: Ancient Images of the Goddess and Her Sacred Animals* (San Francisco: Harper & Row, 1988).

75. See Valeria Gigante Lanzara, *Il segreto delle sirene* (Naples: Bibliopolis, 1986).

76. See Antonella Barina, *La sirena nella mitologia: La negazione del sesso femminile* (Padua: Mastrogiacomo Editore, 1980).

77. Meri Lao, *Le Sirene da Omero ai pompieri* (Rome: Antonio Rotundo Editore, 1985), p. 9.

78. See chapter 8, this work, for black madonnas of the Messina area.

79. Lao, *Le Sirene da Omero,* p. 237.

80. Walker, *The Woman's Encyclopedia,* p. 168.

81. Gennaro Finamore, *Credenze usi e costumi abruzzesi* (Palermo: Adelmo Polla Editore, 1890; repr. Cerchio, 1988), pp. 148–49.

82. See Adolfo Angelucci, ed., "Brevi cenni sulla vita di S. Domenico Abate: Protettore di Cocullo," in *Origine della processione dei Serpari* (Cocullo, n.p., n.d.).

83. See Field, *Celebrating Italy.*

84. Annabella Rossi, in *Le feste dei poveri* (Palermo: Sellerio Editore, 1986), notes that *ciambelle* (the circle bread that recalls the goddess) is a favorite ex-voto offering brought to popular madonnas of Italy (p. 21).

85. "Efficienza concretezza al servizio dell'Abruzzo: Democrazia cristiana," no. 2. *Rosina Giffi.* Elezioni Regionali 1990 (pamphlet).

■ CHAPTER 4

1. The Iblaean area has been studied by anthropologists because it is the locale of fervent saints' cults, notably that of san Sebastiano, whose festa falls on May 1, both the day of the goddess and the international socialist holiday. When they emigrated to the United States, the people of Melilli brought this festa to Middletown, Connecticut. "Pagan" overtones in the celebration have brought the intervention of the church. See Sebastiano Burgaretta, *I 'nudi' di S. Sebastiano ad Avola e Melilli* (Marsala: Nando Russo Editore, 1983), p. 30.

Saint Sebastian may be christian covering for male veneration of the goddess. Burgaretta suggests that the key to the meaning of this nude ritual is a reference to homosexuality (see p. 7). In addition to radical religious beliefs, the region has a historic continuum of radical political beliefs, ranging from the socialist fasci of the 1890s, to the uprising of farmworkers at Avola in the 1970s, to resistance to the presence of NATO nuclear missiles, to contemporary resistance to the mafia.

2. Peter Brown, *Society and the Holy in Late Antiquity* (Berkeley and Los Angeles: University of California Press, 1982), p. 258.

3. Ibid., p. 262.

4. Quoted ibid., p. 265.

5. Ibid., p. 270.

6. Ibid., p. 271.

7. Ibid., p. 281.

8. See Lucia Chiavola Birnbaum, *La religione e le donne siculo americane* (Religion and Sicilian American women) (Syracuse: Casa Editrice–Minori Cappuccini, 1981), and "Religious and Political Beliefs of Sicilian and Sicilian American Women, 1890–Present"

(paper presented at the session Sicilians and Sicilian Americans of the conference of the American Historical Association, San Francisco, December 30, 1983).

9. Birnbaum, *La religione.* See Alberto Varvaro, *Lingua e storia in Sicilia (Dalle guerre puniche alla conquista normanna)* (Palermo: Sellerio Editore, n.d.).

10. Varvaro, *Lingua e storia in Sicilia,* p. 75.

11. Ibid. See also Benedetto Cutello, *U Zoriu* (Ragusa: Editrice Erea, 1978).

12. Varvaro, *Lingua e storia in Sicilia,* pp. 75–81.

13. Ibid., pp. 81–82.

14. Ibid., note, p. 83.

15. The continuum of the earth-mother goddess and saint Anne is conveyed in Masaccio's painting of saint Anne, the virgin, and the child.

16. Varvaro, *Lingua e storia in Sicilia,* pp. 84–86.

17. Ibid., p. 89.

18. Ibid., pp. 97–98.

19. Dacia Maraini, *Viaggiando con passo di volpe: Poesie 1983–1991* (Milan: Rizzoli, 1991), p. 118.

20. In their resistance to church doctrine, southern Italians resemble the gnostics, who challenged the church precept that the Jesus who lived in the flesh was christ. See Elaine Pagels, *The Johannine Gospel in Gnostic Exegesis: Heracleon's Commentary on John* (Nashville, Tenn.: Abingdon Press, 1943).

Resistance to the church is also apparent in Italian profanity; see Giuliano Averna, "Italian and Venetian Profanity," in *The Best of "Maledicta": The International Journal of Verbal Aggression* (vols. 1–8, 1977–1985) (Waukesha, Wis.: Maledicta Press, 1987): "Swearing and cursing are very common in Italy. Although the practice is impolite, and a sin in the eyes of religion, most Italians—regardless of their social level—frequently use blasphemy. Perhaps centuries of religious domination, both temporal and spiritual, in extremely close proximity to the central power of the Catholic Church, have driven them to it" (p. 42). A good deal of the blasphemy refers to disbelief in the virginity of Mary and in the divinity of her son (see p. 40).

The Italian ethnologist Antonino Buttitta reminds us that "what seems to us obscene was in archaic society an essential moment of the sacred, whose rituals aimed to promote the regeneration of nature and of society. In this sense obscene riddles have a function identical to that of an enigma, exhibiting eros they affirm the order of life and the disorder of death." See Giuseppe Pitré, *Ottanta indovinelli popolari siciliani osceni* (Marsala: Nando Russo Editore, 1872), preface.

21. Averna, "Italian and Venetian Profanity."

22. Ibid., pp. 92–93.

23. Ibid., pp. 125–26.

24. Ibid.

25. Ibid., p. 156.

26. Ibid., p. 215; see also *Raccolta di proverbi siciliani ridotti in canzoni dall'abate Santo Rapisarda di Catania,* 4th ed. (Catania: Giannotta Editore, 1924). See Giuseppe Pitré, *Le lettere, le scienze, e le arti in Sicilia* (1870; repr. Palermo: Edizioni Il Vespro, 1979).

27. Carlo Lapucci, *La bibbia dei poveri: Storia popolare del mondo* (Milan: Arnoldo Mondadori Editore, 1985), p. 9.

28. Ibid., p. 16.

29. Ibid., pp. 15–16.

30. Ibid., pp. 36–37.

31. Carmelo Assenza, ed., *400 indovinelli siciliani* (Ragusa: Thomson Editore, 1972).

32. Lapucci, *La bibbia dei poveri,* p. 38.

33. Ibid., p. 39.

34. Ibid., pp. 92–93.

35. Ibid., p. 193.

36. Ibid., p. 107.

37. Ibid., pp. 118–19.

38. Aurelio Bianchi Giovini, *Sulla dominazione degli Arabi in Italia* (Palermo: Edizioni Il Vespro, 1979), p. 68; see also Umberto Rizzitano, *Storia e cultura nella Sicilia saracena* (Palermo: S. F. Flaccovio, Editore, 1975). The classic study is Michele Amari, *Storia dei Musulmani di Sicilia* (1872; repr. Catania: Editrice Giannotta, 1983).

39. See the discussion of Fiorenza's theology in chapter 9, this work.

40. S. Acquaviva et al., *Francesco un 'pazzo' da slegare* (Assisi: Cittadella Editrice, 1983). See also Julien Green, *God's Fool: The Life and Times of Francis of Assisi* (San Francisco: Harper & Row, 1983).

41. Mario Agosta, *Giufà al Bando* (Ragusa: Erea, 1978), p. v.

42. Ibid., p. x.

43. Ibid., p. 241.

44. Lapucci, "Le visite di san Pietro," in *La bibbia dei poveri,* p. 246.

45. Ibid., p. 247.

46. Ibid., p. 261.

47. Ibid., p. 278.

48. Ibid.

49. See Carlo Lapucci, *Il libro delle veglie: Racconti popolari di diavoli fate e fantasmi* (Milan: Garzanti Editore, 1970).

50. Ibid., p. 312.

51. Ibid., p. 327.

52. See discussion of Simeti, *On Persephone's Island,* in *Radcliffe Quarterly,* December 1988.

53. Lapucci, *Il libro delle veglie,* pp. 337–38.

54. Giovanni Selvaggio, *Il culto della sacra famiglia nella città di Ragusa* (Ragusa: Parocchia Sacra Famiglia, 1967). See also Giovanni Selvaggio, *La festa del Battista a Ragusa (1600–1976)* (Ragusa: Erea, 1977), and S. Filippo Rotolo, *La chiesa di S. Francesco all'Immacolata a Ragusa* (Ragusa: Biblioteca Francescana Editrice, 1978).

55. See the discussion of John, below.

56. Selvaggio, *Il culto della sacra famiglia,* p. 290.

57. See chapter 7, this work.

58. Selvaggio, *Il culto della sacra famiglia,* p. 292.

59. Ibid., p. 293.

60. Ibid., p. 291.

61. Ibid., p. 302.

62. Ibid., p. 306.

63. Understanding the Italian vernacular customs of godmotherhood (bonding women together) and godfatherhood (bonding men to one another) may help one to see why attitudes toward homosexuality are considerably more accepting in Italy than in the United States.

64. Selvaggio, *La festa del Battista,* p. 11. In peasant culture, saint John the baptist was invoked during the heavy work of the harvest, when lightning struck, during earthquakes, when troubles threatened a family, and when surgery was necessary (John had experience in this last, since he was beheaded). He is the only saint whose date of birth, June 24, and date of death, August 29, are both popularly celebrated.

65. Ibid., p. 21.

66. In my childhood in Kansas City, Missouri, my Sicilian paternal grandmother and aunts, who had lived near the black madonna of Chiaramonte Gulfi, baked *cuccidati* for all festivals. Not only do the fig-filled semicircular pastries recall the goddess, but I have been told that the meaning of the name cuccidati refers to the value of sharing, a dialectal rendering of "to whom shall I give them?"

67. Selvaggio, *La festa del Battista,* pp. 41–42.

68. Ibid.

69. See Antonio Pasqualino, *I pupi siciliani, piccola biblioteca delle tradizioni popolari siciliane* (Rome: Nando Russo Editore, 1983).

70. Ibid.

71. Ibid., p. 87.

72. Ibid.

73. Francesco Renda, *I fasci siciliani 1892–94* (Turin: Einaudi, 1977), p. vii. See also Giuseppe Giarizzo et al., *I fasci siciliani,* 2 vols. (Bari: De Donato Editore, 1975), Francesco Renda, *Il movimento contadino in Sicilia: E la fine del blocco agrario nel Mezzogiorno* (Bari: De Donato Editore, 1976), and Ernesto Barnabà, *I fasci siciliani a Valguarnera* (Milan: Nicola Teti & C. Editore, 1981).

74. Renda, *I fasci siciliani 1892–94,* p. vii.

75. Giovanni La Terra, *Le sommosse nel ragusano 1944–1945: I fasci siciliani nel ragusano in un processo del 1894* (Ragusa: Coop "Zuleima" Editrice, 1980), p. 78.

76. Ibid., pp. 82–92.

77. Ibid., p. 108.

78. Ibid., pp. 128–45.

79. Ibid.

80. Ibid.

81. Ibid., pp. 126–27.

82. Ibid., p. 42.

83. See Birnbaum, *Liberazione della donna,* pp. 175–77, for feminist anarchists in Sicily.

84. See the discussion of Maria Occhipinti in Birnbaum, *Liberazione della donna,* pp. 175–76.

85. Ibid., p. 91.

86. La Terra, *Le sommosse,* p. 8.

87. See James Joll, *The Anarchists* (New York: Grosset and Dunlap, 1964). Southern Italian vernacular beliefs in anarcho-communism, explored in this chapter, suggest that histories of political thought that refer to the influence of foreign theorists on Italian anarchism disregard the evidence from folklore that Italian anarchism has indigenous, ancient roots.

88. Salomone-Marino, *Costumi ed usanze,* p. 206. Almost all themes touched upon by Guastella can be found in Salomone-Marino's invaluable collection of Sicilian peasant folklore.

89. For the discourse of Amenhemet I, see Carlo Consiglio, *Una società a misura di natura* (Catania: Alfa Grafica Sgroi, 1981).

90. Corrado Catania, "Magic Sicily: An Island within the Island," *Italian Journal: A Bi-monthly Digest of Italian Affairs* 5, no. 1 (1991).

91. See Birnbaum, *Liberazione della donna,* chapter 15.

■ CHAPTER 5

1. Paolo Toschi, *Le origini del teatro italiano* (Turin: Paolo Boringhieri, 1976), p. 8. Toschi's exhaustive investigation of the historical and cultural context of the Italian theater is indispensable to any study of vernacular culture.

2. Bakhtin, *Rabelais and His World,* foreword.

3. Ibid., p. xxi.

4. Ibid.

5. Ibid., p. xix.

6. Ibid., p. 5.

7. See Walker, *The Woman's Encyclopedia,* p. 201.

8. Ibid., p. 10.

9. Ibid., pp. 84–85.

10. Ibid., p. 11.

11. Alvaro Belardinelli, "Uccidere baccanti non è reato," *Avvenimenti,* July 31, 1991.

12. Ibid., p. 26.

13. Bakhtin, *Rabelais and His World,* p. 9.

14. Ibid., p. 10.

15. Mary Ryan, "The Parade in Nineteenth-Century America," in *The New Cultural History,* ed. Lynn Hunt (Berkeley and Los Angeles: University of California Press, 1989).

16. Ibid., p. 142.

17. Toschi, *Le origini del teatro italiano.*

18. See chapter 4, this work, for san Giovanni and the custom of *comparatico.*

19. Toschi, *Le origini del teatro italiano,* pp. 6–7.

20. See chapters 3 and 4, this work.

21. This is similar to the Latin-American custom of breaking a piñata full of sweets for the children.

22. Toschi, *Le origini del teatro italiano,* p. 145.

23. Ibid., pp. 229ff.

24. Alfonso Di Nola, "L'anno degli spettri: Non vi siete sentite un po' strani in questi giorni di festa?" *Il manifesto,* January 8–9, 1989.

25. Ibid.

26. Ibid.

27. See Ginzburg, *Ecstasies.*

28. Donato Morelli, "La festa delle propaggini," in *Nuove ricerche e studi sulla Magna Grecia e la Sicilia antica in onore di Paolo Enrico Arias* (Pisa: Giardini Editori, 1988).

29. A collection of these ribald satirical verses is found in *Stornelli nostrali, opuscoli popolari scelti da Guglielmo Amerighi* (Florence: Stabilimento Grafico Commerciale, 1987).

30. Morelli, "La festa delle propaggini," p. 768.

31. Ibid., p. 769.

32. Quoted in ibid., p. 770.

33. Ibid.

34. Ibid.

35. See Frank Fata, "Understanding Pulcinella," in *Proceedings,* American Association for Italian Studies, 1990, ed. Douglas Radcliff-Umstead (Lowell, Mass.: University of Lowell, 1990).

36. Guglielmo Amerighi, *Le maschere italiane* (Florence: Libreria Editrice Fiorentina, n.d.), p. 5.

37. Ibid.

38. Ibid., p. 15.

39. Ibid.

40. Carnevale di Putignano, 1989, *Le maschere di Giuseppe Balestra,* mostra al Palazzo Municipale, Putignano, February 5–14, 1989.

41. Ibid.

42. For a vivid description of carnival at Venice, see Barbara Lazear Ascher, "Carnival Nights: Venice Full Tilt," *European Travel and Life,* February 1990. Carnivals elsewhere in Italy are similar to those of submerged cultures of the world; e.g., the carnival at Santa Cruz di Tenerife, in the Canaries, was so filled with liberty that the Spanish dictator Francisco Franco prohibited it. In the United States in recent years, the liberation implications of carnivals are discernible, particularly in the Mission District of San Francisco, where third-world peoples live.

43. See "L'AltriTalia," *Avvenimenti,* January 1, 1992, p. 84.

44. Ibid., pp. 151–52.

45. See C. Barbati, G. Mingozzi, and A. Rossi, *Profondo sud: Viaggio nei luoghi di Ernesto De Martino a vent'anni da "Sud e magia"* (Milan: Feltrinelli, 1978). See also Federico D'Agostino, "Immagini della morte e costruzione simbolica della realtà a Colle Sannita," *Sociologia* 1 (1977): 51–80, and "Religion and Magic: Two Sides of a Basic Human Experience," *Social Compass,* no. 27 (1980): 279–83.

46. See DiStasi, *Mal'occhio.*

47. Barbati, Mingozzi, Rossi, *Profondo sud,* p. 153.

48. Salomone-Marino, *Costumi ed usanze,* p. 149.

49. Ibid.

50. Ibid.

51. Quoted in Walker, *The Woman's Encyclopedia,* pp. 360–63.

52. Ibid.

53. See Paola Sensi-Isolani, "Folklore of the Irpinia" (paper presented at the conference Southern Italy and America, State University of New York, Albany, November 17, 1989).

54. I thank Lorraine Macchello for this information.

55. Mario Colangeli and Anna Fraschetti, *Carnevale: I luoghi, le maschere, i riti e i protagonisti di una pazza inquietante festa popolare* (Rome: LatoSide Editori, 1982), pp. 12–13.

56. Ibid.

57. Ibid., p. 14.

58. Ibid., pp. 17–18.

59. Ibid., p. 21.

60. Ibid., p. 22.

61. Ibid., pp. 25–26.

62. Ibid., pp. 18, 12.

63. Ibid., p. 32.

64. Ibid., p. 34.

65. Ibid., pp. 36–37.

66. Ibid., p. 40.

67. Ibid., pp. 48–49.

68. Ibid., p. 71.

69. Ibid., p. 80.

70. Ibid.

71. Ibid., pp. 111–14.

72. For the goddess and poets, see Graves, *The White Goddess:* "My thesis is that the language of poetic myth anciently current in the Mediterranean and Northern Europe was a magical language bound up with popular religious ceremonies in honour of the Moon-goddess, or Muse, some of them dating from the Old Stone Age, and that this remains the language of true poetry—'true' in the nostalgic modern sense of 'the unimprovable original, not a synthetic substitute'. The language was tampered with in late Minoan times when invaders from Central Asia began to substitute patrilinear for matrilinear institutions and remodel or falsify the myths to justify the social changes. Then came the early Greek philosophers who were strongly opposed to magical poetry as threatening their new religion of logic, and under their influence a rational poetic language (now called the Classical) was elaborated in honour of their patron Apollo and imposed on the world as the last word in spiritual illumination: a view that has prevailed practically ever since in European schools and universities, where the myths are now studied only as quaint relics of the nursery age of mankind" (pp. 9–10).

73. Colangeli and Fraschetti, *Carnevale,* pp. 123–24.

74. Ibid., p. 149.

75. Ibid.; see the description of carnival at Barranquilla, Colombia, pp. 102–3.

76. Ibid., p. 154.

77. Gimbutas, *Language,* p. xx.

78. Maureen B. Fant, "The Many Faces of Ancient Sardinia," *Italy, Italy,* July–August 1987.

79. See F. and Bruno Vacca, *Il complesso nuragico di Barumini* (Cagliari: Edizioni V.I.S., n.d.).

80. Colangeli and Fraschetti, *Carnevale,* p. 153.

81. Ibid., p. 272.

82. Ibid., p. 123.

83. Ibid., p. 200.

84. Ibid., p. 36.

85. Ibid., p. 269.

86. Ibid., p. 245.

87. Ibid., p. 241.

88. Ibid., p. 78.

89. Ibid., p. 201.

90. Ibid., p. 202. For Sardinian folklore that transmits values of the goddess, see Clara Gallini, *Dono e malocchio* (Palermo: S. F. Flaccovio, Editore, 1973); in the Sardinian ritual of santa Lucia exorcising the *mal'occhio,* the prayer (p. 177) refers to many Lucias: de Milis, de Arrabi, de Aristanis, de Casteddu, di Barrali, di Oristano, and di Cagliari. For transmission of the folk belief and rituals of exorcism of mal'occhio to the United States, see DiStasi, *Mal'occhio.*

91. Gallini, *Dono e malocchio,* p. 26. See L. Zeppegno and C. Finzi, *Alla scoperta delle antiche civiltà in Sardegna: Un universo di potente, arcaica suggestione* (Rome: Newton Compton Editori, 1984).

■ CHAPTER 6

1. Annabella Rossi, *Il carnevale si chiamava Vincenzo* (Naples, 1977), p. 22.

2. See Lucia Chiavola Birnbaum, " 'A carniliviari semmu tutti aguale' " (paper presented at the conference of the American Italian Historical Association, San Francisco, November 9–11, 1989).

3. Annabella Rossi, *Carnevale si chiamava Vincenzo,* p. 32.

4. Ibid., p. 35.

5. Ibid.

6. Michelangelo came to the Apuan Alps to find white marble for his sculptures.

7. For ancient Viareggio and Versilia, see Quinto del Carlo, *L'Antica Magione . . . Storia preromana di Viareggio e Versilia* (Viareggio: Ruggero Righini, 1988).

8. See Alfredo Morescalchi, *Ricordi di un carnevalaro* (Viareggio: La Nuova Europa, 1981). This *carrista,* who portrayed political themes in carnival floats in Italy, came to the United States and created floats of Disney figures for Macy's Thanksgiving parade in Detroit.

9. See D. H. Lawrence, *Paesi etruschi,* ed. Giovanni Kezich, with an essay by Massimo

Pallottino (Siena: Nuova Immagine Editrice, 1932), and *Apocalypse* (1931; repr. New York: Viking Press, 1966).

10. See Paolo Fornaciari, *Storia del carnevale di Viareggio,* "Speciale Carnevale," *Il tirreno,* February–March 1984.

11. Ibid. See also Scialame, *U ceppone, trenta anni di storia putignanese* (Putignano: Schena Editore, 1981); and *Canti popolari di Terra di Puglia: Testi e musiche di antiche e moderne melodie* (Putignano: Edizioni V. Radio, 1987).

12. Morescalchi, *Ricordi di un carnevalaro,* pp. 15–23.

13. A good overview of themes of Viareggio carnivals may be found in a collection of carnival postcards; see Ettore Settepassi and Moreno Raffaelli, *Città di Viareggio: Il suo carnevale, una particolare storia* (Viareggio: Circolo Filatelico Apuano di Viareggio, 1983). See also Francesco Bergamini and Giuliano Bimbi, *Antifascismo e resistenza in Versilia* (Viareggio: A.N.P.I. Versilia, 1983), pp. 13–14; and Comune di Viareggio, Assessorato alla Cultura, I quaderni del Centro Documentario Storico, Cenni di Storia Viareggina no. 4, *Il carnevale di Viareggio* (Viareggio: Paolo Fornaciari, 1981), p. 3.

14. See *Cento anni di carnevale* (Pisa: Giardini Editori, 1981).

15. Comune di Stazzema, *L'Eccidio di S. Anna* (Massarosa, 1986).

16. See Angelo Malfatti, *Viareggio 1946 . . . e fu subito carnevale* (Viareggio: Comitato Carnevale di Viareggio, 1985).

17. See Mario Tobino, Renzo Pellegrini, and Carlo Alberto di Grazia, *Il carnevale di Viareggio* (Milan: Arnoldo Mondadori Editore, 1988).

18. Carlo Alberto Di Grazia, *Viareggio: Follie di carnevale* (Viareggio: Editrice L'Ancora, 1985), chapter 12, "Nel vento della contestazione."

19. Ibid., p. 251. See also Comune di Viareggio, *Il carnevale di Viareggio,* p. 3.

20. Fondazione Carnevale di Viareggio, *Anteprima: I bozzetti del carnevale di Viareggio* (Viareggio, 1989), p. 1.

21. Ibid.

22. Italians are concerned that children not lose the precious ability to imagine. See Anna Belardinelli, *Un muro pieno di sogni* (Scandicci: Nuova Italia Editrice, 1984).

23. Gimbutas, *Language,* p. 202.

24. Ibid., p. 191.

25. "The Greek Mysteries of Dionysios," in *The Ancient Mysteries,* ed. Meyer.

26. Sensi-Isolani, "Folklore of the Irpinia."

27. See Stanley Brandes, *Metaphors of Masculinity: Sex and Status in Andalusian Folklore* (Philadelphia: University of Pennsylvania Press, 1980).

28. Ibid., p. 139.

29. See chapter 5, this work. The custom of *segare la vecchia,* revealing ambivalence to the goddess, may be found throughout Italy. See Mauro Limiti, *Umbria Folklore* (Perugia: Editrice Sigla Tre, 1985), pp. 110–11.

30. Will Roscoe, "Other Genders: Problems and Possibilities for Feminist Theory" (paper presented at the Scholars' Seminar, Institute for Research on Women and Gender, Stanford University, Stanford, California, February 19, 1992.

31. See "Cenni storici," in *Città Putignano* (Milan: Gruppo Editoriale Weka, 1987), p. 3.

32. See Anton Blok, "Rams and Billy-Goats: A Key to the Mediterranean Code of Honour," *American Ethnologist,* 1985.

33. See Giorgio Burdi, "La 'mascherea,' il desiderio profondo di diventare un 'altro,' " *L'Eco,* Putignano Carnevale Europeo, February 2, 1989, pp. 149, 151.

34. See "Mio marito è cattivo" (My husband is bad), in *Canti popolari,* p. 109.

35. See Birnbaum, *Liberazione della donna.*

36. See Francesca Duranti, *The House on Moon Lake: A Novel* (New York: Random House, 1986). See the discussion of this novel in Lucia Chiavola Birnbaum, "Red, a Little White, a Lot of Green, on a Field of Pink: A Controversial Design for an Italian Component of a Multicultural Canon for the United States," in *From the Margin: Writings in Italian Americana,* ed. Anthony J. Tamburri et al. (West Lafayette, Ind.: Purdue University Press, 1991).

37. Vittorio Tinelli and L. Tinelli, comps., *Racconti nella tradizione popolare* (Putignano: Edizioni V. Radio, 1983), p. 3.

38. Annabella Rossi, *Carnevale si chiamava Vincenzo,* pp. 1, 13, 2, 4, 5, 23, 37, 61.

39. Ibid., p. 61.

40. Gimbutas, *Language,* pp. 241–42.

41. Ibid., p. 200.

42. Ibid., p. 59.

43. "The Egyptian Mysteries of Isis and Osiris," in *The Ancient Mysteries,* ed. Meyer, p. 159.

44. Stone, *Ancient Mirrors of Womanhood,* p. 276.

45. Ibid.

46. Ibid., p. 281.

47. "Acireale non sorride più," ed. Circolo Universitario, *Carnevale* 1989.

48. Clyde Haberman, "Sicilian Mayor Tackles Political System: Popular Palermo Official Battles Coalition of Politicians and Mafia," *San Francisco Chronicle,* May 1, 1991. See Leoluca Orlando, *Palermo,* ed. Carmine Fotia and Antonio Roccuzzo (Milan: Arnoldo Mondadori, 1990).

49. See Franca Fossati, "A Palermo tra agio e disagio," *Noidonne,* June 1990.

■ CHAPTER 7

1. Cristanziano Serricchio, *La cattedrale di S. Maria Maggiore di Siponto e la sua icona* (Bari: Archivio Storico Pugliese), p. 69. See also Cosimo D'Angela, "Storia degli scavi della basilica paleocristiana di Siponto," *Vetere Christianorum* 23 (1986), pp. 337–78. This christian periodical states that the church dedicated to the black madonna of Siponto was built on a temple of Diana (p. 338).

2. Franco Cardini, "La grande madre della repubblica," in *Le grandi madri,* ed. Tilde Giani Gallino (Milan: Editore Milano, 1989), p. 79.

3. Maria Spadone, *La paleontologia del Gargano* (Tesi: Università degli Studi di Milano, Facoltà di Lettere e Filosophia, 1970–71), p. 779.

4. Ibid., p. 770. See also Anna Gaeta, *Fascino di storia sulla rupe garganica: Il Gargano dalla preistoria all'alto medioevo* (Lioni: Tipolitografia Irpina, 1980).

5. Gaeta, *Fascino di storia,* table 41. See also Gimbutas, *Language.*

6. Gimbutas, *Language,* p. 87.

7. Ibid.

8. Apuleius, *The Golden Ass,* trans. Jack Lindsay (Bloomington: Indiana University Press, 1960).

9. See Raffaelle Pettazione, *Italia religiosa* (Bari: Laterza, 1952).

10. Pagels, *Adam, Eve, and the Serpent,* p. xviii.

11. Pagels, "Adam and Eve."

12. Pagels, *Adam, Eve, and the Serpent,* p. xxvi.

13. See the writings of John Adams.

14. Gaeta, *Fascino di storia,* p. 125.

15. Ibid., chapter 5.

16. Ibid.

17. Serricchio, *Cattedrale di S. Maria Maggiore,* pp. 94–95. See also Michele De Filippo, *Società e folclore sul Gargano* (Manfredonia: Michele De Filippo, 1989).

18. Serricchio, *Cattedrale di S. Maria Maggiore.*

19. Ibid., p. 98.

20. "Maria: Donna Obbediente," *Il Rosario* (Siponto: A. N. 3, March 1990). The leaflet contained a letter from the bishop, illustrated with an image of a white, obedient madonna (*"madonna obbediente"*), that warned against "idolatrous instincts not yet spent in our heart." Revealing a layer of ambivalence, the leaflet stated that santa Maria was a symbol of passive resistance and of civil disobedience whenever conscience prompted one to obey god rather than men.

21. Serricchio, *Cattedrale di S. Maria Maggiore,* p. 75.

22. Ibid.

23. Padua was a major center of the red brigades of the 1970s, students inflamed by religious and marxist beliefs. Passionately committed to justice, the red brigades engaged in violent revolutionary acts. In the 1990s, students at the University of Padua are active in nonviolent resistance.

24. See Phyllis Trible, "A Mosaic for Miriam" (E. T. Earl Lecture, Pacific School of Religion, presented at the First Congregational Church of Berkeley, Berkeley, Calif., January 30, 1992).

25. See chapter 10, this work, for a discussion of sibyls.

26. Giuseppe Santarelli, *Loreto arte* (Loreto: Congregazione Universale della S. Casa-Loreto, Anno mariano 1987–1988); see introduction.

27. Ibid., p. 11.

28. *Loreto e il suo messaggio* (Loreto: Basilica della Santa Casa, n.d.).

29. See chapter 10, this work.

30. Santarelli, *Loreto arte,* p. 39.

31. See Fiorenza, *In Memory of Her.* See also Marina Warner, *Alone of All Her Sex: The Myth and the Cult of the Virgin Mary* (New York: Wallaby Pocket Books, 1976); Graves, *The White Goddess;* and Berger, *The Grain Goddess Obscured.*

32. See Alfonso Di Nola, "La femminilità di Dio nel Giudaismo esoterico," in *Le grandi madri* (Milan: Feltrinelli Editore, 1989).

33. Fiorenza, *In Memory of Her,* p. xiii.

34. Ibid., p. 134.

35. Ibid., p. 135.

36. See Adriano Prosperi, "La Pasqua dei lavoratori: Sulla preistoria del Primo Maggio," in *Storia del Primo Maggio,* ed. Renato Zangheri (Rome: Aiep Editore–l'Unità, 1987). This article tracks the origins of the May 1 holiday to prehistory and calls the festival the "easter" of workers.

37. Arnaldo Nesti, *Le fontane e il borgo: Il fattore religione nella società italiana contemporanea* (Rome: Editrice Ianua, 1982), p. 136.

38. Annabella Rossi, *Le feste dei poveri,* pp. 70, 123.

39. *L'Incoronata, cittadella di Maria: 1001 pellegrini verso il millennio 2001* (Foggia: Opera Don Orione, 1990), p. 48.

40. See Giuseppe Angione, *La città del sole: Realtà e sogno di un bracciante,* ed. Giovanni Rinaldi and Paola Sobrero (Foggia: Laboratorio Culturale G. Angione, 1982), pp. 15, 32, 57, 70.

41. See Barbati, Mingozzi, and Rossi, *Profondo sud.* For a patronizing, academic analysis of vernacular Apulian religious beliefs, see Miriam Castiglione, "Sogni, visioni e devozioni popolari nella cultura contadina meridionale," in Gustavo Guizzardi et al., *Chiesa e religione del popolo: Analisi di un'egemonia* (Turin: Claudiana, 1981). Castiglione states that the northern part of Apulia "pullulates with visionaries and healers" (p. 76), attracting peasant-workers, unemployed students, and returning emigrants seeking a direct religious experience. The political implications of these religious experiences, according to Castiglione, are counter to the status quo (p. 76).

Nesti, *Le fontane e il borgo,* is a perceptive account presenting the postmodern world as having become a fable in which it is difficult to say what is good or bad, what is reality and what is appearance (p. 27). Nesti regards this quality as similar to the christian tension between what is already visible and what has not yet appeared (p. 28).

42. Edward Abbey, "Keeping True to Earth," *City Lights Review,* no. 1 (1987): 93–95.

43. Ibid.

44. See "La battaglia di Cerignola," *Il manifesto,* June 17, 1990.

45. *Messaggio del vescovo* (Cerignola: Diocesi di Cerignola–Ascoli Satriano, April 29, 1990).

46. Cipriani, Rinaldi, and Sobrero, *Il simbolo conteso,* p. 48; see also Nesti, *"Gesù socialista."*

47. Justin Vitiello, "Sicily Within," unpublished manuscript, p. 34.

48. Cipriani, Rinaldi, and Sobrero, *Il simbolo conteso,* p. 55.

49. *Stornelli nostrali,* p. 3. Like other compilations, this collection of *stornelli* includes miracles of the madonna, stories of Tuscan brigands, poems for children, women's proverbs, and stories about the rich and the poor.

50. Cipriani, Rinaldi, and Sobrero, *Il simbolo conteso,* p. 33.

51. Ibid., p. 34.

52. Ibid., p. 35.

53. Ibid., p. 56.

54. Ibid., p. 66.

55. Walker, *The Woman's Encyclopedia,* p. 13.

56. Cipriani, Rinaldi, and Sobrero, *Il simbolo conteso,* p. 80.

57. See *Canti popolari.* See also Barwick, "Women as Performers and Agents": "So many performers, both men and women, claim to have learnt the song through the family that it is clear the principal channel of transmission is in the domestic sphere, the woman's domain."

58. Cipriani, Rinaldi, and Sobrero, *Il simbolo conteso,* p. 7.

59. Ibid., p. 20.

60. Ibid.

61. Ibid.

62. Interview with Professor Sansone, April 1990.

63. Ibid.

▪ CHAPTER 8

1. See Falk, *Love Lyrics from the Bible,* poem 2, p. 13.

2. Ibid. For a discussion of the feminist dimension of black madonnas deriving from the Hebrew scriptures, see Gadon, *Once and Future Goddess,* pp. 213–18.

3. Leonard W. Moss and Stephen C. Cappannari, "In Quest of the Black Virgin: She Is Black because She Is Black," in Preston, *Mother Worship.*

4. Ibid., p. 54.

5. Ibid., p. 55.

6. Moss thought the black madonna of Lucera was related to prechristian women divinities brought by Greeks from Crete or Romans from Africa (ibid., pp. 54–55). Today, we know that prechristian women divinities were worshiped in Italy long before the arrival of the Greeks and the Romans. The black madonna of Lucera is located near the site of the Samnite goddess Mefite, whose images may be found in museums of the region. As indicated in the text, indigenous goddesses melded with later ones.

7. Annie Sacerdoti, *Guide to Jewish Italy* (New York: Israelowitz, 1985); see her bibliography. See Carlo Rosella, "L'Ebreo in noi, Grandi Mostre/New York celebra 2000 anni di arte Israelita in Italia," *Panorama,* September 3, 1989.

8. See "Marranos" in *The New Jewish Encyclopedia,* ed. David Bridger and Samuel Wolk (New York: Berman House, 1962), p. 306.

9. Ginzburg, *Ecstasies.*

10. Alix Pirani, ed., *The Absent Mother: Restoring the Goddess to Judaism and Christianity* (Hammersmith: Grafton Books, Mandala, 1991).

11. "Hagar: The Desolation of Rejection," chap. 1 in Phyllis Trible, *Texts of Terror: Literary-Feminist Readings of Biblical Narratives* (Philadelphia: Fortress Press, 1984), p. 9.

12. Quoted in Trible, *Texts of Terror,* p. 17.

13. Ibid., p. 28.

14. Ibid.

15. Ibid.

16. Ibid., p. 39.

17. Ibid., p. 45.

18. Ibid., p. 53.

19. See chapters 3 and 4, this work.

20. Ibid.

21. Raphael Patai, *The Hebrew Goddess* (Detroit, Mich.: Wayne State University Press, 1967), p. 19.

22. Ibid., p. 96.

23. Ibid., p. 116. Examining popular Jewish beliefs of Italy would help solve some conundrums of this study; e.g., the pervasive Italian finger gesture for cuckold (and for the goddess) is two fingers that suggest horns. An image, Astarte of the Horns, 18th–16th century B.C.E., has been found in Nahariya, Israel (see illustrations in Patai, *The Hebrew Goddess*).

24. Roberto Luciani, *Santa Maria in Trastevere* (Rome: Fratelli Palombi Editori, 1987), p. 9.

25. Ibid., p. 11.

26. See Fiorenza, *In Memory of Her*.

27. Falk, *Love Lyrics from the Bible*, p. xiii.

28. Ibid., pp. xiv–xv.

29. Ibid., p. 103.

30. Ibid., p. 113.

31. Ibid., p. 118.

32. Ibid., p. 135.

33. Ibid., p. 141.

34. For a Sicilian history of the Muslim period of Italy, see Giovini, *Sulla dominazione degli Arabi*.

35. Ibid., p. 73.

36. See Rufus and Lawson, *Goddess Sites*.

37. Valentini, *Il nome e la cosa*, p. 162.

38. Ibid., pp. 163–64.

39. Annabella Rossi, *Le feste dei poveri*, p. 123.

40. Tullio Tentori, "An Italian Religious Feast: The Fujenti Rites of the Madonna dell'Arco, Naples," trans. J. Reichman and M. Reichman, in Preston, *Mother Worship*, p. 9.

41. Ibid., p. 99.

42. Ibid., p. 101.

43. Ibid.

44. Ibid., pp. 101–2.

45. Ibid., p. 102.

46. Ibid., p. 104.

47. Ibid., p. 109.

48. Ibid., pp. 101, 102, 108.

49. Ibid., p. 111.

50. Ibid.

51. Ibid., p. 113.

52. Ibid., pp. 113, 117.

53. Ibid.

54. Ibid., p. 119.

55. See Annabella Rossi, Le feste dei poveri.

56. Tentori, "An Italian Religious Feast."

57. Ibid.

58. Quoted in ibid., p. 112.

59. See Fabio Troncarelli, Le streghe, tra superstizione e realtà: Storie segrete e documenti inediti di un fenomeno tra i più inquietanti della società europea (Rome: Newton Compton, 1983).

60. Angelomichele De Spirito, Il paese delle streghe: Una ricerca sulla magia nel Sannio Campano (Rome: Bulzoni Editore, 1976).

61. Ibid.

62. Ibid., p. 88.

63. See Peter Lamborn Wilson, "Evil Eye," City Lights Review, no. 4 (1990). The definitive study of the evil eye is DiStasi, Mal'occhio.

64. Wilson, "Evil Eye," p. 117.

65. Ibid., p. 127.

66. Annabella Rossi, Le feste dei poveri, p. 123.

67. See I Giullari di Piazza, Il viaggio della Madonna Nera.

68. Annabella Rossi, Le feste dei poveri, p. 123.

69. See Il santuario di Montevergine (Montevergine: Edizione del Santuario, n.d.).

70. Film, W. Birnbaum archive. See also Il santuario di Montevergine.

71. See Johnson, Lady of the Beasts.

72. Consalvo Grella, Il Museo Irpino (Avellino: La Provincia Irpina, n.d.).

73. The missini are members of the M.S.I., the small party that recalls Italian fascism; its values are patriarchal—church, state, and family.

74. See Città di Foggia, Settore Cultura, Museo Civico, L'immagine femminile nella Daunia antica: Mostra archeologica (Foggia: DonnArte, 1989).

75. See Gimbutas, Civilization, chapter 5, "Neolithic Cultures of the Adriatic and Central Mediterranean," pp. 159–60.

76. Gimbutas, Language.

77. Gloria Fazia, Il Museo Civico Foggia: Guida, no. 14 (Milan: Federico Garolla Editore, 1987), p. 19.

78. W. Birnbaum film archive.

79. See Birnbaum, "Red, a Little White."

80. For contemporary protestants of Italy and the madonna, see Federazione delle chiese evangeliche in Italia, ed., Maria: Nostra sorella (Rome: Com Nuovi Tempi, 1988).

81. For Waldensians, see Martin Erbstosser, Heretics in the Middle Ages (Leipzig: Edition Leipzig, 1984), p. 96, and Giorgio Tourn, I valdesi: La singolare vicenda di un popolo-chiesa (1170–1976) (Turin: Claudiana, 1977).

82. The Sanctuary of Oropa (Biella: Edizione Eco del Santuario di Oropa, 1963), p. 4.

83. Ibid., pp. 4–5.

84. Ibid.

85. Ibid., pp. 5–6.

86. Ibid., p. 14.

87. See Federazione, *Maria*.

88. Teresa and Francesco Lovecchio, *La festa della Madonna della Sacra Lettera e della Varia a Palmi* (Palmi: C. Pugliese, 1987).

89. Cooperatives, popular in Italy since the socialist *fasci siciliani* of the latter part of the nineteenth century, are Italian feminists' favored mode for transforming the economy (see Birnbaum, *Liberazione della donna*, pp. 238–42). Cooperatives are found all over Italy; see Nadia Tarantini and Roberta Tatafiore, eds., *Donna in Lega: Le inchieste di 'noidonne' tra le cooperatrice* (Pescara: Medium Cooperativa Libera Stampa, 1987), and Omelio Prandini, *La cooperazione* (Rome: Editori Riuniti, 1982).

90. Lovecchio, *La festa,* p. 14.

91. Ibid., p. 10.

92. Ibid., p. 11.

93. Ibid., "La festa di la littara," p. 25.

94. *Invocazione per la novena alla Madonna dei Poveri, regina delle nazione di Seminara* (Seminara: pamphlet, n.d.).

95. Ibid.

96. Pina Piccolo, "Selected Poems" (Berkeley, Calif., 1991). For an interpretation of black madonnas of the Messina area, see the poem "Black Madonnas," by Maria Luisa Spaziani, a major poet of Italy. Born in Turin, she has taught at the University of Messina, where students from nearby villages venerate black madonnas and daily take the ferry from Calabria to Messina. Spaziani's poem, in *La geometria del disordine* (Milan: Arnoldo Mondadori Editore, 1981), translated here by Laura Anna Stortoni, conveys hermetic meanings of black madonnas:

In the darkness the red torches sway
to the rhythm of the procession's psalmodies.
Invisible, the spring genista loans us wings
amidst the bloody smell of lamb.

Black Madonna, coal-like vortex,
visionary poverty, star opposing the sun.
From the well of the irreversible millennium,
you are a river that flows like a blood jet.

A destiny of sand awaits you,
you, heart transfixed by seven swords.
Interior castle, you too are touched
by the wave of the tides.

97. Valentini, *Il nome e la cosa,* pp. 164–65.

98. Comitato Promotore, *Terra di Puglia—Terra di speranza* (Bari: pamphlet, n.d.).

■ CHAPTER 9

An earlier version of this chapter was published in the *Proceedings* of the 1989 international conference Women in Italian Culture, La Trobe University, Melbourne, Australia, June 30–July 2, 1989.

1. Susan Caperna Lloyd, *No Pictures in My Grave: A Spiritual Journey in Sicily* (San Francisco: Mercury House, 1992), p. 41.

2. See Giacomo Panteghini, "Cristiani ed ebrei celebrano la pasqua," *Messaggero di sant'Antonio,* April 1990.

3. *The Daily Planet Calendar* (Berkeley, Calif.: The Nature Conservancy and the Nature Company, 1992). In the Koran, as well as in vernacular catholicism, the olive is regarded as a sacred tree.

4. I thank Solace Sheets for sending me this information.

5. Salomone-Marino, "La Pasqua," in *Costumi ed usanze,* pp. 167–71. See Lucia Chiavola Birnbaum, "Women and Italian Easter Rituals" (paper presented at the session Folklore of the conference of the American Italian Historical Association, City University of New York Graduate Center, New York, N.Y., October 10–13, 1988).

6. Pitré, *Spettacoli,* p. xviii.

7. Susan Caperna Lloyd has filmed the good Friday procession at Trapani, which begins at 3:00 P.M. and continues for twenty-four hours: "In the procession, townsmen called *portatori* carry one-ton statues *(ceti)* depicting the stations of the cross through old Trapani's labyrinth of streets"; see Lloyd, *Processione: A Sicilian Easter* (video; Berkeley: University of California Extension Media Center). See also Lloyd, *No Pictures in My Grave.* Very moved by the figure of the madonna during holy week (as was I), after Susan Caperna Lloyd made the film she became a *portatore* in the good Friday ritual and subsequently searched for the prechristian woman divinity throughout Sicily in pursuit of her own spiritual roots.

8. Pitrè, *Spettacoli,* p. 11.

9. Ibid., p. 42.

10. Ibid., pp. 64–65.

11. Ibid., pp. 110–11.

12. See Fiorenza, *In Memory of Her,* and Pagels, *Adam, Eve, and the Serpent.*

13. Pitrè, *Spettacoli,* p. 125.

14. Vitiello, "Sicily Within," p. 19.

15. Justin Vitiello, "Oral History and Story-Telling: Poetics and Literature of Sicilian Emigration" (unpublished manuscript), p. 14.

16. Ibid., p. 32.

17. Ibid., pp. 22–23.

18. See Willis Barnstone, ed., *The Other Bible: Ancient Esoteric Texts, Including Jewish Pseudepigrapha, Christian Apocrypha, Gnostic Scriptures, Kabbalah, Dead Sea Scrolls* (San Francisco: Harper & Row, 1984).

19. Ibid.

20. "Riso nero," in Simeti, *Pomp and Sustenance,* p. 215.

21. Conversation with Susan Caperna Lloyd, Berkeley, California, April 20, 1992.

22. Author's observation, April 1988. See *Processione dei Misteri* (Trapani: Azienda Provinciale Turismo, 1966), "La separazione" and "L'Addolorata chiude la processione dei Misteri"; see also *Il vomere*, Marsala, March 26, 1988, and Barbara Corrado Pope, "The Origins of Southern Italian Good Friday Processions," in *Italian Americans Celebrate Life: The Arts and Popular Culture*, essays from the twenty-second annual conference of the American Italian Historical Association, ed. Paola Sensi-Isolani and Anthony J. Tamburri (New York: American Italian Historical Association, 1990).

23. Quoted in Toschi, *Le origini del teatro italiano*, pp. 708–9.

24. *Il vomere*, Marsala, March 26, 1988.

25. Author's observation, easter 1988, at Caltagirone.

26. Ibid.

27. "La Settimana Santa in Sicilia: Processioni, rappresentazioni, misteri, canti e simboli della Passione," *Giornale di Sicilia*, supplement, March 30, 1988.

28. Nicolò Gambina, *Origine e storia della processione del 'giovedì santo' in Marsala* (Marsala: Centro Studi Nicola Grillo, Confraternità S. Anna, 1988). See also *Il vomere*, settimale di agricoltura-cooperazione, March 26, 1988, no. 11.

29. See "Incanto segreto di Mozia," in Vladimiro Agnesi, *Alla scoperta della Sicilia antica* (Palermo: S. F. Flaccovio, Editore, 1979).

30. *Encyclopaedia Britannica*, 14th ed., s.v. "Phoenicia."

31. Carlo Palermo, "A Trapani la mafia non esiste," *Avvenimenti*, January 1, 1992.

32. Fatima, the Arabian moon goddess, was considered the "Creatress." Demoted in Islam to the position of Muhammad's daughter, her earlier power seems to be venerated in her incarnation as the Madonna of Fatima.

33. Elisabetta Guggino and Gaetano Pagano, *La mattanza* (Gibellina: Nando Russo Editore, 1977), pp. 36–37. See also *Coro delle Egadi: 50 anni di folklore, 1935–1985* (Trapani: Cooperativa "Coro delle Egadi," 1985).

34. Cusumano, *Pani e dolci*, pp. 14–16.

35. Ibid., pp. 40–41.

36. Ibid., pp. 43–45.

37. Ibid., p. 45.

38. Giovanni Cammareri, *La settimana santa nel trapanese: Passato e presente* (Trapani: Coppolaeditore, 1988), p. 13.

39. See *Venerdì Santo: La processione dei misteri* (Trapani: Azienda Provinciale Turismo, 1966).

40. Ibid., p. 21.

41. Ibid., p. 26; see also pp. 28, 37, and 81.

42. See Lawrence, *Apocalypse*, chapter 15.

43. See Fiorenza, *In Memory of Her*, and Pagels, *Johannine Gospel in Gnostic Exegesis*.

44. Fiorenza, *In Memory of Her*, p. 325.

45. Ibid., p. 326.

46. Ibid., p. 325.

47. Ibid., p. 333.

48. Ibid., p. 334. See also Elisabeth Schussler Fiorenza and Anne Carr, "Teologia femminista," *Concilium: Rivista internazionale di teologia,* June 1987 and June 1989. See also Elisabeth Schussler Fiorenza, *Bread, Not Stone: The Challenge of Feminist Biblical Interpretation* (Boston: Beacon Press, 1984).

49. See *I Misteri e la Settimana Santa in provincia di Trapani,* texts by Alberto Genovese (Trapani: Arpe, 1988).

50. Revelation 12.1–2.

51. Lawrence, *Apocalypse.*

52. "La Settimana Santa in Sicilia," p. 9. For an Italian-American woman's response to holy week in Sicily, see Lloyd, *No Pictures in My Grave.*

53. See Fiorenza, *In Memory of Her.*

54. See *Dalle donne la forza delle donne, Carta Itinerante: Idee, proposte, interrogativi* (Rome, 1986).

55. See Lidia Menapace, *L'economia sessuale delle differenze* (Rome: Edizioni Felina Libri, 1987).

■ CHAPTER 10

1. See Antonio Crocco, *Gioacchino da Fiore e il gioachimismo,* 2d ed. (Naples: Liguori, 1976); see also Delno C. West and Sandra Zimdars-Swartz, *Joachim of Fiore: A Study in Spiritual Perception and History* (Bloomington: Indiana University Press, 1983), and Romano Napolitano, *S. Giovanni in Fiore, monastica e civica: Storia documentata del capoluogo silano,* 2 vols. (Naples: Laurenziana, 1978, 1981).

2. Crocco, *Gioacchino da Fiore,* p. 35.

3. Ibid., p. 79.

4. Ibid., p. 113.

5. Quoted ibid., p. 114.

6. Ibid., p. 160.

7. Ibid., p. 77.

8. Napolitano, *S. Giovanni in Fiore,* vol. 1, *Dalle origini al 1215;* part 2, *L'abate Gioacchino: I tempi,* p. 262.

9. Ibid., p. 268. Another Calabrian prophet, son of a cobbler from Stilo, was Tommaso Campanella, whose *City of the Sun* is often placed in the history of utopian thinking in Italy. He, too, was persecuted (in 1632), after another heretic, Giordano Bruno, had been burned at the stake in 1600. Campanella wanted the thorough reform of all secular and spiritual institutions; his utopian state was a meritocracy in which women enjoyed equal status with men. Their differences and tasks were construed from a male perspective, however. Campanella's idea of pregnancy controlled by the state for eugenic purposes is very hostile to women's self-determination and is the antithesis of liberty. See Tommaso Campanella, *La Città del Sole: Dialogo Poetico/The City of the Sun: A Poetical Dialogue,* trans. Daniel J. Donno (Berkeley and Los Angeles: University of California Press, 1981), p. 17.

10. See Fiorenza, *In Memory of Her.*

11. Antonio Crocco, ed., *L'età dello spirito e la fine dei tempi in Gioacchino da Fiore e nel*

gioachimismo medievale, appendice agli atti del II Congresso internazionale di studi gioachimiti, September 6–9, 1984 (S. Giovanni in Fiore: Centro Internazionale di Studi Gioachimiti, 1986).

12. Ibid., p. 9.

13. Crocco, *L'età dello spirito,* p. 94.

14. Ibid., pp. 94–95.

15. Ibid., p. 121.

16. Saverio Basile, *Leggende Silane* (San Giovanni in Fiore: Saverio Basile Editore, 1987), "La profezia di Gioacchino," pp. 15–16.

17. "Vitalità di un principio," *Quaderni calabresi: Quaderni del mezzogiorno e delle isole,* June 1983.

18. Ibid., pp. 166–67.

19. See Spretnak, *Lost Goddesses of Early Greece;* see also Walker, *The Woman's Encyclopedia,* p. 392.

20. Walker, *The Woman's Encyclopedia.*

21. Ibid., p. 554.

22. Mary Ellen Waithe, ed., *A History of Women Philosophers,* vol. 1, 600 B.C.–500 A.D. (Dordrecht: Martinus Nijhoff, 1987).

23. See Giovanni Pugliese Carratelli, "Tradizione civile della Magna Grecia," in *Magna Grecia: Una panoramica/An Overview* (Rome: Associazione Internazionale Magna Grecia, 1988).

24. Ibid.

25. Waithe, *A History of Women Philosophers,* p. 17.

26. Ibid., p. 25.

27. Ibid., p. 15.

28. Ibid., p. 27.

29. See Luisa Muraro, "La pratica della disparità"; from the Workshop Centro Culturale Virginia Woolf, February 21–22, 1987 (Rome: Centro Culturale Virginia Woolf, 1987).

30. Luisa Muraro, *Guglielma e Maifreda: Storia di un'eresia femminista* (Milan: La Tartaruga, 1985).

31. Ibid., p. 20.

32. Ibid., p. 23.

33. Ibid.

34. Ibid., p. 27.

35. Ibid., p. 28.

36. Ibid., p. 31.

37. Ibid., p. 43.

38. Ibid., pp. 42–43.

39. Ibid., p. 47.

40. Reported to me by Dr. Matteo Sansone, in Mattinata, Apulia, April 1990.

41. Muraro, *Guglielma e Maifreda,* p. 49.

42. Ibid., p. 103.

43. Ibid., pp. 104–5.

44. On persecution of witches in Italy, see A. Bertolotti, *Streghe, sortiere e maliardi nel secolo xvi in Roma* (Florence: Arnoldi Forni Editore, 1883). See also Jeffrey B. Russell, *A History of Witchcraft: Sorcerers, Heretics, and Pagans* (London: Thames and Hudson, 1982); Marina Romanello, ed., *La stregoneria in Europa* (Bologna: Il Mulino, 1975); Barbara Ehrenreich and Deirdre English, *Witches, Midwives, and Nurses: A History of Women Healers* (Old Westbury, N.Y.: Feminist Press, 1973); and Ginzburg, *Ecstasies.*

45. Muraro, *Guglielma e Maifreda,* p. 137.

46. Ibid., p. 151.

47. Ibid., p. 160.

48. Stone, *Ancient Mirrors of Womanhood,* p. 200.

49. Ibid., p. 201.

50. Ibid., p. 202.

51. Peter Dronke, F.B.A., *Hermes and the Sibyls: Continuations and Creations* (Cambridge: Cambridge University Press, 1990), pp. 3–5.

52. Ibid.

53. Ibid.

54. Toschi, *Le origini del teatro italiano,* pp. 611–12.

55. Dronke, *Hermes and the Sibyls.*

56. Ibid., pp. 5–6.

57. Ibid.

58. Joyce Lussu, "La sibilla appenninica," in *Storie* (Bologna: Il Lavoro Editoriale, 1986), pp. 221–39.

59. An important contemporary collection of Italian fables is that edited by Italo Calvino, *Fiabe italiane: Raccolte dalla tradizione popolare duranti gli ultimi cento anni e trascritte in lingua dai vari dialetti,* 2 vols. (Turin: Giulio Einaudi Editore, 1956). See also Birnbaum, "Godmothers and Their Lore," in *Liberazione della donna,* p. 324.

60. Stone, *Ancient Mirrors of Womanhood,* p. 381.

61. See Johnson, *Lady of the Beasts.*

62. Ibid., pp. 273–74.

63. Charles W. Jones, *Saint Nicholas of Myra, Bari, and Manhattan: Biography of a Legend* (Chicago: University of Chicago Press, 1978).

64. Laura Marchetti, ed., *Il femminile nella fiaba,* atti del convegno, Bari, January 27–29, 1989 (Bari: Arci Donna; l'Assessorato alla Cultura della Provincia di Bari, 1989).

65. Ibid., p. 14.

66. Many of these fables have been published in editions available to schoolchildren; a series from Savelli includes fables collected by Pitré. See Giuseppe Pitré, . . . *o salti questa finestra,* ed. Cecilia Codignola (Milan: Savelli Editori, 1979).

67. Lidia Menapace, "Le storie, la storia, alcune conclusioni," in *Il femminile nella fiaba,* ed. Laura Marchetti.

68. Ibid., p. 16.

69. From the Alphabet of Ben Sira, 23 a–b, quoted in *Lilith* 3 (Summer 1991): 16.

70. Quoted in Roberto Sicuteri, *Lilith la luna nera* (Rome: Astrolabio, 1980), p. 27.

See also Sylvia Brinton Perera, *La Grande Dea: Il viaggio di Inanna regina dei mondi* (Como: Red Edizioni, 1987).

71. Alphabet of Ben Sira, 23 a–b.

72. See Giovanni Mongelli, O.S.B., *Gli angeli,* vol. 2, *Gli angeli cattivi: Nostri avversari nell'opera della salvezza* (alla scuola di S. Tommasso). Monte S. Angelo, Edizioni "Michael" Santuario S. Michele Arcangelo. (Foggia: Leone Editrice, 1990). See Lilith listed among the demons, p. 49.

73. Ibid., p. 53.

74. Ibid., p. 58.

75. Ibid., p. 63.

76. Ibid., p. 67.

77. Ibid., p. 103.

78. Ibid., p. 114.

79. See Perera, *La Grande Dea.*

80. Susan Staats, "Lilith," in *Goddesses,* a 1991 calendar of the paintings of Susan Seddon Boulet (Petaluma, Calif.: Pomegranate Calendars and Books, 1990).

81. For the "Venere di Chiozza" near Scandiano, see Bernardini, *L'Italia preistorica,* p. 209; see also the "Venere di Savignano," p. 215.

82. Luisa Muraro, *La Signora del Gioco: Episodi della caccia alle streghe* (Milan: Feltrinelli Editore, 1976).

83. See Ginzburg, *Storia notturna* and *Ecstasies.*

84. *La Gana,* introduction by Carla Sanguinetti and Centro Donna, story by Nives Fedrigotti (Venice: Centro Internazionale della Grafica di Venezia, in collaboration with Centro Donna di Arcola, Assessorato alla Cultura—Provincia della Spezia, Centro Ligure di Documentazione per la Pace di Genova, Centro di Documentazione Internazionale di Sarzana, 1990).

85. Ibid., p. 7.

86. Ibid., p. 8.

87. Ibid.

88. Ibid., p. 11.

89. See Gustafson, *The Black Madonna.*

90. Ibid., p. 12.

91. See Pitré, *Medici, chirurgi, barbieri.*

92. *La Gana,* pp. 27–28.

93. Ibid., p. 28.

94. Ibid., p. 67.

■ CHAPTER 11

1. See contents, *MicroMega: Le ragioni della sinistra,* April 1987.

2. See *Operazione Gladio: Il segreti del Sid parallelo* (Rome: Avvenimenti Documenti, 1991).

3. D. Breschi et al., *L'immaginario mafioso: La rappresentazione sociale della mafia* (Bari: Edizioni Dedalo, 1986).

4. See "Donne e studenti contro la mafia," *Segno,* September–November 1988; see also Silvia Neonato and Monica Lanfranco, "Donne a Genova: Mobilitate per affetto," *Noidonne,* October 1989. Since 1985 women have protested in the streets of Genoa carrying babies, beating pans, and holding laundry as banners. Not worried about feminist categories, they have demonstrated as mothers against the danger of drugs for their children, as wives of unemployed dockworkers, and as housewives tired of pollution that grays their laundry.

5. See Filippo Gentiloni, "Sorella, non madre," *Com nuovi tempi,* no. 8, April 24, 1988. Gentiloni contrasts conservative church uses of the image of Mary to the positive Mary he finds in Luke's Magnificat, where she is not subordinated and obedient, but a "prophet of liberation" and witness, disciple, and sister in a community of equals.

6. See Brown, *The Cult of the Saints.*

7. Giorgio Marlin, "The Mouth of Truth," *Italian Journal: A Bi-Monthly Digest of Italian Affairs* 5, no. 1 (1991).

8. Walker, *The Woman's Encyclopedia,* p. 158.

9. Marco Capitello, ed., *La pantera siamo noi, 1: Cronache, immagini, documenti e storie dell occupazioni universitarie del '90* (Rome: Instant Books–C.I.D.S., 1990), p. 15.

10. Ibid., p. 17.

11. Ibid., p. 19.

12. Ibid., p. 31.

13. Ibid., p. 39.

14. Ibid., p. 43.

15. Ibid., p. 44.

16. Ibid., p. 55.

17. See Birnbaum, *Liberazione della donna,* pp. 238–42.

18. Capitello, *La pantera siamo noi,* p. 57.

19. Ibid., pp. 68–69.

20. Ibid., p. 101.

21. Ibid., p. 155. See also Lidia Menapace et al., eds., *Le scomode figlie d'Eva: Le comunità cristiane di base si interrogano sui percorsi di ricerca delle donne* (Rome: Edizione Com Nuovi Tempi, 1989).

22. See Michael J. Eula, "Gramsci's View on Consent and Its Basis as an Alternate Political Route," *Differentia* 1 (Autumn 1986), discussing Gramsci's view that revolution is the process of reaching the deepest beliefs of the people.

23. Capitello, *La pantera siamo noi,* p. 157.

24. Ibid., p. 221.

25. Mariano Cirino and Raimond Michetti, "La natura della pantera," *Arancia blu,* April 4, 1990.

26. Ibid.

27. Ibid.

28. Ibid.

29. See Birnbaum, *Liberazione della donna.*

30. See slogans for the demonstration of Unione Donne Italiane, "La Goccia,

Rome," in Paola Bono and Sandra Kemp, eds., *Italian Feminist Thought: A Reader* (Oxford: Basil Blackwell, 1991). The historical context of Italian women and nonviolence can be found in Birnbaum, *Liberazione della donna,* chapter 15, "Violence and Peace."

31. Vivere Lesbica, broadsheet, in Bono and Kemp, *Italian Feminist Thought.*

32. "Gente di cuore contro gente di malaffare," *Avvenimenti,* August 7, 1991.

33. Ibid., p. 17.

34. Yuki Maraini, ed., *Siamo in tante . . . la condizione della donna nelle canzoni popolari e femministe* (Milan: Savelli, n.d.).

35. See Dacia Maraini, *I sogni di Clitennestra e altre commedie* (Milan: Bompiani, 1981).

36. Dacia Maraini, guest editor, "The Monster's Mother: The Makings of Women's Theatre in Italy," *New Observations,* July–August 1989.

37. Dacia Maraini, *La lunga vita di Marianna Ucria: Romanzo* (Milan: Rizzoli Libri, 1990).

38. "Al vaglio delle donne: Un'analisi a' più voci della 'Mulieris dignitatem,' " *Com nuovi tempi,* December 18, 1988.

39. See Mary Collins, O.S.B., "Daughters of the Church: The Four Theresas, Women Invisible in Church and Theology," in *Concilium: Religion in the Eighties* (Edinburgh: T. & T. Clark, 1985).

40. Pia Bruzzichelli, "Un sinodo sfiorito," *Noidonne,* January 1986.

41. Hans Küng and Norbert Greinacher, eds., *Contro il tradimento del concilio: Dova va la chiesa cattolica?* (Turin: Claudiana, 1987).

42. *Uomini nuovi per un futuro di pace,* atti del 5 convegno giovanile (Genoa: Centro Cultura "Don Bosco" e Gioventù Aclista di Genova, 1986).

43. "Al vaglio delle donne."

44. Ibid.

45. Franca Bimbi, "Tre generazioni di donne: Le trasformazioni dei modelli di identità femminile in Italia" (paper presented at the Women in Italian Culture conference, Melbourne, Australia, June 30–July 2, 1989).

46. Franca Bimbi and Grazia Castellano, eds., *Madri e padri: Transizioni dal patriarcato e cultura dei servizi* (Milan: Franco Angeli, 1990); see also Maria Cristina Marcuzzo and Anna Rossi-Doria, eds., *La ricerca delle donne* (Turin: Rosenberg & Sellier, 1987).

47. See Muraro, "La pratica della disparità."

48. Ibid., p. 192. See also Franca Bimbi, *Parenthood in Italy: Asymmetrical Relationships and Family Affection* (Padua: University of Padua, 1990). Bimbi analyzes the decline in birth rate and the increase in life expectancy that places Italy in the forefront of demographic change. The pattern of the Italian family that is now emerging features a strong bond between the generations, along with a sense that each person is responsible for his or her own self-fulfillment (p. 12). The modern Italian parent is affectionate. The father is no longer the only breadwinner, nor is he the center of the family "decisional hierarchy"—"In this sense, the cultural model of the patriarchy has lost its legitimacy" (p. 18). See also Franca Bimbi et al., *Il filo di Arianna: Letture della differenza sessuale* (Rome: Cooperativa Utopia, 1987).

49. Bimbi, "Tre generazioni di donne."

50. Tina Lagostena Bassi, "Violence against Women and the Response from Italian Institutions" (paper presented at the conference Women in Italian Culture, La Trobe University, Melbourne, Australia, June 30–July 2, 1989).

51. See Sylvia J. Yanagisako, "Gender and the New Industrialization of Italy" (paper presented at Associates' Day, Institute for Research on Women and Gender, Stanford University, Stanford, Calif., January 21, 1982).

52. See Birnbaum, *Liberazione della donna,* chapter 8. See also Margherita Repetto Alaia, "The Historical Background of Change in Italy of Women's Status from the Turn of the Nineteenth Century to the Present" (paper presented at the session "Italian Americans and Their Public and Private Life," American Italian Historical Association, New Haven, Conn., November 14–16, 1991).

53. Ida Dominijanni, "Controcanto femminile," *Il manifesto,* December 31, 1989. See also Adriana Cavarero, "Il modello democratico nell'orizzonte della differenza sessuale," in *Democrazia e diritto,* Associazione Centro di Studi e Iniziative per la Riforma dello Stato, March–April 1990.

54. See Renate Holub, *From Double-Militancy to Double-Alterity: Feminist Theory in Italy* (New York: Routledge, forthcoming); see also Birnbaum, *Liberazione della donna.*

55. Luce Irigaray, *Una probabilità di vivere: Limite al concetto di neutro e universale nelle scienze e nelle tecnologie,* supplemento al no. 5, September–October 1986, *Donne e Politica,* Rome.

56. See Luce Irigaray, *Il tempo della differenza: Diritti e doveri civili per i due sessi, per una rivoluzione pacifica* (Rome: Editori Riuniti, 1989).

57. Ibid., p. 84.

58. Braidotti, *Patterns of Dissonance,* p. 261.

59. Libreria delle Donne di Milano, *Non credere di avere dei diritti* (Milan: Rosenberg & Sellier, 1987); see epigraph.

60. See Renate Holub, "For the Record: The Non-Language of Italian Feminist Philosophy," *Romance Language Annual* 1 (1990): 133–40. See also the following works by Holub: "The Politics of 'Diotima,'" *Differentia* 5 (May 1991): 161–73; *From Double-Militancy;* and "Strong Ethics and Weak Thought." See Luce Irigaray, *Etica della differenza sessuale* (Milan: Feltrinelli Editore, 1985); Anna Rita Calabrò and Laura Grasso, eds., *Dal movimento femminista al femminismo diffuso: Ricerca e documentazione nell'area Lombarda* (Milan: Franco Angeli, 1986); Franca Bimbi et al., *Il filo di Arianna* (Rome: Cooperativa Utopia, 1987); Franca Bimbi, "Il movimento femminista e le sue forme di azione collettiva," *Quaderni della Fondazione Feltrinelli,* no. 32 (1986): 205–13; Franca Bimbi, "Specchio delle mie brame: Immagini e riflessioni sulle trasformazioni della comunicazione erotica," in Bimbi et al., *Il filo di Arianna,* pp. 13–36; and Adriana Cavarero et al., *Diotima: Il pensiero della differenza sessuale* (Milan: La Tartaruga, 1987). Particularly important are the publications of the Centro Culturale Virginia Woolf at Rome and the various publications of the Libreria delle Donne at Milan; e.g., *Erotica: 21 fotografe rappresentano l'immaginario erotico* (Florence: Grafica Style, 1984). See Lucia Chiavola Birnbaum, "The Goddess, Black Madonnas, and *Socialismo Autogestito,*" *Proceedings,* 1990 conference of the American Italian Historical Association (forthcoming).

61. *Dalle donne la forza delle donne.* See Livia Turco, "Dalle donne alle donne," *L'unità,* September 12, 1986. An excellent collection of major articles on the subject of women's representation in politics is the publication of Casa delle Donne di Pesaro, *Rappresentanza o rappresentazione? Come costruire il mondo comune delle donne nel mondo degli uomini* (Pesaro: Rassegna Stampa, 1989); see also *Reti: Pratiche e saperi di donne* (Rome: Editori Riuniti Riviste, 1987–1991). See Ida Magli, *Viaggio intorno all'uomo bianco: Antropologia giorno per giorno* (Milan: Rizzoli Libri, 1986).

62. See the discussion of Menapace in Birnbaum, *Liberazione della donna.*

63. Lidia Menapace, *L'economia sessuale delle differenze* (Rome: Edizioni Felina Libri, 1987), p. 98.

64. Ibid.

65. Ibid., p. 17.

66. Ibid., p. 23. Menapace's thinking is part of a large philosophic discourse in which crisis and criticism imply a difference, a change, and "the activity of choosing among a given number of possibilities," among them "a reconsideration of Marxism as social project devoid of totalizing claims." See Peter Caravetta, "Thresholds: Crisis and Criticism in Contemporary Italian Philosophy," *Italian Journal* 2, no. 4 (1988).

67. Caravetta, "Thresholds," p. 25. See also Alessandro Dal Lago, "The Demise of the Revolutionary Imaginary?" *Differentia* 1 (Autumn 1986): One significance of the concept of differences is that it puts an end to deducing the existence of an object from its contrary, deducing the subject from the object, deducing society from the state, and deducing the state from society. Dal Lago states, "Each of us must speak as his own tiny self, not in the name of the Proletariat" (p. 49).

68. Dal Lago, "Demise," p. 105. See also Lidia Menapace, "Il movimento delle donne negli anni Settanta e Ottanta: Fra emancipazione e liberazione," in Menapace et al., eds., *Le scomode figlie d'Eva,* and Filippo Gentiloni and Marcello Vigli, *Chiesa per gli altri: Esperienze delle CdB Italiane* (Rome: Edizioni Com Nuovi Tempi, 1985).

69. This section of the chapter, in another version, was published as my review of the Menapace volume in *Differentia: Review of Italian Thought,* Spring–Autumn 1989, pp. 315–19. See also Angela Cattaneo and Marina D'Amato, *La politica della differenza: Dati e analisi per uno studio del rapporto donne/partiti* (Milan: Franco Angeli, 1990). Italian feminists do not regard the concept of differences as implying "essentialism"; differences are regarded as deriving from dissimilar historical and life experiences. Lina Mangiacapre, *Faust-Fausta* (Florence: L'Autore Libri, 1990), dedicated to *"tutte le Sibille,"* is a parable of Persephone's descent to the unconscious, where androgyny is explored and women's difference and the rapport between men and women become infinitely complex. Mangiacapre is the founder of the Neapolitan feminist group *Le nemesiache,* named for the goddess who destroyed arrogance. Nemesis, sometimes called the "inescapable one," "gave birth and death to all gods"; see Walker, *The Woman's Encyclopedia,* pp. 721–22.

70. "Primo mese di guerra: Chi si abitua e chi no," *Avvenimenti,* February 20, 1991.

71. Ibid.

72. See *Avvenimenti,* January 22, 1992.

73. See "Sandokan e i ribelli della facoltà," *Avvenimenti,* February 5, 1992.

74. Vitiello, "Sicily Within," p. 55.

75. Lidia Menapace has pointed out that women are not pacifists in the sense of fearing death, because they have always been caretakers of the dead. Italian feminists have become fierce antagonists to war to the extent that they have taken control of their own sexuality and make their own decisions about having children—"New human lives are no longer an infinite resource at the disposition of generals; reproduction is a scarce and precious good"; see Menapace, "La maternità non tollera nè exerciti nè guerre," *Azione nonviolenta,* December 1991.

76. Capitini's thinking on nonviolence is, in part, a reaction to the neorealism enunciated by the North American protestant theologian Reinhold Niebuhr, who, behind a great deal of intellectual mystification involving paradox, influenced the cold-war generation of U.S. intellectuals and political leaders to espouse a culture of death and killing and conditioned the public to these beliefs.

77. Norberto Bobbio, review of Aldo Capitini, *Elementi di un'esperienza religiosa* (Bologna: Cappelli Editore, 1990), in *Azione nonviolenta,* April 1991.

78. Adriana Zarri, "Barbari antichi e moderni," *Avvenimenti,* February 27, 1991.

79. "Signornò, e l'obiezione diventa un diritto," *Avvenimenti,* January 29, 1992.

80. See "Concordia Sagittaria: Primo comune nonviolento d'Italia," *Azione nonviolenta,* November 1991.

81. Sergio Turone, "Parlare ai potenti mediante sciacquone," *Avvenimenti,* November 13, 1991.

82. "Il sedicesimo congresso del movimento nonviolento," *Azione nonviolenta,* April 1991.

83. Ibid., p. 10.

84. Ibid.

85. *L'unità, Il manifesto,* and *La repubblica.*

86. "Il sedicesimo congresso," p. 10.

87. Ibid., p. 11.

88. See Luisa Muraro, "La libertà di nominarlo," in "Scusi, lei crede?" *Noidonne,* November 1988.

89. Simone Weil, *The Need for Roots: Prelude to a Declaration of Duties towards Mankind,* trans. A. F. Willis, preface by T. S. Eliot (London: Ark Paperbacks, 1952), p. 7.

90. Ibid., p. 11.

91. Ibid., p. 33.

92. Ibid., p. 41.

93. Ibid., p. 282. See also M. Esther Harding, *I misteri della donna* (Rome: Astrolabio, 1973), p. 184.

94. Weil, *The Need for Roots,* p. 288. The best interpretation of Simone Weil is that of Clare B. Fischer, "Our Mother Country Is Hope: Simone Weil's Ethic of Work" (1992).

95. Gesualdo Bufalino, *The Plague Sower* (Hygiene, Colo.: Eridanos Press, 1988). This section appeared in different form as a review in *Differentia: Review of Italian Thought,* Spring–Autumn 1989.

96. Ennio De Santis, *Exhibit and Reading,* Italian Institute of Culture, San Francisco, April 11, 1991. For a different example of masculine interest in recovering culture, see Gaetano Cipolla, *Giovanni Meli: Moral Fables, a Bilingual Edition* (Ottawa: Biblioteca di Quaderni d'italistica, no. 6, 1988).

97. See Lucia Chiavola Birnbaum, "Women of South Italy and Women of the United States: Regional, Cultural, and Political Life" (paper presented at session three, The Regions of the Mezzogiorno, conference on Southern Italy and America, State University of New York, Albany, November 17, 1989).

98. This theme informs two recent Italian films, *Cinema Paradiso* and *Siamo Tutto Bene.*

99. An excellent survey of this literature is in Franco Pignatoro, "La letteratura meridionalista, dal folclore . . . a una lucida coscienza politica," *Rocca,* May 15, 1981.

100. Ibid.

101. Giuseppe Jovine, "Racconti popolari anomi molisani" (paper presented at the conference on Southern Italy and America, State University of New York, Albany, November 17, 1989).

102. See "Matera/sassi di ieri sassi di domani," *Avvenimenti,* January 22, 1992.

103. I am indebted to Maria Gloria Rando for telling me of her mother's devotion to this dark madonna.

104. Jovine, "Racconti popolari anomi molisani."

105. Ibid.

106. Max Jaggi et al., *Red Bologna* (London: Writers and Readers Publishing Cooperative, 1977).

107. D. H. Lawrence, *Paesi etruschi,* and *Apocalypse.*

108. Gimbutas, *Language,* pp. 230–31.

109. See discussion in Braidotti, *Patterns of Dissonance,* p. 258.

110. Valentini, *Il nome e la cosa,* p. 72.

111. See Birnbaum, *Liberazione della donna.*

112. See Roberta Tatafiore, "Quelle del sì, del no e le perplesse," *Noidonne,* January 1990.

113. See Gad Lerner, "Pcidramma: La svolta del Pci al congresso di Bologna," *L'Espresso,* March 11, 1990.

114. Valentini, *Il nome e la cosa,* p. 39.

115. Ibid., p. 41.

116. Ibid.

117. Ibid., passim.

118. Giancarlo Zizola, "L'uso politico della fede: La religione nel sistema di guerra," *Com nuovi tempi,* no. 6, April 6, 1986.

119. Ibid., p. 57. For a masculine view of the change, see Salvatore Biasco et al., *Sinistra e cambiamento: Una agenda* (Milan: Feltrinelli, 1987).

120. Biasco et al., *Sinistra e cambiamento,* p. 103.

121. Chiara Valentini, "Il partito è mio e lo gestisco io," *L'Espresso,* March 18, 1990. The slogan of some women of the Pds, It Is My Party and I Shall Manage It, is a play on the words of the slogan of Italian feminists of the 1970s, who worked for legalized abortion with the theme It Is My Uterus and I Shall Manage It.

122. "La cultura e la politica della differenza nel Pds," interview with Livia Turco by the Women's Collective of *Confronti,* April 1991, p. 20.

123. See *Le donne cambiano i tempi: Una legge per rendere più umani i tempi del lavoro, gli orari della città, il ritmo della vita* (Rome: Sezione Femminile Nazionale del Pci, 1988).

124. "La cultura e la politica," p. 21. See also Livia Turco, "La democrazia del socialismo," *Reti: Pratiche e saperi di donne,* no. 6, November–December 1988.

125. Turco, "La democrazia del socialismo."

126. Ibid., p. 22.

127. Ibid.

128. "Tutte al centro della scena," *Noidonne,* Unedited Pages, June 1991.

129. See Norberto Bobbio, *The Future of Democracy: A Defense of the Rules of the Game,* ed. Richard Bellamy, trans. Roger Griffin (Minneapolis: University of Minnesota Press, 1987). See also the interview with Bobbio in *L'Espresso,* October 22, 1989, "Norberto Bobbio parla dei suoi 80 anni: La sinistra del duemila." Bobbio is important in the contemporary Italian discussion of a genuinely democratic socialism because he has always aligned liberal values with socialism. He regards the last few decades in Italy as ones of emancipation, in which the effort of women for self-management is the most significant factor. See also Norberto Bobbio, *Which Socialism? Marxism, Socialism, and Democracy,* ed. Richard Bellamy, trans. Roger Griffin (Minneapolis: University of Minnesota Press, 1987).

130. When Guttuso died a few years ago, he was buried with a traditional catholic funeral.

131. "Movimento nonviolento," *Azione nonviolenta,* no. 5, May 1986. For Italy's contemporary nonviolence movement, see Lucia Chiavola Birnbaum, "European Disarmament Movement: Stage 2," *Journal of Women and Religion of the Graduate Theological Union* (Spring 1983).

132. Ramón A. Gutiérrez, *When Jesus Came.*

133. See Alba Gonzales, *Myths, Metamorphoses, Memory, and Augury* (San Francisco: Istituto Italiano di Cultura, 1990).

134. Ibid.

135. Ibid. See Gonzales's sculpture *Totem Ambiguo* (1985).

136. For an excellent collection of studies of the condition of the women of Umbria, see Consulta Regionale sui Problemi della donna, *Raccolta delle principali normative dello stato, della CEE e della regione dell'Umbria, relativi alla condizione della donna* (Perugia: I Ristampa, September 1988); see also Consulta Regionale per le celebrazione del 30 della Liberazione, "La 'dimensione donna' nella Resistenza Umbra," primi risultati di una ricerca condotta nella Provincia di Perugia (Perugia: Regione dell'Umbria, Testimonianze/ Quaderni, 1972).

137. Anna Belardinelli, *Simulacra* (San Francisco: Istituto Italiano di Cultura, 1990), p. 20.

bibliography

I hope that this book will stimulate others to study black madonnas, and other dark women divinities, in their many cultural contexts. The titles in this bibliography refer, primarily, to black madonnas of Italy.

Abbey, Edward. "Keeping True to Earth." *City Lights Review*, no. 1 (1987): 93–95.

"Acireale non sorride più." Edited by Circolo Universitario, *Carnevale* 1989.

Acquaviva, Sabino. *Francesco un 'pazzo' da slegare*. Assisi: Cittadella Editrice, 1983.

Adams, Henry. *Mont Saint Michel and Chartres*. 1904. Reprint. New York: Viking/Penguin, 1986.

Agosta, Mario. *Giufà al Bando*. Ragusa: Erea, 1978.

"Al vaglio delle donne: Un'analisi a' più voci della 'Mulieris dignitatem.'" *Com nuovi tempi*. December 18, 1988.

Alaia, Margherita Repetto. "The Historical Background of Change in Italy of Women's Status from the Turn of the Nineteenth Century to the Present." Paper presented at the session "Italian Americans and Their Public and Private Life." American Italian Historical Association, New Haven, Conn., November 14–16, 1991.

Albert, Michael, Leslie Cagan, Noam Chomsky, Robin Hahnel, Mel King, Lydia Sargent, and Holly Sklar. *Liberating Theory*. Boston: South End Press, 1986.

"L'AltriTalia." *Avvenimenti*, January 1, 1992.

Amari, Michele. *Storia dei Musulmani di Sicilia*. 1872. Reprint. Catania: Editrice Giannotta, 1983.

Amerighi, Guglielmo. *Le maschere italiane*. Florence: Libreria Editrice, n.d.

Amin, Samir. *Delinking: Towards a Polycentric World.* Translated by Michael Wolfers. London: Zed Books, 1985.

———. *Eurocentrism.* Translated by Russell Moore. New York: Monthly Review Press, 1989.

Angeletti, Claudia. *Briganti e Madonne.* Florence: Libreria Editrice, 1982.

Angelucci, Adolfo, ed., "Brevi cenni sulla vita di S. Domenico Abate: Protettore di Cocullo," in *Origine della processione dei Serpari.* Cocullo, n.p., n.d.

Angione, Giuseppe. *La città del sole: Realtà e sogno di un bracciante.* Edited by Giovanni Rinaldi and Paola Sobrero. Foggia: Laboratorio Culturale G. Angione, 1982.

Anzaldúa, Gloria. *Borderlands: La Frontera: The New Mestiza.* San Francisco: Spinsters/Aunt Lute, 1987.

———. *Making Face, Making Soul: Haciendo Caras: Creative and Critical Perspectives of Women of Color.* San Francisco: Aunt Lute Foundation, 1990.

Appunti per la storia dell'antropologia culturale: Materiali antropologici. Series edited by Tullio Tentori. Rome: Editrice Ianua, n.d.

Apuleius. *The Golden Ass.* Translated by Robert Graves. New York: Farrar, Straus and Giroux, 1951.

———. *The Golden Ass.* Translated by Jack Lindsay. Bloomington: Indiana University Press, 1960.

Ascher, Barbara Lazear. "Carnival Nights: Venice Full Tilt." *European Travel and Life.* February 1990.

Assenza, Carmelo, ed. *400 indovinelli siciliani.* Ragusa: Thomson Editore, 1972.

Associazione Teologica Italiana. *Teologia e progetto/Uomo in Italia.* Assisi: Cittadella Editrice, 1980.

Atkinson, Clarissa W., Constance H. Buchanan, and Margaret R. Miles, eds. *Immaculate and Powerful: The Female in Sacred Image and Social Reality.* Boston: Beacon Press, 1985.

Averna, Giuliano. "Italian and Venetian Profanity." *The Best of "Maledicta": The International Journal of Verbal Aggression* (vols. 1–8, 1977–1985). Waukesha, Wis.: Maledicta Press, 1987.

Bakhtin, Mikhail. *Rabelais and His World.* Translated by Hélène Iswolsky. Bloomington: Indiana University Press, 1984.

Barbati, C., G. Mingozzi, and A. Rossi. *Profondo sud: Viaggio nei luoghi di Ernesto De Martino a vent'anni da "Sud e magia."* Milan: Feltrinelli, 1978.

Barina, Antonella. *La sirena nella mitologia: La negazione del sesso femminile.* Padua: Mastrogiacomo Editore, 1980.

Barnabà, Ernesto. *I fasci siciliani a Valguarnera.* Milan: Nicola Teti & Co. Editore, 1981.

Barnstone, Willis, ed. *The Other Bible: Ancient Esoteric Texts, Including Jewish Pseudepigrapha, Christian Apocrypha, Gnostic Scriptures, Kabbalah, Dead Sea Scrolls.* San Francisco: Harper & Row, 1984.

Barolini, Helen. *Festa: Recipes and Recollections of Italian Holidays.* New York: Harcourt Brace Jovanovich, 1988.

Barwick, Linda. "Critical Perspectives on Oral Song in Performance: The Case of Donna Lombarda." Ph.D. dissertation, Flinders University of South Australia, 1985.

————. "Women as Performers and Agents of Change in the Italian Ballad Tradition." Paper presented at the conference Women in Italian Culture, La Trobe University, Melbourne, Australia, June 30–July 2, 1989.

Basile, Saverio. *Leggende Silane.* San Giovanni in Fiore: Saverio Basile Editore, 1987.

Bassi, Tina Lagostena. "Violence against Women and the Response from Italian Institutions." Paper presented at the conference Women in Italian Culture, La Trobe University, Melbourne, Australia, June 30–July 2, 1989.

"La battaglia di Cerignola." *Il manifesto,* June 17, 1990.

Begg, Ean. *The Cult of the Black Virgin.* London: Arkana, 1985.

Belardinelli, Alvaro. "Uccidere baccanti non è reato." *Avvenimenti,* July 31, 1991.

Belardinelli, Anna. *Un muro pieno di sogni.* Scandicci: Nuova Italia Editrice, 1984.

————. *Simulacra.* San Francisco: Istituto Italiano di Cultura, 1990.

Bellah, Robert N., and Philip E. Hammond. "The Five Religions of Modern Italy." In *Varieties of Civil Religion.* San Francisco: Harper & Row, 1980.

Bergamini, Francesco, and Guiliano Bimbi. *Antifascismo e resistenza in Versilia.* Viareggio: A.N.P.I. Versilia, 1983.

Berger, Pamela. *The Grain Goddess Obscured: Transformation of the Grain Protectress from Goddess to Saint.* Boston: Beacon Press, 1985.

Bernal, Martin. *Black Athena: The Afroasiatic Roots of Classical Civilization.* Vol. 1, *The Fabrication of Ancient Greece, 1785–1985.* New Brunswick, N.J.: Rutgers University Press, 1987.

————. *Black Athena: The Afroasiatic Roots of Classical Civilization.* Vol. 2, *The Archeological and Documentary Evidence.* New Brunswick, N.J.: Rutgers University Press, 1991.

Bernardini, Enzo. *L'Italia preistorica.* Rome: Newton Compton, 1983.

Bertolotti, A. *Streghe, sortiere e maliardi nel secolo xvi in Roma.* Florence: Arnoldi Forni Editore, 1883.

Biasco, Salvatore, Gianni De Michelis, Giorgio Napolitano, Riccardo Perboni, Giorgio Ruffolo, Gian Enrico Rusconi, and Michele Salvati. *Sinistra e cambiamento: Una agenda.* Milan: Feltrinelli, 1987.

Bimbi, Franca. "Il movimento femminista e le sue forme di azione collettiva." *Quaderni della Fondazione Feltrinelli,* no. 32 (1986): 205–13.

————. *Parenthood in Italy: Asymmetrical Relationships and Family Affection.* Padua: University of Padua, 1990.

————. "Specchio delle mie brame: Immagini e riflessioni sulle trasformazioni della comunicazione erotica." In Bimbi, Franca, Laura Grasso, Maria Zancan, and Gruppo di Filosofia Diotima. *Il filo di Arianna: Letture della differenza sessuale.* Rome: Cooperativa Utopia, 1987.

————. "Tre generazioni di donne: Le trasformazioni dei modelli di identità femminile in Italia." Paper presented at the Women in Italian Culture conference, Melbourne, Australia, June 30–July 2, 1989.

Bimbi, Franca, and Grazia Castellano, eds. *Madri e padri: Transizioni dal patriarcato e cultura dei servizi.* Milan: Franco Angeli, 1990.

Birnbaum, Lucia Chiavola. "Black and Other Madonnas." *La bella figura: The Literary Journal Devoted to Italian American Women,* no. 3 (Fall 1988).

———. "A carniliviari semmu tutti aguale." Paper presented at the conference of the American Italian Historical Association, San Francisco, November 9–11, 1989.

———. "Enlightened Behaviorists and American Democracy" (1992).

———. "European Disarmament Movement: Stage 2." *Journal of Women and Religion of the Graduate Theological Union,* Spring 1983 (Berkeley, Calif.)

———. "The Goddess, Black Madonnas, and *Socialismo Autogestito.*" *Proceedings,* 1990 conference of the American Italian Historical Association (forthcoming).

———. *Liberazione della donna—Feminism in Italy.* Middletown, Conn.: Wesleyan University Press, 1986.

———. "Red, a Little White, a Lot of Green, on a Field of Pink: A Controversial Design for an Italian Component of a Multicultural Canon for the United States." In *From the Margin: Writings in Italian Americana,* edited by Anthony J. Tamburri, Paolo A. Giordano, and Fred L. Gardaphe. West Lafayette, Ind.: Purdue University Press, 1991.

———. *La religione e le donne siculo americane.* (Religion and Sicilian American women) Syracuse: Casa Editrice–Minori Cappuccini, 1981.

———. "Religious and Political Beliefs of Sicilian and Sicilian American Women, 1890– Present." Paper presented at the session Sicilians and Sicilian Americans of the conference of the American Historical Association, San Francisco, December 30, 1983.

———. Review of *Economia politica della differenza sessuale,* by Lidia Menapace. *Differentia* (Spring–Autumn 1989): 315–19.

———. "Women and Italian Easter Rituals." Paper presented at the session Folklore of the conference of the American Italian Historical Association, City University of New York Graduate Center, New York, N.Y., October 10–13, 1988.

———. "Women of South Italy and Women of the United States: Regional, Cultural, and Political Life." Paper presented at session three, The Regions of the Mezzogiorno, of the conference on Southern Italy and America, State University of New York, Albany, November 17, 1989.

Blok, Anton. "Rams and Billy-Goats: A Key to the Mediterranean Code of Honour." *American Ethnologist,* 1985.

Bò, Vincenzo. *La religiosità popolare: Studi, ricognizione storica, orientamenti pastorali, documenti.* Assisi: Cittadella Editrice, 1979.

Bobbio, Norberto. *The Future of Democracy: A Defense of the Rules of the Game.* Edited by Richard Bellamy. Translated by Roger Griffin. Minneapolis: University of Minnesota Press, 1987.

———. *Il futuro della democrazia.* Turin: Einaudi, 1984.

———. *Quando la teologia ascolta il povero.* Assisi: Cittadella Editrice, 1984.

———. Review of *Elementi di un'esperienza religiosa,* by Aldo Capitini. *Azione nonviolenta* (April 1991).

———. *Saggi su Gramsci.* Milan: Feltrinelli, 1990.

———. *Teologia della cattività e della liberazione.* Brescia: Editrice Queriniana, 1976.

———. *Which Socialism? Marxism, Socialism, and Democracy.* Edited by Richard Bellamy. Translated by Roger Griffin. Minneapolis: University of Minnesota Press, 1987.

Boff, Leonardo. *Liberating Grace.* Translated by John Drury. Maryknoll, N.Y.: Orbis Books, 1981.

Bono, Paola, and Sandra Kemp, eds. *Italian Feminist Thought: A Reader.* Oxford: Basil Blackwell, 1991.

Braidotti, Rosi. *Patterns of Dissonance: A Study of Women in Contemporary Philosophy.* Translated by Elizabeth Guild. New York: Routledge, 1991.

Brancato-Scammaca. *La terra feudale della Milicia nella storia della Sicilia.* Undated pamphlet.

Brandes, Stanley. *Metaphors of Masculinity: Sex and Status in Andalusian Folklore.* Philadelphia: University of Pennsylvania Press, 1980.

Breschi, D., and G. Lo Cascio. *L'immaginario mafioso: La rappresentazione sociale della mafia.* Bari: Edizioni Dedalo, 1986.

Brown, Peter. *The Cult of the Saints: Its Rise and Function in Latin Christianity.* Chicago: University of Chicago Press, 1981.

———. *Society and the Holy in Late Antiquity.* Berkeley and Los Angeles: University of California Press, 1982.

Bruzzichelli, Pia. "Un sinodo sfiorito." *Noidonne,* January 1986.

Bufalino, Gesualdo. *Le menzogne della notte: Una favola di rutilante invensione.* Milan: Bompiani, 1988.

———. *The Plague Sower.* Hygiene, Colo.: Eridanos Press, 1988.

Burdi, Giorgio. "La 'mascherea,' il desiderio profondo di diventare un 'altro.'" *L'Eco.* Putignano Carnevale Europeo. February 2, 1989.

Burgaretta, Sebastiano. *I 'nudi' di S. Sebastiano ad Avola e Melilli.* Marsala: Nando Russo Editore, 1983.

Calabrò, Anna Rita, and Laura Grasso, eds. *Dal movimento femminista al femminismo diffuso: Ricerca e documentazione nell'area Lombarda.* Milan: Franco Angeli, 1986.

Calvino, Italo, ed. *Fiabe italiane: Raccolte dalla tradizione popolare duranti gli ultimi cento anni e trascritte in lingua dai vari dialetti.* 2 vols. Turin: Einaudi, 1956.

Cammareri, Giovanni. *La settimana santa nel trapanese: Passato e presente.* Trapani: Coppola-editore, 1988.

Campanella, Tommaso. *La Città del Sole: Dialogo Poetico/The City of the Sun: A Poetical Dialogue.* Translated by Daniel J. Donno. Berkeley and Los Angeles: University of California Press, 1981.

Canti popolari di Terra di Puglia: Testi e musiche di antiche e moderne melodie. Putignano: Edizioni V. Radio, 1987.

Capitello, Marco, ed. *La pantera siamo noi, 1: Cronache, immagini, documenti e storie dell occupazioni universitarie del '90.* Rome: Instant Books–C.I.D.S., 1990.

Capitini, Aldo. *Elementi di un'esperienza religiosa.* Bologna: Cappelli Editore, 1990.

Capuana, Luigi. *Versi giovanili.* Reprint. Palermo: Vito Cavallotto Editore, 1978.

Caravetta, Peter. "Thresholds: Crisis and Criticism in Contemporary Italian Philosophy." *Italian Journal* 2, no. 4 (1988).

Carbonaro, Antonio, and Arnaldo Nesti. *La cultura negata: Caratteri e potenzialità della cultura popolare.* Florence: Guaraldi Editore, 1975.

———. *La diversità culturale.* Rimini and Florence: Guaraldi Editore, 1975.

Cardini, Franco. "La grande madre della repubblica." In *Le grandi madri,* edited by Tilde Giani Gallino. Milan: Editore Milano, 1989.

Carlo, Quinto del. *L'Antica Magione . . . Storia preromana di Viareggio e Versilia.* Viareggio: Ruggero Righini, 1988.

"Carlo dei lupi." Interview with Carlo Ginzburg. *Il manifesto,* April 1989.

Carnevale di Putignano, 1989. *Le maschere di Giuseppe Balestra.* Mostra al Palazzo Municipale, Putignano, February 5–14, 1989.

Carratelli, Giovanni Pugliese. "Tradizione civile della Magna Grecia." In *Magna Grecia: Una panoramica/An Overview.* Rome: Associazione Internazionale Magna Grecia, 1988.

Carroli, Piera. "Major Themes of the Lullabies of Emilia-Romagna and Toscana." Paper presented at the conference Women in Italian Culture, La Trobe University, Melbourne, Australia, June 30–July 2, 1989.

Casa delle Donne di Pesaro. *Rappresentanza o rappresentazione? Come costruire il mondo comune delle donne nel mondo degli uomini.* Pesaro: Rassegna Stampa, 1989.

Castelli, Raffaele. *Credenze e usi popolari siciliani.* Palermo: Il Vespro, 1980.

Castiglione, Miriam. "Sogni, visioni e devozioni popolari nella cultura contadina meridionale." In Gustavo Guizzardi, Carlo Prandi, Miriam Castiglione, Enzo Pace, and Antonio Morossi. *Chiesa e religione del popolo: Analisi di un'egemonia.* Turin: Claudiana, 1981.

Catania, Corrado. "Magic Sicily: An Island within the Island." *Italian Journal: A Bi-monthly Digest of Italian Affairs* 5, no. 1 (1991).

Cattaneo, Angela, and Marina D'Amato. *La politica della differenza: Dati e analisi per uno studio del rapporto donne/partiti.* Milan: Franco Angeli, 1990.

Cavarero, Adriana. "Il modello democratico nell'orizzonte della differenza sessuale." In *Democrazia e diritto,* bimestrale dell'Associazione Centro di Studi e Iniziative per la Riforma dello Stato, March–April 1990.

———. *Nonostante Platone: Figure femminili nella filosofia antica.* Rome: Editori Riuniti, 1990.

Cavarero, Adriana, Cristina Fischer, Elvie Franco, Giannina Lungobardi, Veronica Mariaux, Luisa Muraro, Anna Maria Piussi, Wanda Tommasi, Anita Sanvitto, Betty Zanardi, Chiara Zamboni, and Gloria Zanardo. *Diotima: Il pensiero della differenza sessuale.* Milan: La Tartaruga, 1987.

"Cenni storici." *Città Putignano.* (Milan: Gruppo Editoriale Weka, 1987.

Cento anni di carnevale. Pisa: Giardini Editori, 1981.

Cherchi, Placido, and Maria Cherchi. *Ernesto de Martino: Dalla crisi della presenza alla comunità umana.* Naples: Liguori Editore, 1987.

Christ, Carol P. "Embodied Thinking: Reflections on Feminist Theological Method." *Journal of Feminist Studies in Religion* 5, no. 1 (Spring 1989).

Cipolla, Gaetano. *Giovanni Meli: Moral Fables, a Bilingual Edition.* Ottawa: Biblioteca di Quaderni d'italistica, no. 6, 1988.

Cipriani, Roberto, Giovanni Rinaldi, and Paola Sobrero. *Il simbolo conteso: Simbolismo politico e religioso nelle culture di base meridionali.* Preface by Alfonso Maria Di Nola. Rome: Editrice Ianua, 1979.

Cirino, Mariano, and Raimond Michetti. "La natura della pantera." *Arancia blu,* April 4, 1990.

Città di Foggia. Settore Cultura. Museo Civico, *L'immagine femminile nella Daunia antica: Mostra archeologica.* Foggia: DonnArte, 1989.

Cocchiara, Giuseppe. *The History of Folklore in Europe.* Translated by John N. McDaniel. Philadelphia: Institute for the Study of Human Issues, 1952.

————. *Preistoria e folklore.* Palermo: Sellerio Editore, 1978.

————. *Storia del folklore in Italia.* Palermo: Sellerio Editore, 1981.

Colangeli, Mario, and Anna Fraschetti. *Carnevale: I luoghi, le maschere, i riti e i protagonisti di una pazza inquietante festa popolare.* Rome: LatoSide Editori, 1982.

Colinon, Maurice. *Les Saintes Maries de la Mer: Ou les Pelerins du clair de lune.* Paris: Editions S.O.S., 1975.

Collins, Mary, O.S.B. "Daughters of the Church: The Four Theresas, Women Invisible in Church and Theology." In *Concilium: Religion in the Eighties.* Edinburgh: T. & T. Clark, 1985.

Comitato Promotore. *Terra di Puglia—Terra di speranza.* Bari: n.d. (via Bellomo 94, 80124).

Comune di Stazzema. *L'Eccidio di S. Anna.* Massarosa, 1986.

Comune di Viareggio, Assessorato alla Cultura, I quaderni del Centro Documentario Storico, Cenni di Storia Viareggina no. 4. *Il Carnevale di Viareggio.* Viareggio: Paolo Fornaciari, 1981.

Comunità di base. *La chiesa cresce dal basso.* Turin: Cooperativa Tempi di Fraternità, 1978.

"Concordia Sagittaria: Primo comune nonviolento d'Italia." *Azione nonviolenta,* November 1991.

Confronti: Mensile di fede, politica, vita quotidiana. Rome: Cooperativa Com Nuovi Tempi.

Consiglio, Carlo. *Una società a misura di natura.* Catania: Alfa Grafica Sgroi, 1981.

Consulta Regionale per le celebrazione del 30 della Liberazione. "La 'dimensione donna' nella Resistenza Umbra." Primi risultati di una ricerca condotta nella Provincia di Perugia. Perugia: Regione dell'Umbria, Testimonianze/Quaderni, 1972.

Consulta Regionale sui Problemi della donna. *Raccolta delle principali normative dello stato, della CEE e della regione dell'Umbria, relativi alla condizione della donna.* Perugia: I Ristampa, September 1988.

Conti, Carmelo. *Il vento a corde dagli Iblei: Autori del novecento.* Catania: Edizioni Greco, 1987.

Cordelier, Pierre. *Les Gitans.* Rennes: Editions Ouest-France, 1983.

Cornelisen, Ann. *Women of the Shadows: A Study of the Wives and Mothers of Southern Italy.* New York: Penguin Books, 1976.

Coro delle Egadi: 50 anni di folklore, 1935–1985. Trapani: Cooperativa "Coro delle Egadi," 1985.

Correnti, Santi. *Leggende di Sicilia.* Milan: Longanesi & Co., 1975.

Cristiani di base oggi: Atti del VI Convegno Nazionale delle Comunità Cristiane di Base, Roma, 30/31 ottobre e 1 novembre 1982. Naples: Segreteria tecnica nazionale delle CdB, 1983.

Crocco, Antonio. *Gioacchino da Fiore e il gioachimismo.* 2d ed. Naples: Liguori Editore, 1976.

Crocco, Antonio, ed. *L'età dello spirito e la fine dei tempi in Gioacchino da Fiore e nel gioachimismo medievale.* Appendice agli atti del II Congresso internazionale di studi gioachimiti. September 6–9,1984. S. Giovanni in Fiore: Centro Internazionale di Studi Gioachimiti, 1986.

Cultrera, E., ed. *Venuta da Lontano: L'antico culto della madonna di Gulfi, storie e tradizione.* Ragusa: Utopia Edizioni, 1990.

"La cultura e la politica della differenza nel Pds." Interview with Livia Turco by the Women's Collective of *Confronti,* April 1991.

Cuore: Settimanale di resistenza umana. Milan: Arnoldo Mondadori.

Cusumano, Antonino. *Pani e dolci della valle del belice.* Marsala: Nando Russo Editore, 1981.

Cutello, Benedetto. *U Zoriu.* Ragusa: Erea, 1978.

D'Agostino, Federico. "Immagini della morte e costruzione simbolica della realtà a Colle Sannita." *Sociologia* 1 (1977): 51–80.

————. "Religion and Magic: Two Sides of a Basic Human Experience." *Social Compass,* no. 27 (1980): 279–83.

The Daily Planet Calendar. Berkeley, Calif.: The Nature Conservancy and the Nature Company, 1992.

Dal Lago, Alessandro. "The Demise of the Revolutionary Imaginary?" *Differentia* 1 (Autumn 1986).

Dalle donne la forza delle donne, Carta Itinerante: Idee, proposte, interrogativi. Rome, 1986.

Daly, Mary. *Gyn/Ecology: The Metaethics of Radical Feminism.* With a new intergalactic introduction by the author. Boston: Beacon Press, 1990.

————. *Pure Lust: Elemental Feminist Philosophy.* Boston: Beacon Press, 1984.

D'Angela, Cosimo. "Storia degli scavi della basilica paleocristiana di Siponto." *Vetere Christianorum* 23, 1986.

Davis, Natalie Zemon. *Society and Culture in Early Modern France.* Stanford, Calif.: Stanford University Press, 1975.

De Filippo, Michele. *Società e folclore sul Gargano.* Manfredonia: Michele De Filippo, 1989.

De Martino, Ernesto. *La fine del mondo: Contributo all'analisi delle apocalissi culturali.* Edited by Clara Gallini. Turin: Einaudi, 1977.

————. *Il mondo magico: Prolegomeni a una storia del magismo.* 4th ed. Turin: Boringhieri, 1986.

————. *Morte e pianto rituale nel mondo antico: Dal lamento pagano al pianto di Maria.* Turin: Einaudi, 1958.

————. *Naturalismo e storicismo nell'etnologia.* Bari: Laterza, 1941.

————. *Sud e magia.* Milan: Feltrinelli, 1959.

————. *La terra del rimorso: Contributo a una storia religiosa del Sud.* Milan: Il Saggiatore, 1961.

De Martino, Ernesto, ed. *Magia e civiltà: Un'antologia critica fondamentale per lo studio del concetto di magia nella civiltà occidentale.* Texts and commentary by Garin, Paolo Rossi, Frazer, Durkheim, Lévy-Bruhl, Cassirer, Freud, Jung, Piaget, Eliade, Volmat, Malinowski, Lévi-Strauss, Jensen, and De Martino. Milan: Garzanti Editore, 1962.

De Palma, Claudio. *La Magna Grecia: Storia e civiltà dell'Italia meridionale dalle origini alla conquista romana.* Rome: Newton Compton, 1985.

De Spirito, Angelomichele. *Il paese delle streghe: Una ricerca sulla magia nel Sannio Campano.* Rome: Bulzoni Editore, 1976.

Delaney, John J., ed. *A Woman Clothed with the Sun: Eight Great Appearances of Our Lady.* New York: Doubleday, 1960.

Di Grazia, Carlo Alberto. *Viareggio: Follie di Carnevale.* Viareggio: Editrice L'Ancora, 1985.

Di Nola, Alfonso. "L'anno degli spettri: Non vi siete sentite un po' strani in questi giorni di festa?" *Il manifesto,* January 8–9, 1989.

——. *L'arco di Rovo: Impotenza e aggressività in due rituali del sud.* Turin: Boringhieri, 1983.

——. *Gli aspetti magico-religiosi di una cultura subalterna italiana.* Turin: Boringhieri, 1976.

——. "La femminilità di Dio nel Giudaismo esoterico." In *Le grandi madri.* Milan: Feltrinelli, 1989.

——. *Gesù segreto: Ascesi e rivoluzione sessuale nel cristianesimo nascente.* Rome: Newton Compton, 1989.

Di Segni, Riccardo. *Il vangelo del ghetto: Le storie di Gesù, leggende e documenti della tradizione medievale ebraica.* Rome: Newton Compton, 1985.

Discorsi sopra l'antica e moderna Ragusa con una biografia di Giovan Battista Odierna per Filippo Garofalo. Ragusa: Libreria Paolino Editrice, 1980.

DiStasi, Lawrence. *Mal'occhio: The Underside of Vision.* Berkeley, Calif.: North Point Press, 1981.

"Divided Italy: Fear of New Europe." *San Fancisco Chronicle,* February 6, 1991.

Dominijanni, Ida. "Controcanto femminile." *Il manifesto,* December 31, 1989.

Le donne cambiano i tempi: Una legge per rendere più umani i tempi del lavoro, gli orari della città, il ritmo della vita. Rome: Sezione Femminile Nazionale del Pci, 1988.

"Donne e studenti contro la mafia." *Segno,* September–November 1988.

"Dopo le elezioni/gli scenari: Vicini e lontani." *Avvenimenti,* April 22, 1992.

Dronke, Peter. *Hermes and the Sibyls: Continuations and Creations.* Cambridge: Cambridge University Press, 1990.

Dundes, Alan, ed. *The Evil Eye: A Casebook.* Madison: University of Wisconsin Press, 1981.

Duranti, Francesca. *The House on Moon Lake: A Novel.* New York: Random House, 1986.

DWF. *donnawomanfemme,* no. 16. "Prova d'Ascolto." Rome: Cooperativa Utopia, 1992.

Eberstadt, Fernanda. "Annals of Place: The Palace and the City." *New Yorker,* December 23, 1991.

"Efficienza concretezza al servizio dell'Abruzzo: Democrazia cristiana," no. 2. *Rosina Giffi.* Elezione Regionale 1990 (pamphlet).

Ehrenreich, Barbara, and Deirdre English. *Witches, Midwives, and Nurses: A History of Women Healers.* Old Westbury, N.Y.: Feminist Press, 1973.

Eisler, Riane. *The Chalice and the Blade: Our History, Our Future.* San Francisco: Harper & Row, 1987.

Elizondo, Virgil. *The Future Is Mestizo: Life Where Cultures Meet.* New York: Crossroad, 1992.

Ennio De Santis, Exhibit and Reading. Italian Institute of Culture, San Francisco, April 11, 1991.

Erbstosser, Martin. *Heretics in the Middle Ages.* Leipzig: Edition Leipzig, 1984.

"The Eternal Etruscans." *National Geographic* 173, no. 6 (June 1988): 696–743.

Eula, Michael J. "Gramsci's View on Consent and Its Basis as an Alternate Political Route." *Differentia* 1 (Autumn 1986).

Fagiuoli, Gianfranco. *Le apparizioni della madonna di Medjugorje.* Grandi Opere Peruzzo, Supplemento. Milan: Ferruccio Spena, 1985.

Falassi, Alessandro. Preface to *Spettacoli,* by Giuseppe Pitré. Palermo, 1870. Reprint. Palermo: Il Vespro, 1978.

Falk, Marcia. *Love Lyrics from the Bible: "The Song of Songs," a New Translation and Interpretation.* San Francisco: HarperSanFrancisco, 1990.

Fant, Maureen B. "The Many Faces of Ancient Sardinia." *Italy, Italy,* July–August 1987.

Fata, Frank. "Understanding Pulcinella." In *Proceedings,* American Association for Italian Studies, 1990. Edited by Douglas Radcliff-Umstead. Lowell, Mass.: University of Lowell, 1990.

Fazia, Gloria. *Il Museo Civico Foggia: Guida,* no. 14. Milan: Federico Garolla Editore, 1987.

Federazione delle chiese evangeliche in Italia, ed. *Maria: Nostra sorella.* Rome: Cooperativo Com Nuovi Tempi, 1988.

Ferrara, Corrado. *L'Ignota provenienza dei canti popolari in Noto.* Noto: Tipografia Zammit, 1908.

———. *La musica dei Vanniaturi: Gridatori di Piazza Notigiani.* Noto: Off. Tip. Di Fr. Zammit, 1896.

Field, Carol. *Celebrating Italy: The Tastes and Traditions of Italy Revealed through Its Feasts, Festivals, and Sumptuous Foods.* New York: William Morrow, 1990.

Filo del Arianna. *La differenza non sia un fiore di serra.* Atti del convegno organizzato a Verona, December 1–2, 1990. Milan: Franco Angeli, 1991.

Finamore, Gennaro. *Credenze usi e costumi abruzzesi.* Palermo: Adelmo Polla Editore, 1890. Reprint. Cerchio, 1988.

Finegan, Jack. *Myth and Mystery: An Introduction to the Pagan Religions of the Biblical World.* Grand Rapids, Mich.: Baker Book House, 1989.

Fiorenza, Elisabeth Schussler. *Bread, Not Stone: The Challenge of Feminist Biblical Interpretation.* Boston: Beacon Press, 1984.

———. *In Memory of Her: A Feminist Theological Reconstruction of Christian Origins.* New York: Crossroad, 1983.

Fiorenza, Elisabeth Schussler, and Anne Carr. "Teologia femminista." *Concilium: Rivista internazionale di teologia.* June 1987 and June 1989.

Fiori, Gabriella. *Simone Weil: Una donna assoluta.* Milan: La Tartaruga, 1991.

Fischer, Clare B. "Our Mother Country Is Hope: Simone Weil's Ethic of Work" (1992).

Fischer, Corey. *Sometimes We Need a Story More than Food.* A Traveling Jewish Theatre presentation.

Fiume, Marinella. *Vita di Orazia, contadina e guaritrice.* Palermo: La Luna Edizione, 1988.

Fondazione Carnevale di Viareggio. *Anteprima: I bozzetti del Carnevale di Viareggio.* Viareggio, 1989.

Fornaciari, Paolo. *Storia del Carnevale di Viareggio.* "Speciale Carnevale." *Il tirreno,* February–March 1984.

Fossati, Franca. "A Palermo tra agio e disagio." *Noidonne,* June 1990.

Gabaccia, Donna Rae. *Militants and Migrants: Rural Sicilians Become American Workers.* New Brunswick, N.J.: Rutgers University Press, 1988.

Gadon, Elinor W. *The Once and Future Goddess: A Symbol for Our Time.* San Francisco: Harper & Row, 1989.

Gaeta, Anna. *Fascino di storia sulla rupe garganica: Il Gargano dalla preistoria all'alto medioevo.* Lioni: Tipolitografia Irpina, 1980.

Galland, China. *Longing for Darkness: Tara and the Black Madonna, a Ten-Year Journey.* New York: Viking/Penguin, 1990.

Galli, Giorgio. *Occidente misterioso.* Milan: Rizzoli, 1987.

Gallini, Clara. *Dono e malocchio.* Palermo: S. F. Flaccovio, Editore, 1973.

Gallino, Tilde Giani, ed. *Le grandi madri.* Milan: Feltrinelli, 1989.

Gambina, Nicolò. *Origine e storia della processione del 'giovedì santo' in Marsala.* Marsala: Centro Studi Nicola Grillo, Confraternità S. Anna, 1988.

La Gana. Introduction by Carla Sanguinetti and Centro Donna. Story by Nives Fedrigotti. Venice: Centro Internazionale della Grafica di Venezia, in collaboration with Centro Donna di Arcola, Assessorato alla Cultura—Provincia della Spezia, Centro Ligure di Documentazione per la Pace di Genova, Centro di Documentazione Internazionale di Sarzana, 1990.

Gebara, Ivone, and M. Clara Bingemer. *Maria Madre di Dio e madre dei poveri.* Assisi: Cittadella Editrice, 1987.

"Gente di cuore contro gente di malaffare." *Avvenimenti,* August 7, 1991.

Gentiloni, Filippo. "Il ritorno del'etica." *Il manifesto,* March 4, 1990.

———. "Sorella, non madre." *Com nuovi tempi,* no. 8, April 24, 1988.

Gentiloni, Filippo, and Marcello Vigli. *Chiesa per gli altri: Esperienze delle CdB Italiane.* Rome: Edizioni Com Nuovi Tempi, 1985.

Germino, Dante. *Antonio Gramsci, Architect of a New Politics.* Baton Rouge: Louisiana State University Press, 1990.

Gharib, Georges. *Le icone Mariane: Storia e culto.* Rome: Città Editrice, 1987.

Giarizzo, Giuseppe, Gastone Manacorda, Francesco Renda, Paolo Manganaro. *I fasci siciliani.* 2 vols. Bari: De Donato Editore, 1975.

Gimbutas, Marija. *The Civilization of the Goddess: The World of Old Europe.* Edited by Joan Marler. San Francisco: HarperSanFrancisco, 1991.

———. *The Goddesses and Gods of Old Europe, 6500–3500 B.C.: Myths and Cult Images.* New and updated ed. Berkeley and Los Angeles: University of California Press, 1982.

———. *The Language of the Goddess.* San Francisco: Harper & Row, 1989.

Ginzburg, Carlo. *The Cheese and the Worms: The Cosmos of a Sixteenth-Century Miller.* Translated by John and Anne Tedeschi. Baltimore, Md.: Johns Hopkins University Press, 1980.

———. *Ecstasies: Deciphering the Witches' Sabbath.* Translated by Raymond Rosenthal. New York: Pantheon Books, 1991. Originally published as *Storia notturna: Una decifrazione del sabba.* Turin: Einaudi, 1989.

———. *Il giudice e lo storico: Considerazioni in margine al processo Sofri.* Turin: Einaudi, 1991.

————. Introduction. *Quaderni storici* 41 (1979).

————. *The Night Battles: Witchcraft and Agrarian Cults in the Sixteenth and Seventeenth Centuries.* Translated by John and Anne Tedeschi. Baltimore, Md.: Johns Hopkins University Press, 1966. Originally published as *I Benandanti: Stregoneria e culti agrari tra cinquecento e seicento.* Turin: Einaudi, 1966.

————. "Stregoneria e pietà popolare." In *Miti emblemi Spie: Morfologia e storia.* Turin: Einaudi, 1986.

Giovini, Aurelio Bianchi. *Sulla dominazione degli Arabi in Italia.* Palermo: Il Vespro, 1979.

I Giullari di Piazza (Italian folk music and theater), *Il viaggio della Madonna Nera: The Voyage of the Black Madonna.* Musical and theatrical pageant written by Alessandra Belloni and Dario Bollini, with music by John La Barbera, and masks, puppets, and frescoes by Antonio Romano.

"Going to See the Virgin Mary." *New York Times Book Review,* August 11, 1991.

Gonzales, Alba. *Myths, Metamorphoses, Memory, and Augury.* San Francisco: Istituto Italiano di Cultura, 1990.

Gramsci, Antonio. *Antonio Gramsci: Lettere dal carcere.* Edited by Paolo Spriano. Turin: Einaudi, 1971.

————. *An Antonio Gramsci Reader: Selected Writings, 1916–1935.* Edited by David Forgacs. New York: Schocken Books, 1988.

————. *Elementi di politica.* Rome: Editori Riuniti, 1964.

————. *Folclore e senso comune.* Rome: Editori Riuniti, 1992.

————. *The Modern Prince and Other Writings.* Translated by Louis Marks. New York: International Publishers, 1957.

————. *Passato e presente.* Turin: Editori Riuniti, 1975.

————. *Quaderni del carcere.* Vol. 3. Edited by Valentino Gerratana. Turin: Einaudi, 1975.

————. *La questione meridionale.* Edited by Franco De Felice and Valentino Parlato. Rome: Editori Riuniti, 1962.

————. *Il Risorgimento.* New, rev. ed. Turin: Editori Riuniti, 1975.

Grant, Michael. *The Rise of the Greeks.* New York: Charles Scribner's Sons, 1987.

————. *The World of Rome.* New York: Praeger, 1969.

Grant, Robert M. *Gnosticismo e cristianesimo primitivo* (Bologna, 1976).

Graves, Robert. *The Greek Myths.* 2 vols. New York: Penguin Books, 1955.

————. *The White Goddess: A Historical Grammar of Poetic Myth.* Amended and enlarged ed. New York: Farrar, Straus and Giroux, 1966.

Green, Julien. *God's Fool: The Life and Times of Francis of Assisi.* San Francisco: Harper & Row, 1983.

Grella, Consalvo. *Il Museo Irpino.* Avellino: La Provincia Irpina, n.d.

Griffin, Susan. *Made from This Earth: An Anthology of Writings.* New York: Harper & Row, 1982.

Groth-Marnat, Barbara. *A Pilgrimage to the Black Madonnas.* Santa Barbara, Calif.: Red Rose Publications, 1990 (P.O. Box 50160, Santa Barbara, CA 93150).

Guardiani, Francesco. "Neo-barocco e post-moderno." Paper presented at the session Mythology and Literature of the ninth annual conference of the American

Association for Italian Studies, University of Lowell, Lowell, Mass., April 13–16, 1989.

Guastella, Serafino Amabile. *L'antico carnevale della Contea di Modica: Schizzi di costumi popolari.* 2d ed. Ragusa: Piccitto & Antoci Editori, 1887.

———. *Le domande carnescialesche e gli scioglilingua del circondario di Modica.* Ragusa: Piccitto & Antoci Editori, 1888.

———. *Le parità morali.* Ragusa, 1884. Reprint. San Casciano: Cappelli Editore, 1968.

Guggino, Elisabetta, and Gaetano Pagano. *La mattanza.* Gibellina: Nando Russo Editore, 1977.

Guggino, Elsa. *La magia in Sicilia.* Palermo: Sellerio Editore, 1978.

Guidi, Oscar. *Gli streghi, le streghe: Antiche credenze nei racconti popolari della Garfagnana* (Lucca: Maria Pacini Fazzi Editore, 1990.

Guizzardi, Gustavo, Carlo Prandi, Miriam Castiglione, Enzo Pace, and Antonio Morossi. *Chiesa e religione del popolo: Analisi di un'egemonia.* Turin: Claudiana, 1981.

Gulino, G., and E. Scuderi, eds. *Questioni del dialetto: Atti del convegno di studi sul dialetto siciliano.* Pachino, May 29–31, 1981. Catania: Aldo Marino Editore, 1981.

Gullace, Gino. *Back to the Roots: A View of Magna Graecia.* Rome: International Association Magna Grecia, 1987.

Gustafson, Fred. *The Black Madonna.* Boston: Sigo Press, 1990.

Gutiérrez, Gustavo. *The Power of the Poor in History.* Translated by Robert R. Barr. Maryknoll, N.Y.: Orbis Books, 1983.

Gutiérrez, Ramón A. *When Jesus Came, the Corn Mothers Went Away: Marriage, Sexuality, and Power in New Mexico, 1500–1846.* Stanford, Calif.: Stanford University Press, 1991.

Haberman, Clyde. "Sicilian Mayor Tackles Political System: Popular Palermo Official Battles Coalition of Politicians and Mafia." *San Francisco Chronicle,* May 1, 1991.

Harding, M. Esther. *I misteri della donna.* Rome: Astrolabio, 1973.

Herm, Gerhard. *I bizantini.* Milan: Garzanti Editore, 1985.

Hobsbawm, E. J. *Primitive Rebels: Studies in Archaic Forms of Social Movements in the Nineteenth and Twentieth Centuries.* New York: W. W. Norton, 1959.

Holub, Renate. *Antonio Gramsci: Beyond Marxism and Postmodernism.* (London: Routledge, 1992).

———. "Cultural (Il)literacy: Humanism, Heidegger, Anti-Humanism." *Differentia,* no. 3–4 (1990): 73–90.

———. "The Cultural Politics of the CPI from 1944–56." *Yale Italian Studies* 2 (1978): 261–83.

———. "For the Record: The Non-Language of Italian Feminist Philosophy." *Romance Language Annual* 1 (1990): 133–40.

———. *From Double-Militancy to Double-Alterity: Feminist Theory in Italy.* New York: Routledge, forthcoming.

———. "Gramsci's Theory of the Intellectual in the U.S. Today." *Working Papers in Cultural Studies,* no. 17 (1991): 1–39 (Cambridge: Massachusetts Institute of Technology, Cultural Studies Project).

———. "The Politics of 'Diotima.' " *Differentia* 5 (May 1991), 161–73.

————. "Strong Ethics and Weak Thought: Feminism and Postmodernism in Italy." *Annali d'Italianistica* 9 (1991): 124–43.

————. "Towards a New Rationality? Notes on Feminism and Current Discursive Practices in Italy." *Discourse* 4 (1982): 89–107.

Hourani, Albert. *A History of the Arab Peoples.* Cambridge, Mass.: Harvard University Press, Belknap Press, 1991.

Iacono, Giuseppe, ed. *Folklore religiosa nella Contea di Modica.* Ragusa: Criscione Tecnoplast Graficarta, 1989.

"Incanto segreto di Mozia." In Vladimiro Agnesi. *Alla scoperta della Sicilia antica.* Palermo: S. F. Flaccovio, Editore, 1979.

L'Incoronata, cittadella di Maria: 1001 pellegrini verso il millennio 2001. Foggia: Opera Don Orione, 1990.

Invocazione per la novena alla Madonna dei Poveri, regina delle nazioni, di Seminara. Seminara: pamphlet, n.d.

Irigaray, Luce. *Etica della differenza sessuale.* Milan: Feltrinelli, 1985.

————. *The Irigaray Reader.* Edited by Margaret Whitford. Oxford: Basil Blackwell, 1991.

————. *J'aime à toi: Esquisse d'une félicité dans l'histoire.* Paris: Bernard Grasset, 1992.

————. *Una probabilità di vivere: Limite al concetto di neutro e universale nelle scienze e nelle tecnologie.* Supplemento al no. 5, September–October 1986, *Donne e Politica,* Rome.

————. *Il tempo della differenza: Diritti e doveri civili per i due sessi, per una rivoluzione pacifica.* Rome: Editori Riuniti, 1989.

Jaggi, Max. *Red Bologna.* London: Writers and Readers Publishing Cooperative, 1977.

Johnson, Buffie. *Lady of the Beasts: Ancient Images of the Goddess and Her Sacred Animals.* San Francisco: Harper & Row, 1988.

Joll, James. *The Anarchists.* New York: Grosset and Dunlap, 1964.

Jones, Charles W. *Saint Nicholas of Myra, Bari, and Manhattan: Biography of a Legend.* Chicago: University of Chicago Press, 1978.

Jovine, Giuseppe. "Racconti popolari anomi molisani." Paper presented at the conference Southern Italy and America: Regional, Cultural, and Political Life, State University of New York, Albany, November 17, 1989.

Judd, Elizabeth. "The Myths of the Golden Age and the Fall: From Matriarchy to Patriarchy." In *Views of Women's Lives in Western Traditions,* edited by Frances Richardson Keller.

Jung, Carl G. *The Essential Jung.* Edited by Anthony Storr. Princeton, N.J.: Princeton University Press, 1983.

————. "The Psychological Aspects of the Kore." In Jung and Kerényi, *Essays on a Science of Mythology.*

Jung, Carl G., and Karl Kerényi. *Essays on a Science of Mythology: The Myths of the Divine Child and the Mysteries of Eleusis.* Bollingen Series 20. Princeton, N.J.: Princeton University Press, 1963.

Kaplan, Temma. *Anarchists of Andalusia, 1868–1903.* Princeton, N.J.: Princeton University Press, 1977.

Keller, Frances Richardson, ed. *Views of Women's Lives in Western Tradition: Frontiers of the Past and the Future.* Lewiston, N.Y.: Edwin Mellen Press, 1990.

Kerényi, Karl. "The Kore in Eleusis." In Jung and Kerényi, *Essays on a Science of Mythology.*

King, Karen L., ed. *Images of the Feminine in Gnosticism.* Philadelphia: Fortress Press, 1988.

Kinsley, David. *Hindu Goddesses: Visions of the Divine Feminine in the Hindu Religious Tradition.* Berkeley and Los Angeles: University of California Press, 1988.

Küng, Hans, and Norbert Greinacher, eds. *Contro il tradimento del concilio: Dova va la chiesa cattolica?* Turin: Claudiana, 1987.

La Terra, Giovanni. *Le sommosse nel ragusano 1944–1945: I fasci siciliani nel ragusano in un processo del 1894.* Ragusa: Coop "Zuleima" Editrice, 1980.

Laboratoire de Préhistoire du Musée de l'Homme, Muséum National d'Histoire Naturelle. *Art et civilisations des chasseurs de la préhistoire 34 000–8 000 ans av. J. C.* Paris: Palais de Chaillot, 1984.

Ladurie, E. Le Roy. *Les paysans de Languedoc.* 2 vols. Paris: S.E.V.P.E.N., 1966.

Lanternari, Vittorio. "Religione popolare: Prospettiva storico-antropologica." In *Folklore e dinamica culturale: Crisi e ricerca d'identità.* Naples: Liguori Editori, 1976.

Lanzara, Valeria Gigante. *Il segreto della sirene.* Naples: Bibliopolis, 1986.

Lao, Meri. *Le Sirene da Omero ai pompieri.* Rome: Antonio Rotundo Editore, 1985.

Lapucci, Carlo. *La bibbia dei poveri: Storia popolare del mondo.* Milan: Arnoldo Mondadori, 1985.

———. *Il libro delle veglie: Racconti popolari di diavoli fate e fantasmi.* Milan: Garzanti Editore, 1970.

Lawrence, D. H. *Apocalypse.* 1931. Reprint. New York: Viking Press, 1966.

———. *Paesi etruschi.* Edited by Giovanni Kezich, with an essay by Massimo Pallottino. Siena: Nuova Immagine Editrice, 1932.

Leggio, Giuseppe. *Ibla Erea.* Ragusa: Tipografia Leggio e DiQuattro, 1977.

Lerner, Gad. "Pcidramma: La svolta del Pci al congresso di Bologna." *L'Espresso*, March 11, 1990.

Levi, Carlo. *Cristo si è fermato a Eboli.* Turin: Einaudi, 1945.

———. *Le parole sono pietre: Tre giornate in Sicilia.* Turin: Einaudi, 1945.

Levi, Primo. *The Drowned and the Saved.* Translated by Raymond Rosenthal. New York: Summit Books, 1986.

Libreria delle Donne di Milano. *Erotica: 21 fotografe rappresentano l'immaginario erotico.* Florence: Grafica Style, 1984.

———. *Non credere di avere dei diritti.* Milan: Rosenberg & Sellier, 1987.

Limiti, Mauro. *Umbria Folklore.* Perugia: Editrice Sigla Tre, 1985.

Lloyd, Susan Caperna. *No Pictures in My Grave: A Spiritual Journey in Sicily.* San Francisco: Mercury House, 1992.

———. *Processione: A Sicilian Easter.* Video. Berkeley: University of California Extension Media Center.

Loreto e il suo messaggio. Loreto: Basilica della Santa Casa, n.d.

Lovecchio, Teresa and Francesco. *La festa della Madonna della Sacra Lettera e della Varia a Palmi.* Palmi: C. Pugliese, 1987.

Luciani, Roberto. *Santa Maria in Trastevere*. Rome: Fratelli Palombi Editori, 1987.

Lussu, Joyce. "La sibilla appenninica." In *Storie*. Bologna: Il Lavoro Editoriale, 1986.

Magli, Ida. *La femmina dell'uomo* Bari: Laterza, 1985.

————. "Le funzioni culturali della donna." In *La donna, un problema aperto: Guida alla ricerca antropologica*. Florence: Vallecchi Editore, 1974.

————. *Viaggio intorno all'uomo bianco: Antropologia giorno per giorno*. Milan: Rizzoli, 1986.

Malfatti, Angelo. *Viareggio 1946 . . . e fu subito Carnevale*. Viareggio: Comitato Carnevale di Viareggio, 1985.

Mangiacapre, Lina. *Faust-Fausta*. Florence: L'Autore Libri, 1990.

Maraini, Dacia. *La lunga vita di Marianna Ucria: Romanzo*. Milan: Rizzoli, 1990.

————. *I sogni di Clitennestra e altre commedie*. Milan: Bompiani, 1981.

————. *Viaggiando con passo di volpe: Poesie 1983–1991*. Milan: Rizzoli, 1991.

————, guest editor. "The Monster's Mother: The Makings of Women's Theatre in Italy." *New Observations*, July–August 1989.

Maraini, Yuki, ed. *Siamo in tante . . . la condizione della donna nelle canzoni popolari e femministe*. Milan: Savelli, n.d.

Marchetti, Laura, ed. *Il femminile nella fiaba*. Atti del convegno, Bari, January 27–29, 1989. Bari: Arci Donna; l'Assessorato alla Cultura della Provincia di Bari, 1989.

Marcuzzo, Maria Cristina, and Anna Rossi-Doria, eds. *La ricerca delle donne*. Turin: Rosenberg & Sellier, 1987.

Mari, Giovanni, ed. *Moderno postmoderno: Soggetto, tempo sapere nella società attuale*. Milan: Feltrinelli, 1987.

"Maria: Donna Obbediente." *Il Rosario*. Siponto: A. N. 3, March 1990.

Marlin, Giorgio. "The Mouth of Truth," *Italian Journal: A Bi-Monthly Digest of Italian Affairs* 5, no. 1 (1991) (New York, Italian Academy Foundation Inc.).

Mason, Tim. "Italy and Modernization: A Montage." *History Workshop Journal*, Spring 1988.

"Matera/sassi di ieri sassi di domani." *Avvenimenti*, January 22, 1992.

Maulucci, Francesco Paolo. *Il Museo Archeologico Nazionale di Napoli*. Naples: Carcavallo Editore, 1988.

Menapace, Lidia. *L'economia sessuale delle differenze*. Rome: Edizioni Felina Libri, 1987.

————. "La maternità non tollera nè exerciti nè guerre." *Azione nonviolenta*, December 1991.

————. "Il movimento delle donne negli anni Settanta e Ottanta: Fra emancipazione e liberazione." In *Le scomode figlie d'Eva: Le comunità cristiane di base si interrogano sui percorsi di ricerca delle donne*, edited by Lidia Menapace et al. Rome: Edizione Com Nuovi Tempi, 1989.

————. "Le storie, la storia, alcune conclusioni." In *Il femminile nella fiaba*, edited by Laura Marchetti. Atti del convegno, Bari, January 27–29, 1989. Bari: Arci Donna; l'Assessorato alla Cultura della Provincia di Bari, 1989.

Merry, Bruce. "Women in Modern Italian Literature: Four Studies Based on the Work of Grazia Deledda, Alba De Cespedes, Natalia Ginzburg, and Dacia Maraini." *Capricornia*, no. 8 (Townsville, Australia).

Messaggio del vescovo. Cerignola: Diocesi di Cerignola–Ascoli Satriano, April 29, 1990.

Meyer, Marvin W., ed. *The Ancient Mysteries: A Sourcebook.* San Francisco: Harper & Row, 1987.

Milano, Attilio. *Storia degli ebrei in Italia.* Turin: Einaudi, 1992.

I Misteri e la Settimana Santa in provincia di Trapani. Texts by Alberto Genovese. Trapani: Arpe, 1988.

Mongelli, Giovanni, O.S.B. *Gli angeli.* Vol. 2, *Gli angeli cattivi: Nostri avversari nell'opera della salvezza* (alla scuola di S. Tommasso). Monte S. Angelo, Edizioni "Michael" Santuario S. Michele Arcangelo. Foggia: Leone Editrice, 1990.

Morelli, Donato. "La festa delle propaggini." In *Nuove ricerche e studi sulla Magna Grecia e la Sicilia antica in onore di Paolo Enrico Arias.* Pisa: Giardini Editori, 1988.

Morescalchi, Alfredo. *Ricordi di un carnevalaro.* Viareggio: La Nuova Europa, 1981.

Morton, Nelle. "The Goddess as Metaphoric Image." In *The Journey Is Home.* Boston: Beacon Press, 1985.

Moss, Leonard W., and Stephen C. Cappannari. "In Quest of the Black Virgin: She Is Black because She Is Black." In *Mother Worship,* edited by James J. Preston.

"Movimento nonviolento." *Azione nonviolenta,* no. 5, May 1986.

Muir, Edward, and Guido Ruggiero. *Microhistory and the Lost Peoples of Europe.* Baltimore, Md.: Johns Hopkins University Press, 1991.

Muraro, Luisa. *Guglielma e Maifreda: Storia di un'eresia femminista.* Milan: La Tartaruga, 1985.

————. "La libertà di nominarlo." In "Scusi, lei crede?" *Noidonne,* November 1988.

————. *L'Ordine simbolico della madre.* Rome: Editori Riuniti, 1991.

————. "La pratica della disparità." From the Workshop Centro Culturale Virginia Woolf, February 21–22, 1987. Rome: Centro Culturale Virginia Woolf, 1987.

————. *La Signora del Gioco: Episodi della caccia alle streghe.* Milan: Feltrinelli, 1976.

Murray, Margaret A. *The God of the Witches.* London: Oxford University Press, 1931.

Museo di storia e cultura contadina genovese e ligure. *Catalogo.* Genoa: Consorzio Agricolo Intercomunale, 1984.

Napolitano, Romano. *S. Giovanni in Fiore, monastica e civica: Storia documentata del capoluogo silano.* Vol. 1, *Dalle origini al 1215;* part 2, *L'abate Gioacchino: I tempi.* Naples: Laurenziana, 1978, 1981.

Neonato, Silvia, and Monica Lanfranco. "Donne a Genova: Mobilitate per affetto." *Noidonne,* October 1989.

Nesti, Arnaldo. *Una cultura del privato: Morfologia significato della stampa devozionale italiana.* Turin: Claudiana, 1980.

————. *Le fontane e il borgo: Il fattore religioso nella società italiana contemporanea.* Rome: Editrice Ianua, 1982.

————. *"Gesù socialista," una tradizione popolare italiana, 1880–1920.* Turin: Claudiana, 1974.

————. *Utopia e società: Per una sociologia dell'utopia.* Rome: Editrice Ianua, n.d.

Neumann, Erich. *The Great Mother: An Analysis of the Archetype.* Translated by Ralph Manheim. Princeton, N.J.: Princeton University Press, 1955.

"Norberto Bobbio parla dei suoi 80 anni: La sinistra del duemila." *L'Espresso,* October 22, 1989.

Operazione Gladio: Il segreti del Sid parallelo. Rome: Avvenimenti Documenti, 1991.

Origine della Processione dei Serpari. Cocullo, n.d.

Orlando, Leoluca. *Palermo.* Edited by Carmine Fotia and Antonio Roccuzzo. Milan: Arnoldo Mondadori, 1990.

Pagels, Elaine. "Adam and Eve and the Serpent in Genesis 1–3." In *Images of the Feminine in Gnosticism,* edited by Karen L. King. Philadelphia: Fortress Press, 1988.

––––––. *Adam, Eve, and the Serpent.* New York: Random House, 1988.

––––––. *The Gnostic Gospels.* New York: Random House, 1979.

––––––. *The Johannine Gospel in Gnostic Exegesis: Heracleon's Commentary on John.* Nashville, Tenn.: Abingdon Press, 1943.

Palermo, Carlo. "A Trapani la mafia non esiste." *Avvenimenti,* January 1, 1992.

Panteghini, Giacomo. "Cristiani ed ebrei celebrano la pasqua." *Messaggero di sant'Antonio,* April 1990.

Pasqualino, Antonio. *I pupi siciliani, piccola biblioteca delle tradizioni popolari siciliane.* Rome: Nando Russo Editore, 1983.

Pasquier, Alain. *The Louvre: Greek, Etruscan, and Roman Antiquities.* Paris: Scala Publications, 1991.

Passerini, Luisa. *Storia e soggettività: Le fonti orali, la memoria.* Perugia: La Nuova Italia Editrice, 1988.

Patai, Raphael. *The Hebrew Goddess.* Detroit: Wayne State University Press, 1967.

Perera, Sylvia Brinton. *La Grande Dea: Il viaggio di Inanna regina dei mondi.* Como: Red Edizioni, 1987.

Perniola, Mario. "Post-Political Styles." *Differentia* 1 (Autumn 1986): 39.

Perry, Mary Elizabeth. "The Black Madonna of Montserrat." In *Views of Women's Lives in Western Tradition,* edited by Frances Richardson Keller.

Pettazione, Raffaelle. *Italia religiosa.* Bari: Laterza, 1952.

Piccola biblioteca delle tradizioni popolari siciliane. Edited by Antonino Buttitta. Palermo: Coopesa, n.d.

Piccolo, Pina. "Selected Poems." Berkeley, Calif., 1991.

Pignatoro, Franco. "La letteratura meridionalista, dal folclore . . . a una lucida coscienza politica." *Rocca,* May 15, 1981.

Pintor, Luigi. "Pci, le cose sono due." *Il manifesto,* March 11, 1990.

Pirani, Alix, ed. *The Absent Mother: Restoring the Goddess to Judaism and Christianity.* Hammersmith: Grafton Books, Mandala, 1991.

Pitré, Giuseppe. *I gesti dei siciliani: Piccola biblioteca delle tradizioni popolari siciliane.* Edited by Antonino Buttitta. 1871. Reprint. Marsala, 1983.

––––––. *Le lettere, le scienze, e le arti in Sicilia.* 1870. Reprint. Palermo: Il Vespro, 1979.

––––––. *Medici, chirurgi, barbieri e speziali antichi in Sicilia, secoli XIII–XVIII: Curiosità storiche e altri scritti.* Edited by Giovanni Gentile. 1876. Reprint. Rome: Casa Editrice del Libro. 1942.

––––––. *. . . . o salti questa finestra.* Edited by Cecilia Codignola. Milan: Savelli Editori, 1979.

————. *Ottanta indovinelli popolari siciliani osceni.* Marsala: Nando Russo Editore, 1872.

————. *Spettacoli e feste popolari siciliane: Biblioteca delle tradizioni popolari siciliane.* Edited by Aurelio Rigoli. Preface by Alessandro Falassi. Palermo, 1870–1913. Reprint. Palermo: Il Vespro, 1978. Vols. 1–2, Popular Sicilian songs; 3, Popular poetry; 4–7, Fables, novels, and popular stories; 8–11, Sicilian proverbs; 12, Popular Sicilian representations and festivals; 13, Children's games in Sicily; 14–17, Customs, beliefs, and prejudices of the Sicilian people; 18, Fables and popular legends in Sicily; 19, Popular medicine in Sicily; 20, Riddles, doubts, questions, tongue twisters of the Sicilian people; 21, Saints' festivals in Sicily; 22, Studies of popular legends in Sicily; 23, Proverbs, mottoes, and exorcisms of the Sicilian people; 24, Lampoons, songs, legends, usages of the Sicilian people; and 25, The family, the house, the life of the Sicilian people.

Plaskow, Judith. "Jewish Anti-Paganism." *Tikkun,* March–April 1991.

Pope, Barbara Corrado. "The Origins of Southern Italian Good Friday Processions." In *Italian Americans Celebrate Life: The Arts and Popular Culture,* essays from the twenty-second annual conference of the American Italian Historical Association. Edited by Paola Sensi-Isolani and Anthony J. Tamburri. New York: American Italian Historical Association, 1990.

Prandi, Carlo. *Religione e classi subalterne.* Rome: Coines Edizioni, 1977.

Prandini, Omelio. *La cooperazione.* Rome: Editori Riuniti, 1982.

Preston, James J., ed. *Mother Worship: Theme and Variations.* Chapel Hill: University of North Carolina Press, 1982.

"Primo mese di guerra: Chi si abitua e chi no." *Avvenimenti,* February 20, 1991.

Processione dei Misteri. Trapani: Azienda Provinciale Turismo, 1966.

Prosperi, Adriano. "La Pasqua dei lavoratori: Sulla preistoria del Primo Maggio." In *Storia del Primo Maggio,* edited by Renato Zangheri. Rome: Aiep Editore–l'Unità, 1987.

Quasimodo, Salvatore. "Vento a Tindari." In Carmelo Conti, *Il vento a corde dagli Iblei: Autori del novecento.* Ragusa and Catania: Edizioni Greco, 1987.

Raccolta di proverbi siciliani ridotti in canzoni dall'abate Santo Rapisarda di Catania. 4th ed. Catania: Giannotta Editore, 1924.

Ragusa, Giovanni. *Chiaramonte Gulfi nella storia di Sicilia (dalle origini ai nostri giorni).* Modica: Franco Ruta Editore, 1986.

Renda, Francesco. *I fasci siciliani 1892–94.* Turin: Einaudi, 1977.

————. *Il movimento contadino in Sicilia: E la fine del blocco agrario nel Mezzogiorno.* Bari: De Donato Editore, 1976.

Reti: Pratiche e saperi di donne. Rome: Editori Riuniti Riviste, 1987–1991.

Rich, Adrienne. *Of Woman Born.* New York: W. W. Norton, 1976.

Riger, Stefanie. "Epistemological Debates, Feminist Voices: Science, Social Values, and the Study of Women" (1991).

Rizzitano, Umberto. *Storia e cultura nella Sicilia saracena.* Palermo: S. F. Flaccovio, Editore, 1975.

Rohrlich, Ruby. "Prehistoric Puzzles." Review of *The Language of the Goddess,* by Marija Gimbutas. *Women's Review of Books,* June 1990.

Romanello, Marina, ed. *La stregoneria in Europa.* Bologna: Il Mulino, 1975.

Roscoe, Will. "Other Genders: Problems and Possibilities for Feminist Theory." Paper presented at the Scholars' Seminar, Institute for Research on Women and Gender, Stanford University, Stanford, Calif., February 19, 1992.

Rosella, Carlo. "L'Ebreo in noi, Grandi Mostre/New York celebra 2000 anni di arte Israelita in Italia." *Panorama,* September 3, 1989.

Rosenau, Pauline Marie. *Post-Modernism and the Social Sciences: Insights, Inroads, and Intrusions.* Princeton, N.J.: Princeton University Press, 1992.

Rosengarten, Frank. "Gramsci's Arrest." *Italian Culture* 7 (1986–89).

Rossi, Annabella. *Il carnevale si chiamava Vincenzo.* Naples, 1977.

———. *Le feste dei poveri.* Palermo: Sellerio Editore, 1986.

Rossi, Pietro, ed. *Gramsci e la cultura contemporanea: Atti del convegno internazionale di study gramsciani tenuto a Cagliari il 23–27 aprile 1967.* Rome: Editori Riuniti, 1969.

Rotolo, S. Filippo. *La chiesa di S. Francesco all'Immacolata a Ragusa.* Ragusa: Biblioteca Francescana Editrice, 1978.

Rufus, Anneli S., and Kristan Lawson. *Goddess Sites: Europe.* San Francisco: HarperSan-Francisco, 1991).

Russell, Jeffrey B. *A History of Witchcraft: Sorcerers, Heretics, and Pagans.* London: Thames and Hudson, 1982.

Ryan, Mary. "The Parade in Nineteenth-Century America." In *The New Cultural History,* edited by Lynn Hunt. Berkeley and Los Angeles: University of California Press, 1989.

Sacerdoti, Annie. *Guide to Jewish Italy.* New York: Israelowitz, 1985.

Salerno, Salvatore. *Red November, Black November: Culture and Community in the Industrial Workers of the World.* Albany: State University of New York Press, 1989.

Salomone-Marino, Salvatore. *Costumi ed usanze dei contadini di Sicilia.* Palermo: Remo Sandron–Editore, 1879.

———. *Le reputatrici in Sicilia nell'età di mezzo e moderna.* 1879. Reprint. Palermo: Il Vespro, 1979.

The Sanctuary of Oropa. Biella: Edizione Eco del Santuario del Oropa, 1963.

"Sandokan e i ribelli della facoltà." *Avvenimenti,* February 5, 1992.

Santarelli, Giuseppe. *Loreto arte.* Loreto: Congregazione Universale della S. Casa-Loreto, Anno mariano 1987–1988.

Santayana, George. *Scepticism and Animal Faith: An Introduction to a System of Philosophy.* In *The Philosophy of Santayana,* edited by Irwin Edman. New York: Modern Library, 1942.

Santuario della Madonna di Milicia. Undated pamphlet.

Il santuario di Montevergine. Montevergine: Edizione del Santuario, n.d.

Sarti, Roland. *Long Live the Strong: A History of Rural Society in the Apennine Mountains.* Amherst: University of Massachusetts Press, 1985.

Satriani, Luigi M. Lombardi. "Gramsci e il folclore: Dal pittoresco alla contestazione." in *Gramsci e la cultura contemporanea,* edited by Pietro Rossi.

———. *Il silenzio, la memoria e lo sguardo.* Palermo: Sellerio Editore, 1979.

Scammaca, Brancato. *La terra feudale della Milicia nella storia della Sicilia*. Milicia; undated pamphlet.

Schemann, Alexander. *Historical Road of Eastern Orthodoxy*. Crestwood, N.Y.: St. Vladimir's Seminary Press, 1977.

Scholem, Gershom. *Kabbalah*. New York: Dorset Press, 1974.

Scialame. *U ceppone, trenta anni di storia putignanese*. Putignano: Schena Editore, 1981.

"Il sedicesimo congresso del movimento nonviolento." *Azione nonviolenta*, April 1991.

Selvaggio, Giovanni. *Il culto della sacra famiglia nella città di Ragusa*. Ragusa: Parocchia Sacra Famiglia, 1967.

———. *La festa del Battista a Ragusa (1600–1976)*. Ragusa: Erea, 1977.

Sendler, Egon. *The Icon: Image of the Invisible*. Translated by Fr. Steven Bigham. Redondo Beach, Calif.: Oakwood Publications, 1988.

Sensi-Isolani, Paola. "Folklore of the Irpinia." Paper presented at the conference Southern Italy and America, State University of New York, Albany, November 17, 1989.

Seppilli, Tullio. "Le Madonne arboree: Note introduttive." In *Le grandi madri*, edited by Tilde Giani Gallino.

Serricchio, Cristanziano. *La cattedrale di S. Maria Maggiore di Siponto e la sua icona*. Bari: Archivio Storico Pugliese, n.d.

Settepassi, Ettore, and Moreno Raffaelli. *Città di Viareggio: Il suo carnevale, una particolare storia*. Viareggio: Circolo Filatelico Apuano di Viareggio, 1983.

"La Settimana Santa in Sicilia: Processioni, rappresentazioni, misteri, canti e simboli della Passione." *Giornale di Sicilia*. Supplement, March 30, 1988.

Sicuteri, Roberto. *Lilith la luna nera*. Rome: Astrolabio, 1980.

"Signornò, e l'obiezione diventa un diritto." *Avvenimenti*, January 29, 1992.

Silone, Ignazio. *L'avventura d'un povero cristiano*. Milan: Arnoldo Mondadori, 1968.

———. *Fontamara*. Milan: Arnoldo Mondadori, 1949.

———. *Severina*. Edited and with articles by Darina Silone. Milan: Arnoldo Mondadori, 1981.

Simeti, Mary Taylor. *On Persephone's Island*. New York: Alfred A. Knopf, 1986.

———. "Riso nero." In *Pomp and Sustenance: Twenty-Five Centuries of Sicilian Food*. New York: Alfred A. Knopf, 1989.

Simonson, Rick, and Scott Walker, eds. *The Graywolf Annual, Five: Multi-Cultural Literary*. Saint Paul, Minn.: Graywolf Press, 1988.

Società Italiana delle Storiche. *Discutendo di storia: Soggettività, ricerca, biografia*. Turin: Rosenberg & Sellier, 1990.

Solari, Adalberto. *Viaggio a Loreto: Nuova guida della città e del santuario della S. Casa*. Rimini: Edizioni Pama Graphicolor, n.d.

Solarino, Raffaele. *La Contea di Modica: Ricerche storiche*. 2 vols. Ragusa: Libreria Paolino Editrice, 1982.

Spadone, Maria. *La paleontologia del Gargano*. Tesi: Università degli Studi di Milano, Facoltà di Lettere e Filosophia, 1970–71.

Spaziani, Maria Luisa. "Black Madonnas." In *La geometria del disordine*. Milan: Arnoldo Mondadori, 1981.

Spera, Salvatore. *Maria, storia e simbolo: Atti della VII primavera di Santa Chiara 1988.* Rome: Edizioni Vivere, 1989.

Spretnak, Charlene. *Lost Goddesses of Early Greece: A Collection of Pre-Hellenic Mythology.* Berkeley, Calif.: Moon Books, 1978.

Staats, Susan. "Lilith." In *Goddesses*, a 1991 calendar of the paintings of Susan Seddon Boulet. Petaluma, Calif.: Pomegranate Calenders and Books, 1990.

Starhawk. *Truth or Dare: Encounters with Power, Authority, and Mystery.* San Francisco: Harper & Row, 1987.

Stasak, Alyson. "The Spiral: The Symbol of the Goddess." Paper presented to class in feminist cultural history, California College of Arts and Crafts, Oakland, December 2, 1991.

"Lo statuto del PDS: Istruzioni per l'uso." *Avvenimenti*, February 20, 1991.

Steinfels, Peter. "Idyllic Theory of Goddesses Creates Storm: Was a Peaceful Matriarchal World Shattered by Patriarchal Invaders?" *New York Times*, February 13, 1990.

Stone, Merlin. *Ancient Mirrors of Womanhood: A Treasury of Goddess and Heroine Lore from around the World.* Boston: Beacon Press, 1979.

Stornelli nostrali, opuscoli popolari scelti da Guglielmo Amerighi. Florence: Stabilimento Grafico Commerciale, 1987.

"The Struggle Continues." *Black Panther: Black Community News Service* 1, no. 1 (Spring 1991).

"A Survey of Italy: Awaiting an Alternative." *Economist*, May 26, 1990.

Tarantini, Nadia, and Roberta Tatafiore, eds. *Donna in Lega: Le inchieste di 'noidonne' tra le cooperatrice.* Pescara: Medium Cooperativa Libera Stampa, 1987.

Tatafiore, Roberta. "Quelle del si, del no e le perplesse." *Noidonne*, January 1990.

Tentori, Tullio. "An Italian Religious Feast: The Fujenti Rites of the Madonna dell'Arco, Naples." Translated by J. Reichman and M. Reichman. In *Mother Worship*, edited by James J. Preston.

Teubal, Savina J. *The Lost Tradition of the Matriarchs: Hagar, the Egyptian.* San Francisco: HarperSanFrancisco: 1990.

Thomas, Brook. *The New Historicism and Other Old-Fashioned Topics.* Princeton, N.J.: Princeton University Press, 1991.

Tinelli, Vittorio, and L. Tinelli, comps. *Racconti nella tradizione popolare.* Putignano: Edizioni V. Radio, 1983.

Tobino, Mario, Renzo Pellegrini, and Carlo Alberto di Grazia. *Il Carnevale di Viareggio.* Milan: Arnoldo Mondadori, 1988.

Toschi, Paolo. *Le origini del teatro italiano.* Turin: Boringhieri, 1976.

Tourn, Giorgio. *I valdesi: La singolare vicenda di un popolo-chiesa (1170–1976).* Turin: Claudiana, 1977.

Trible, Phyllis. *God and the Rhetoric of Sexuality.* Philadelphia: Fortress Press, 1984.

———. "Hagar: The Desolation of Rejection." Chap. 1 in *Texts of Terror: Literary-Feminist Readings of Biblical Narratives.* Philadelphia: Fortress Press, 1984.

———. "A Mosaic for Miriam." E. T. Earl Lecture, Pacific School of Religion, presented at the First Congregational Church of Berkeley, Berkeley, Calif., January 30, 1992.

Troncarelli, Fabio. *Le streghe, tra superstizione e realtà: Storie segrete e documenti inediti di un fenomeno tra i più inquietanti della società europea.* Rome: Newton Compton, 1983.

Turco, Livia. "Dalle donne alle donne." *L'unità*, September 12, 1986.

————. "La democrazia del socialismo." *Reti: Pratiche e saperi di donne,* no. 6, November–December 1988.

Turone, Sergio. "Mai voto in Italia fu migliore di questo." *Avvenimenti,* April 22, 1992.

————. "Parlare ai potenti mediante sciacquone." *Avvenimenti*, November 13, 1991.

"Tutte al centro della scena." *Noidonne,* Unedited Pages, June 1991.

Uomini nuovi per un futuro di pace. Atti del 5 convegno giovanile. Genoa: Centro Cultura "Don Bosco" e Gioventù Aclista di Genova, 1986.

Vacca, F., and Bruno Vacca. *Il complesso nuragico di Barumini.* Cagliari: Edizioni V.I.S., n.d.

Valentini, Chiara. *Il nome e la cosa: Viaggio nel Pci che cambia.* Milan: Feltrinelli, 1990.

————. "Il partito è mio e lo gestisco io." *L'Espresso,* March 18, 1990.

Varvaro, Alberto. *Lingua e storia in Sicilia (Dalle guerre puniche alla conquista normanna).* Palermo: Sellerio Editore, n.d.

Vattimo, Gianni. *La fine della modernità: Nichilismo ed ermeneutica nella cultura post-moderna.* Milan: Garzanti Editore, 1985.

Venerdì Santo: La processione dei misteri. Trapani: Azienda Provinciale Turismo, 1966.

Vercoutter, Jean. *Antico Egitto: Archeologia di una civiltà.* Trieste: Electa/Gallimard, 1992.

Verga, Giovanni. *I malavoglia.* Trier, 1881. Reprint. Verona: Edizioni Scholastiche Mondadori, 1968.

————. *The She-Wolf and Other Stories.* 2d ed. Edited and translated by Giovanni Cecchetti. Berkeley and Los Angeles: University of California Press, 1978.

————. *Tutte le novelle.* Milan: Arnoldo Mondadori, 1942.

"Vitalità di un principio." *Quaderni calabresi: Quaderni del mezzogiorno e delle isole.* June 1983.

Vitiello, Justin. "Oral History and Story-Telling: Poetics and Literature of Sicilian Emigration" (Philadelphia, 1992).

————. "Sicily Within." Unpublished manuscript, 1992.

"Vivere Lesbica." In *Italian Feminist Thought,* edited by Paola Bono and Sandra Kemp.

Waithe, Mary Ellen, ed. *A History of Women Philosophers.* Vol. 1, 600 B.C.–500 A.D. Dordrecht: Martinus Nijhoff, 1987.

Walker, Barbara G. *The Woman's Encyclopedia of Myths and Secrets.* San Francisco: Harper & Row, 1983.

Wallerstein, Immanuel. *Geopolitics and Geoculture: Essays on the Changing World-System.* Cambridge: Cambridge University Press, 1991.

Warner, Marina. *Alone of All Her Sex: The Myth and the Cult of the Virgin Mary.* New York: Wallaby Pocket Books, 1976.

Weil, Simone. *The Need for Roots: Prelude to a Declaration of Duties towards Mankind.* Translated by A. F. Willis. Preface by T. S. Eliot. London: Ark Paperbacks, 1952.

West, Delno C., and Sandra Zimdars-Swartz. *Joachim of Fiore: A Study in Spiritual Perception and History.* Bloomington: Indiana University Press, 1983.

Wilson, Peter Lamborn. "Evil Eye." *City Lights Review,* no. 4 (1990).

Yanagisako, Sylvia J. "Gender and the New Industrialization of Italy." Paper presented at Associates' Day, Institute for Research on Women and Gender, Stanford University, Stanford, Calif., January 21, 1982.

Zarri, Adriana. "Barbari antichi e moderni." *Avvenimenti,* February 27, 1991.

Zeppegno, L., and C. Finzi. *Alla scoperta delle antiche civiltà in Sardegna: Un universo di potente, arcaica suggestione.* Rome: Newton Compton, 1984.

Ziegler, Christiane. *The Louvre: Egyptian Antiquities.* Paris: Scala Publications, 1990.

Zimdars-Swartz, Sandra L. *Encountering Mary: From La Salette to Medjugorje.* Princeton, N.J.: Princeton University Press, 1991.

Zizola, Giancarlo. "L'uso politico della fede: La religione nel sistema di guerra." *Com nouvi tempi,* no. 6, April 6, 1986.

"Lo 'zoccolo duro' non abita più qui." *La repubblica,* January 31, 1991.

Zuntz, Gunther. *Persephone: Three Essays on Religion and Thought in Magna Graecia.* 2d ed. Oxford: Clarendon Press, 1971.

index

265